'Miss Bedford has done a fine pi⟨...⟩
subject. Aldous Huxley is likely to ⟨...⟩
to come, and those interested in ⟨...⟩
abundant material for further thoug⟨...⟩
a stimulator of thought himself).'
Christopher Sykes, *The Listener*

'The treatment of his character is as masterly as anyone alive could
have managed. She had many advantages, she lived in his
ambiance for years, stayed for long periods with him and his first
wife Maria, was able to study some of Maria's private writings.
Miss Bedford, though a young woman at the time, didn't lose her
balance. She has a percipience about them both, which is tolerant,
experienced, and the reverse of sentimental. This picture of Aldous
is as accurate as we are ever likely to get.'
C. P. Snow, *Financial Times*

SYBILLE BEDFORD

Aldous Huxley
A Biography

Volume Two
The Turning Points 1939–1963

PALADIN
GRAFTON BOOKS
A Division of the Collins Publishing Group

LONDON GLASGOW
TORONTO SYDNEY AUCKLAND

Paladin
Grafton Books
A Division of the Collins Publishing Group
8 Grafton Street, London W1X 3LA

Published in Paladin Books 1987

First published in Great Britain by
William Collins Sons & Co. Ltd and
Chatto & Windus Ltd 1974

ISBN 0-586-08548-0

Printed and bound in Great Britain by
Collins, Glasgow

Set in Baskerville

To
MATTHEW

He was scientist and artist in one—standing for all we most need in a fragmented world where each of us carries a distorting splinter out of some great shattered universal mirror. He made it his mission to restore these fragments and, at least in his presence, men were whole again.

YEHUDI MENUHIN

CONTENTS

CONTENTS

ILLUSTRATIONS

Photographs reproduced by kind permission of Matthew Huxley
except Aldous and Cyril Connolly by courtesy of the
BBC Hulton Picture Library

AUTHOR'S NOTES

A number of quotations in this book are not entirely accurate: none are without full authority. In quoting from Aldous Huxley's books and letters I have freely extracted, eliminated, juxtaposed, conflated as best suited my immediate purpose. I have never put words into his mouth.

From the many sources whose help I have gratefully acknowledged I have often supplemented the printed sources by the private correspondence and conversation with which particular passages may have been fused or even substantially modified.

Maria Huxley (*née* Nys) had three sisters, Jeanne, Suzanne and Rose.

Jeanne had two daughters; Sophie, by her first husband René Moulaert, a theatrical designer, and Noële by her second husband the French playwright Georges Neveux.

Suzanne married the Dutch artist Joep Nicolas and had two daughters Claire and Sylvia. Rose married twice: she had one daughter, Olivia, by her first husband the French *surréaliste* poet, Eric de Haulleville, and, by her second husband, a son Sigfrid (Wessberg).

Acknowledgements

The author wishes to thank the following for permission to reprint excerpts from copyright material:

Cyril Connolly and the British Broadcasting Corporation for an interview with Aldous Huxley.

Mrs Laura Huxley, Chatto & Windus Ltd, and Farrar, Straus & Giroux, Inc., for *This Timeless Moment: A Personal View of Aldous Huxley*.

Mrs Laura Huxley, Chatto & Windus Ltd, and Harper & Row, Inc., for the complete works of Aldous Huxley.

Professor Roy Lamson and The Massachusetts Institute of Technology for *Ancient Views of Human Nature* and *Modern Views of Human Nature*.

John Lehmann and the British Broadcasting Corporation for an interview with Aldous Huxley.

John Morgan and the British Broadcasting Corporation for an interview with Aldous Huxley.

The Peace Pledge Union.

Denis Preston and Record Supervision Ltd. for taped interviews with Aldous Huxley from *Speaking Personally*, record number LRS 003-4.

Professor Grover Smith, Harper & Row, Inc., and Chatto & Windus Ltd. for *The Letters of Aldous Huxley*.

Mrs Betty Wendel for recollections of Aldous Huxley.

PART EIGHT

In Another Country: 1939-1945

". . Whereas here we just listen and
cannot believe."

MARIA HUXLEY in a letter to
Edward Sackville-West

Chapter One

Limbo

DURING the six years of the war, Aldous and Maria remained in Southern California. They did not travel; they moved house only once. Aldous started and abandoned one more utopian novel, found it hard to write, and during the worst time could not write at all, wanted to do something, did not know what; eventually wrote four books, three of them different in substance from what he had done before; ground out some work for the films when occasions arose. Matthew was drafted into the Medical Corps of the U.S. Army, became seriously ill, was consequently discharged. Maria's family took to the roads before the advancing German armies and there were many months with no news from them at all. Maria's health worsened; the doctors discovered signs of t.b., prescribed a very dry climate, and they went to live in a small oasis in the Mojave desert. There they led an existence of long solitudes punctuated by a little family life. Aldous saw less of Gerald Heard who was founding his own community, Trabuco College, gasoline and tyre rationing imposing separations in an area where distances were on an inhuman scale and public transport negligible; there were other reasons definable perhaps as shades of ideological estrangement. Aldous's own health continued precarious and he went through one long bad patch, a flare-up of the bronchial and other troubles. Such money as he was able to earn—and there were alarmingly lean years as well as very good—was needed for the responsibilities he kept taking on. Jeanne's child was sent over in time, lived with them, finished her education, went off to join the Free French forces. Joep and Suzanne Nicolas, too, had listened to Cassandra in the nick of time; Maria's mother and youngest sister with baby, after many hardships reached the U.S.A. The two German Jewish children Aldous had tried to rescue did not, but they had got as far as England where his cousin Joan and her husband, General Buzzard, took them in and brought them up, Aldous contributing to their education. A large amount of Maria's time and energy was spent in trying to get food to Europe. Aldous persisted with his Bates training and saw Mrs Corbett when work and transport allowed. His sight continued to improve. And this, well beyond the purely personal level, was the most heartening thing for him in those years: one tangible hint that men could help themselves. His other solace was Maria, her unfailing devotion, companionship, lightness of touch.

Of the war, six thousand miles away, he would not speak at all. Not during the first bad years. On the day Paris fell, Anita Loos wrote later, his face was dead white and he bore the expression of someone who was peering into hell; but the talk that evening was mostly some scientific discussion between him and Edwin Hubble; nobody mentioned Paris. (The few references found in his letters are either remote and pessimistic or on the conventional personal level, expressions of concern for Julian's son, Francis, who was serving in a destroyer; Lewis Gielgud's safe escape from France.) What went on behind the silence even Maria did not always know, though some of it we can perhaps imagine. The consciousness—the consciousness of a sensitive if under-emotional man—that the victims and the instruments of *this* war *that is now* are living men and women; the consciousness of great present suffering that must be followed by yet more suffering. The sense of waste and folly. The sense of utter horror. Physical and moral. Unalleviated by any sense of right. For Aldous never changed the conviction he had arrived at: that war, in *any* cause, in *any* circumstances, must always by its own nature be evil and lead to further evil. When the war went badly, he grieved; when it went "well", he could not rejoice. He foresaw famine, massacres, destruction and whatever the present outcome, abolition of the decencies—an age of tyranny before us. Throughout, he remained unsustained by any sense of solidarity or achievement, of shared hopes and aims. Again, as he had been during the First World War, in a very different way, Aldous was cut off from the mass of his contemporaries.

He took no direct action. He did not preach on platforms, or sign manifestoes or write any more pamphlets or letters to the press. The way he chose now was oblique, less open—the long way round. The approach to the perennial philosophy is a quiet one. The first book he wrote, the book he found bearable—and useful —to write at this time, was the biographical study of a man who was a contemplative mystic who chose, for the greater glory of France, to immerse himself in power politics: a cautionary tale about the illusions of the human will and the horrors and catastrophic consequences of the Thirty Years War. Aldous's own ends (in day to day conduct) might be defined as harmlessness: doing the work at hand, giving such individual material help as he could. His long-term end, his absolute end: discovery. The discovery of what we are. His life was mainly what, for want of a better word, we must call the inner life: a process of gradual self-transformation, the fruits of which are traceable, perhaps, in his books (Aldous left no journal) and were evident to those who met the man he had become. There were of course other, lighter, sides. The inner life was being refreshed by his curiosity about the outer one; and there was the daily fact that Aldous and Maria seldom ceased to laugh at themselves. In spite of the nightmare six thousand miles away, and in psychological distance immensely further still, there were pleasures. There was the Californian sunshine. There was the pleasure he took in the animals they kept, and in the two young human animals, a new nephew and niece; the pleasure and reassurance of the austere beauty of their desert landscape. Aldous's love and need of nature was greater even than the love he bore for art as a young man. As the turning points were passed and it became possible to believe in an end to the German terror and an end to the war itself, when it was evident that England would survive in far more than the physical sense and that in some parts of the world at least the chances for a tolerably free and decent life had not all been destroyed, Aldous's own mood lightened and he was able to advance again towards the serenity that was inherent in his nature.

What if Aldous and Maria had in fact returned to Europe in 1938 or 1939? Perhaps it might be worth thinking about for a few moments. Aldous appeared to attach little conscious importance to the matter; he never tried to justify or explain. (He did express the view that it was selfish of any woman, invalid or child to remain in Europe if they had the means to leave, because they would be using food and medical resources.) Yet might he not have been moved in part by the syndrome of the First World War which he did spend in England and in circumstances of much personal unhappiness—Trevenen's death, the desolation of Oxford, separation from Maria, reclusion in an underpaid and uncongenial job, the jingoism of the public mood, the prevailing hypocrisies that jarred so bitterly on his generation and the revulsion which brought forth such works as *Antic Hay*? For the older Aldous, too, *that* England would have been intolerably claustrophobic and distasteful, whereas now, in the present war, he and Maria would have been non-combatants living, very likely, in the country. Their physical danger would have been negligible. (Though of course they could not have known this while the Battle of Britain was on.) It is unsound to predict anyone's reactions but I doubt whether either of them would have been particularly affected by personal fear. (One recalls Aldous writing letters about French poetry to Juliette in 1917 while "being pestered by these German aeroplanes .. a fiendish banging of bombs eastward towards St Paul's ..".) Maria, though, would have had some very anxious hours on the days Aldous went up to London.

Food rationing, clothes rationing, shortage of drink, drabness and the rest wouldn't have mattered a scrap to them. On the contrary. And essentially they would have led the kind of life they led anywhere. Instead of talking to Edwin Hubble he would have talked to Julian, Joad and Haldane . . . It would have been marginally easier to go to see someone at an English university than getting to U.C.L.A. or Berkeley in war-time California. The Peace Pledge Union was soldiering on with admirable courage and good sense (and allowed to soldier on— up to a point—with no less admirable tolerance) for such things as a declaration of War Aims and a change in the policy of Unconditional Surrender. It is unlikely that Aldous would have been active in the first-hand ways of his novitiate in 1936 (though he never resigned his sponsorship of the P.P.U., indeed confirmed it by a letter in the 1950s), but he would have seconded the movement with the prestige and the respect he might well have held had he been present. Nor is it at all unthinkable that he might have filled some niche in the B.B.C. Meanwhile he would have written the same kind of books in a slightly different way. The intrinsic fact of war would of course have been unchanged. Yet nightmare at a lesser distance loses some of its obsessive power. To see people live through it, not as the doomed and passive victims in one's imagination, but with courage, humour, spirit, might have been revealing and consoling. By "being there" Maria would have been spared much anguish. One cannot speak for Aldous. There also remains the question whether, given their state of health, they might not have been killed off by six English winters. (Or perhaps their health might never have reached such a stage?) That, too, it is impossible to tell.

I have given an outline, a kind of scaffolding, of these years in Aldous's life. Years are made of days. In the three chapters which follow, I shall try to fill in some of these with glimpses from Maria's letters and with what comes through in Aldous's own, and with some eye-witness's accounts.

Chapter Two

Pacific Palisades

ALDOUS had signed on with M.G.M. for *Pride and Prejudice* in August 1939. Now that the war was actually there, he felt he could not go on with it. He talked to Krishnamurti; he telephoned (with Maria on the extension) to Anita Loos. She wanted to know why.

"Because it pays fifteen-hundred dollars[1] a week," he answered in deep distress. "I simply cannot accept all that money to work in a . . studio while my family and friends are starving and being bombed in England."

"But Aldous," I asked, "why can't you accept that fifteen-hundred and send the larger part of it to England?"

There was a long silence at the other end of the line, and then Maria spoke up.

"Anita," she said, "what would we ever do without you?"[2]

On 10th September Maria wrote to Rosalind Rajagopal, ". . . Aldous had taken up his job and I am quite certain it was the right thing to do, for the moment anyway . . . he is going to do it good-heartedly . . . Tell Krishnaji. He was a great help. Tell him we thank him. He probably knows anyway."

After the first shock, after Poland had fallen but Western Europe was still ticking over, the Huxleys, too, succumbed to the lull. The R.A.F. was bombarding Germany with propaganda pamphlets, Aldous and Gerald took it as a hopeful sign. Sophie arrived safely in November. Waiting for her, Maria had promised Jeanne, "She shall never be lost, or lonely or sad." She was sixteen:

I hope she will be young and indifferent and discover her new life instead of regretting the old. I know that during the last war I had an immense indifference for it, was only out to discover life.

The Huxleys thought of adopting her. "In case we shall all be killed. We would want her to inherit the little we have with

[1] Upped to $2,500 in Miss Loos's text. The actual sum was $1,500.
[2] Anita Loos in *Aldous Huxley, A Memorial Volume.* Chatto & Windus, 1965. Hereafter cited as *Mem Vol.*

Matthew. We can count on Matthew treating her like a sister.
But what if Matthew marries a wife who does not want to share
with Sophie?"[1] Meanwhile she was to be called Miss Huxley. Then
Aldous had the pleasure of a visit—all too brief—from Gervas.
The Nicolas's, Joep and Suzanne with their two small daughters,
Claire and Sylvia, landed in New York. Next, "an unexpected
piece of good news!" (wrote Aldous), Julian announced himself
for Christmas. It was almost as if there were no war.

Maria had to "switch everything up and down the week because
Julian kept contradicting his telegrams and letters . . And he had
said that he wanted to see people . . At last he arrived, and he
hurricaned us.

> But he was exciting and amusing and so nice. Even though he
> never realizes other peoples' existences. He must also be as strong as
> all of us put together . . . Well, I gave three parties . . . The last
> party was the largest and I stayed in my bedroom—like a queen
> you may say [this is to Eddy], but like a rabbit I think . . . When
> they had gone I collected the cigarette ends for 23 minutes . . .
> And so the nonsense went on . . . I could see Aldous was bored too.
> On my first evening I had seated Sophie next to Charlie Chaplin . .
> when to my dismay at the last minute and a flurry of white pleats
> she runs in to me and whispers she *must* sit opposite Charlie! You
> can imagine how that upset the orthodoxy of the never very orthodox
> table in my house . . . You see that my life was very complicated about
> nothing at all . . And Julian had to have a row of presents for
> everyone on Sunday when the shops were closed . . . And then he
> would insist on going on picnics at very early hours of the day—
> while my family would still be oversleeping and I would make
> breakfast in an aura of disapprobation and grunts. But all went well
> finally. Julian loved us and we loved him. And he flew off on
> Tuesday.

Aldous's sight has so much improved "that Julian could almost
not believe it . . . When I am tired or feel sad or depressed, it is
always that which encourages me most."

Aldous's work on *Pride and Prejudice* stopped after the New Year.
In February the studio recalled him for revisions; on half-pay.
This turned out most welcome. The American royalty accounts
came in and Aldous, for a wonder, read them. He knew that
After Many A Summer, published in October, had already sold

---

[1] All unassigned quotations in this and the next chapters will be from letters
by Maria Huxley.

10,000 copies. Now he found out that in spite of this he was in the red with Harpers, and to the tune of 9,000 dollars. (His old books had always been selling in England; in America they did not.) It was a blow. And not easily made up. Even if he did get a new job at a studio at full pay it would take—what with Federal income tax, State tax, agents' fees—about three months of film work. Meanwhile the future of the book-trade in England looked entirely uncertain. M.G.M. assured Aldous that they would always have work for him for the asking.

> Which by the way is not just niceness on their part. [Maria to Jeanne] It's because Aldous has learnt to do their kind of thing extremely well, as he does anything he really wants to. The only thing I find that he has still to learn is to pay some attention to his own finances; the kind of surprise we just had simply shouldn't have happened. It proves that he doesn't even look at his accounts ...

Nevertheless, Aldous did not accept any more film work for the next eighteen months. When *P. & P.* (M.G.M.'s working title for Jane Austen) was done with, he remained at home (he could never come to terms with the sealed windows, the air-conditioning at the studio) trying to work out a framework for a novel linking the present with a future: a forerunner, it would seem, of the Good Utopia, the antidote to *Brave New World*.

"We go for walks again, and there is some sense in our lives ..." Maria could take Aldous to Mrs Corbett and the tailor and the osteopath; she took him and Gerald to have their hair cut: "They are equally difficult to get to the hairdresser, so I take them at the same time." She drove Sophie to her lessons. She (having been led to all their doctors) was now finishing her French schooling under private tutors, Aldous seeing to Eng. Lit.

> I would like to save her [Maria wrote to Sophie's mother] all those painful experiences Lady Ottoline might have saved me at that age if she had taken the trouble to advise me ...

One of the things Maria did not realize in her turn was the effect of that strange and gloomy house. Sophie usually went out with them in the evening, but

> sometimes it was not possible and I[1] was terrified in that awful house at night. So it was decided to buy me a watch-dog. It was to be a great surprise and when it arrived, the surprise was mine, because they had bought me a toy-pomeranian, and I was of course

---

[1] From a memoir written by Sophie Moulaert, the present Mrs W. Welling.

expecting something like a German sheep-dog! Aldous adored this silly but intelligent little female dog. [But it was Maria who brushed it, washed it, fed it.] He would go on the floor to play with her, walk in the garden with her on a leash . . . and talk about the proper way of having her trimmed. He wanted to call her Mae West because she always wriggled her behind and was very seductive . . She was finally called Loulou after the cartoons of "Little Lulu" which Aldous followed. The evening Loulou joined the family, we went to show her off to Anita Loos who owned a male pomeranian called Cagney (after the actor). There was quite a large dinner party and everybody sat in a circle around the two dogs. Loulou was extremely charming . . Cagney was most disagreeable and growled. Aldous then revealed that Loulou had been acquired to be a wife to Cagney, but Anita told him that Cagney was castrated. Aldous was so disappointed that we all had to laugh.

Gerald, at the moment, was being difficult.

Il est d'une intransigeance incompréhensible, and [to continue in a free translation of Maria's letter to her sister Jeanne] Aldous says he has taken up the attitude of "the Buddhist Party", meaning that he's become as rigid as if he'd joined the Communist Party . . . Gerald has become the priest of this "party-religion" and so one may no longer laugh even about his person . . . He can't see us because he will not leave his house for more than two hours at a time because of his meditations . . . Meditation takes for him the place of drugs. When it's time he throws us out . . .

Aldous's own criticism was more general. Writing to Julian about Gerald's book *Pain, Sex and Time*, he said,

I have always thought it unfortunate that Gerald should have consistently chosen to employ historical and pre-historical terms for the discussion of psychological and philosophical problems. The result is a quite unnecessary confusion of issues and the casting of a haze of dubiety over matters of plain psychological fact . . .

Gerald's writing, or rather manner of writing, had ever been a stumbling block. In 1929, the year of their first meeting, Aldous had written to Robert Nichols:

I've not ventured yet to attack Heard's book. It seemed to be written in such a frightful way . . And anyhow does one—or ought one—to believe in these great generalizations? I make so many myself that I have a personal and intimate reason for distrusting them!

9

At present Gerald was beginning to give what Maria called lectures in churches. ". . Whether Hindu Temple or Baptist Hall, [he] has a large following. [This is again to Eddy] He speaks well, but we don't go often." When Gerald comes to the house they have "far more interesting talks than the preachings—quicker—less hammed—well, you know, and full of those facts that both of them always find everywhere . . . Chris Isherwood often joins us now; we like him very much indeed. On Tuesdays we all meet for lunch at a market . . and we can eat our vegetarian and medical faddist foods under olive trees. And talk for ever under umbrellas . . ."

Bertrand Russell was still being subjected to the abominable witch hunt that had arisen over his appointment to City College, New York.[1] Aldous sent him this note (19th March)[2]

> Dear Bertie,
>   Sympathy, I'm afraid, can't do much good; but I feel I must tell you how much I feel for you . . in the midst of the obscene outcry that has broken out around your name in New York.
>   Ever yours,
>   Aldous H.

The phony war still held; able to write to France, Maria described an idyllic outing with their dog and goats:

> Nous avons été en pick-nick avec les Rajagopal, Krishnamurti, leur petite fille et deux oies; nous avons apporté Loulou, Jaja et Blanchette . . nos petites chèvres . . .
>   Il y avait aussi des humains: Chris et Gerald et Peggy avec ses enfants et ses parents mais en comparaison des bêtes cela ne comptait pas du tout. Dans la campagne il faisait beau et doux et ensoleillé. Nous étions dans un bosquet d'eucalyptus sur une herbe succulente . . . Enfin c'était charmant . . .

In April the world changed. The German invasion of Norway and Denmark began on the 9th. Soon after, Aldous became ill. The trouble appeared to be some old and deep-seated low infection which now manifested itself in turns by intestinal upsets, urticaria, bronchitis, myocardiac weakness, and for the next three or four months Aldous was not fit enough to attempt any work. After

---

[1] See *The Autobiography of Bertrand Russell*, Volume II, Chapter II, George Allen and Unwin, 1968; and *The Bertrand Russell Case*, ed. by John Dewey and Horace M. Kallen, Viking Press, 1941.
[2] Published in Russell's autobiography as above.

the invasion of Belgium there was no more news of Maria's mother,
or of Rose and Eric de Haulleville and their baby; after the fall
of France there was no more news from Jeanne. Weeks later,
they had word that the Belgian party had left Brussels on foot
in the general exodus, and after frightful days on the road—
machine-gunned from the air, caught in a panicking crowd—had
got to Bordeaux; and that Jeanne had been out of Paris when the
Germans came.

. . We heard from them briefly . . . [Aldous to Julian, 7th July] we
were making arrangements to get money through, when the curtain
drops again. Goodness knows where they are now . . . and goodness
knows how or when any communication is to be established with
them. For the moment no money can be sent . . . And, of course, if
the war goes on, there will be famine conditions in Belgium by the
winter.

Aldous was now in the hands of Christopher Isherwood's
Austrian doctor, Kolish, slowly getting better under his (rather
experimental, I gathered) treatment, and trying to get over his
inability to write.

. . all political and social speculation looks silly and irrelevant
before the ink is dry on the paper. However, I seem at last to have
something significant crystallizing in my mind—something which
may permit itself to be written. I hope I may soon be well enough
to begin . . .

In July I arrived in California (a refugee—having been in
France, with a minor anti-fascist record, at the time of the German
breakthrough and got away on an American ship). I found Aldous
and Maria very changed. There was of course Aldous's new sight
—there he was without his spectacles, walking, reading (still holding the print close to his eyes), but this was not as impressive as
it might have been because of his looking so drawn and strained,
like a man with a great burden of unhappiness severely locked
away. I had often seen him look ill or withdrawn or quietly sad,
but even during the great insomnia of 1935 he had always kept
his air of equanimity. And poor Maria was so thin, so worn, so
nervous—and so resolutely cheerful. One felt that everything was
too much for her, physically too much, every minute. It was of
course a deeply unhappy time for most of us, but it seemed to
me that the Huxleys were almost deliberately, if not consciously,
putting themselves under the greatest possible strain, submitting
themselves to some rigorous process of repression; a process, I

thought even then, that must have been of longer standing, must have ante-dated the catastrophic news of the last weeks.

Their house indeed was sinister, and quite unfunny. They did not live on stale crusts and squashy fruit, or shut their doors at fixed hours, yet there was now in their life (unlike before and unlike later on) something of that same element of *retrécissement* Maria had commented on in Gerald's. The ease had gone, the blessed lack of tension. What had been a framework was now a timetable. Start for Mrs Corbett; start for Dr Kolish; dinner not in the cool of the evening but on the dot of 7 p.m. Bedtime at ten. Most of it *was* imposed by geography or health, but there was rigorism in the execution. Maria's protectiveness, that had been so discreet, was now compulsive. There were a number of taboos. "Don't talk war to Aldous." One had to accept everything American, never show longing for Europe— . . *je regrette l'Europe aux anciens parapets* . . . *that* was unmentionable. I *could* not have spoken of the war to Aldous; once I manoeuvred our mutual English friend, Allanah Harper, into asking him, "Aldous, don't you want England to win? Wouldn't it be *better* if England won?" Aldous remained mute for a second, then he said in a colourless voice, "There won't be any England as we knew it". To Maria, Europe had already become unreal, a remote hell. Allanah who had come out of France with me had brought her dog; this Maria could not understand. I explained that since one had been *able* to take the dog, it would have been wrong and cruel, quite apart from any personal attachment, to have abandoned him. She would not see it. "You could have brought a baby instead." "Maria, what baby?" "*Any* baby." Go up to a Frenchwoman with a pram, "Madame, donnez-moi votre bébé, je le porterai en Amérique"? Maria remained convinced that this could and should have been done.

Yet they doted on Loulou. This funny little thing was the incongruous element in their household. When Gerald came, the dog would sit on his lap—it was a kind of dare. I can still see Gerald, rocking to and fro in a wicker-chair, talking a blue streak to Aldous, clasping the toy pom to his knees. (If one wants an idea of the cadences and subject matter of his conversations, one should go to Christopher Isherwood's novel *Down There on a Visit* and listen to Augustus Par.) Aldous and Maria were now vegetarians. One could not get out of them how much of it was due to diet and how much to not eating living things. At any rate, unlike Gerald, they still ate fish. There were meat and wine on the table for Matthew, Sophie and unregenerate guests. Life was being kept resolutely "normal" for the young. Matthew had just come home for the summer months (having got through his second pre-medical year at Colorado University), was taking some scientific course and going about quite independently with his friends. Sophie had passed her baccalaureat (at the Lycée Français in New York where Maria had taken her during the bad days in June). "What good it will do her now, I don't quite know!" wrote Aldous. Maria wished that Sophie, too, would study medicine —it was a way to anything: even writers such as Maugham and Céline had begun by being doctors. Sophie thought she'd like the stage and enrolled as a dramatic student at the Max Reinhardt School at Hollywood.

In August Aldous began research for *Grey Eminence*: a mass of reading on the religious and political seventeenth-century background, most of it aloud by Maria (they got through five volumes of Bremond's—admirably readable—*Histoire du Sentiment Réligieux en France*, Gustave Fagniez huge and indigestible work, *Le Père Joseph et Richelieu*, and so on and on). By the end of September Aldous started writing. ("The whole story has an obliquely topical interest," he wrote to Harold Raymond, "for Joseph was as much responsible as anyone for prolonging the Thirty Years War, which is in the direct line of ancestry to the present disasters.") The atmosphere became more relaxed; they went again for their long walks on beach and hills, and visited such Huxleyan haunts as the pier at Santa Monica where Aldous would consult the lady fortune teller (The World's Largest Drug Store came later on).

In October, after the first full month of the Blitz on London, Aldous wrote this much to Lewis Gielgud:

As for the future—*quien sabe*? The one enormous lesson of it all . . is that unless things are done in time, the most ghastly events will occur. There is a tide in the affairs of men—which no politicians ever take. There were 15 years after 1918 during which something cd have been done, either along purely Machiavellian lines or else along lines of genuine co-operation. Nothing was done and the world drifted into the state of a man with a neglected cancer, who will die if he is left alone and will die under the knife if operated. The fable of the Sibylline books is appallingly apposite—less and less at a higher and higher price . . .

For the rest one tries to alleviate, however infinitesimally, some tiny fragment of the general misery; one writes . . . one tries to understand a little of this extraordinary universe . . .

The year's money troubles were not over. Aldous's British agent was Ralph Pinker, head of J. B. Pinker & Sons, "one of the two or three oldest literary agencies in London—highly regarded and supposedly uncorruptible." (I owe the inside of this story to Cass Canfield of Harper's, whom I shall be quoting.) Pinker's elder brother, Eric, founded the American branch of the firm in the 1930s.

> . . Eric Pinker seemed to me a kind of "Mr Salteena" but agreeable nevertheless—a sporty type with gambling proclivities. Things went along well with him until E. Phillips Oppenheim could not collect from Eric $100,000 owed in royalties. Eric was sentenced to a term in Sing Sing . . .
>
> A year or two after Eric's release I lunched with his brother, Ralph, at the Savoy in London. This was a bibulous and sentimental occasion. Ralph elaborated on how many of the great authors who let the Pinker agency take care of their affairs had stuck by him. This affected him deeply.

However, by the summer of 1939 even Aldous noticed that Ralph Pinker's payments were short of nearly £900, and wrote him a stiff letter.

> . . I am at a loss to understand why money which was paid to you on my behalf as much (in some cases) as a year ago should still be withheld from me . . .

To this and other letters there had been no satisfactory answer. In October Julian cabled that Pinker's was going into liquidation. Like his brother, Ralph had hung on to some of his clients' earnings and was in due course sentenced to a term in Wormwood Scrubs. "The Pinker situation sounds fantastically worse than one could have imagined," Aldous wrote in December when the details had come in.

> . . I suppose the poor imbecile started speculating to offset an overdraft and didn't stop till he'd reached minus thirty-six thousand. It is difficult to see how else he could have spent so much, seeing that he has always made an excellent income out of his business . . .

Some of Pinker's clients were badly stung; so Aldous was relatively lucky to get away with a loss of £500.

News again of Maria's family—two long and wonderfully vivid letters from Rose—all were re-united in Sanary for the present, though fearing re-patriation to Belgium by Vichy France. "But one of my brothers-in-law [young Eric de Haulleville] cannot live long," Maria wrote to Eddy,

> Because the strain of the walks and nights and starvations and fears has ruined the heart and the kidneys. He is a surréalist poet and had

14

to drop, along with a bicycle, all his manuscripts . . that must have broken his heart too.

And Jeanne was married again. To Georges Neveux (at the Mairie in Sanary). The Huxleys started cabling money . . .

During the Presidential Elections in November (Roosevelt *v.* Wendell Wilkie) when the rest of the European colony was putting their hopes on F. D. R., Aldous remained wearily aloof—one *politician* against another . . .

Before the end of the year, Maria wrote one of her summing-up letters. She was sending a Christmas hamper to Eddy and Raymond Mortimer, "if it ever gets there, remember it was sent with love and melancholy . . Melancholy because it is really impossible to write anything. Yet I think much about you and all the unguessable part of English life becomes like a burden." But the letter went on. She told Eddy about Aldous's illness, "Such a good excuse to lead a quieter and quieter life." But he is cured now. About his work, "It is the first work he has been able to do since the war. It means he can work now in spite of the war." And he found the book "more difficult than he thought he would; the arranging and presentation at the right place." About the Californian seasons—"It is the time when fires destroy whole hillsides and villages. And the air crackles with electricity . . ." About Matthew, who will be with them for three weeks again at Christmas.

He has become such an adorable person—his intellect . . has solidified, and he is so like Aldous, and so like Julian too, that it makes me laugh. He writes articles on population which he sends to Aldous, and short stories which he sends to me.

. . We all live far, and all are ridiculously busy. Last year and for the whole year I was so rushed and driven that I don't think I could have kept it up and remained quite sane. Now Aldous is better and Sophie has a car . . .

We have both changed a good deal. Aldous definitely smoother and more relaxed and even more gentle and so well looking, whereas of course I have not got any younger; women don't!

. . Then when it is over, we cannot probably make up for it; we shall be completely out of the most fatal years of our lives and there will be an uncommunicableness that only a long long time can make up. [Sad to say, Eddy and Maria only met once more, and very briefly.] I went through it after the last war; when after five years of growing-up and roaming through the world I found my grandmother again whom I admired and loved. They had worked hard on the spot under the invasion. Very important work for soldiers in German prisons; and I came back so futilely busy living a selfish girl's life;

I did not even realize at the time why I was so out of tune, tactless and thoughtless; it took many years to make up for that. But of course it is highly improbable that we shall want to go to Europe ever.

There was one piece of news Maria had not been able to give Eddy. In France, on Christmas Day, Jeanne had had a baby.

Jeanne, wisely, had not told them before the event. Then, with communications as uncertain as they were, Aldous and Maria only got the news of Noële Neveux's birth in March.

. . I am very near the point of tearing my heart out with hesitation and imagination. [To Eddy] In three successive days I have heard that my sister in Nice had a baby; that the baby was between life and death for three weeks, and when the telegram announcing its survival came, it went on saying "Send us food."

And my mother's letter begs for food and all the packages are stopped by the blockade!

. . Another ray of hope is that we might get them all over here.

But if we do succeed in getting them over here, who is going to keep them all? Should I ask Aldous to work for them? Should I leave them in distress and hunger while we live in comfort? Aldous is feverishly lost in finishing his book. Gerald is much too busy preaching. Krishnamurti is full of sympathy but cannot make my decisions for me. So here I am telling you about it who are under God knows what circumstances in England. For the news was bad tonight. [15th March] It comes on those loud excited voices and yet I must know before I go to sleep because sometimes too it is good. And you have fog and too many clouds for attacks.

. . I do find letter writing extremely difficult now . . one's feelings are so . . strained and also changing . . outside circumstances alter so rapidly . . . But when you say you like to hear from me that pleases me . . . Those very far days when we seemed so young are far enough gone for me to say how fond I was of you . . . I remember one cold night when the lights had gone out and we sat under capes and coats and you said that when we were both eighty we would reminisce. Well, now I am not eighty but one hundred and eighty. So excuse the affection I express . . . It is not very well in keeping with the rules of English reticence. But then, nor am I English. Never very English, was I? Nor did the English like me. I think you were an exception.

My heart is as heavy as my grandmother's heart must have been. And I think we must get used to that too. Never will our hearts ache less . . . Once last week, it was so beautiful as I drove down through

the canyons covered with white scented brush, that I think I sang . . .
But it was not happiness or light-heartedness. Something very
different. Nor did it last.

And to me a few days later, Maria wrote (I had left California
the month before):

It is horrible to be asked for food and not be able to give it. I know
you can imagine the situation. Now that Jeanne has that baby too,
it is tragic. Tell Suzanne that the baby is saved. The cable said,
"Noële sauvée mais envoyez nous nourriture." You can imagine
what I felt like. I am torn between asking Aldous to help and you
know at what cost that is. He has never been willing to "make
money" for ourselves and now to "have to make money" for my
family is too much to ask him. He feels strongly about asking favours
from people too and so on. Also if I were not busy and striving and
pushing all the time, they would all forget and let go and nothing
would be done . . . The same is happening now. Poor Aldous.
    I know that if I cannot get the affidavits, I can ask the Saxtons or
even Willi [Seabrook] . . . When I say I can ask that means I feel I
may ask . . Curiously enough there are so many people I *cannot* even
ask. One has the answer before asking.

Then came some details about how often to send food, and about
money because I had heard about a way of sending parcels from
New York.

We ought to send once a week, don't you think. (Eddy liked the
canned ham and butter.) Chocolate is what my mother asks for.
Some disastrous letters arrived at the same time as the telegrams.
Obviously the situation has suddenly become much worse. Ask
Suzanne to read my mother's letter. It is very touching. But we must
get them out too. God knows how I will manage that. I am terrified
of the burden.
    If you have any bright ideas about their coming over, let me
know . . . I am very anxious . . . but I think I let myself be less
destroyed by things now than I used to. All the teachings have
taught me that little anyway.

And again to me a few days later:

I know how awful asking is; that is why I so often overdo helping
people; to spare them the asking . . . Everyone encourages us to get
all of them out. Except Anita and her brother. Who also made us
waver for a day when they said the first duty etc. but Aldous says
that we only hesitated because there was nothing immediate to do.

The minute we could do something we did [everything] to further the chance of getting them out . . . I believe we may succeed . . . I want to sleep and forget a while. I still can sleep as many hours as I can get . . .

Georges Neveux will get help here because "he is an honourable man" as well as everything else . . . isn't it the most wonderful thing to be able to trust people. I think it must be a better feeling than being trusted. I feel it so anyway. When those one loves or even friends come up to scratch. But how painful, how uncomfortable when one fears they may not . . .

. . If you have time, in your troubles, wish me well in my undertaking. Eric died. Good night.

Eric de Haulleville died at Vence, like D. H. Lawrence. He was not yet forty.

Presently, Aldous spoke the liberating word. He told Maria casually, "If they weren't your family but six Chinese who had only us to save them, we would do it." Maria in her immense relief reported it at once in a letter to Suzanne.[1] *He* was confident and calm. "But—why hasn't it occurred to him to tell me this at once?"

I who was in despair believing that the whole decision was to be my own.

He thinks it inconceivable that I hesitated; he thinks we've only got to live like poor refugees because we *are* refugees, which is quite true after all. De là à mourir de faim, il dit, qu'il y a du chemin.

And the week after in a hand-written scribble to me:

. . So many unnecessary complications . . . Now I hear that Rose is pregnant too! One cannot judge them but it is difficult to understand. And tonight as I was listening to short waves, I was haunted by the Greeks . . . [April 1941—the war had reached the Balkans] The news . . . [illegible] a new type of horror . . .

Sophie is more seriously in love than ever. She does not tell me.

[1] Maria's letters to her sisters were always in French; whenever their contents are essential to the narrative, I have—freely—translated them. My decision to leave some letters, or passages of letters, in the original was based on two reasons. Maria's French had a very particular flavour and some of the things she wrote would have lost the shade of meaning she intended in translation; she would either have left them unsaid or put them in a different way in English. So the choice was really between leaving out such passages or keeping them in the original. My second reason was that consistent English would not have been true to the essentially bi-lingual nature of the Huxley household. When alone, Aldous and Maria usually spoke French to one another.

But what a muddle we are all in . . . Oh, I am well again. Not my
health—my interest somehow. I understand Virginia. [We had just
heard of the death of Virginia Woolf.] For I suppose she did it
deliberately. Only now we must not do it any more. I have learnt
it is not a way out—there is no way out—I can't even say it is
frightening, just tiring, tiring . . .

Joep and Suzanne Nicolas, in New York, were working hard
to establish themselves. Joep was getting big commissions, such
as the stained-glass windows for Holland House, Suzanne had
orders and gave sculpture classes, but to do their work they
needed a studio, materials, assistants, and they had to live (at a
certain standard). They asked Aldous and Maria to help them
out with $500 a month for the next four months. They did. (This
was faithfully re-paid after the war.)

Aldous was due to enter his seventh Three Years' agreement
with Chatto & Windus. The sixth, in 1938, had been identical
with the one before (made at the time he was stuck with *Eyeless
in Gaza*), three works of fiction or non-fiction within the three
years and an annual advance of £1,250. Now the situation had
changed. For one, with the collapse of Pinker's, Aldous was without an agent. This was of little matter. For some time already
he had had no literary agent for America (though indeed he used
one for his film jobs) and had been dealing with Harper's directly.
He was very glad to do so from now on with Chatto's, as in fact
he had long done for all practical purposes. Ralph Pinker had
earned his salt only with translation rights, and translation rights
were at a standstill. The two things that had really changed were
that Aldous could no longer bind himself to writing even one
book every year, and that Chatto's were no longer able to let
him have any regular income whatsoever. (Wartime regulations
did not allow advances to be paid to a non-resident author; all
he was entitled to receive—ahead of actual earnings—was £50
for a delivered MS.) His English royalties for the year, moreover,
had shrunk to £843 before taxes.

The crisis about their coming . . . has been crowned by their
refusal to come. [Maria to Sybille in May] I had a letter which
explained why yesterday. A very nice letter from Georges who must
be a very decent man and Jeanne is well with him. They won't come
because he won't be a refugee on our shoulders. He does not think it
is fair. And I can sympathize so readily with that. But I shudder at
the future unknown to us all.

Then there is Rose who won't come because she wants to stay with
her friends, and particularly with one friend. Mother can't bear to

be separated from Rose's child. Meanwhile, one, the quickest and smallest (two I mean) of Mrs Ebert's food parcels arrived. [A woman in New York who managed to get food into France from Portugal.] . . I did send mother some money via a Quaker friend just when you told me you could do it . . Now, because . . of the great possibility of France and the U.S. finding themselves at war it seems to me urgent I should send more money. I herewith enclose a cheque for five hundred dollars. Send it to Jeanne Neveux, Villa les Flots . . Sanary. If you think it better to send in smaller sums or wait or anything else do. I trust your judgement entirely on these matters. I have an adorable photo of Jeanne with Noële who is now quite well though miniscule. A lively-looking adorable little child. And a photo of Georges with her. I like his face very much.

. . The book is almost finished; one can say it is. We went on a holiday thinking it was, then Aldous started changing some things. He will probably go into the movies for a bit. He is extremely well . . . Matthew will be back. I believe I am very tired but otherwise all right. I long and long to get away and hide but probably it must be from myself I should hide to get a rest. Too much imagination and too much concern for other people's business. We are again in love with the Mojave desert where the flowers have grown in such profusion this rainy year . . .

. . We don't see Eva [Herrmann] often but it is always nice to see her. We were polite to the Feuchtwangers and the Manns live exactly opposite so we meet on our walks. The poodle has been shorn . . and looks much nicer . . .

Indeed, the Sanary pattern had curiously repeated itself, the Thomas Manns in Pacific Palisades, Bruno Frank in Beverly Hills, Heinrich Mann and Feuchtwanger—in safety after hairbreadth escapes—working at M.G.M. (Like Goethe, Mann liked to be attended by a faithful black poodle; we rather had it in for Nicko, the present one, because he made up to everyone when the Magician's back was turned: by his side, he cut us.)

In June Aldous had the sad news that his Aunt Ethel Collier, The Dragon, the youngest of T. H. Huxley's daughters, had died at the age of seventy-five. "Dear Dragon . . ." He wrote an affectionate letter to his cousin Joan (still minding his two refugee children) talking of Aunt Ethel's noble stoicism, light-heartedness and humour.

Grey Eminence was finished and Aldous uncertain what to turn to next. By July,

Aldous, poor Aldous is making a little urgently needed money at the Fox studios . . . [to Sybille] he is correcting proofs which come in like punishment. And that combined with the movie work is a lot for him. But this time he is doing some sort of nonsense for Fox and Fox is nice. They don't expect him to go there and sit every day, so our life is much as ever.

. . A long letter from Victoria [Ocampo in Buenos Aires] . . she is running some sort of French review as well . . . Malraux is at Roquebrune having escaped from a prison camp. There is a price. Usually ten thousand francs. Once in unoccupied France apparently they are left alone . . . As for the Russian affair none can even guess at the truth or the future.

. . Matthew is working with Mr Barrett's tools in his house. [Mrs Barrett was a very nice woman who cooked part-time.] Loulou and I are looking out of an undimmed dining-room window towards a placid sea and many swinging trees and clouds . . . I have always had this tendency to look out of the window for ever and was already laughed at when I arrived in England with the last war.

. . Oh wooden shacks! I could fall in love with them too! And we may still escape into one bang on the desert slopes of these hills. But I should not whisper about it! It was so beautiful last time I went, I almost could not return.

. . From Marjorie [Seabrook] regular letters . . . But I don't understand Americans. Why they have no money and why everything. They bob up and down like mad corks. We may bob up and down in our hearts but anyway the polish on the shoes was always there and shiny.

Gerald and Christopher Isherwood and all that gang have gone to a camp with some Quakers and others and are having prayer meetings and talks for a whole month. We are going to Rosalind [Rajagopal] for the weekend. She and Krishnamurti and the children have been away for a month and we have missed them a great deal. Her blue innocent eyes . . . Now it is time for me to go and fetch his lordship and we come back via the barber and the tailor. It is very like being in a job suddenly. Aldous actually gave Antonio [the gardener] some shoes he should have had two years ago. Still some from England I believe. But so we become avaricious too. The Mrs Ebert packages were ruinous but you should have read the letters they sent when receiving the food. Their news is good and Jeanne is happy. They all tell me how nice he is and he does look it.

More photographs had arrived and again Maria says how much she likes Georges Neveux's face.

To me like a monk's face yet he is anything but a monk so I am wrong.

. . . My mother and youngest sister . . are expecting their papers to come to the U.S. [To Eddy six days later] . . even through the help

of some people in Washington it seems eternally slow . . . I also hear
that the Quakers are coming home because they cannot get food in
to feed the children. Meanwhile we are full of hope again for
England. That is to say I am. I never dare say what Aldous thinks
because I suppose I don't always know, but it seems as if she has at
last got a worse stick to beat them back with.

. . His biography of Father Joseph . . I was astonished to see with
what interest Matthew read it, and continuously, for three days.
I expected him to be bored . . I, on the contrary, thought it pretty
tough reading because of the packed historical background so
incongruously mad; but it may have been because it is just the sort of
thing I cannot remember. Gerald likes it immensely and it is the
first book of A he has liked whole-heartedly; but that is special too.

Now that the book is finished he could not write another though he
thought he had an idea. He says he cannot sit down and write
fiction in the middle of it all and so well I understand . . . No money
of course comes to us from England . . .

Maria mentioned The Dragon:

. . She wrote the most free letters . . Small details one does not
think about . . She had remained in London all the time in her large
lonely house. Maids extinguishing fire-bombs in the garden as
silently, I suppose, as English maids do everything.

Iris Tree, too, friend of Aldous's London youth, had drifted to
California.

We see [her] a lot and she gets interesting letters from her son.
[Yvon Moffat] Do you know him? He must be very intelligent . .
He is a friend of Matthew's and we liked him . . . Iris herself is full
of charm and sweetness; the vagueness does not matter. She lives in
a tiny house with two enormous dogs and no money to feed herself
yet always enough for the dogs and the vets. She goes to stay in the
forest and breaks all the rules by feeding bears honey and milk on
her back porch but she gets by with everything. She found a tame
blue-bird that had settled on her hand from nowhere . . She lives
next to our friends the Krishnamurti bunch and you know the
horror Brahmins have of dogs . . But they forgave Iris for bringing
the dogs and sitting all over their car, leaving trails of smell and
white hairs . . . K. has travelled everywhere and speaks all the
languages which is so nice too. One single language becomes very
boring.

Christopher Isherwood had written to say that Gerald's prayer
camp was being a success: he was

radiantly happy and radiantly well in spite of the heat because the camp was interesting and everything was going well. So that is good. They are released on the 7th [August] and will all come here on the 8th . . . I must say they are doing pretty well to be able to correspond. When I was in my convent and we were "en retraite" we could not send or receive letters . .

Eva [Herrmann] is still painting and living in lonely comfort in a too large house and overspending as usual. But she is nice. Then there is Maugham whom Gerald sees and who came here and who asks us to lunch . . he seems . . much mellowed and gentler though tired. . . Tonight is one of those rare occasions when Aldous went to dine with the Ronald Colmans. You must know him on the pictures and he is a nice man. But Matthew was here and he is so grown-up now that I could not resist having too much of a head-ache to go out. It is the rarest thing for me to have a free evening.

One might note here that with the Huxleys *nice* was a strong word used with deliberation. When Aldous said that someone was a nice man, it meant a good deal; as for instance in his letter of 1918 when he speaks of "the marvellous niceness common to all Beerbohms".

I have a comic little dog now which I spoil and Aldous spoils. . . While I type its hair gets caught in my fingers. And she is a great nuisance . . It is because she looks like a fox and has such impertinent and observing eyes that I cannot resist her.

Matthew is back from college as adorable as ever only more so and handsome . . But I don't know much about him. He is affectionate and easy, yet reserved. He seems so definite and yet so muddled and imprecise and yet intelligent. I wonder what his life will be. I cannot guess but would not be surprised if he surprised us all one day.

When we left Raymond thought it would be Aldous and Gerald who abandoned me for a column in the desert. Now I have fallen in love with a "Cabonan" in the middle of the desert . . .

Send us your news, dear Eddy . . . Raymond never writes at all so I don't either. You give him the news and my love . . . That is best. Nor have any of the Hutchinsons ever answered me and it is best to leave that too. Naomie writes. Do you remember Naomi Royde-Smith? You liked each other.

Dined with father and mother Mann, last night [To Marjorie Seabrook, 4th September] Golo was there [Thomas's second son, the professor]; trying to keep up the grumpiness of an honest philosopher. Mony, the one whose husband was drowned under her eyes, was there and completely silent. Matthew, so alert and trying so hard to talk to Madame: they liked each other so that was all right. Aldous had on a new suit, his first in America, and I could not keep my eyes from him . . . All the old ones are tight and shrunken but nice too in a way. Mann himself has learned English admirably and reads it with interest. He was peaceful and pacifying; she was hating and violent and we would not discuss it; besides to be rude about America while you *have* to remain in it. Eva was there.

. . I can't urge you to come here [California]—so many people detest it. Though, if I dare to presume to say so, they are all wrong. And Sybille is a silly little snob about it—so don't believe her.

Aldous, in his better suit no doubt, had been conscientiously attending Sophie's every public theatrical performance at the Reinhardt School. "He never excused himself," she wrote, "because of work—or because it bored him. One evening I found on my pillow a little note saying: 'Ce soir j'ai été fier de toi. A.' " Nevertheless, not wanting "to be a burden to them any longer—they were spending lots of money and energy on all the family and friends," Sophie decided to give it all up and went to take a secretarial course. In October I had a dispirited letter from Maria:

. . Avarice will have to play a bigger and bigger role in our lives [after talking about people using air-mail stamps] . . . God will help us I am sure when the slump comes and there will be no more movies . . .

I have heard today to my great relief but with a growing sense of responsibility that the Visa Department at Washington have cabled mother and Rose and Olivia their visas for this country. I was very worried about their situation as Belgian refugees in France . . . Only the great problem will only begin once mother and Rose are here . . . But I am trying hard not to think of anything before they are here. Except that I have knitted each of them a jersey like yours.

. . You have often scolded me about mail: now . . . it is worse than ever. We are looking out only for the French mail and for a letter from Washington . . . Flying thoughts in my heart are still so fond, but they never materialize. The loathing of letter writing grows. I also cannot bear writing about myself any more. Chiefly because what we do is so unimportant and unamusing . . . So the day will soon come when I write nothing at all to nobody . . . Now I still make an effort . . but it won't be possible much longer. Then there is of course the dreariness of the actual typing. The noise and the hours I spend at it. Now I seem busy too. Aldous has had to go back to the studio but it won't be for long. We have been often to stay with Rosalind and Krishnaji in Ojai and to see Gerald who now lives in Laguna. Chris [Christopher Wood] has bought a most lovely and comfortable large house there, very Italian looking . . .

Hazel the black one has accompanied them and even you would approve of the cooking. Chris has a wine cellar with a key and Gerald's bed (they got the furniture with the house) is pink and blue cretonnes all padded and stitched. The dining-room is an octagon with large windows onto the sea, very civilized.

Reading aloud a life of Tolstoi after having read some of his journals. What a strange man . . . Much more passionate than I realized. To myself, War and Peace for the 5th time . . .

Got hold of Marjorie's story at last. Excellent, don't you think? I hope you will see her a little . . Do be a bit nice and consoling . . . Aldous heard from Jeremy [Hutchinson] who is stationed in Plymouth Virginia while his boat is being repaired. He is a lieutenant and has a wife, Peggy Ashcroft, and a three months baby and sounds sad but peacefully so. A letter from Eddy same as ever and one from Raymond. Very affectionate but differing much in opinion, he says, with Aldous and Gerald and regretting *that*. Sad too, but again, peaceful . . But above all an affectionate letter. Dear Raymond. He sent his most beloved pictures to America for safe-keeping with a friend and they all burned, in the friend's flat.

. . Sophie does secretarial courses—so anyhow she won't ever quite be one of the starving actresses but will be able to type for a crust of bread and a bad bed in a tenth-rate boarding house if the very worst comes to the very worst. Perhaps I am gloomy but perhaps tired because it is late and I shall go to bed.

In November Aldous, for the first time since 1934, wrote again to his unmet correspondent Starkey;[1] a long letter about war in which he stated some of his most consistently held views. ". . when war is waged on a large scale and for a long time between equally matched powers, all attempts at a solution of the problems involved become equally disastrous.

Thus, it is clear that to make peace now with the Germans on their terms will lead to catastrophic results. And to go on fighting until the Nazi regime is overthrown . . . will lead, in all probability, to results hardly if at all less catastrophic. We live under the illusion that all problems are at all times susceptible to a reasonable satisfactory solution. They are not.

And he said this on pacifism. "In wartime . . psychological conditions

are such that the application of pacifism to politics is for all practical purposes impossible. There can only be the personal pacifism of

[1] Mrs Flora Strousse of Philadelphia who wrote under the pseudonym of Floyd Starkey. She and Aldous had sporadically corresponded since 1928.

individuals. That . . such personal pacifists cannot produce any large scale amelioration of social conditions is obvious. Nevertheless, they fulfil a real social function, particularly when their pacifism is based upon a "theocentric" religious experience. The world would be even more horrible than it actually is, if it were not for the existence of a small theocentric minority working along quite other lines than the anthropocentric majority. It is immensely to the credit of the English and American governments that they should have recognized the existence of personal pacifists, and provided for their functioning as integral parts of the democratic society. No democratic society can exist without an opposition—the ordinary political opposition, and an infinitesimal opposition of men and women who are simply not concerned with the things that preoccupy the great mass of human beings . . .

The men and women of the margin, as Aldous called them in *Grey Eminence*.

. . England and America owe an incalculable debt to the Quakers for the way in which they have educated successive generations of rulers to realize that a theocentric opposition is a thing of enormous value to the society containing it . . .

Good must be worked for (as he again developed in *Grey Eminence*) by individuals and organizations small enough to be capable of moral, rational and spiritual life.

Aldous now had the bad news about Drieu la Rochelle. He explained it to himself in a letter to Julian.

My old friend Drieu has, alas . ., become, as the new editor of the *Nouvelle Revue Française*, an ardent advocate of collaboration. He is an outstanding example of the strange things that happen when a naturally weak man, whose talents are entirely literary, conceives a romantic desire for action and a romantic ambition for political power and position. Rushing in where angels fear to tread, he does the most insensate things. It is the greatest pity; for there was something very nice about Drieu and I had a real affection for him. We occasionally hear from Charles de Noailles . . . The family camps in a few rooms of their huge house in Paris . . .

Grey Eminence, A Study in Religion and Politics had been published in October. It is the history of a man who set out to become a saint and ended up as Richelieu's right-hand man; François Leclerc du Tremblay, known in religion as Father Joseph of Paris and to anecdotal history as l'Eminence Grise, who began life as a mystic and got involved "in more and more frightful power policies, which resulted in the destruction of a third of the population of Central Europe, guaranteed the rise of Prussia . . . paved the way for Louis XIV, the Revolution, Napoleon and all the rest". Father Joseph, who had been a pupil of Benet of Canfield, was a man of genuine spiritual gifts, without desire for personal power; what moved him was nationalism, the passionately held conviction that the glory and supremacy of France were willed by God—the French were the chosen people. A barefooted Capuchin monk, Father Joseph never ceased to practise great austerities; part of his days and half his nights were spent in prayer and contemplation. And after prayer and contemplation,

> back he had to go to the hideous work to which his duty to the Bourbons had harnessed him, the work of spreading famine and cannibalism and unspeakable atrocities across the face of Europe . . .[1]

To the very end he made a desperate effort to make the best of both worlds. Needless to say, he failed. He failed because this *must* fail—and that is the dominant theme of Aldous's book. What made him write it?

> No episode in history can be entirely irrelevant to any other subsequent episode. But some events are related . . more significantly than others. This friar . . . we shall find if we look into his biography a little closely, [that] his thoughts and feelings and desires were among the significantly determining conditions of the world in which we live today . . . [They] led to August 1914 and September 1939. In the long chain of crime and madness which binds the present world to its past, one of the most fatally important links was the Thirty Years War . . . [Father Joseph] was one of the forgers of one of the most important links in our disastrous destiny; and at the same time he was one of those to whom it has been given to know how the forging of such links may be avoided. Doubly instructive in the fields of politics and religion, his life is further interesting as the strangest of psychological riddles . . .

Aldous finished his present movie work in November "—tiresome work, but unavoidable, since Books at the moment don't keep wolves very far from doors, and the movie work is on the whole preferable to the continual shallow improvising of articles and stories . . ." Presently he was able to write to Julian, "I have started preliminary work on a new book, a kind of novel."

[1] *Grey Eminence*. Chatto & Windus, 1941.

Chapter Three

Llano del Rio

TWO months later the novel began to flow. "..Enfin ça marche. He always has trouble at the beginning." Maria to Suzanne. "He breaks off, starts again, change—dropping the idea that seemed so good a few weeks ago."

One present concern was Matthew. The doctors found him in such poor health—anaemia, low blood pressure—that he was forbidden to return to college and ordered at least a year of rest and feeding up. Hard on him, Maria said, as it isn't natural to live at home at his age. (Rising twenty-two.) Luckily he appeared to be looking forward to his leisure and cheerfully settled down to a regime of reading and nursery food.

Aldous was writing, well enough to do just that, for the rest his own health was ticking over. To Suzanne, Maria for once took off the lid. "Je me suis tout à coup rendu compte que probablement il ne sera jamais vraiment normal.

I fear that for the whole of his life he will never be really well. I don't think he'll even mind. He is more and more absorbed by his books and ideas. And a nice walk once a day. He doesn't even notice that he hasn't used his hands or his body for the last two or three years. The slightest effort, the slightest change in routine brings about a relapse, depression, fatigue. The one thing that consoles me is that it doesn't seem to bother him. He isn't quite aware of it, I think.

It is discouraging for me—I felt very sad the other day when I had realized that it might be like this for ever . . .

I telephone for him. When Loulou barks at night I have to force myself to shut her up, I even hide her under my sheets. I'm always full of apprehension and remorse. One has to plot to make him go to bed early or keep his siesta as one does for a child. Because he won't even bother to think about such things, or to plan and organize. At the end of a day this can be as exhausting as physical work—only I have to admit that I think he is happy. That is to say: relatively.

He's recovered from the shock of the Japanese war [Pearl Harbour], and the moment his work gets going he is so absorbed that he forgets the world. He forgets Mère, and Noële and Matthew, and the house and our bank account, and to take his medicine and not to tire himself and to answer his letters.

I believe that he is outside life more than he ever was. There used

to be a time when he made some kind of contact through his
curiosity about material things . . . Now when I try to reach him,
I'm reminded of the fishermen in the Bible . . . But he is so touching, because he is trying so hard to help me, he wipes the plates for
instance when I'm washing up . . .

The note of discouragement, in another key, is sounded in a
letter of Aldous's (to me; à propos of something I had written
about *Grey Eminence* and Mr Micawber). "I was born between
two worlds, one dead, the other powerless to be born, and have
made, in a curious way, the worst of them both.

For each requires that one should be whole-heartedly *there*, at the
moment—with Micawber, as he is and for his own sake, while he is
drinking his punch: with the Clear Light of the Void as it is and for
its own sake, in an analogous way. Whereas I have always tended to
be somewhere else, in a world of analysis, unfavourable equally to
Micawberish living, Tolstoyan art and contemplative spirituality.
The title of my first book . . *Limbo*, was, I now see, oddly prophetic!

Slowly, quietly, they had been going on with their idea of
moving into the desert. The wooden shack was bought, made
habitable and a second little house was a-building. The original
house, not quite a shack, stood under a clump of large trees
beside running water—an irrigation ditch planted with poplars;
there were fruit trees and almond trees and vines, and this was
what had caught them, this and the beauty of the Sierra far away
on the horizon. On 11th February 1942 they left the monstrous
house in Pacific Palisades and moved into the Mojave, to Llano.

That is, Maria and Matthew went to get things into shape,
Aldous followed when the new house was ready and meanwhile
stayed at Eva's. Gerald, too, was building; a monastery, as Aldous
called it. The official name was Trabuco College. He and Maria
drove over to see the site. "It is a huge estate," Aldous wrote to
Christopher Isherwood, ". . in a very beautiful, rather English
country-side behind Laguna . . . one rather serious problem will
be communication with the outside world. The nearest store is
about twenty miles away . . ." (The war-time rubber shortage
was just starting.)

In March Aldous did some movie work (on Jane Eyre), and
when that was done moved out to Llano. Some time before this
he had already come to an impasse in the novel and laid it aside
for the moment. Instead, he had started on "a little book of pure
utility," as he wrote to Eugene Saxton, about the Bates Method.

"I am anxious to get this out pretty quickly; for the optometrists are lobbying their hardest . . to get it legislated out of existence, nominally because the teachers of the method are 'unqualified', actually because theirs (the optometrists') is an overcrowded profession and they fear the inroads of rivals who may cause a diminution in the sale of optical glass. A little book by a reasonably sane and responsible person might help to keep this unquestionably very valuable technique alive and contribute towards its official recognition as a branch of education . . . The title I have chosen is *The Art of Seeing*."

Llano was still far from finished—water problems, lighting problems (they had to generate their own electricity)—but there was a marvellous sense of solitude.

> Car l'immensité et la nudité d'un désert se sent même sur une route encombrée de camions de l'armée; c'est quelque chose de pénétrant comme des ondes invisibles. . . L'hombre entoure la maison et les feuilles sont encore jeunes et d'un vert que l'on peut croire transparent. Car je n'habite pas un désert, j'habite une oasis. [Maria to her niece, Claire Nicolas.[1]]

There were nine kittens playing under the trees while rats gambolled in the little cellar below. "Matthew is with me. He is happy here and his room is large and green, a Chinese green . . . he has his encyclopaedia, we each have our own. Opposite is Aldous's room where he works, it is the sun-burnt colour of the drawing-room in Sanary, with book shelves and ten windows . . but with shutters like European windows . . . He has a Louis Philippe desk with brass feet which we replaced with castors. Because we are putting everything on castors. The kitchen table and the beds and the desks. Of course the beds roll away when we make them, and the dining-table too when the meat is tough and I hope Aldous's desk won't roll off into the desert . . .

". . To the East, among the poplars and the vines, one jump across the brook, you would find a little house, white inside and out, stuffed with wall-cupboards and easy to sweep. That is my house . . I cook in an aquarium, I am the fish and outside are the mountains and the snow and the plain and the leaves that shade us, for the trees are very big. My bedroom is minute—if I want to sit by the window I must roll away the bed . . . Above is a blue attic with a very long bed, like the bed at Sanary. That is for Aldous. But under the thickest and greenest of the poplar trees there stands a silvered caravan which might comfortably house one day a young poet . . .

---

[1] Claire White (Mrs Robert Winthrop White), the writer.

". . There is no prospect of getting new tyres so we use our car only when strictly necessary and then so slowly that I risk falling asleep and into a ravine. Fortunately this obliges us to stay here where I am so happy."

The Nicolas children, Claire and Sylvia, were talented and precocious girls. To Claire, the prospective poet of the silver caravan, Aldous sent this message.

Aldous has asked me to tell you that he advises you to write "poetry" strictly in accordance with the rules. He would like you to follow these with great care because he says this leads to an enrich-ment of the language. The most difficult for example are sonnets. Take Hérédia. Since you like Rimbaud at the moment he advises you to study him à fond so that you will realize that *he* did not allow himself any liberties . . . Aldous thinks that you have enormous facility and talent and that you've got to exercise restraint in order to achieve *quality* . . . Il t'embrasse en confrère.

In another letter to Claire, Maria formulated advice to the rebellious young. "From your letters and your poems I would guess that you were *distraite, rêveuse et révoltée*. Am I right? Vague and dreamy because a poet wishing to escape from life; in revolt b*e*cause of life; and here lies the great danger.

Life is and will be the reality. Rebels are ineffectual, unless they manage to put their feelings in a harness . . . What I'm trying to say to you is that you will have to live this life for a good many years, with human beings as they are, and with humdrum tasks—but tasks which if they are not performed will take on a terrible importance . . . For, to give you an irritating example, the over-independent artist who doesn't wash, smells; the one who leaves his drawings all over the place, loses half of them. The brilliant and egotistical creature who enchants in company has no friends and is wretched at home . . . Rebels never succeed in making their Peace with life, they end up by being obliged to live on the Charity of life. And it is just that which one must avoid. Read biographies. Read the biography of Verlaine, of Rimbaud. After that, I hesitate, but, Claire, do try to understand, read the lives of the saints. You see it's quite a programme. Adieu ma chérie.

Ta Coccola.

At Llano, in his ten-windowed room, at his roller-skating desk, Aldous worked so well that he had finished the new book, *The Art of Seeing* in July, and then went back almost at once to the deferred novel. And now there was the sudden news that Rose, too, was married again and actually *in* America.

> . . by some miracle of which we haven't yet heard the details, [she] managed to get on to the S. S. *Drottingholm* with her husband [Billy Wessberg] and baby. They are now in New York.

Another piece of good news, Aldous went on, "was a cable from M's mother, saying that she expected to get to Lisbon this month —after 18 months of wrestling with visas, etc., and more than a year after we had aeroplane tickets for her passage."

Meanwhile Aldous went off to a seminar at Gerald's.

> . . He is delighted . . and Gerald writes me just as enthusiastically about Aldous; Aldous says that Gerald is at his most brilliant and Gerald says that Aldous is in his very best form and *full of* initiative; this is startling . . . This is the best news I could have and perhaps once again they will become the devoted friends and work together as they once did. The split, although never actually mentioned, always made me sad and seemed so unnecessary. [Maria to Rosalind Rajagopal.]

And in August Mère arrived in New York. "I know what would give her the greatest pleasure in the world," Maria wrote to Claire.

> If you could get her interviewed and have the interview published with her photograph! Do you see? She always suffered from being nobody and this is perhaps the one occasion in her life. I suppose I could arrange it here . . but Aldous wouldn't understand, would be horrified etc. But I can see nothing bad about it. You must know some journalists? Mother of four daughters—refugees during the last war—dramatic escapes—mother-in-law of four remarkable men, Aldous, Joep, Eric and Georges; all well-known. You yourself known, well, what more can a newspaper want?
>
> Three attempts to get to America go wrong; the tickets I send to Bordeaux never reach her; Washington loses her papers; a second lot of papers arrive the week America enters the war; we give up all hope—and *here* she is.
>
> Staying in the studio of her sculptress daughter; going to live in the oasis of a desert (romantic description) with another daughter. One grand-daughter is a pupil at Max Reinhardt's (sounds more romantic than secretarial course and Sophie still goes there sometimes). Well, you see. I think it's a brilliant idea and Mère would adore it.

At Llano the summer, their first desert summer, had been very hot.

. . terribly hot, but I stood it. [Maria to Sybille] Aldous and Matthew were away for most of July and half of August which helped . . . He spent three hard weeks at Gerald's monastery and only lost a bit of weight . . . Then at the end of August came a terrific storm . . now the nights are long and cool . . .
But the news. Oh dear. It is so good that as we confided to each other yesterday, it is rather disquietening. We were walking towards sunset, the Joshua tree immensely slender and tufted, Loulou ahead, Tom the cat behind and we shared our thoughts.
Because Aldous is very very well. Stood the summer without a murmur . . The eyes are improving; the book on the eyes is coming out this autumn. The novel is progressing well. The moods are excellent and his interests are growing to such an extent that I am amazed. He does pick the figs for his own fun; he goes and gets the tomatoes; does all the drying in a box outside his terrace . . . He makes his bed so well that I only go up once a week to change it. He scrapes his shoes on the irrigation days before coming in and he shakes the carpets every morning without being asked to. He loves it all and for the first time knows the joy of things growing and of doing with his hands; that is because he sees better, I am sure.
Then Matthew . . is helpful with ideas that he never puts into practice. Luckily he drinks so much milk and cream that even if he does not like my rapidly improving cooking I know he is well enough fed. Now he will have to go to the army soon; he is a non-combatant as his plea for objection was refused; the only choice being prison, and Matthew and Aldous and me, all three thinking that useless; nor has the child the strength, morally as well as physically, to go through with that. But we have had difficult days over it. Everyone has. He may go to U.C.L.A. for a term unless they call him up before. I don't know.

Maria was writing the day after her birthday and described how she had spent the eve in Los Angeles with her devoted friend Pepe (Weissberger) distributing fruit from Llano.

. . Some delicious, some beautiful, but never both at the same time— huge, lusciously rosé bunches of grapes that taste of nothing but remind one of the passage in the *Après midi* . . . Mrs Corbett with a note from Aldous was the first stop. Then Mrs Barrett's German shoe-making friend, and Mrs Wallace the fat cook you remember, then to my mad French dress-maker . . . then a long dash to the negro quarter where my dear old Hazel received the largest case . . .

but she, typically of her kindness, had gone to hospital giving me up and assisting a dying friend. Then [spending the night in Hollywood] I did a very unusual thing. Matthew had left a detective novel about; I was curious, I looked, I read till 3.15 and .. it was so bad I could not understand or believe it—so ignorant and stupid . . . I was more than a year older by the time my birthday came, and after some medical visits and shopping [I] came home to Aldous for a walk and dinner and a quiet desert night. We now have a huge, blue enamel bedstead standing in the middle of the desert and it looks quite well really. Misses a *pot de chambre* or an immense clock to make it quite a Dali, and a shell. Eva telegraphed, and Anita. That was nice. I was astonished. I forgot all about it till I got your letter from Aldous.

The bedstead was not the only outdoor objet d'art at Llano. In the middle of their yard, on the trap-door over the pit that housed their generating engine, stood a terra cotta bust of Gerald Heard. This ensemble was referred to as Gerald's Tomb. Maria had broken off the letter; she went on next day:

Mañana es otrà dia, to the extent that the tomatoes have ripened, the peaches too; that I shall have to think of peeling them for preserving and so on—basketsful of tomatoes and I feel it is my duty to turn them into tomato purée .. There is no doubt that transportation is getting scarcer and scarcer and that this winter we may get stuck for vegetables and fruit .. So I sit for many hours in my cool kitchen through which the desert extends .. and peel and core and chop. But the sun does the rest. I just put out some sliced peaches covered with honey and they go into a contraption Matthew made with glass and mirrors and black paint and out comes the jam .. Sun cookery is Aldous's hobby, marvellous because it isn't tiring. He puts the teapot in the box in the morning . . . soft eggs take two hours . . .

.. We read aloud a good deal but not your style of books . . . No more time to knit .. Rose's little baby will need some and I wonder when I will do that . . . Why, oh why, must they go in for procreation so in my family? But the whole of America is doing it; I'm haunted by the pregnant women, they are all young, even childish .. They will be bad mothers and be divorced many times and so what of the little children? But all that is in the ways of the world. Our cat must have a wife and they will have babies too, and really it is very cruel not to allow Loulou to have them. When all is quiet .. birds come; they come in the evenings to drink as we are one of the only pools for many square miles; the road-runner has a little chick running after it for many weeks; the quails with long families in their coveys, pheasants yesterday from the next ranch and gluttoning on the grapes; ugly young ones; but the migrating birds stop. Six ducks one evening with blue-tipped wings and then, making me think I had gone mad, five large white cranes in our dark apple tree! Such is desert life. I delight in it. It seems utterly inexplicable when all the papers and magazines and friends are filled with the horrors of war and internal stresses. When Matthew himself may have to go any day and when food has to be sent to Jeanne and in Belgium my family is starving and sick. They are sick all around us; we don't have to think so far, and most people so unhappy, so muddled; so craving and scrambling that it is truly inexplicable that we should have so much and I so much delight. Because if it is egoism it is certainly a form which does not hurt anyone. Nor was I any help to people when I got all excited and distressed and muddling. So now I live this mood until another time may or may not come. Perhaps you do not understand, perhaps you disagree, perhaps you condemn. But I have sent a letter you asked for and I know that you will always be fond . . . Don't forget to write at Christmas! Let us be conventional about traditions.

Maria ended this letter—a long one even for her, of which I have transcribed about one-third—with this passage:

Mother is in New York. With Suzanne at the moment, proposing, on my suggestion, to come and live with us. I trust and hope that we will behave well and stand it. I think so. And the day may yet come when Aldous and I will be alone in our desert as it was meant; by us; because who knows about fate.

The little book of pure utility came out in October in America (and in England some months later selling 10,000 copies in the first few days). Aldous had written *The Art of Seeing* to repay a debt of gratitude:

. . gratitude to the pioneer of visual education, the late Dr W. H. Bates, and to his disciple, Mrs Margaret D. Corbett, to whose skill as teacher I owe the improvement in my own vision.[1]

There was also his hope that the book might suggest help to the thousands and thousands of people who suffer from eye defects and do not get complete relief from spectacles. (He was not offering help or cure, it must be made clear, for any of the acute diseases of the eyes that are treated by surgery or medication, but confined himself—as reputable teachers of the method do—

[1] This and subsequent quotations are from *The Art of Seeing*. Chatto & Windus, 1943.

to the much more commonplace visual defects now treated by means of lenses.) I shall attempt to sum up, in compressed form, Aldous's case for the Bates Method.

> *Medicus curat, natura sanat* . . the whole scope and purpose of medicine is to provide sick organisms with the internal and external conditions most favourable to the exercise of their own self-regulative and restorative powers.

It remains to determine what *are* the most favourable conditions for a given disorder.

> In the early years of the present century Dr W. H. Bates, a New York oculist, became dissatisfied with the ordinary symptomatic treatment of eyes. Seeking a substitute for artificial lenses, he set himself to discover if there was any way of re-educating defective vision into a condition of normality.
>
> As the result of his work with a large number of patients he came to the conclusion that the great majority of visual defects were functional and due to faulty habits of use. These faulty habits were invariably related, he found, to a condition of strain and tension . . . Other causes, he found, were strictly psychological: grief, anxiety, irritation, fear may cause a temporary, or, if chronic, an enduring condition of mal-functioning.
>
> Dr Bates discovered that, by means of appropriate techniques, the condition of strain could be relieved. When it had been relieved— when patients had learnt to use their eyes and mind in a relaxed way —vision was improved and refractive errors tended to correct themselves . . .
>
> Now, it can be laid down as a general physiological principle that improvements in the functioning of a part of the body always tend to be followed by organic improvements within that part. The eye, Dr Bates discovered, was no exception to this general rule. When the patient learnt to relax his tenseness and acquired proper seeing-habits, the *vis medicatrix naturae* was given a chance to operate—with the result that, in many cases, the improvement of functioning was followed by a complete restoration of the health and organic integrity of the diseased eye.

Now if this is so, why is there such widespread, to put it mildly, scepticism about this method in the medical world? One answer, Aldous said, can be summed up in three words: "habit, authority and professionalism.

> [orthodox] symptomatic treatment of defective sight has been going on for a long time, has been carried to a high degree of perfection,

and, within its limitations, is reasonably successful. If it fails in a certain proportion of cases to provide even adequate palliation of the symptoms, that is nobody's fault, but a condition inherent in the nature of things. For years, the highest medical authorities have all asserted this to be the case—and who will venture to question a recognized authority? . .

Another stumbling block (beside the opticians' vested interests) is the very fact that the Bates Method lies outside the pale of recognized medicine—an open invitation to charlatans to cash in.

. . There exist, scattered about the world, some scores or perhaps hundreds of well-trained and thoroughly conscientious teachers of Dr Bates . . But there are also, unfortunately, a number of ignorant and unscrupulous quacks, who know little more of the system than its name . . . no standards of competence are legally imposed upon [them] . . .

As for potential patients,

Visual re-education demands a certain amount of thought, time and trouble. But thought, time and trouble are precisely what the overwhelming majority of men and women are not prepared to give, unless motivated by a passionate desire or an imperious need.

Aldous draws an analogy between Bates and the treatment of infantile paralysis developed by Sister Elizabeth Kenny. Both methods "protest against the immobilization of sick organs. Both insist on the importance of relaxation. Both affirm that defective functioning can be re-educated towards normality by proper mind-body co-ordination. And, finally, both work."

Work if you work. Having stated the case, Aldous got down— he tried to keep the book as brief and clear and practical as he could—to the actual techniques of teaching the eyes to move and relax, the Batesian exercises of palming, shifting, flashing, the way to read, or to watch a film, without strain. Never mind the medical hypotheses on which the theory is based, is his refrain, our knowledge of the human mind-body *is* limited, theories may be inadequate or turn out wrong: does it matter as long as it works in practice?

. . Bates's theory of accommodation may be as incorrect as were the eighteenth and nineteenth-century explanations of the efficacy of lime-juice in cases of scurvy. Nevertheless scurvy was cured by lime-juice . . .

(In this context it is worth mentioning that during the war Mrs Corbett and her teachers were training young men who had been turned down by the U.S. Navy and Air Force but were determined to have another try. "They are so anxious to normalize their vision," Aldous reported to Julian,

> that they are ready to take a lesson every day and to practise intensely for hours at a stretch. The result is that scores of them get through their tests after only a few weeks, sometimes even a few days, of training. The doctors still oppose the whole method on *a priori* grounds; but a number of air force and navy officers responsible for recruitment are now actually recommending young men who can't pass the tests, but whom they would like to have, to go and get themselves normalized by Mrs Corbett. In another twenty or thirty years, even medical orthodoxy may come round to it.)

Mme Nys was about to start on her journey West. Maria sent her a warning word.

> . . J'ai un peu peur que tu ne devines pas la simplicité de notre vie. Car, par exemple, pas de radio; impossible de lire au lit parceque la machine qui produit l'electricité est précieuse et caduque. Nous mangeons très sainement mais vaguement. Enfin c'est solitaire, et nous y tenons . . .

In October she arrived. Inevitably, perhaps, the old conflict flared up again. "Mère hasn't been here a week," Maria wrote to Suzanne, "and already I have become insufferable, irritable and nasty.

> . . The presence of the poor woman, so sweet and calm now and full of good will, is enough to make me shrivel up like a spider . . . *Que faire? Que faire?* I had the best intentions in the world . . And I reproach her with exactly the same faults which she makes rise in me; and I look at myself with horror.
> I fell under the spell of this desert and thought I'd become an angel. At the first temptation I find myself as intolerant as ever. When I'm with Mère everything goes to pieces, Mère who hasn't spoken ill of anyone yet, who hasn't done any harm to the dogs or the cats, or to Olivia who adores her, or to Aldous or to me. And I can find neither affection nor tenderness for her in myself. As soon as she is out of the house, I'm filled with repentance and pity; as soon as she comes through the door again and opens her mouth, I find something to make me boil with anger . . . So it is easier to preach to others than to behave well oneself. Remember the letter I wrote to Claire—I could weep with shame . . .

Poor Mme Nys did not love the desert, and this saddened and upset Maria. Mme Nys didn't like the vague and healthy eating habits or having to read by candle light. Least of all she liked the solitude. This was the kind of situation that arose:

Mère offers to bake us a cake. Instead of saying Yes—because I know that she's longing for some—I say of course you can bake a cake but don't do it for us as neither Aldous nor I want to eat any cake. Which is true. But couldn't I have pretended? To anyone else I would have, out of sheer politeness . . . but there is a demon in me which interferes . . . Hélas!

Now Matthew went down with acute appendicitis. Luckily he happened to be in Los Angeles and could be operated on within hours. When he came home again, Aldous and Maria had decided to set up Mme Nys on her own. "My mother came, I failed, and she went," Maria wrote to me. "A passage we might as well forget. As she is now very agreeably and satisfactorily living in a little apartment in Beverly Hills near the Library and has already many friends.

. . Alas Rose has also decided for the nth time that mother is impossible in the house. I do so wonder if the poor woman does realize . . . I can't say what it is that turns me into a shattered bundle of nerves.

Aldous, who always treated his mother-in-law with the greatest courtesy, sent this little note in December:[1]

Chère Mère,
    Gràce a mes dix jours de travail chez Fox, je me sens (ce qui est très à propos à cette saison) un peu riche. Je vous prie donc d'accepter ce petit cadeau du Père Noel cinémafotographique; et j'espère que vous trouverez quelque chose de joli pour pendre à votre Christmas Tree, ou pour mettre dans le bas des autres.
                              Affectueusement,

                                                   Aldous

Rose's little girl, Olivia de Haulleville, a charmer but a handful, was spending the winter at Llano while Rose was expecting another baby[2] by her second husband. Matthew was drafted into the Medical Corps of the U.S. Army (having done his pre-medical years at Colorado University) and was off to his training

---

[1] Unpublished.
[2] A boy. Sigfrid Wessberg. Maria was godmother.

in Abilene, Texas. (Maria, in a letter to me dated 8th March, set down the family news, or newses as she sometimes spelt it.)

. . Matthew takes it all in his stride and is filled with his usual interests . . . He looks handsome and is very happy because he has found an adorable woman to love. I shall have few letters of course. In spite of being as Blimpish as you are some times he is interesting and liked. So we laugh together and also listen to him. I miss him a lot but am so very pleased at the whole solution of a difficult situation and am glad if he is strong enough now to stand the life that all other men must have to stand.

Aldous is admirably well and is writing the best novel yet. He is also enchanted with all our houses and gardens and sheds and trees, and several times a day he goes visiting the large irrigation reservoir which a silver mill pumps water into . . . He is also very anxious to plant vegetables and so it shall be . . Once more, but without the interest, you would find me painting the artichoke leaves . . . Everyone talks of the food shortage which here is more serious than in town and we fare badly always but what of it; I know we won't starve just as I knew we would always have enough money until Aldous got ill and frightened me in his insomnias and there were so many people to support. I hope he will not frighten me into planting beans . . . Since Matthew went, Sophie has been staying here . . . She has typed [parts of] Aldous's novel beautifully and retires each night to read Havelock Ellis and burns a huge log fire that scents the mild air wafted into my windows . . .

From Jeanne no news whatsoever since the total occupation of France following the Allied North African landings last year. Her last letter was dated 29th November.

And all my letters were returned; even some things sent 1941 Xmas! Rose, I don't know, I see her so little. I think she loves the new blond husband who is very authoritative . . . 6 foot high and 34 years old.

And the books we read are fascinating and we do every evening after dinner as ever . . . Read W. Sheldon's last book on Temperaments and you will see why you need privacy and I am driven crazy by my mother and why Aldous cannot take physical exercise . . .

There are few news . . We rarely go to town . . Now we go next week and visit Ojai, we saved our gas for that. We are better friends all the time with Rosalind and Krishnaji and miss seeing them. Then Aldous goes to Laguna to visit Gerald who now owns a large monastery on top of a beautiful hill . . He is happy as far as I can make out but I have not seen him for more than a year. Gas and other things. We write sometimes.

40

As it turned out both Aldous and Maria went to see Gerald at
Trabuco in April.

.. And he was sweet. [Maria to Rosalind] He is very, profoundly,
sad. Poor Gerald. He feels he muddled many of his friendships and
does not understand ... Aldous will stay with him in May and he
asked me to go and so now slowly he may have his family back. I
told you he sees the swami ...

Matthew was now transferred from Texas to Denver, Colorado,
to start training as an Army laboratory technician. This was
excellent news as it was the work he wanted. Then, hardly started,
he caught measles, followed by a throat infection. Aldous was
worried. "Measles is a horribly treacherous disease", he wrote to
Julian, ".. and I hope very much that this may not prove to be
something unpleasant with long-range consequences.

.. One can only pray that the army doctors aren't merely pumping
him full of toxic sulphanilamide for lack of knowing any other
treatment—which is what so many medicos do nowadays, since the
sulfa drugs became fashionable. They even give sulfa-pills to six
months old babies for a cold in the head. The cold is short-circuited
of course; but so is the baby ... One day I should like to write a
little book on fashions in medicine ... fortunately no animal species
possesses anything approaching the toughness of man.

Now something rather sad was happening to Aldous, although
they did not realize it at the time. "A ridiculous accident", wrote
Maria; "he was doing some weeding .. and getting a poisoning
of the skin comparable to poison ivy. Not knowing anything about
it except that there is no poison ivy here, we neglected it."
Aldous's blood stream became infected and he had to leave the
desert for Los Angeles and treatment. Matthew meanwhile in
his army hospital was severely ill. They *had* pumped him full of
sulphanilamide—and this on top of massive immunization shots
for tetanus, typhoid, smallpox and the rest. Shots, as Aldous
said, which don't do one much harm if one is strong, but which,
if there is a constitutional weakness, may play havoc. Matthew
got worse and the doctors believed that he had rheumatic fever;
then again that he had not. After seven weeks of it, still undiag-
nosed, he was medically discharged from the army. He had lost
forty pounds and reached home in June in a very low condition.
  Aldous, too, had returned to Llano, believing himself cured of
the skin trouble. Twelve hours later it flared up—very badly—
and he had no choice but to leave again. It was thought that the
thing had been brought on originally by his handling of some

particularly virulent kind of burr weed, and that he had become allergic to the very presence of this weed which was quite common in the desert. Maria stayed on without him "because Matthew has to be looked after, also because I love it."

On 26th June Aldous's old friend Eugene Saxton died. Aldous wrote to his wife, ". . I always thought of him as one among the best of my friends.

> It was as though he possessed some quality stronger than absence and distance—an essential lovableness and reliability and warmth . . . In a curious, hardly analysable way Gene was, for me, a living proof of the triumph of character over matter . . .

Slowly, Matthew improved. Aldous, inoculated, was back at Llano: "Gay in spite of the poison-ivy-poison which is at last subsiding." (It was not.) "We are all three very happy and sometimes I wonder at it all." (Maria to Rosalind in July.) Their friend Peggy[1] came to stay with them.

> . . The visit was a great success. She looks as fresh and pretty as any girl in love and we were very gay and it was like having one of my sisters here. (I suppose you know that she is going to marry the doctor [Kiskadden] *I* wished for her two years ago—rather frightening . . . He impresses one as being extremely nice . . .) Her visit was most valuable as she saw many ways to improve my treatment of Matthew . . who has a great affection for her.
> We are reading the autobiography of Nehru.

Then Aldous went off for two weeks at Trabuco.

> He likes it there [still to Rosalind] and is fairly well looked after, not as well as when he goes to stay with you. There is another seminar and he goes earlier to see a man, Evan Wents . . It is nice to think that he and Gerald are good friends again. Gerald was for so long stimulating to Aldous that when there came a lull I was sad. Now it seems they are very pleased with each other and so I keep out of it all. I gather it is entirely intellectual and on "principles". But that is all right too . . .

What is one to think about that "lull", that intangible rift between Aldous and Gerald Heard? My guess is that the cause of it was that Aldous would not go along with Gerald's personal involvement in the religious life—the preaching in temples, the assumption of spiritual directorship; Aldous, to put it very bluntly,

---

[1] Peggy, the future wife of the late Dr William Kiskadden, had already been a great friend of Gerald Heard's in England (when she was Mrs W. Curtis Bok) where both had been connected with Dartington.

could neither believe in or approve of Gerald as a guru figure. Both he and Maria saw it as a grave mistake and feared for Gerald. What, if anything aside from "theological" argument, ever came into the open, I do not know. Most likely Aldous silently withdrew; while Gerald, affected by implied disapproval and the loss of coadjutor or disciple—both implausible roles for Aldous—may have seen it (this is guesswork) as a typical failure to commit himself. Whatever happened, there never was a break, the whole thing *was* a lull, an estrangement; it was bridged and their friendship survived, though their companionship, I believe, never quite returned to what it had been during their last English and their first American years.

In 1943 Maria, too, took to spending a few days now and then in what they called Gerald's monastery.

. . Aldous says Gerald has the whole thing, ways of life as well as philosophy, very clearly worked out and on the tips of his fingers which I gather means "tip of the tongue" and that people here find it extremely stimulating . . .

. . It is an extremely beautiful place [to Sybille] and the little convent is built rather like an Italian one. The bells ring and we slip into the Oratory wearing blue jeans and red dresses . . . Iris Tree—the irresponsible Iris—has been out there for three months, most reliably preparing the meals. Deliciously out of beans and starch with sometimes the help of a Boulestin cookery book. She is always on time and always plentiful and angelic. An untidy and sometimes a little dirty angel with blown hair at the early morning meditation . . . She writes hymns in the morning sun and runs wildly with the goats in the afternoon. But she is tired as we all are— and weather-beaten—as we all are even more.

The botanical intolerance started up each time Aldous went back to Llano, disruptive to his work and to their lives. For the rest of the summer he drifted about from place to place, undergoing new treatments, always expecting to be cured and able to return next week. In the autumn he and Maria moved into a furnished apartment in Beverly Hills and tried to make the best of it. At least it was restful to be able to sleep all night without "rushing a flash-light at the howling coyotes", Maria wrote to Matthew who had remained at Llano, "lovely but lonely". Sophie, too, had an apartment in town and was earning not the stale crust of Maria's prediction but an agreeable independent living.

[She] is very pretty, very well, very nice and very happy. She is secretary at Warners for all the dubbing in French and is much appreciated. In fact she is much more than a secretary and loves it and works very hard and very willingly. She has her hair done at Sax's and buys fourteen dollar shoes . . .

Before the year was out, Aldous had got within forty pages of the end of his novel: all but the epilogue to *Time Must Have A Stop* was written. He was still waiting to go back to Llano, but his particular weed was slow to die. It was so strong Maria wrote to me sadly on 13th December, that it had resisted the first snows. "The Christmases that I thought would string themselves out on a desert gold and silver for the rest of my life till we reached the golden little cemetery above us have already been interrupted . . ."

The weed gave up and Aldous and Maria had a long, quiet winter and spring at Llano. The novel was finished in February. Rose's husband was taken for the army, Rose with her two children moved into the desert, to a small house six miles away Aldous had bought. Matthew was well enough to stay in town. When he came out to see his parents every other week or so, he would bring their provisions—a shopping list, Maria sent him, has turned up amongst his papers. A shopping list can be more individual than a love letter.

30/Jan/44
Lettuce (2 as I cook it) romaine,
those snub-nosed little squat
2 artichokes
2 bunches of small carrots and fresh radishes.
And pears and a few tangerines and apples.
Also CHEESE. And a loaf of bread.
And, if possible, a bottle of Nestlé coffee.

Matthew was well enough in fact to return to the university, take his degree and get down to his medicine. He had been on the point of going back to Colorado when it all came out (the Huxleys, it may be remembered, had always counted on their son's medical career)—Matthew did *not* want to be a doctor, had never really wanted to be one, and his pre-medical years had made him loathe the whole idea. Aldous and Maria were badly shocked. At themselves. How *could* they have been so obtuse? They said yes at once. So Matthew was now looking for a job on the technical side of the movies. (At the same time Aldous and Christopher Isherwood were working together on an original film story. The studio never bought it—perhaps it was too good; Matthew, however, eventually landed a job as reader at Warner Brothers.)

On Easter Day Aldous wrote to Cass Canfield, the president of Harper's, who since the death of Saxton was dealing with his affairs:

.. I hope to be able to get down to a project which I have had in mind for some time, which is an anthology with comments, along the lines of *Texts and Pretexts*, but devoted to what has been called the Perennial Philosophy—the Highest Common Factor underlying all the great religious and metaphysical systems of the world. It would bring together, under a series of headings, quotations from Western and Oriental sources of every period . . .

Grace Hubble kindly and most competently did most of the proof corrections of *Time Must Have A Stop*. "Professional proof reading", Aldous wrote her, "has now reached a pitch of ineptitude undreamed of in happier times and my own talents in this direction have not improved correspondingly . . ." Relieved of this chore he was able to begin work on the anthology in May.

Almost at once he interrupted himself again to write the article on William Sheldon's classification of human types[1] which he always regarded as of extreme importance and as the first serious advance of the science of man since Aristotle. Sheldon, after some forty years of research, has devised a typology based upon three factors present to a varying degree in every individual. To these factors he gave the names of endomorphy, mesomorphy and ectomorphy. The endomorphic physique is soft and round and dominated by the digestive tract; the mesomorphic hard, heavy-boned and dominated by the muscles; the ectomorphic is a linear physique, like Aldous's, with slender bones, stringy muscles and a thin-walled gut. Each of them is very closely correlated with specific patterns of temperament—viscerotonia, in Sheldonian terms, somatotonia and cerebrotonia. Now *all* three physical factors are constitutional components in every individual, although in very varying combinations and degrees. Sheldon evolved a system of calculating the relative amounts of each component by dividing the body into five zones, taking a number of measurements of each and subjecting the results to certain

---

[1] *The Varieties of Human Physique* (1940) and the companion volume *The Varieties of Temperament* (1942) followed by *The Varieties of Delinquent Youth* (1949). Though the closeness of the relation between physique and temperament is still a matter of controversy Sheldon's classification of physique is now a standard part of Human Biology and occupies a chapter in a principal current textbook *Human Biology* by G. A. Harrison, J. S. Weiner, J. M. Tanner and N. A. Barnicot (1964).

mathematical procedures which yield a three-digit formula expressing the amount of each component present in the organism measured.

Thus the formula 7-1-1 indicates that the individual . . exhibits endomorphy in the highest possible degree, combined with the lowest degree of mesomorphy and ectomorphy. In practice, he would probably be extremely fat, gluttonous and comfort-loving, without drive or energy, almost sexless . . How different from the well-balanced 4-4-4, the formidably powerful and aggressive 3-7-1, the thin, nervous, "introverted" 1-2-7![1]

"For the first time", [Aldous to Grace Hubble] "the old insights and intuitions about the different kinds of human beings have been clarified and put on a firmly objective and measurable basis." And to E. S. P. Haynes:

. . All other psychologists are merely psychological, and talk as though the mind were unrelated to its muscles, intestines and bones. Sheldon considers human beings as they really are—psycho-physical wholes . . . The gut of a round fat man, like G. K. Chesterton, may be as much as forty feet long. The gut of a thin man, like myself, may be as little as eighteen feet long and weigh less than half . . It would obviously be miraculous if this physical difference were not correlated with a mental difference. And yet these asinine psychiatrists and sociologists continue to talk of minds and characters as though they existed in a vacuum.

The question now posing itself is whether these physical differences are unalterable and absolute? Is there any way—hormone therapy, dieting, exercise—by means of which the physique of, say, a 1-1-7 can be changed into a 7-1-1 or 3-4-3? "The answer would seem to be no. An individual's basic formula cannot be modified . . .

. . Our fundamental physical pattern is something given and unalterable, something we can make the best of but can never hope to change.[2]

Something we can make the best of. Or, by refusing to acknowledge it for instance, the worst.

For example, less than ten boys out of every hundred are sufficiently mesomorphic to engage with even moderate success in the more

[1] Aldous Huxley "Who Are You?" *Harper's Magazine*, November 1944.
[2] "Who Are You?" cit.

strenuous forms of athletics . . Hence the almost criminal folly of
encouraging all boys, whatever their hereditary make-up, to
develop athletic ambitions . . . A rational policy . . would be to tell
all boys the simple truth, which is that . . excellence [in the more
violent sports] depends primarily on a particular inheritance of size
and shape, and that persons of other shapes and sizes . . have as good
a right to realize their own *natural* capacities . . .[1]

And this leads of course to one of the most serious problems
of society—individuals with an inborn propensity to violence.

There exists . . a certain percentage of people, [Aldous to Julian] . .
"Somatotonics" . . who are constitutionally aggressive, who love risk
and adventure . . who lust for power and dominance, who are
psychologically callous and have no squeamishness about killing,
who are insensitive to pain and tirelessly energetic. How can these
be prevented from wrecking the world?

Sheldon's concept of constitutional analysis, Aldous held, has
provided us with a new and extremely efficient instrument for
thinking about human affairs. (Aldous's own article was published in *Harper's Magazine* with "pictorial comments" by James
Thurber.)

At Llano at the moment all was well. In June Maria wrote
to Matthew that Aldous would like to plant two fig trees. "He
has seen some advertised at ten dollars a piece. Apparently he
has been longing for years to get them." Then the weed returned
and he was chased away. Once more it was the pattern of last
summer and autumn: flight; inoculations; hopeful return; flight.
Only now, having kept on the town apartment, Aldous had a
place to escape to.

. . Really quite large [Maria to Sybille] two large bed-rooms,
large sitting-room and dining-room, and Matthew lives in it all the
time. I keep my respectable clothes there and as I never wear them
they never wear out and it is a great economy. And Aldous keeps
his hat there . . .

South Doheny Drive is a street astride the demarcation line
between Los Angeles and Beverly Hills. The Huxleys' apartment,
number 145 1/2 was on the West side and had a Beverly Hills

[1] "Who Are You?" cit.

postman; the East side had a Los Angeles postman who simply consigned any letter, book or contract with a Beverly Hills address to the dead-letters office. Aldous thought it was "preposterous" that one postman would not walk across the street, or the other make no effort at an interception.

For his birthday, Aldous was at Llano. Matthew had sent him some Corelli records which he unwrapped and played before the day. Maria wrote to him, "I don't suppose you knew it was Aldous's 50th Birthday yesterday? The only mail was a letter . . saying that the story [the movie story] is not selling."

Summer 1944 and news at last from France. Paris had been liberated. Jeanne, Georges and Noële were there. "A postcard to say they are well. Alive anyways. How protected we have been." Sophie came out to Llano to announce her decision to join the Free French forces and return to Europe. She expected opposition. Instead, Maria leapt out of her chair and cried Bravo. Aldous agreed to let her go. ("In his absent-minded, cool and charming way." she wrote, "I knew he loved me. I amused him . . .") Presently she left for a training camp in Baltimore. Matthew sent her off with an orchid, her first.

> Sophie went off in a glory. [To Sybille] After those . . five years all ended in perfection . . . She is leaving with nothing but good memories from this stay in a country that will become a fairy-tale episode in her life . . . Now she has gone back to Jeanne and what? Perhaps a man, devotion, self-sacrifice and a perfect mother and wife. It would not astonish me.

Now Rose's husband in turn was medically discharged from the U.S. Army "and they are living happily ever after—we hope. They paint, they sculpt, they sing and they admire their children. Olivia goes to the local school in a yellow bus but speaks French at home and has an English accent."

In November the doctors allowed Aldous to return to Llano for the winter. And now he did something he had often longed to do, he learnt to drive. Maria taught him.

> . . Yes, it's wonderful about the car. [To Sybille] He will not take a licence or drive on the main highways and in town but he adores it and still likes speed. Nor did he ever make a mistake; not when learning to back or enter the garage. Even the cattle stare in wonderment when he drives through them and our gate neatly into a crowded garage. And he smiles and his cap is always on one side or the other for the setting of the sun and you know how comic and rakish and adorable he looks then. Also like a little boy because he is very preoccupied to do it well—and does.

Christmas they spent with Rose, and Maria was able now to describe it to Jeanne:

> . . un beau Noël chez Rose. We are all so fond of one another that it was charming and even Mère (who is no longer afraid of us and therefore not on the defensive) has become a good kind granny to the children who adore her . . . [Rose's boy] Siggy is superb, and like Holbein's portrait of the little English prince in red and gold. Olivia will have looks . . . Rose was beautiful . . .

And on their way home, Matthew told Maria "avec une conviction qui faisait pitié, 'If I could have a wife like Rose I would be happy.' . . . He has a horror of divorce and loves family life just as though he'd been brought up with brothers and sisters."

January 1945. Once more Maria sent me her news report from Llano.

> . . The spring is in full sweetness. A spring with snow in the mountains, water in the rivers and green over the desert . . . So we are lazy as in the Sanary winter days; all the more in the expectations of Mistrals. Mistral there and Mistral here. One's fate, even in winds, varies little. Now I hate it less. It has so many values in summer for coolness and windmills.
> My mother was staying here and Rose came with the children . . .
> I have patience with my mother too and can be fond of her now, after 46 years, which is a great relief.
> Aldous is just finishing another book. A fascinating one: a Text and Pretexts of Philosophy. It will be out in the autumn and very much your cup of tea even though you may not agree with it. Philosophia Perrenis. (It would be unlike me to have spelled it properly.) Then he is going to have a painting bout. He has not painted since we are in this country and now is going to try . . . His skin is getting steadily better and next year we hope not to have to go away in the summer . . . We have long walks in the evenings and after dinner we read. But we dine very late and until then we live in our houses. The nights under the same roof but the days well apart . . .
> Since my cure I am less abominably tired . . .

This is one of Maria's rare references to her health. Very few people knew that there had been anything to be cured.

> . . My health is excellent again. It is a bug with a tail; a flagellate and has a face like a tadpole. Usually . . makes children ill but not

grown-ups . . . It caused all the fatigue, the stupidity, the discouragement, the pains and discomforts. After a week of atabrin, which the soldiers take in the Pacific, I was . . so stimulated instead of sleeping fourteen hours a day I could not sleep at all. All the energy has come back . . . This is the most wonderful climate and life for health. We shall all live to be two hundred and shall we want it then? Do I want it now? Shall I ever want it? At the moment it would feel like a punishment but I must say I never think about it. Used to bother me and horrify me when I was always tired. But it is one of the old habits you teased me about—living in the present. . . How much one fundamentally alters I do not know. It seems that things which were always there come up in turns. Sometimes they wilt, sometimes they grow . . . It is just this getting older . . . which gives you some steadiness. If one can get old without resentment or holding back I believe it is worth much more than the beautiful losses. I know I feared it for a long time. Then I forgot about it because I was so busy with other things . . .

Every three weeks Matthew comes for a long weekend and has plans. Now he is installing an invented telephone . . . He is full of wonderful ideas—usually too wonderful . . . We adore each other in a comic and in a tender way. And sometimes we insult each other because the dishes are badly wiped or washed or there is some ash on the table. He is as finicky as I am but we each have our specialities as well as a great many in common. He and Aldous are excellent friends and then, we think he is a queer fish! I don't really know. Because he is both reserved and not at all. And he has queer lazinesses and absences; and then is the most conscientious and thoughtful person.

He reads trash for Warner Bros. But earning his living and finding that he is very much appreciated . . . Many women but thank God no wives or babies. His chief interests are social and political. Very active . . . I am nice and see the likeable side of every new woman: even when one had greasy hair! He is very "sérieux" and could lack a sense of humour if he did not have to live with me who let not a blimpishness pass and he is good-natured about it . . . He is also good looking in a very strange way and . . that straw hair is now much darker . . . He is bound to go to New York . . He has too much of Aldous's integrity for me to ever give a thought to the dangers . . . I think it will be "girls"—il a d'ailleur de qui tenir.

I have a little more patience with cooking and don't mind any more . . . No meat for either of us. Eggs from our chickens and a wonderfully healthy bread. Cream for Aldous and our complete satisfaction with monotony.

Gerald we hardly ever see . . . We see Christopher Isherwood. He is a sort of habitué sans habitudes. Part of the family. But no successor to Eddy—or Raymond. Somehow those days are all over . . .

Eva . . . I asked her whether she would like to come to a séance
which a famous man whose name I do not know is offering to give
us in our flat . . . Only eight people. I never went to a séance except
the sitting we had with Mrs Garrett and that was not successful.

. . May the horrors of this world not disturb your peace-of-mind.
It is the most haunting world and particularly haunted me while
the Germans re-advanced. Now it is relieved a little . . . That peace
will be a misery and misery. Nothing but overwhelming pity if one
went back. I read about it a bit. But one can only have a true
picture through experience . . .

. . Now it is bed-time. A bed which stands in a bow-window and
looks out onto the stars. But not until the eyes have travelled up the
dark trees which are like fountains towards the sky; more beautiful
than with their leaves even . . . Then, further, the snow-covered
hills. The nights are usually very still; even if the wind blows during
the day. So I look out and the silence is so silent it will mean much.
Tomorrow I will have a long day . . . Then Aldous will come back
late with news and books from the library.

Chapter Four

Time Must Have A Stop

"WHICH of your novels, Mr Huxley, has been most real to you?" John Chandos asked in 1961. "You mean the actual characters?" said Aldous. "The actual characters, and the ambience—is there any one novel that became most alive to you?"

"In a way—somehow the one—*Time Must Have A Stop* was the one I most enjoyed doing."

Whereupon Chandos asked about the Fifth Earl and carp gut and living to a hundred, and Aldous had to say, No, no, not that one; and we heard no more.

Time Must Have A Stop took nearly two and a half years—more than the actual writing time of *Eyeless in Gaza*, a book twice the length; two and a half years, that is, passed between start and finish. But the interruptions here were external interruptions—beneficial if anything to the book a-simmering—due to other work and ill health. Although he ran into trouble now and then, Aldous was never intrinsically held up. From the beginning he knew where he was going and what he wanted to say. There remained the—horribly difficult—job of finding the way of doing it. The novel was perhaps his most integrated one to date and it does not lend itself to anthologizing. In spite of extracts from note-books and the usual discursive dialogue, the burden is conveyed essentially by a story, and Aldous's own summary of it says about as much—or falls as short, as anyone's.

. . About half way through the story, [to Cass Canfield] which I have deliberately kept light, with events on a small scale minutely described, the principal comic character dies, and all that follows takes place against the background of his posthumous experience, which is, of course, wholly and disquietingly incompatible with the life he was leading . . . The other principal character is a very precocious and talented boy of only 17 during the main story—whose date is 1929—and whom we meet again in an epilogue, of present date, as a young man, maimed in the war, and concerned with the problem of the relationship between art (for he is a poet) and religion, the aesthetic and the spiritual life. Altogether it is an odd sort of book; but I hope it has come off.

Later he was heard saying once or twice that he thought it had. To Ted Haynes he wrote at the time:

I am very glad you liked the book. I liked it pretty well myself—though I remain sadly aware that I am not a born novelist, but some other kind of man of letters, possessing enough ingenuity to be able to simulate a novelist's behaviour not too unconvincingly. To put the matter physiologically [Sheldonianly], I am the wrong shape for a story teller . . .

Aldous's later books are fully acceptable, and intelligible, only to those who have had, or wished to have, some intimation of what Jeremy Pordage, in *After Many A Summer*, dismissed with distaste as *timeless good*—it is a matter of having bought, or of having at least the intention of buying one day, your ticket to Athens. What Aldous was trying to say—in differing ways, on differing levels of intensity, is what he began to say in *Eyeless in Gaza*. Does *Time Must Have A Stop* bring home the walled-in daily nonsense of the lives of most of us? How credible, how capable of moving—transforming moving—is the character of Bruno, Bruno Rontini, the enlightened and, thereby, the *good* man? How potent is the scene where Bruno has the flash of insight about Eustace Barnack who will die in a few hours, or the scene where he first reaches the boy Sebastian, or the last scene where Sebastian adult meets his father? Do the chapters of the after-death experience come off? For a (personal) answer one has to read the book. I shall only quote two passages. One because it gives the key to Aldous's choice about his own writing during the later half of his working life; the choice to withhold some substance or vitality from his writing for the sake of something else. Bruno Rontini and Sebastian have been talking about poets and writers. They express their knowledge of reality, Bruno has been saying, but themselves very rarely act on their knowledge. Why not?

"Because all their energy and attention are absorbed by the work of composition. They're concerned with writing, not with acting or being. But because they're only concerned with writing about their knowledge, they prevent themselves from knowing more."

"What do you mean?" Sebastian asked.

". . You know in virtue of what you are; and what you are depends on three factors: what you've inherited, what your surroundings have done to you, and what you've chosen to do with your surroundings and your inheritance. A man of genius inherits an unusual capacity to see into ultimate reality and to express what he sees. If his surroundings are reasonably good, he'll be able to exercise his powers. But if he spends all his energies on writing and doesn't attempt to modify his inherited and acquired being in the light of what he knows, then he can never get to increase his knowledge . . . he'll know progressively less instead of more."

The other passage is the last paragraph but one in the novel.

> Sebastian smiled and, standing up, ran a finger-nail across the grille of the loud-speaker.
> "One can either go on listening to the news—and of course the news is always bad, even when it sounds good. Or alternatively one can make up one's mind to listen to something else."

Time Must Have A Stop was published in America in October 1944 (where it sold at once some 40,000 copies) and in England in the February following.

Spring 1945: news coming in from the continent of Europe. Drieu la Rochelle imprisoned in France waiting to stand his trial for collaboration. "When I read of this," Aldous wrote to Victoria Ocampo, "I thought of the possibility of escape by suicide.

> And now it has happened. I had known him and been fond of him since 1919, and these last tragic chapters of his life, with their violent ending, make me feel very sad as I think of him.

There was news of Rina (her own name, one might recall, was Rontini). Rina was re-married, to Marcel Eustration; had spent part of the war in Sanary at Renée Kisling's, heroic in procuring food for Jeanne and other friends in desperate straits. When her husband joined the Maquis, she had gone to work on the land to help feed his comrades. The Villa Huley had been sold. (It was uninhabitable in war-time, converted as it had been to bottled cooking gas: there was no gas.) Jeanne had bought another house for them instead, La Rustique, on the main road between Sanary and Bandol, and transferred the furniture. Rina and Marcel were living there at present. Here is Maria's first letter:

> Chère, chère Rina, Tu ne peux croire combien j'ai été touchée en apprenant par Madame Neveux l'amitié et le devoument que tu as eu pour elle et pour moi durant ces horribles années de guerre. Je sais que tu habite maintenant La Rustique . . je m'imagine que tu t'assoie dans les grands fauteuils, à la table en verre . . et cela me donne envie de pleurer.
>
> J'ai souvent pensé à toi avec tendresses car nos années de jeunesse ne peuvent s'oublier: lorsque nous voyagions ensemble dans la Fiat

et dans la Bugatti. Lorsque tu étais avec nous à Londres et à Paris.
Lorsque tu soignais Pussy et Miquette . . . et je suis toute heureuse
de savoir que . . tu est restée parmis mes affaires à Sanary et si amie
avec ma sœur.

Ici nous menons une vie bien différente de notre vie en France . . .

Maria describes their life at Llano, their animals and cats, the
desert flowers, the poisonous snakes they meet on walks.

. . Mathieu est un très grand garçon qui aura 25 ans la semaine
prochaine. Mais nous avons encore toujours des fraises pour son dîner
d'anniversaire . . . Il a été dans l'armée pendant quelques mois
seulement y étant tombé gravement malade. Maintenant il travaille
dans un studio de cinéma . . je ne sais pas ce qu'il fera après la
guerre.

Then she talks about Aldous, his health and work. He has
written many new and successful books and a few stories for the
cinema.

Mais cela ne lui plait pas . . . Rose habite à 13 kilomètres d'ici . . Sa
fille a déjà sept ans, le petit garçon et tout blond et gras et rose . . .
J'espère que tu aura le temps de m'écrire et que tu me donneras
toutes tes nouvelles . . . concernant ton mari, nos amis et ta famille
en Italie. Je n'ai encore rien reçu de Mme Peterich [Costanza] mais
je sais que Monsieur Fasola est mort. Je n'ai plus de nouvelles
d'Angleterre. Le Comte de Noailles m'écrit que Monsieur Mortimer
était à Paris et un homme très important maintenant dans le
journalism. "Il Signorino Duca" [this was the Italian household's
nickname for Eddy Sackville-West, who sometimes had the look of a
fragile and ageless princely child] parle à la TSF et m'écrit quelques
fois. Mrs Hutchinson jamais . . . Mme Gielgud va bien . . . Le fils
aîné de Madame Kisling est Pilote Français dans un camp américain
. . . Ma sœur Nicolas est à New York . . . Monsieur Seabrook est
remarié et Madame Sybille est à New York. Eva à Hollywood.
Mais la première de nous que tu reverras sera Sophie . . car elle est
dans l'armée Française . . . Je termine en t'embrassant très très
tendrement et en te remerciant de toute ton amitié et de ce que tu
as fait pour nous. Je t'envoie un tout petit colis de chocolat; nous ne
sommes jamais trop vieux pour cela. J'écris à Marcel par le même
courier . .

                                                    Ta Maria

A few weeks before the armistice in Europe, Aldous finished
The Perennial Philosophy. Its greatest merit, Aldous wrote to Starkey,

"is that about forty per cent of it is not by me, but by a lot of saints, many of whom were also men of genius." By Chinese Taoist philosophers, by followers of Buddha, by Christian mystics; by Lao Tsu, Asoka, Plotinus and St John of the Cross, by François de Sales, by Eckhart, St Teresa, by Boehme and George Fox, by William Law, by Christ . . . It was useful, Aldous thought, and timely to show precisely what the best and most intelligent human beings had agreed upon in the last three thousand years. "Seeing that it is perfectly obvious that we shall never get more than a temporary truce until most men accept a common *weltanschauung*." For the blurb (which he re-wrote) Aldous insisted on the insertion of this line,

Mr Huxley has made no attempts to "found a new religion".

". . it may take the wind out of the sails of some of the ecclesiastical critics who will want to say that I am another Mrs Eddy."
The Perennial Philosophy is about the nature of ultimate reality and the ends of man, about how to apprehend this reality and to attain these ends.

But the nature of this one Reality is such that it cannot be directly . . apprehended except by those who have chosen to fulfil certain conditions, making themselves loving, pure in heart and poor in spirit. Why should this be so? We do not know.[1]

Aldous, who has been accused not only of being another Mrs Eddy but of letting down the intellect, goes on:

It is just one of those facts which we have to accept, whether we like them or not and however implausible and unlikely they may seem. Nothing in our everyday experience gives us any reason for supposing that water is made up of hydrogen and oxygen . . Similarly, nothing in our everyday experience gives us much reason for supposing that the mind of the average sensual man has, as one of its constituents, something resembling, or identical with, the Reality substantial to the manifold world; and yet, when that mind is subjected to certain rather drastic treatments, the divine element, of which it is in part at least composed, becomes manifest, not only to the mind itself, but also, by its reflection in external behaviour, to other minds.
It is only by making physical experiments that we can discover the intimate nature of matter and its potentialities. And it is only by making psychological and moral experiments that we can discover

[1] This and subsequent quotations are from *The Perennial Philosophy*. Chatto & Windus, 1946.

the intimate nature of mind and its potentialities. In the ordinary circumstances of average sensual life these potentialities of the mind remain latent and unmanifested. If we would realize them, we must fulfil certain conditions and obey certain rules, which experience has shown empirically to be valid.

. . few professional philosophers and men of letters . . did very much in the way of fulfilling the necessary conditions of direct spiritual knowledge. When poets or metaphysicians talk about the Perennial Philosophy, it is generally at second hand. But in every age there have been some men and women who chose to fulfil the conditions . . and of these a few have left accounts of the Reality they were thus able to apprehend and have tried to relate, in one comprehensive system of thought, the given facts of this experience with the given facts of their other experiences . . .

The fulfilment of the necessary conditions—it always comes back to that; the steps we must take to annihilate, however gradually and painfully, the self-regarding ego: self-will, self-interest, self-centred thinking, wishing and imagining.

Extreme physical austerities are not likely to achieve this . . . But the acceptance of what happens to us (apart, of course, from our own sins) in the course of daily living is likely to produce this result . . . self-denial should take the form, not of showy acts . . but of control of the tongue and the moods—in refraining from saying anything uncharitable or merely frivolous (which means, in practice, refraining from about fifty per cent of ordinary conversation), and in behaving calmly and with quiet cheerfulness when external circumstances or the state of our bodies predisposes us to anxiety, gloom or an excessive elation.

Also:

Sufficient not only unto the day, but also unto the place, is the evil thereof. Agitation over happenings which we are powerless to modify, either because they have not yet occurred, or else are occurring at an inaccessible distance from us, achieves nothing beyond the inoculation of here and now with the remote or anticipated evil that is the object of our distress. Listening four or five times a day to newscasters and commentators . . . St John of the Cross would have called it indulgence . . and the cultivation of disquietude for disquietude's sake.

. . The twentieth century is, among other things, the Age of Noise. Physical noise, mental noise and noise of desire . . . All the resources of our miraculous technology have been thrown into the current assault against silence . . .

. . One of the most extraordinary, because most gratuitous, pieces of twentieth-century vanity is the assumption that nobody knew anything about psychology before the days of Freud. But the real truth is that most modern psychologists understand human beings less well than did the ablest of their predecessors. Fénelon and La Rochefoucauld knew all about the surface rationalization of deep, discreditable motives in the subconscious, and were fully aware that sexuality and the will to power were, all too often, the effective forces at work under the polite mask of the *persona*. Macchiavelli had drawn Pareto's distinction between "residues", and "derivations"— between the real, self-interested motives for political action and the fancy theories . . . Like Buddha's and St Augustine's, Pascal's view of human virtue and rationality could not have been more realistically low. But all these men, even La Rochefoucauld, even Macchiavelli, were aware of certain facts which twentieth-century psychologists have chosen to ignore—the fact that human nature is tripartite, consisting of a spirit as well as of a mind and body; the fact that we live on the border-line between two worlds, the temporal and the eternal, the physical-vital-human and the divine; the fact that, though nothing in himself, man is "a nothing surrounded by God, indigent of God, capable of God and filled with God", if he so desires.

To be filled with God. And what is the point of that? The average sensual, the average rational man may ask. Aldous attempted to give an answer in *Grey Eminence*—where there is no vision, the people perish . . .

A totally unmystical world would be a world totally blind and insane. From the beginnings of the eighteenth century onwards, the sources of mystical knowledge have been steadily diminishing in number all over the planet. We are dangerously far advanced into the darkness . . .[1]

And yet even now

the existence at the heart of things of a divine serenity and goodwill may be regarded as one of the reasons why the world's sickness, though chronic, has not proved fatal . . .

"But the goods of eternity cannot be had except by giving up at least a little of our time to silently waiting for them." Not merely on the economic level income must balance expenditure. Just as "we cannot put forth physical energy unless we stoke our body

[1] *Grey Eminence*, cit.

with fuel in the form of food [or] .. utter anything worth saying, unless we read and inwardly digest the utterances of our betters. We cannot act rightly and effectively unless we are in the habit of laying ourselves open to leadings of the divine Nature of Things . . .

> This means that the life in which ethical expenditure is balanced by spiritual income must be a life in which action alternates with repose, speech with alert passive silence . . . "What a man takes in by contemplation," says Eckhart, "that he pours out in love." The well-meaning humanist and the merely muscular Christian, who imagines that he can obey the second of the great commandments without taking time even to think how best he could love God with all his heart, soul and mind, are people engaged in the impossible task of pouring unceasingly from a container that is never replenished.

Aldous, for his part, had learned this early. *Silently waiting, Taking time to think*—hours of solitude and quiet were part of the disciplines of his profession. In his later years the disciplines served other ends as well. I do not think that Aldous, unlike Gerald Heard, meditated in any formal, stated way, only that in his later life not all his private hours were spent over typewriter or note-book—how often Matthew or Maria had come upon him, sitting quietly, head in hand . . .

That Maria, for her part, followed—possibly preceded— Aldous on this road there is no doubt. But she only spoke about it obliquely; spontaneous, and articulate, though she was, her medium was not words. The question of her beliefs was made more complex by her cradle Catholicism—her Catholicism discarded, her Catholicism retained. Christopher Isherwood, who loved her well, once said, "What Maria believed in nobody knew. Certainly not in words.

> 'Off to Trabuco, Chris?' she asked me.
> 'Not this week. Oh, no.'
> Maria: 'Why?'
> 'I'm so fed up, sick and tired of hearing them yacking about God.'
> Maria like lightning. '*How* I understand you.' "

That June the Huxleys were still in the desert but it was becoming evident that Aldous would never be rid there of the botanical allergy. What happened next, Maria related in a letter to Rosalind.

> We have actually bought, rather suddenly and vaguely the most hideous little house at Wrightwood .. It is twenty-three miles from

here in the hills above us next to Big Pines. A small [mountain] resort with crowded ugly cabins though not of the lowest type. All facilities such as water, electric light, gas deliveries . . a very good little store.

For there were other grounds that made Llano difficult to live in: periodical water shortages, the great heat in summer, the capricious electricity supply.

> One day we went for a walk, enquired to rent, saw a house which was the right size, furnished and clean and in three days we owned it.
> Then we discovered it was monstrously painted and shaped and draped; stupidly and lazily kitchened and bathroomed; and sadly that the two upper bedrooms were really very small and Noah's arky . . .
> Wonderful walks and flowers and surprises of just escaping to tread on a rattler [a rattle snake] and running nose to nose with a mother and baby bear; not so nice and I was terrified because of stories Frieda [Lawrence] told me about mother bears.
> . . Meanwhile Aldous is full of energy and initiative and with white paint he has done very good alterations. I laugh when I see the smears and the crusts and the brush hairs and his finger prints and the paint over the floor and his face! Also he has painted at last a very good and lovely picture . . .
> . . I tell you very secretly that this wonderful place [Llano] is for sale again . . . Pangs of regret for the beauty—should it be allowed to play such a part in one's life?

The first post-war visitor from England arrived in July. "Madge Garland,[1]" a very old friend, of the fluffy pretty type who worked on Vogue for years. [Maria to Rosalind]

> Still pretty and gay but so serious, so much more with a sense of values and that sadness in her eyes which so many seem to have. But she was also kind and sweet in the old days; only more so now; none of that malicious wit and brilliance of that milieu in our young days. She thought Aldous was wonderfully "transformed". Not only changed and looking well and so on. But transformed. I forget so often how badly he did see. How green and stoopy he used to be . . .

And this is Madge Garland's own account.[2] "It was quite extraordinary—when I arrived, Maria took me out into the garden at Llano. Aldous was pottering about across a little bridge: he called

---

[1] The present Lady Ashton.
[2] In conversation with S. B.

out, 'Hallo Madge.' He *saw* me. Then he crossed the narrow plank bridge without stick or specs."

10th August 1945. Aldous writes to Victoria Ocampo: "Thank God we are to have peace very soon.

But . . peace with atomic bombs hanging overhead . . National states armed by science with superhuman military power always remind me of Swift's description of Gulliver being carried up to the roof of the King of Brobdingnag's palace by a gigantic monkey: reason, human decency and spirituality, which are strictly individual matters, find themselves in the clutches of the collective will, which has the mentality of a delinquent boy of fourteen in conjunction with the physical power of a god.

14th August 1945.

Janin, ma Chérie! Le jour de Paix est arrivé . . . It has been official for the last 4 hours. This is something one will not forget! Everybody was smiling—or crying. There is much grief made harder to bear by this exuberance of deliverance. All the shops closed spontaneously . . Mère brought me roses . . . I went to a little church in the Mexican quarter, and I was moved in that poor church because the people were really praying . . .

PART NINE

Sufficient Unto The Day: 1945-1951

"One is compelled willy nilly to adopt
the advanced Christian attitude of 'one
step enough for me', for the good reason
that circumstances don't permit the
seeing of a second step, much less the
distant scene . . ."

ALDOUS HUXLEY in a letter to
Naomi Mitchison

Chapter One

Wrightwood

IN August 1945 Aldous and Maria went out to camp in their new house. Wrightwood stood at an altitude of 6,000 feet in a landscape of pinewoods and sage brush, below a chain of close and spectacular mountains. The nights were noisy with the yelpings of foxes and ranch dogs. It was their first American summer of 1937 all over again, chaotic and strenuous as the settling in at Frieda's ranch. The wooden house was not insulated, the electric light unconnected, Aldous's future room still a stable; workmen appeared, vanished within a few hours; there being no window-glass to be had, they used windows lifted from Llano. "Please," Maria wrote to Rosalind, "like it when you come."

Aldous loved it from the first. "Aldous loves the mountains wherever he sees them. His enthusiasm for the walks are like those of a little boy and make me think how strongly he remembers the holidays in Switzerland with his mother.

> [I] for choice would go back to the expanses reminiscent no doubt of the plains of Flanders—which does not mean that I am not perfectly happy here. You know how happily I can fit into any situation which is not London—or Paris—or New York . . . The altitude used to make me sick but that is better and can be taken care of.

Throughout it, workmen's clatter, hayfever—the form his allergies took that year—Aldous was working away on a slim book on science, liberty and peace. Daily living had become easier within weeks of the end of the war; gasoline flowed again, Maria got hold of five tyres and the promise of a reconditioned engine ("Krishnaji will drive me to the garage"). This new mobility made them more busy and restless, "the long monotonous stretches are no more . . ." But the overwhelming thing, "the actual joy, each day, is peace. Bad as it is. Ominous too as it is. But to know that they are not burning, smashing, torturing at the moment, is a continual and active realization."

The Perennial Philosophy was published in America in September, and sold 23,000 copies within weeks. (Pleasing to Aldous, Maria wrote, as an "expression of interest in it".) Matthew had become an American citizen, and went off to the University of California at Berkeley to continue his education, specializing now in Latin-American studies.

> [He] has been the big happiness and joy of my life lately [Maria to Sybille] because he very rapidly has become just the sort of man I wanted him to become. Self-assured; and self-directed. Definitely on the side of all that we care for and his personal integrity is beyond doubt. He will make small mistakes; not big ones—I think . . . His health is excellent . . . I suppose that you think me quite a doting mother—but Aldous has turned into a doting father. And Matthew is extremely useful to him sometimes. Helped him out instantly over a deep jam in the Alice situation. Then Matthew presses him to more activity than he would have otherwise in worldly matters.

The Alice situation: Aldous had been asked to work with Walt Disney on a film about *Alice in Wonderland*—part a cartoon version of Tenniel's drawings, part flesh-and-blood episodes from the life of Lewis Carroll, the Rev. Charles Dodgson. The project came off and Aldous and Maria returned to their town apartment for November and December. Aldous thought that something rather nice might be made out of it—Dodgson, the "fascinating mid-Victorian eccentric" and "the old, unreformed Oxford of the eighteen-sixties".

> . . My mother was brought up there as a child—[he wrote to Victoria Ocampo] and incidentally Dodgson, who was a passionate amateur photographer, made a number of delightful pictures of her, some of which are reproduced in the volume of Dodgson's letters to his child friends. Also my aunt, Mrs Humphrey Ward, lived there as a young married woman and has left a very lively account of the place in her *Recollections of a Writer*. [Which Maria was then reading aloud] It would be nice to be able to reconstruct the university of the period, with its long-drawn struggles between Tory High Churchmen and Liberal Modernists, under Jowett and Pattison. But, alas, there is no time in an hour of film—and even if there were time, how few of the millions who see the film would take the smallest interest in the reconstruction of this odd fragment of the past!

All the same, Maria said, "this is the first movie he likes doing". When it was over they retreated once again to Llano for the winter and spring. In May Maria sent off one of her situation reports, this time to Harold and Vera Raymond, apologizing for Aldous's silence. It used to be my business, she said, "writing the letters to friends. Now I have hoped he did some of it because I have been so busy . . . But this evening [Aldous was in town] I long to write to you both and give you the many messages which I know Aldous too feels for you.

. . Perhaps Aldous never writes to Gervas either. His very favourite cousin. But then: we are all so busy . . . Nor is anything improving here with the strikes. There are no queues because nothing is rationed and therefore one just simply does not get anything that is short. There is a double kind of black market here; the regular one and the one which is just favouring the habitual customer—which is fair. But desert rats as we are, no one has our customship and it is lucky that we need so few things . . . You say you just received my parcel . . It must be the Xmas one. I am very discouraged with sending to England as such a small percentage arrive . . Particularly in London . . I spend my whole days making parcels . . Since last year when France was opened I have not stopped or relaxed. Luckily for me the countries did not open all at once. Then the needs grew less urgent while others grew so much worse. Belgium is now actually flourishing. In France my sister can get along fairly well too. She has a delicate little girl which complicates matters. And now I do all I can for Italy. [For Costanza Fasola, for Rina's family, for so many others.] There also it is disheartening because so much is stolen . . . And I know that I have stood in front of my table with the weighing scales for as many hours as the continental mothers have in their queues . . but with the difference that I did it with joy . . .

Has Aldous told them that they usually lived in a desert and that "we loved it? That it was [and the *was* crossed out and made into *is*] the most beautiful place on earth?" But now they are thinking of selling because there is this new house in the mountains.

We shall go there soon . . . our dearest friend Krishnamurti will be there all June . . .
. . We are a gay and intimate family. Matthew is very different. Yet he has so much of Aldous, the kindness . . . Yes, Aldous still has no glasses. In fact he sees better and better. Enough now to drive the car on these country roads. He can read large print with the eye that was blind. If you notice on the photographs, the eyes are never retouched now . . . He is planning two novels. I suppose he told you at least that. But we are not planning to visit Europe. Sometimes I long to. To go to Florence again. To see the roofs on the French houses. The mists over the dark tree trunks of the London Parks. We are not likely to go soon. Mostly because we cannot bear the miseries. The begging officers in London streets after World War I were bad enough. And the Viennese. So we just went where there

were no beggars and forgot. Now the despair will be in every country
. . . also we think it is not fair to go and eat your food. Certainly one
day we shall go back. To visit or to stay . . .

. . My little niece is upstairs [Olivia] . . and I can hear her sleep.
She has come to keep me company. It helps remarkably . . I do not
like to be entirely alone somehow even though there are not the
ghosts of the flat in Albany. [Maria used to be certain that E2
Albany was haunted; indeed during the time I stayed there alone I
was uneasy, without tangible cause, every night.] But only cats are
little company. All the dogs have died. Many cats too, but we have
two left . . . snakes, thieves, coyotes, even owls; just the desert. It is
hard on those soft little things. And I mind very much each time.
We started out with eleven [cats] and added up to fifteen . . . and
only two left. One is pale and streaky ginger with golden eyes . . .
Here ends the paper and the tales but never the many messages of
good wishes and much love that we send you both and to the boys
too . . .

It was Aldous who felt aloof and gloomy about Europe. As
Maria had said about him earlier in the war: "Aldous has no
wish to go to England any more. He loved Italy, he loved France,
but his home-sickness was only for England. That has gone now.
It's dried up." To Victoria Ocampo he wrote:

Yes, how remote it seems, the time of our first meeting, and what a
strange, unsatisfactory kind of existence I was leading! And what a
strange Decline-and-Fall world it was we were living in! What
Europe must be like now, after the Fall, is hard to imagine. And of
course it must get much worse . . . as the hunger grows more intense
in the coming months. I was sent a number of French books recently
—all rather horrifying, I thought. Novels about the Resistance—
half heroism, half unutterable moral squalor; essays by existentialists,
which are just Kierkegaard without God and also without genius.
I hope, and presume, that there must be something better . . .

Science, Liberty and Peace[1] came out in America that March and
in England a year later. It said, Aldous thought, some things
that needed saying, "absurdly simple things such as 'the Sabbath
is made for man, not man for the Sabbath', things which men
of science like to forget because it is such enormous fun inquiring
into the processes of nature and designing bigger and better
gadgets that they do not wish to realize that human beings are
sacrificed to applied science . . the pious talk about science serving

[1] Written at the request of Nevin Sayre of the Fellowship of Reconciliation
to whom Aldous made over the royalties.

mankind is (as things are at present) pure nonsense and hypocrisy
. . . I have said all this as drily and unemphatically as possible,
as nothing is gained in this sort of case by rhetoric."

The slim book opens with this paragraph:

If the arrangement of society is bad (as ours is), and a small number
of people have power over the majority and oppress it, every victory
over Nature will inevitably serve only to increase that power and
that oppression. This is what is actually happening.[1]

Actually happening. In 1946? In 1900. That paragraph was
written not by Aldous but by Tolstoi some seventy years ago.
No social evil, Aldous then went on, can possibly have only one
cause. "All that is being maintained here is that progressive science
is one of the causative factors involved in the progressive decline
of liberty and the progressive centralization of power, which have
occurred during the twentieth century."[1] Now is there any way
in which the advantages of a new technology can be enjoyed
without consequent loss of freedom? "My own view," says Aldous,

which is essentially that of the Decentralists, is that, so long as the
results of pure science are applied for the purpose of making our
system of mass-producing and mass-distributing industry more
expensively elaborate and more highly specialized, there can be
nothing but ever greater centralization of power in even fewer
hands. And the corollary . . is the progressive loss by the masses of
their civil liberties, their personal independence and their opportunities for self-government. But here we must note that there is
nothing in the results of disinterested scientific research which makes
it inevitable that they should be applied for the benefit of centralized
finance, industry and government. If inventors and technicians so
chose, they could just as well apply the results of pure science for the
purpose of increasing the economic self-sufficiency and consequently
the political independence of small owners, working either on their
own or in co-operative groups, concerned not with mass-production
but with subsistence and the supply of the local market . . .

. . Ralph Borsodi's studies[2] have shown that mass-producing and
mass-distributing methods are technologically justified in about one-
third of the total production of goods. In the remaining two-thirds,
the economies effected by mass-producing are offset by the increased

[1] *Science, Liberty and Peace.* Chatto & Windus, 1947 (and subsequent
quotations).
[2] Ralph Borsodi—set up a "School of Living" in the East (U.S.) in the
1930s to do research into methods of small-scale production and decentralization.

cost involved in mass-distribution over great areas, so that local production by individuals or co-operating groups, working for a neighbourhood market, is more economical than mass-production in vast centralized factories.

But of course, as Aldous pointed out, it is highly unlikely that this so desirable process of decentralization and de-institutionalization will be carried out. *Quis custodiet custodes?*

. . What is needed is a restatement of the Emersonian doctrine of self-reliance—a restatement, not abstract and general, but fully documented with an account of all the presently available techniques for achieving independence within a localized, co-operative community . . .

Inevitably we come to the results of pure science as applied to war. Armaments, as Aldous pointed out, are the only goods that are given away without consideration of costs or profits.

Modern war is, among other things, a competition among nations as to which can hand out, free, gratis and for nothing, the largest amount of capital goods in the shortest time. These capital goods are all maleficent and unproductive; but the thought occurs to one that something resembling wartime prosperity might be made permanent if there were more giving away at cost, or even for nothing, and less selling at a profit and paying of interest.

To this Aldous added a warning note. If it were to happen we should find ourselves with a political system approximating state socialism. Preferable, most likely, in some ways to the present dispensation. But

we must remember that any government enjoying a monopoly of political and economical power is exposed to almost irresistible temptations to tyranny.

There is no way of escaping Acton's dictum.

. . The most important lesson of history . . is that nobody ever learns history's lesson. The enormous catastrophies of recent years have left the survivors thinking very much as they thought before. A horde of Bourbons, we return to what we call peace, having learned nothing . . .

If our rulers were sincere in their desire for peace, "they would do all they could to by-pass the absolutely insoluble problems of power by concentrating all their attention . . on the one great problem which every member of the human race is concerned to solve . . . The first item on the agenda of every meeting . . should be: *How are all men, women and children to get enough to eat?*"

During the first half of 1946 Aldous was engaged in short-term work, articles for *Vedanta in the West*, a series of essays for the Encyclopaedia Britannica (finally not published). In June he started on a film version of his 1921 short story, "The Gioconda Smile". He was working with Zoltan Korda, Alexander Korda's brother, and found this very pleasant. "He is a nice, intelligent fellow," he wrote afterwards to Anita Loos, "and we were able to co-ordinate our respective specialities of writer and director without the interference of a producer. Consequently the work was done quickly and efficiently, without being held up by retired button-manufacturers using the Divine Right of Money to obstruct the activities of those who do the actual work."

In July Aldous and Maria moved up to Wrightwood again, where the house had become livable enough. The place was agreeable, Maria wrote, "but there is no immensity . . . The beautiful desert is out of my life though it will never be out of my inner eyes." In the evenings they were visited by a charming racoon who took food from their hands. "He holds it in his front paws and carries it to the bird-bath to wash it before eating." Deer trustingly came down the slopes at night, but also swarms of large mice who settled in the caravan, and there was always the fear that Aldous might step on one of the rattle snakes on his walks. After dinner they re-read Proust—alas, their enthusiasm of twenty-five years ago seems incomprehensible now, almost inexplicable. What does Georges think of Proust? Maria inquires of Jeanne (in fact twenty years ago, Aldous had already asked himself this question). "The most curious feature of [Proust's] mentality is his complacent acceptance of the 'intermittences of the heart' and all the other psychological discontinuities which he so subtly and exhaustively describes.

No author has studied the intermittences of the spirit with so much insight and patience, and none has shown himself so placidly content to live the life of an intermittent being . . . *The idea of using his knowledge in order to make himself better never seems to have occurred to him* [my italics].[1]

In August they are expecting Suzanne and her girls. Maria had not seen them for six years; of Claire and Sylvia, Aldous

[1] Personality and Discontinuity of the Mind, *Proper Studies*, 1927.

had only had brief glimpses when they were little: now they were
young women, twenty-one, eighteen. They drove all the way
from New York through the height of the American summer in
an old station wagon loaded to the gills with Suzanne's statues.
Joep Nicolas had gone to Holland for his first post-war show,
and the party was escorted by Claire's fiancé, Bobby White. One
morning early in mid-country they saw a notice stuck against a
tree:

SUZANNE C'EST ICI

"We arrived [Claire wrote[1]] while Aldous and Maria were
having a breakfast of stewed fruit, delicious bread and tea. Aldous
came like a huge insect out of a tiny pod, his silver caravan, I
was struck by how much more handsome he had grown since
those years ago in Holland when his forehead was tensely furrowed
and his posture stooped (. . as a child I was taken along on a
sight-seeing tour and remember his knocking his head on all the
doors and his passionate interest in unicorns . . .) Maria, looking
at my now husband Bobby asleep in a hammock, whispered to
Suzanne: 'Comme il est beau, on dirait un Picasso!' and little
Olivia said: 'Qu'est-ce que c'est un Pique Oiseau?' "
  Soon they were all in a great bustle. Aldous sat to Suzanne
for a head, then Maria; Sylvia painted, Bobby sculpted. Claire
wrote and drew. Very sweet, amusing, talented girls, Aldous
called them, the elder a wraith-like being, the younger with her
feet firmly planted on the ground, the two "equally gifted and
charming, and equally unaffected and unspoiled." Claire was a
little afraid of Aldous, "feeling one must talk—on those marvellous
family walks in the mountains—whereas with Krishnamurti . . I
was terribly relieved at not having to say one word and feeling
completely at ease. I got my first rise out of Aldous, typically, by
a naïve remark. These salt blocks in the meadows for the cows,
were they for making salt butter rather than sweet butter? Actually
what happened was that Sylvia adopted Maria and was relaxed
with Aldous who delighted in her and said she had the same figure
as Maria at that age." Indeed Aldous was enchanted and amused,
Maria told Jeanne, describing what she called "ce centre de
travail et de joie.

  I cannot tell you the pleasure these three "sisters" are giving us
(for Suzanne seems to be her children's age, and they seem to be
nearly hers) . . . Les enfants sont belles et gracieuses . . douces,

<hr />
[1] Claire Nicolas White in a letter to S. B. 1969.

71

intelligentes et facile à vivre et affectueuses. Je ne sais pas combien Claire est fiancée mais . . elle a bien choisi. Et tous travaillent et ne parlent que de travail. On croirait à peine à une réunion de trois femmes. Elles ne boivent ni ne fument et ne semblent s'intéresser à aucunes sottises de leur âge. Je trouve que Suzanne a une chance incroyable. Et qu'elle les as joliment bien élevées. Suzanne elle même est heureuse parcequ'elle travaille.

And what they have seen of Suzanne's work is good, very good, "Pas de génie peut-être mais de premier ordre quand même." It is difficult to believe this about one's own sister, but Aldous says so too. And what does she look like now Suzanne, who used to turn all the heads? "Elle est mince . . . Son visage est beau—je trouve qu'il a gagné de la personalité en vieillissant." Her English is excellent with a slight accent, a Dutch accent. "It seems we have the same voice on the telephone. Matthew falls for it.

Nous nous ressemblons tellement—et si peu. [This was exactly true.] Suzanne est plus vivante, je crois. On se connait si peu . . .

The girls adore Rose, are for ever running in and out of her house, painting away on her verandah, roping in Siggy and Olivia, sketching wherever they go . . .

They all tell me that Rose is happy. And I know that this will please you, Janin. That her life is agreeable and amusing . . .

Maria, so concerned about Rose with two small children, a husband out of work and practically no money, would like to believe it. "Bobby and the girls dream of living in the desert on love and spring water . . . And that old wash-tub of Rose's, the tub with the mangle—*my* nightmare is the thought of that weekly wash—well, it's precisely that old wash-tub which enchants Suzanne!" Aldous's head has started very well; but poor Suzanne does not foresee the difficulty she is going to run into with Maria's.

I give an impression of being young; but then, in detail, the face is tired and shows its age, 48, and Suzanne, whose mind is still full of the me of her youth, is lost. I am not telling her this but I can feel it.

Now for glimpses of Maria by Suzanne. In the evenings, of course, one read to Aldous. Tolstoi. "Poor Coccola who did not see very well and, because of the Bates system, wouldn't wear spectacles, tried to hold the book close to her eyes and then far again, and was enchanted when we took her turn . . . She was tremendously active, living entirely on her nerves . . . using the

money saved by having no domestic help to send parcels to an
Italian orphanage . . . And all those fortune-tellers—she and
Aldous were fascinated by fortune-tellers. And yet Coccola would
go and pray in that little Mexican church . . and read St François
de Sales . . . Once she said to me 'If I weren't married to Aldous,
I would be a Catholic.' . . She also admitted that she suffered from
not having developed a talent of her own. Instead she devoted
herself body and soul to Aldous's talent . . . But then there is his
gentillesse for her—the way he comes running from his study when
she gets home from marketing and relieves her of the parcels . . ."

Presently Claire's fiancé had to return to New York; Aldous
commissioned him to sculpt a new bird-bath which paid for his
train fare. In the midst of it all, Aldous finished the Gioconda
script and switched to the stage version and to note-taking for
a novel about fourteenth-century Italy. In the intervals he wrote
several long letters to his brother about world affairs, letters to
Middleton Murry about demoniac possession, to Cyril Connolly
about Palinurus, to Professor Rhine about para-normal perception and to Anita Loos about the toughness of the problems of
the stage. To Victoria Ocampo, who had asked him for an article
on T. E. Lawrence, he demurred: he had read a quarter of the
Seven Pillars some fifteen years ago.

. . I found it as hard to read now as I found it in the past . . . even
in his writing, Lawrence was a man of the conscious will. He *wanted*
to write well, and he wrote about as well as a conscious will can make
one write. But the consciously willed style always . . stops short of
the best, the genuinely good. It is always what the other Lawrence
calls "would-be" . . . not all artificial styles are of the "would-be"
variety. To some people it comes natural to write artificially; they
are artificial with freshness and unction—like Milton, for example.
Nothing could be more artificial than "Lycidas", but nothing could
be more deeply spontaneous, less of the surface. "Lycidas" is as
much a product of the Tao as are the "wood-notes wild" of more
natural poets. But with T. E. Lawrence I never felt any freshness or
spontaneity . . . freshness, the free-working of the Tao, the something
not ourselves that makes for beauty and significance—these are the
things I find myself valuing more and more in style. And these are
the things I don't find in the *Seven Pillars*, which I read with admiration for the man . . . As a character, I find Lawrence extremely
interesting . . . If one wants a demonstration of the basic *misère de
l'homme*, one could hardly choose better than Lawrence; for he had
everything that the human individual, as an individual, can possess
—talent, courage, indomitable will, intelligence, everything, and
though his gifts permitted him to do extraordinary, hardly credible
things, they availed him nothing in relation to "enlightenment",

"salvation", "liberation". Nothing burns in hell except self-will says the author of the *Theologica Germanica*. Lawrence had a self-will of heroic, even of Titanic, proportions; and one has the impression that he lived for the most part in one of the more painful corners of the inferno. He is one of those great men for whom one feels intensely sorry, because he was nothing but a great man.

In a letter to Victoria earlier in the year (also à propos of the *Seven Pillars*) Aldous had explained the lines guiding his own reading. ". . I don't read very much in the way of general literature. My eyes make it impossible for me to keep up . . .

and at the same time my primary preoccupation is the achievement of some kind of over-all understanding of the world, directly and, at one remove, through the building up of some hypothesis that accounts for the facts and "saves the appearances". Most of the limited reading I am able to do is aimed at the refinement and clarification of the guiding hypothesis. In regard to belles lettres—outside the few stupendous things, whose periodical re-perusal throws fresh light on the central problem—I read what chance brings to hand, paying attention only to what contributes in one way or another to the furthering of my underlying purpose.

Asked by the honorary librarian of the Peace Pledge Union to write a preface to the translation of Godel's *La Paix Créatrice* Aldous replied (in an unpublished letter of 16th September) that he would think about it. Meanwhile,

I feel more and more that the best way of advocating and securing peace at present is to insist in and out of season on the world's basic and most difficult problem—that of feeding a population already too large to feed adequately and destined to increase from two thousand millions to three thousand millions in a lifetime. Everybody wants to eat. All the resources in intelligence and good will are needed to make it possible for everybody to eat. Power politics guarantee that the world shall *not* be fed properly. Human beings seem incapable of coming to an agreement except in the face of a common enemy—and the only common enemy who is not another human being or society is hunger. Only by concentrating on the basic problem of humanity can we by-pass the non-basic problems, those of nationalism and power.

And to Julian, that same autumn, he put it rather more succinctly:

And of course this business of population is the one thing these bloody politicians should be thinking about at this time . . . Poverty

74

in the midst of plenty is largely bosh. There is poverty in the midst of poverty . . . All this criminal haggling as to who shall bully whom, which is all the peace conferences can think about, seems pretty silly to say the least. Just gangsterizing while the world starves . . .

The happy families left Wrightwood for Los Angeles in late September ("beautiful abandoned Llano was passed on the way, with its gardens brimming with fruit" [Claire]). Suzanne's show opened at the Taylor Galleries on 3rd October. "A good show, with some excellent things in it, and we rounded up quite a good collection of people," Aldous wrote to Anita Loos. "Let's hope to goodness they will do some buying and ordering of portraits. Grace and Edwin were there . . Constance has been a great help and stand-by . . ." The three sisters went to live in Mme Nys's Beverly Hills apartment, eating their suppers at Aldous and Maria's. At noon once or twice a week, as was the Huxleys' custom, they met at the Town and Country Market—that pleasant, shaded place at Fairfax and Third—Aldous and Maria had a friend there, Yolanda, an Italian woman with a lively face and eyes and worn scrubbed hands, who ran a spaghetti and fried chicken stall. She came from Rome and had married an American, Louis Robert Loeffler. They first met at one of Swami Prabhavananda's services at the Vedanta Temple of which Yolanda was a member. At the market she found time to sit with the Huxleys over their coffee, the three of them talking away happily in Italian. It was at Yolanda's one day that, according to Claire,

Sylvia and I spotted Stravinsky whom we had met at a friend's party and had both flirted with, I think. We went over to talk to him, and Aldous, with his usual courtliness, joined us and introduced himself by saying, "I'm a friend of Victoria Ocampo's." This is how their great friendship began.

Presently the Nicholas's ran out of money. Claire decided they must all take jobs.

I found one in the papers for Sylvia as an usherette in a local movie house and for myself at the Marian Hunter book store. Could not persuade Suzanne to be a cashier in a restaurant. For one month Aldous went every night to fetch Sylvia after the evening show and walk her home. I think he found it terribly amusing to escort her in black satin pants and a green military type jacket with huge padded shoulders, her uniform.

In December they had saved enough money and drove back to New York. (A hazardous journey with half a ton of sculpture in the car and a difficult boy for escort, a beau of Sylvia's who had turned Buddhist and refused to consult a map. In Texas their station wagon overturned: much against the odds, humans and statuary escaped uncrushed.)

Aldous learned that Julian had been elected to the permanent secretaryship of Unesco. He was delighted and sent a letter of good wishes and hopes. Might it not be possible for Julian to persuade the technologists that human beings have certain physical and psychological needs, and that applied science should serve those needs?

The ideal would be if technologists and pure scientists could meet, consider the human situation, evaluate human needs in the way of food, clothing, shelter, peace, individual liberty, group self-government etc; and then frame a policy of research designed to fulfil those needs.

E.g. it is perfectly obvious that atomic energy, being generated from uranium, which is a natural monopoly, is a power-source no less politically unsatisfactory than petroleum. Like petroleum, uranium may occur within the territories of powerful nations—in which case it increases their power and their tendency to bully others; or it may be found within the borders of weak nations—in which case it invites aggression and international chicanery, as is now the case with the oil of the Middle East.

Now how about developing a source of power which is *not* a natural monopoly? Nor a wasting asset, like uranium, or petroleum, or even coal?

The most obvious power source hitherto inadequately exploited is wind. I gather that the experimental wind turbine which has been producing fifteen hundred kilowatts in Maine has proved entirely satisfactory. If scientists genuinely wanted to contribute to peace and well being, they can collectively and intensively consider the yet more efficient development of such wind turbines and thereby end natural monopolies and remove one of the standing temptations to aggression, war and foreign burrowing from within. But they prefer to concentrate on atomic power, which creates unparalleled temptations . . .

That winter Cyril Connolly came to California, the first English (non-expatriate) writer after the war, the first to see Aldous, their first new meeting since those barren encounters at Sanary in the past. So much had happened. Cyril had gone on from the love of his youth for the early books ("the brilliant destructive period"), had felt let down by *Point Counter Point*, had pounced on *Eyeless in Gaza* with a savage parody, and then become captivated again by *Ends and Means*, which he reviewed, and been "strangely moved by passages in *After Many A Summer* and almost all of *Time Must Have A Stop*."[1] Meanwhile Aldous had written a fan letter to the author of *Palinurus* (there was a distinctive flavour about its *Weltanschauung* which, like Byronism, might become contagious— "future historians of literature may discover lingering strains of palinuremia"). And now here they met. "I loved him again," Cyril said; and in print, "I was at once struck by the strange new quality of sublimated sensuality, intellectual pity, spiritual grace . . ."[2] He found nothing Americanized about Aldous (".. unlike the younger expatriates, he speaks better English than you or I, with a silvery and almost extinct intonation—sounding the 'o' in petrol like a bell").[1] Hollywood, Los Angeles, Aldous's environment, Cyril like so many Europeans found unlovely, alien— "those who have loved the Mediterranean will not be reconciled here and those who really care for books can never settle down to the impermanent world of the cinema . . ." Yet there are exceptions, he goes on to say, and of these Aldous is the most remarkable.

> The California climate and food creates giants but not genius, but Huxley has filled out into a kind of Apollonian majesty; he radiates both intelligence and serene goodness, and is the best possible testimony to the simple life he leads and the faith he believes in, the only English writer, I think, to have wholly benefited by his transplantation and whom one feels exquisitely refreshed by meeting.

One day after the two men had been lunching together, Cyril had a dream in which Aldous appeared to him in a blue light and from which he woke with an extraordinary sense of serenity and consolation. When he told Aldous about it, Aldous said very simply, "Yes, I thought about you a good deal. I felt you were unhappy."

In January 1947 Aldous and Maria began the process of moving their possessions into Wrightwood: they were pulling out of Llano for good. (Though it was still unsold and hard to sell.)

"First night in Wrightwood," Maria wrote to Jeanne on 26th

---

[1] Cyril Connolly in *Picture Post*, 6th November 1948.
[2] Cyril Connolly in *Horizon*, No. 93/94, October 1947.

February, "since it has become my only refuge; and I am sad."
But now that they have put in central heating and gas and
Aldous's very special light-bulbs, it really ought to be quite satisfactory. And there is the good news that Matthew has just had his
degree at Berkeley, "an excellent degree . . one couldn't do better.
I am proud and happy." *But*: Matthew got himself involved with
a woman who adores him and he not, "and he doesn't seem to
be able to get rid of her." And Aldous has been in a muddle over
the dramatic rights of the Gioconda. It is sorting itself out but
has made him nervous and tired. And he had strained his heart
again in the autumn and doesn't seem to get over it. Maria's
next letter a week later is even more discouraged. Aldous has a
toothache, his general health *is* low and Wrightwood so ugly and
the house uncomfortable and too small and there is no proper
help. "I often ask myself why life should be so complicated for
two people of simple tastes who are rich and free? It must be
our fault somehow . . . If only Aldous would take a secretary or
perhaps a taxi once in a while . . . But then we've just been
spending so much on this house . . . I try my best to *feel* as reasonable as I appear and keep telling myself that even if we are going
to live here for the rest of our days, time passes quickly. Too
quickly to waste it over the hundred and one things I do . . .
Forgive this letter . . it's only to you that I dare open my heart . . .
It must be largely fatigue. I'm constantly struggling with details:
you see, Aldous *will* not have anything to do with practical and
financial matters. He doesn't want to talk about them, he doesn't
want to *think* about them . . . And yet he has an excellent practical
intelligence on the rare occasions he chooses to employ it." Now
they've been asked to go to Russia for the Quakers. So interesting
. . . "I should like to go; with Matthew for instance. But for Aldous
at the moment it's out of the question."

Jeanne for her part was in London. She had not returned to
journalism after the war but had decided, on Aldous's advice, to
acquire an entirely new trade. Her little girl Noële had begun
life with defective sight, she had been able to help her with the
techniques from *The Art of Seeing*, and so became interested in the
wider applications of the method. Now she had gone to be trained
as a Bates teacher by the Misses Scarlett, who were practising in
Portman Square (with Aldous and Maria commenting on her
every step from California). In a third and even more open letter,
Maria admitted that she herself was taking Bates lessons again
as she had been seeing very badly. "Reading lately has been
torture.

How well I understand what you say about nervous fatigue . .
Sometimes I have the sensation that if I were pushed a little further,

or a little faster, I would go mad. Whereas I *can* cope with physical
fatigue. I have no longer any trace of tuberculosis and though I
definitely strained my heart several times this winter, I seem to have
recovered from both these troubles. (Obviously, you must not say a
word of this to *anybody*, so don't even refer to it in your letters . . . I
couldn't bear the offers of advice and help . . . Je m'arrange très bien
pour me soigner en secret.)

What with a house in the country and a flat in town and Aldous
the most absent-minded of men, this isn't too difficult.

. . Il est si bon et si affectueux que toute ma vie en est comblée.
Mais la fatigue causée par les êtres humains m'est insupportable et
insurmontable. Une promenade m'est *tout*. This, by the way, is one
of the reasons why I'm so afraid of a journey to Europe. Which in
any case is out of the question for me for at least another year . . .

How she envies Jeanne. To be able to do work of one's own.
Whereas, "I don't see how I can ever stop being general maid.
If we lived in Los Angeles all year round, we could have domestic
help; even here we could." It's the double existence, one day
here and one day there, "it's our love of LIBERTY that makes me
a slave. So I cannot complain . . it's voluntary . . and so calm to
be alone all day and so nice to be à nous deux at night . . . And
now I must go to bed.

Je vais me coucher tout en sachant que je ne verrai même pas les
trois étoiles habituelles . . . je me souviens qu'un hiver à Londres
dans un troisième étage d'hôpital je me suis liée intimement avec le
haut d'un arbre denudé, sur un ciel rose de brouillard . . la beauté
de cet arbre était intense et amical. On peut trouver son plaisir
partout et toujours.

Meanwhile Aldous was still struggling with the *Gioconda Smile*:
". . this translation and development of an old theme", he wrote
to Leon M. Lion who had produced *The World of Light* in London,
"into and through two different media . . a play and also a movie
script . . ." He was finding it interesting as a literary problem but
was growing tired of "the endless jig-saw puzzle and carpentry
work . . . Also . . one gets tired . . of having to express everything
in terms of dialogue. This would be all right if one were Shakespeare
. . . But not being Shakespeare, and working in the realistic medium
of the modern play, one has to stick to conversational verisimilitude
and to be, therefore, even less poetical than one is capable of being
in narrative . . ." Aldous had not yet had any theatrical opinion,

but feels that he has learnt a good deal by the current experiment and will not, in future, "make as many obvious mistakes as I made in my first essays."

And then this job is done and Aldous's health is better and his mood is gay. On their evening walk he tells Maria that this morning, 19th March, he has sat down to his new novel. He speaks about it with passion. Fourteenth-century Italy, the age of *Decameron*, the Black Death, the condottieri, Sienese painting . . . "Petrarch will be a character in the novel . . disguised, of course . . and Catherine of Siena . . . The real saints, Aldous says, are so much more improbable than anything one could invent.

> It must be sad for him [Maria to Jeanne] to talk to someone who knows so little about the fourteenth century . . . But he assured me that he never misses his brilliant friends . . . He doesn't want conversational fireworks any more . . . Aldous, you know, has become a very remarkable human being . . . I wish you knew him now.
> But often we just have fun on our walks, or we're silent; today was different.

Only a few days later, Aldous has his doubts, he wonders whether he knows enough about the period. "Going to the other extreme," he writes to Anita, "I think perhaps I may write something about the future instead . . a post-atomic-war society in which the chief effect of the gamma radiations had been to produce a race of men and women who don't make love all the year round, but have a brief mating season. The effect of this on politics, religion, ethics etc. would be something very interesting and amusing to work out."

Aldous had just signed his ninth three-year agreement with Chatto & Windus. The eighth in 1944 had been identical with the seventh in 1941—no fixed number of books, no annual advance. Now there was one last change: a flat royalty rate of 20% on non-fiction as well as fiction. He and Chatto's continued to enter into an agreement every three years for the rest of Aldous's life. The terms never changed and I shall not refer to the matter again.

In April Maria was still very dejected. "Aldous tells me that my spirit is broken. It happened slowly but surely . . . whenever I dare hope to have some time to myself, or allow myself some personal interest, I am punished. Whenever I relax my tension vis à vis of Aldous, he falls ill or over-tires himself or something . . ." On 9th May Aldous left Wrightwood and his desk—he is on salary again, this time with Universal at $1,560 a week. They are going to shoot the Gioconda this summer with Zoltan Korda directing and Charles Boyer in the principal part.

Matthew had prospects of a job in the East and was ready for a change of scene. His young woman was still clinging. Aldous himself took a hand in engineering a smooth and sudden departure. One dead of night, Matthew, solo, was sent off in his car to New York with parental blessings. On arrival, at Suzanne's, he found a letter of admonishment from his mama:

> . . It is an encouragement to marriage to keep such an affair going . . . the minute it becomes as domestic you give hopes . . . Remember that for the future and I hope this chapter is closed and that you are already in the arms of a plump, gay and unfaithful blond!

She also advised him to write only once, ". . that is, an answer to the first letter she will probably send after the break."

Claire Nicolas was officially engaged now to Bobby White, the grandson of the late Stanford White, the New York architect. "An aristocratic family, in the American sense," Maria wrote, "which means among other things, well brought-up . . important after all . . . Bobby is charming and has an enormous talent . . ." The wedding was in July. The Huxleys did not go because of Aldous's work at the film studio, which was expected to go on all summer; besides "we have less and less desire to travel."

Aldous had some recent news of T. S. Eliot from Ted McKnight Kauffer whom he answered, "I'm glad Tom Eliot was well when you saw him.

> He is a man for whom I have always had a great affection, (though I have never been very intimate with him, in spite of nearly thirty years of acquaintance) as well as a profound admiration.

In July Maria wrote to Matthew, "Strange, sad news—Gerald has said that God's will was to end Trabuco and Trabuco ended . . .

> A very nice man called Kelly came to tea and told us all about it . . . He spoke with no resentment or judgement. But there is no doubt that Gerald really made a mess of the whole thing, chiefly by having favourites and then dropping them to take up another and so often making the dropped favourite despair of everything and leave Trabuco and God; forgetting that God and Gerald were not the same thing.
> . . Peggy had heard vaguely and did not know it had happened yet. It transpired that Gerald was even more of an autocrat than we had thought: and more self-satisfied too . . .
> It is sad . . . Poor Gerald, I suppose.

Seen from the side lines it makes a queer story. Perhaps Gerald Heard's[1] biographer will be able to sort it out clearly and charitably one day. Trabuco itself was eventually acquired by the Vedanta Society.

By September the Gioconda film was done and Aldous pleased with the final version which, "thanks to the untiring resourcefulness of Zoltan Korda, came through the cutting rooms without losing anything from any of the essential scenes [To Gervas]." The one unfortunate thing was that the title had been changed, as nobody was supposed to have heard of the Gioconda. "The all-powerful Jewish gentlemen in charge of distribution have elected to call the thing *A Woman's Vengeance*, and there's nothing to be done about it." To his brother-in-law, Georges Neveux, Aldous wrote a detailed description of the cast in which he said, "Boyer a su créer une atmosphère de tendresse très simple et sans aucune sentimentalité." (Neveux—author of *Plainte contre Inconnu*, *Zamore* etc., adapter of the French dramatic version of *Anne Frank's Diary*—was for his part translating and tailoring Aldous's *Gioconda* play.)

In the course of the year Aldous wrote an article "The Double Crisis", some 10,000 words long, about a subject to which even politicians and industrialists have since had to pay at least lip-service. Twenty-five years ago very few people thought about it or considered it worth thinking about. The subject is ecology. The human race, Aldous postulated already then, is passing through a time of demographic and ecological crisis. There were in fact, he said, two crises—a political and economic crisis of which we were conscious and which was being discussed, and a crisis in population and world resources of which "hardly anything is heard in the press, on the radio or at the more important international conferences. The Big Three or Four hardly deign to discuss it . . ." Indeed so feeble was the interest that Aldous had some difficulty in getting the article placed. One editor of a large-circulation magazine turned it down with the private comment that its hot air content was high. What Aldous was insisting on was (*a*) that world resources were inadequate to world population, (*b*) that world population was rising, (*c*) that the discernible upper level problems could not be solved without reference to the problems that were shaping up in the cosmic and biological basement.

. . *Après moi le déluge*. Industrialism is the systematic exploitation of wasting assets. In all too many cases, the thing we call progress is

---

[1] He died in California in the summer of 1971.

merely an acceleration in the rate of that exploitation. Such prosperity as we have known up to the present is the consequence of rapidly spending the planet's irreplaceable capital.

Sooner or later mankind will be forced by the pressure of circumstances to take concerted action against its own destructive and suicidal tendencies. The longer such action is postponed, the worse it will be for all concerned . . . Overpopulation and erosion constitute a Martian invasion of the planet . . .[1]

. . . Treat Nature aggressively, with greed and violence and incomprehension: wounded Nature will turn and destroy you . . . if, presumptuously imagining that we can "conquer" Nature, we continue to live on our planet like a swarm of destructive parasites— we condemn ourselves and our children to misery and deepening squalor and the despair that finds expression in the frenzies of collective violence.

[1] "The Double Crisis" first published in *World Review*, 1948, republished in *Themes and Variations*. Chatto & Windus, 1950.

Chapter Two

Reversions

AND then they do decide to go to New York—Aldous's first move after nine and a half solid years of California. They left on 15th September, by car of course, staying with Frieda on the way. A month later Maria writes to Rosalind from West 59th street: "We are not lost or dead or even tired. We are simply having a wonderful adventure on this glorious Eastern shore.

. . The journey was fascinating . . usually it had been winter when I drove across . . . The climate was kind; the trees green and heavy with fruit and there were flowers in little old-fashioned gardens. We right away forgot the West and the deserts.
. . We are far from that now. Because we also drove through the large cities which always have parks and rivers for the rich and slums and smoke for the poor . . . Then New York was horribly disappointing at first because our large-roomed and beautiful flat is also horribly old, dilapidated and not organized for a tidy person such as myself. By now, of course, all is perfect. The view over all the roofs and the sun pouring in is what matters most.
May I tell you that I have an absolute horror of California. I would not mind if I never went back . . . *nothing* there holds me, nothing invites me back. And I would have no more qualms if I lost Wrightwood with the books and the kitchen than I had when the house in the South of France went . . . Seen from here . . it seems quite a mad life. Not the years at Llano. Those were peaceful.
. . I can't tell you how well Aldous is. [The life] we are leading . . is very far from our lazy, now I almost think self-indulgent California life. He seems stimulated by the climate, the people and things.

In the morning Aldous went down and had breakfast at the Automat where he could get tea and porridge. Victoria Ocampo was in New York. He ran into John Gielgud—who was playing opposite Judith Anderson[1]—"looking romantically battered." There were Julian and Juliette—on their way to a Unesco Conference in Mexico—Julian "better and more relaxed than I had expected he would be under the strain of his job . . ." There was an unexpected meeting with Gervas, travelling on tea business

[1] In Robinson Jeffers' adaptation of *Medea*. Gielgud played Jason, Miss Anderson, Medea.

and "nicer than ever"; and when those six united Huxleys—
Gervas, J. & J., Aldous, Maria, Matthew—were having dinner
at a restaurant, in walked their young cousin Jill, arrived that
afternoon from England with another party (promptly abandoned). She found Aldous rounded out, "much less up in the
air than he used to be . . ." And Gervas found that he still had
"that tremendous zest—that gift of being interested in everything—almost too much so . . . But the lovely air with which he
talked and talked about all those things . . . One wasn't frightened
by that extraordinary knowledge he had—he brought one *into* it
—did you feel that? And people think of him as aloof. He wasn't
really, you know. *He was more and more concerned.* And how nice
Matthew was to him—I took a very good view of Matthew."
(Who was about to start a job with the Elmo Roper polls and
had found himself a nice apartment in the West Seventies.)

Fridays to Tuesdays Aldous and Maria spent at the Nicolas's
who now lived at Islip, on the South shore of Long Island. "Today
[13th October] is Sunday at Suzanne's. Victoria and her sister
came for the day and are resting . . .

> It is a very large house, full of their paintings . . and so very com-
> fortable as well as agreeable . . . We walk to the sea and in the parks
> of the neighbouring houses . . . Claire is living a charming life; the
> husband sculpts, she writes . . and their house is a small one standing
> on the estate of their parents [the Stanford Whites] whose grand-
> father owned and built the mansion—everything is so much more
> like Europe; it might bore me later—so far it is like being at home;
> I meet old-fashioned English people who might be all Aldous's
> aunts; and very intelligent and sober at that.
>
> I like the different look the faces have in the street, and the vacuity
> of the faces of Los Angeles crowds grows more and more so in
> retrospective. However, all this does not mean that we are here for
> ever. Aldous has a novel to finish; and after all I have a house . . . I
> wonder about the apples. Rose wrote there are a great many . . now
> is the time to pick them . . . It seemed to me always ridiculous that
> people should need holidays . . . until America put me to work. So
> now I am having what every American woman talks about—and
> enjoying every minute of it . . . Wonderful also to be so near Europe
> that all I have to do is walk into a grocery or Bloomingdale, order
> the food for Europe and it is gone. No weighing and strings and
> papers to glue. It seems so easy and I feel so near! Near what is
> difficult to tell you.

The dam is broken, they are up to their plans again. Thinking
of the Argentine: "Victoria has often asked us. Now we shall go."
But the ships are booked up till the autumn of 1948. So they think

of taking the car and crossing Central America from the Pacific·
"Would it tempt you?"

They left the East in the middle of November. On 3rd December
Maria wrote to Matthew from the Los Angeles flat.

Darling Matthew, I want to tell you that Aldous is wonderfully
well, full of spirits and "happy to be back". I don't mind about
"being back" because it is now so obvious that I must revolutionize
our life that all will be well in the end. For that reason alone I am
glad we went. I was slowly getting obsédée by the narrowing of my
life . . . now I give it no more thought because it will change. Not
suddenly, that it can't, but it will.

So think of us quite happy here. Aldous is working well [on the
post-atomic-war novel; Catherine of Siena abandoned] and reading
quite a bit in spite of going to Mrs Corbett every day and I go to
Miss MacGavin [one of Mrs C's assistants] every day. You see, I
already indulge myself too . . . Aldous also goes to [Dr?] Leaf every
day; there is no doubt that . . . treatment is immediately resultful for
Aldous's coughs. That time it was the allergic cough, this time it is
the last bit of bronchitis which left after two treatments; but Aldous
goes every day of this week all the same. There have been dentists
too . . .

In the evenings they are being very gay.

Monday night dined at Constance's [Constance Collier] who
risked having the Chaplins and the Colmans. Charlie always refused
to see Ronnie. While Ronnie has a rather sentimental admiration
and love for Charlie. Charlie very Left and provocative and Ronnie
very Right but never picked up the gloves Charlie threw quite
unnecessarily several times—people have such a need to air their
views always. But all went well; they were very polite to each other
at first but luckily their children are of the same age and play
together. So very soon that table of old people (except Oona) was
dotingly talking of their children . . . Aldous and I could not get a
word in about you because you were definitely out of date. Then
Charlie did the usual acting but with much tact and let Ronnie tell
and act (very badly and shyly) about his Othello film. Charlie was
stupendous doing the Chopin film . . .
Benita [Colman] very beautiful in her plantureuse way and not
ashamed of being the Juno type; beautifully dressed in the only
dress I admired in New York in a Saks window . . Her warm
voice, her healthy laughter . . and the kindness with which she
extremely tactfully brings Ronnie out and to the fore. They are

obviously two very happy ménages. And all under the grand wing
of Constance . . . And Aldous ate a slice of ham . . .

Yesterday we stayed at home, today we had a most delightful
dinner with the Stravinskys. Berman[1] only there . . And I must say
it was delightful to listen to Stravinsky. He pours out—what pours is
very intelligent—it is often very new—sometimes quite difficult to
explain but always immensely worth listening to and the French,
not perfect, is intelligent and colourful. There were also books, and
reproductions; and everything. A vegetarian dinner for Aldous, just
right, simple, good. She is so easy and very nice. Berman, I don't
know. Clever, certainly. He showed us a whole book of drawings
from Mexico. Competent, but not nice. Somehow—méchant. An unpleasant line, harshness . . But the house is nice, easy, straggling,
full of things . . . Stravinsky is so extremely polite, I suppose the old
school of politeness but quite all right and unnoticeable at the same
time. Then suddenly at ten, they asked me if I wanted some champagne? It startled me so much. Of course I said no, so did Aldous,
but when they opened it all the same we of course had it and it was
such a symbolic thing somehow. We quite easily and unostentatiously
drank each others health—but I felt it was a gracious act of hospitality and also a gesture of particular friendship. I believe they
have real friendship for us. We like them very much.

And who else do you think has come back into our life—Gerald.
Not only physically (he has bought a house in the Valley, where
Ventura and Sepulveda meet) but actually he has already asked
Aldous twice to go for walks with him. And he is so nice and there is
so much of the old Gerald in him *without* the old tension in the hands
and eyes! So we are very happy about that . . Dear Gerald, perhaps
he has gone through enough hell by now.

. . . I realized more and more during the journey how little I liked
California. Even the sun I loathe and it gives me head-aches and the
way of life with distances one cannot walk, with help who will only
work eight hours a day [or not at all] . . . It is very unfair because the
sun is wonderful for Aldous's eyes. He knows it. But Mrs Corbett
says the eyes are very good and that the holiday did him, the eyes,
a lot of good. Aldous says no; so I suppose he knows best . . He lost
a bit of weight . . now he has porridge every morning because I
noticed he liked it at the blessed automat.

. . We have not started readings yet. We shall get a gramophone
tomorrow to take with us. Both Peggy and Stravinsky recommend a
small portable Philco which Aldous heard in the shop and liked so
don't criticize it to him. I hope it has *volume* because that matters so
much to Aldous that it makes the neighbours' life intolerable . . . Good
bye my darling. I wish I were Suzanne and saw you for weekends!

---

[1] Eugene Berman, the Russian painter and stage designer.

Then after two weeks of Wrightwood, Maria wrote to Matthew again: "This is a letter to ask you to help me . . .

. . My behaviour during the last five years has become apparent to me . . . for some unknown reason I have been piling upon myself a kind of punishment which took the form of work, physical work that is. I should have realized that indirectly it was a much greater punishment on Aldous who thereby lost help for his own work. When we cleared out of the desert I thought we got out of the situation; but because I had not understood my own psychological reasons, or because there were some unconscious reasons as well . . the situation remained the same.

Because I personally disliked Wrightwood and all mountains I punished myself by trying to live here for Aldous's sake. It is now clear that Wrightwood is going to be a much greater burden than Llano because not only do we both feel the altitude but because the snow and ice make an extra problem . . We have to keep [the house] warm all the time so that it does not freeze. I can rely on no one for friendship or money to turn everything on and off. No one . . has time to be conscientious . . . We made a mistake when we thought we could find help here . . . Even if we could find help, that fact that we live irregularly means we have to pay it for doing nothing . . . or not get it when we want it . . . The same problem in town; the laundry cannot call, the milk neither . . .

We are doubling expenses of living, that is evident. We have here a great capital engaged which would have been well employed if we had been living here most of the time. The house is superbly equipped for permanent residence. *But*, Aldous needs to work for the movies to make a living—he says so in so many words. When there is snow we don't wish to live here, when it is too cold we don't wish to live here. When we *do* live here we are always rushing to town [the best of two hours' drive] for my dentist or Aldous's or something. It is restless . . . For a long time I have felt it catching up with me. For a long time I have told all of you in a joke or in despair that I was going mad; mad or ill, it will be one or the other and now I know it and I told Aldous and we are going to sell Wrightwood.

We must centralize our efforts . . . It will be very hard to find a house in town. It may even be entirely too expensive. But this time I hope I will remember that perfection is out of the question. That I must stick to essentials. Aldous's needs. That I do not need a wonderful kitchen . . . The entire mistake in this house is that I perfected it so that I could run it. I am through with running houses myself. We shall take holidays in expensive hotels . . This habit of economizing on ourselves is ludicrous. And my freedom, my strength, my gaiety are really Aldous's. So I am going to indulge in it. While I punished myself he bore the consequences. Why I have felt the need of punishing myself is fairly clear to me, no need to waste time over it; stupidity, selfishness and misunderstanding are at the base of it.

(By the way, do not think I am ill—[Dr] Hawkins thinks me better than I have been for a long time, so all I do is preventive. Hawkins is *very* clever with me in many ways I notice . .) But to remain well, I know better than any doctor can tell me, that *I must stop*. Just as I knew better than any doctor, when I was young, that I was not going to die unless I did stop. You can trust me to keep fit for Aldous's sake.

In town we shall need something like the house on Crescent Heights. Everyone is very kind and will help. Peggy and Bill [Kiskadden] understand. And Stravinsky has been curiously kind and considerate to me; gone out of his way to be kind about nothing in particular as though he had a second sight about my despair. Because despair it was . . .

Now come figures about what Wrightwood has already cost them. Bills for 20,000 dollars. "Plus all we forget. Shall we ever get it back? We are incapable fools.

. . . Please wish them all a happy Christmas . . Don't spend too much on anyone. You are not rich and we are not either. Aldous has to earn every penny of it.

Then it is Aldous who goes on, in hand-writing, on the same page:

Dearest M, I know you will approve this necessary decision. The next problem is to find something in town . . .

We saw "Monsieur Verdoux" the other day. What an aesthetic mess! He passes from a mime about murder which depends on *not* being taken seriously, to attempts at serious psychology which are supposed to be taken seriously & consequently make the murder-farce seem intolerable—because after all murder once removed from the world of childish make-believe, is not conceivably a subject for comedy. One feels terribly sorry for Charlie—such talents, such a mess—in art no less than in life. And all because he refuses to take anyone's advice about anything, but believing that, like the Pope, he is infallible.

Love from

Aldous

(Here one might note that Chaplin, in his autobiography, records that Thomas Mann and Lion Feuchtwanger gave him a standing ovation at this same private showing of *Monsieur Verdoux*.)

Aldous published no new book in 1947; Harper's, however, brought out *The World of Aldous Huxley: An Omnibus of His Fiction and Non-Fiction Over Three Decades* with an introduction by Charles J. Rolo, and Suzanne's bust of Aldous on the cover. And in February 1948, both Chatto's and Harper's published the Gioconda play (Harper's confusingly, under yet another previous title, *Mortal Coils*).

In January Aldous gave a quote to the publishers of *Our Plundered Planet* and at the same time wrote to Fairfield Osborn, the author: "The great question now is: will the public and those in authority pay any attention to what you say, or will the politicians go on with their lunatic game, . . ignoring the fact that the world they are squabbling over will shortly cease to exist in its old familiar form, but will be transformed, unless they mobilize all available intelligence and . . good will, into one huge dust bowl . . .

I have been trying to put this question . . for the last year or two—even succeeding in planting it in the *Bulletin of the Atomic Scientists* this summer, pointing out that, while mankind could do very well without atomic energy, it cannot dispense with bread. But hitherto I have had no audible response from any quarter. I hope very much that you, with your scientific authority and your beautifully organized collection of facts, will be able to make some impression in influential quarters . . .

. . I see this problem of man's relation to Nature as not only an immediate practical problem, but also as a problem of ethics and religion. It is significant that neither Christianity nor Judaism has ever thought of Nature as having rights in relation to man . . You will find orthodox Catholic moralists asserting . . that animals may be treated as things. (As though things didn't deserve to be treated ethically!) The vulgar boast of the modern technologist . . that man has conquered Nature has roots in the Western religious tradition, which affirms that God installed man as the boss, to whom Nature was to bring tribute. The Greeks knew better than the Jews and Christians. They knew [about] hubris towards nature . . . Xerxes is punished, not only for having attacked the Greeks, but also for having outraged Nature in the affair of bridging the Hellespont.

But for an ethical system that includes animate and inanimate Nature as well as man, one must go to Chinese Taoism, with its concept of an Order of Things, whose state of . . balance must be preserved . . . Whitman comes very close to the Taoist position. And because of Whitman and Wordsworth and the other "Nature Mystics" of the West, I feel that it might not be too difficult for modern Europeans and Americans to accept some kind of Taoist philosophy of life, with an ethical system comprehensive enough to take in Nature as well as man. People have got to understand that the commandment, "Do unto others as you would that they should do unto you" applies to animals, plants and things, as well as to people; and that if it is regarded as applying only to people . . then the animals, plants and things will, in one way or another, do as badly by man as man has done by them . . .

On the 22nd of February 1948, Maria wrote to Matthew:

I must tell you of a great event—the book was finished last night. Aldous arrived in the kitchen saying he was late for dinner, which I had not realized, and then, walking around as you know he does, he suddenly said, "I think I finished the book!"

It was *Ape and Essence*, his second Utopia, the gruesome Utopia set in an enclave of survivors after atomic war.

. . I decided I would read it all night. Take coffee and then take the manuscript to bed. Of course Aldous said no and silly and so on. But after dinner he asked me, "We might read it aloud if you like." This is the first time he allowed me to read anything [of his] aloud, except the play.

And then we settled down in our first class carriages. Aldous's is long and comfortable and he can stretch out, but usually I wriggle and get cramps because mine is that silly short green sofa . . but the first time I moved was at page 70 and Aldous thought of going to bed which I would not—he gave in easily and we finished at one thirty. It read for four hours and a quarter without a lag of interest . . .

My feeling was awe when I had finished. Not fear and horror . . that was coming in waves during the reading; but awe at the possibilities and at Aldous. He looked so well and pink and rested from lying down . . in his blue jersey and the cotton blue shirt . . Though he so often looks old now he looked young and a bit shy and pleased: you know his air of a little boy. Honest, innocent, humble and so clever and knowing so much.

. . All you have been told about [the book was] the destructive side, and it is also constructive. It is also in a very interesting medium. The scenario form giving room for very beautiful descriptions of nature, for music, for poetry. Excellent medium for cutting out all that he does not actually need and for getting in, via the narrator, all he needs to say. Then also a very clever use of the religion that prevails. But I won't spoil it. I shall have an extra copy made and sent to you at once . . .

Aldous is so sweet. When we had finished I was dazed of course, I had . . a violent head-ache in the eyes . . and I felt sick. All I could say was, "Well, I am impressed."

But when I came up with my hot-water bottles he was walking around still in his blue jersey and asked, "What do you think of it? Is anything wrong? Must I change anything?" "No!" Most emphatically . . . Not that I am a good judge but often my quick reactions do help him to see something. His corrections go farther and deeper than I can see for myself. But this . . size, shape, form . . is absolutely perfect.

At first the typescript made me halt and read it badly; I was also nervous—that I would spoil it for him. But then . . I got so deeply interested that it read well and fluently . . . I had not even remembered to drink any coffee . . . Oh, and when I think what I am made to read sometimes. Those interesting books so buried in twaddly language. Or those odious personalities coming through what they say about others . . .

I suggest you read it when you have *time* . . not at night, when you have been tired . . If you had someone to read it with it would add to the pleasure I believe. Aldous enjoyed my reading of it; I am astonished he often says he likes the way I read—*when* I read properly. Knowing him so well and every thought and his language too, I suppose it was much as he thinks it aloud. I suppose about forty or fifty-thousand words.

Ape and Essence—the form, a scenario (a rejected script rescued on its way to the studio incinerator); the time, the post-atomic twenty-first century; the setting, the Los Angeles plain. "Dissolve to street: under the porches of ruined filling-stations lie heaps of human bones . . ." "Cut to medium close shot of the Unholy of Unholies . . ." It is some decades since the Bomb, "the Thing", has wasted most of our known world; active radiation has ceased, but food is still short, and everything else. The books from the former L.A. Public Library are used to stoke communal ovens; labour gangs dig up and plunder the corpses of the dead. Four babies out of five are born deformed and are destroyed (and their mothers savagely punished); sex is loathed and feared, only periodical public orgies are permitted by Church and State.

> *But man, proud man,*
> *Drest in a little brief authority—*
> *Most ignorant of what he is most assur'd.*
> *His glassy essence—like an angry ape,*
> *Plays such fantastic tricks before high heaven*
> *As make the angels weep.*

The state religion is a cult of Belial, government absolute by a hierarchy of castrated priests. The Arch-Vicar, a figure reminiscent of the Controller in *Brave New World*, explains the new theology to the explorer from unbombed New Zealand. All things foreseen by Belial inevitably come to pass:

> "The overcrowding of the planet . . . the land . . ruined by bad farming. Everywhere erosion . . the deserts spreading, the forests dwindling. Even in America, even in that New World which was once the hope of the Old . . . Bigger and better, richer and more powerful—and then, almost suddenly, hungrier and hungrier. Yes, Belial foresaw it all . . . The New Hunger . . of enormous industrialized proletariats, the hunger of city-dwellers with money, with all the modern conveniences, with cars and radios, . . the hunger that is the cause of total wars and the total wars that are the cause of yet more hunger."

And remember this, the Arch-Vicar adds,

> ". . even without the atomic bomb, Belial could have achieved all his purposes. A little more slowly perhaps . . men would have destroyed themselves by destroying the world they lived in . . . From the very beginning of the industrial revolution He foresaw that men would be made so overwhelmingly bumptious by the miracles of their own technology that they would soon lose all sense of reality. And that's precisely what happened. These wretched slaves of wheels and ledgers began to congratulate themselves on being the Conquerors of Nature. Conquerors of Nature, indeed! In actual fact, of course, they had merely upset the equilibrium of Nature and were about to suffer the consequences. Just consider what they were up to during the century and a half before the Thing. Fouling the rivers, killing off the wild animals, destroying the forests, washing the topsoil into the sea, burning up an ocean of petroleum, squandering the minerals it had taken the whole of geological time to deposit. An orgy of criminal imbecility. And they called it progress. Progress! . . . Progress and Nationalism—those were the two great ideas He put into their heads . . ."

You mean, you think—it was the *Devil*? says the explorer from New Zealand.

> "Who else desires the degradation and destruction of the human race?"
> "Quite, quite," Dr Poole protests. "But all the same, as a Protestant Christian, I really can't . . ."
> ". . Well, what are the facts? . . Nobody wants to suffer, wants to be

degraded, wants to be maimed or killed . . [yet] the overwhelming majority of human beings accepted beliefs and adopted courses of action that could not possibly result in anything but universal suffering . . The only plausible explanation is that they were inspired or possessed by an alien consciousness . . .

". . consider all the other evidence. Take the First World War, for example. If the people and the politicians hadn't been possessed, they'd have listened to Benedict XV or Lord Lansdowne—they'd have come to terms, they'd have negotiated a peace without victory; but they couldn't, they couldn't. It was impossible for them to act in their own self-interest . . the Belial in them wanted the Communist Revolution, wanted the Fascist reaction . . wanted Mussolini and Hitler and the Politburo, wanted famine, inflation and depression; wanted armaments as a cure for unemployment; wanted the persecution of the Jews and the Kulaks; wanted the Nazis and the Communists to divide Poland and then go to war with one another. Yes . . He wanted concentration camps and gas chambers and cremation ovens. He wanted saturation bombing (what a deliciously juicy phrase!); He wanted the destruction overnight of a century's accumulation of wealth and all the potentialities of future prosperity, decency, freedom and culture. Belial wanted all this, and, being the Great Blowfly in the hearts of the politicians and generals, the journalists and the Common Man, He was easily able to get the Pope ignored even by Catholics, to have Lansdowne condemned as a bad patriot, almost a traitor. And so the war dragged on for four whole years; and afterwards everything went punctually according to plan . . . men and women became progressively more docile to the leadings of the Unholy Spirit. The old beliefs in the value of the individual human soul faded away; the old restraints lost their effectiveness; the old compunctions and compassions evaporated. Everything that the Other One had ever put into people's heads oozed out, and the resulting vacuum was filled by the lunatic dreams of Progress and Nationalism . . ."

The Arch-Vicar chuckles shrilly.

". . Take the scientists, for example. Good, well-meaning men, for the most part. But He got hold of them all the same—got hold of them at the point where they ceased to be human beings and became specialists. Hence . . those bombs . . .

". . And finally, of course, there was the Thing. Unconditional surrender and bang! . . ."

The Post-the-Thing community in *Ape and Essence* is unspeakably bestial, unspeakably horrible. Affection, joy, compassion have withered, only hunger, fear, lust, cruelty, malicious glee are left. Aldous strained to pile horror upon crass horror—the narrator's blank verse, the Arch-Vicar's donnish discourse, alternate with scenes of orgies, whippings, cruel ritual, presented in the harsh distorting medium of black musical comedy. The book, it always seemed to me, achieves a high degree of unbearableness. Unbearable: is it correspondingly effective? (It appears to be very much so among American students today, the one book by Huxley to which the majority of them profess itself to be able to "relate". Matthew, in his own twenties at the time he read the advance copy, recoiled and wrote a long argumentative letter to his father.) Aldous, wrote the book as a warning—*this* is what human beings are capable of becoming, *this* is the degradation we may reach . . . Yet beside the undoubted element of prophecy, there is also one of hindsight in *Ape and Essence*. Aldous chose to postulate (with all the artifice this entailed) his diabolical community in the future. Why? Unutterably horrible though they are, the doings of those post-atomic apes of California don't come near the toll of pain, waste and final human outrage that had already happened in places such as Auschwitz.

Maria said that she looked with awe at Aldous. It is hard to imagine her reading this book to Aldous, stretched out on their long chairs in their wooden house at Wrightwood, hard to imagine Aldous asking for this particular book to be read to him. One must suppose that if he could bear to write it, he could bear to hear it. Did Maria protest too much about the pleasures of that reading?

Chapter Three

"As If We Had Never Left"

ALDOUS and Maria were at Wrightwood; Aldous, not ready to embark upon another book, thinking about a film. "On Saturday Anita, Paulette [divorced from Chaplin, remarried to the actor Burgess Meredith], Burgess and the Huckles came out to lunch [Maria on 12th April] . . because Burgess wants to make a scientific film on hypnotism, Aldous to write the story. Aldous saw demonstrations here by a man who uses hypnotism to short-cut psychoanalysis and deals very successfully with sleep." Meanwhile Zoltan Korda proposed a script of another old short story of Aldous's, "The Rest Cure" from *Brief Candles*, to be filmed, if all went well, with Michèle Morgan, Alexander Korda putting up the money. And after that perhaps, they might do *Point Counter Point* . . .

> Aldous is entirely thinking and behaving as if we had never mentioned selling Wrightwood. [Maria to Matthew] So I let him be. If he likes it that much—Well, I'm quite prepared to enjoy its good sides . . . Please do not mention this. I know when it is dangerous to disturb Aldous. This is one of those times. If I bothered him about selling the house or reminding him of it, he might have a new type of allergy or something else which would necessitate an immediate and prolonged stay at Wrightwood. Do we know what tricks we play on ourselves?

Tricks or not, a couple of weeks later Aldous went down with virus pneumonia. This, however, was efficiently dealt with and for once did not seem to bring an aftermath. Nor did it interfere with the plans which sprang up like a sudden wind. The Korda brothers decided that Aldous should write the screen play of "The Rest Cure" in Italy, paying for the story rights by financing his and Maria's journey. "The Rest Cure" was the elaboration of an anecdote that had happened to a woman who lived opposite Costanza Fasola's, and the Kordas wanted Aldous to give it an up-to-date Italian post-war background. Aldous said yes; Cunard promised a passage for mid-June. On the 10th they were at the Hotel St Regis in New York (Aldous attending a round table conference on modern art got up by *Life Magazine*).

Meanwhile *The Gioconda Smile* had opened at the New Theatre in London on 3rd June, with Clive Brook as Henry Hutton,

Pamela Brown as Janet Spence, Brenda Bruce as Doris Mead and Noel Howlett as Dr Libbard. The notices were mixed (good in the *Mail*, the *Standard* and the *Spectator*, poor in *The Times* and the *New Statesman*).

Aldous and Maria sailed for Cherbourg on the *Queen Mary*. On the second morning out Maria, after breakfast in bed and Aldous standing by in a dressy suit, scribbled a note to Matthew, "My Wild Western Bovarism did not really work." Dissolve and cut to Jeanne Neveux's journal. Tuesday 29th June 1948.

Ils arrivent! Nous sommes à la gare St Lazare. Georges, Sophie, Noële et moi. L'attente est longue, nous n'avons pas le droit d'aller sur les quais, et nous les guettons—Aldous est le plus grand.

There is Juliette, too, waiting by the exit. Cut to Georges Neveux's journal.

Enfin les voici. J'ai lu tant de lettres de Maria à Jeannot et si longtemps vecu au milieu des souvenirs et des livres d'Aldous à Sanary, que j'ai l'impression de les voir sortir non de l'inconnu, mais du fond de ma mémoire. Aldous ressemble assez à sa photo, Maria ressemble à Rose; même sourire, même conversation sautillante qui n'écoute jamais la réponse mais qui épie sur le visage de l'interlocuteur le reflet de ce qu'elle vient de dire.

They are borne off to the Neveux's flat in the rue Bonaparte, between St Germain-des-Près and St Sulpice.

Everybody is tired. We go to bed quite early. Maria is to have our room (Jeannot and I moving into my study) and Aldous to sleep in Noële's room . . . Noële. Maria has given her a wristwatch. A real watch. Noële is very surprised to see the hands go round all the time. The idea of those hands never stopping disturbs her.

The Neveux ask in French writers who want to meet Aldous. "Il est fêté." Maria goes off to see their old friend Mimi, Lewis Gielguid's ex-wife at Passy. Aldous and Georges are asked to do a talk on the French Radio. It is to be recorded Sunday evening; in the morning they rehearse.

I suggest a number of questions to Aldous. He nearly always rejects them. He does not want to take too definite a position on any point. He is afraid of being cornered, pinned down like a butterfly on the cork of an idea. He slips through our fingers, takes wing, becomes vague, alternates.

And above all he dreads irony. Why? Because for so long he himself used to handle irony with such skill . . .

At last we manage to set up four large pages, a long dialogue which we copy out and read aloud in turn, straight-faced like two popes . . .

Afterwards they go out with Maria, are photographed outside the *Deux Magots*, look at the *Musé d'Art Moderne*. On the way back, Georges and Aldous go and have a look at the inside of the Church of St Sulpice and the frescos by Delacroix which seem to Aldous (and to Georges as well) "*bien emphatiques*.

On our return, Aldous becomes animated, smiles, charms. He recites Mallarmé, Rimbaud, Shelley. (Il a un certain respect devant l'obscurité poétique. Ça, c'est la zone sacrée, que son esprit scientifique n'a jamais pu entamer. Et c'est de cette zone là qu'est sorti son mysticisme actuel.) 5 Juillet. Il me parait d'une grande modestie naturelle. Et cette modestie n'est pas le revers d'un orgueil dissimulé, mais le complément, le gardien de son travail. Ça le dérange dans ses opérations intellectuelles de se sentir vu et commenté. Les articles qui paraissent sur lui, il ne les lit jamais. Le livre qui vient de paraître à Paris sur lui, je le lui ai acheté. Il l'a soupesé, regardé avec méfiance, et reposé. Il ne l'a pas lu—pas même feuilleté. Il m'explique que ça ne pourrait pas lui être utile.[1]

On 9th July, the evening French Radio broadcast the Huxley-Neveux conversation, Aldous and Maria left for Siena. Now Maria sends some scrawls to Matthew.

. . It is as if we had never left. There are two worlds, and will remain so . . . We don't miss the orange juice, the ice-water, the cellophane wrappings, we laugh at the flies in the streets, the smell of urine, the horse-dung . . I also hope that you will marry a European, selfishly but perhaps also for your pleasure: the difference is infinite and I think for the better.

. . Aldous is at his best for health but annoyed at having to work and it is a shame when you see the pleasure he gets out of wandering in streets and the churches and the museums and countryside . . . it seems more and more inconceivable to live in California. Jeanne

---

[1] Thus Aldous did not as much as cut the pages of a book about himself. Since the publication of Volume I, I am often asked about the effect on his work of adverse criticism of the calibre of Wyndham Lewis's devastating use of the first page of *Point Counter Point* in *Men without Art* or Cyril Connolly's parody of *Eyeless in Gaza*. I am almost certain (one cannot prove a negative) that he never read either. "Were they kept from him then?" No. Aldous omitted to read about himself partly out of a protective instinct for his work (he would ask and take advice, but did not believe in the constructiveness of most published comment), partly out of natural incuriosity and detachment.

and Costanza made it so clear to me. Now I even doubt the only favourable angle—that is climate. For as they point out Aldous was *never* ill in Europe—and certainly this European climate, so much more temperate, has so far produced *no* allergy—*no* cough—*no* hives—*no* skin troubles and, what he minds most of all, *no* hayfever. Of course winters are cold, but again everyone agrees that with money one can buy fuel—no more black market, so no unpleasant business relations . . . So now there is our *great plan* for which we begin to prepare now—next May you either quit or ask for a six months vacation—so we three can leisurely explore Italy or maybe Spain. We take a new Ford with a four-shift gear box (essential) and an extra loud horn, and at the end of it we decide on where we should live—probably in Sanary . . . This is not considering politics— how can one—tell me what you think and that you will love it . . . I will buy you rings and belts and shirts, Aldous will adore to show you everything—it is touching to see how he enjoys it, every leisurely look at paintings and statues, and how gay and well he looks. Yet sad, because I notice how little he sees, and how much he deserves to see.

By chance Georges Neveux was also making a film in Italy and arrived in Rome with Jeanne and Noële. Aldous and Maria joined them on 2nd August. They stayed at the Hotel de Ville above the Spanish Steps, the Huxleys in a suite on the eighth floor (booked by the Rank organization) with a terrace of incomparable view.

The four of us dine at the Grappola d'Oro. [Georges Neveux's journal] We drink to our reunion. *"Enfin nous voici en Europe,"* says Maria. "In Europe at last." Which goes to show that for the Nys sisters Europe is Italy . . .

5th August. [Jeanne's diary] We dine at Professor Cherubini's (the Marquis de St Amour), Costanza's first lover . . .

18th August. Georges and Aldous . . dine in the charming little Trattoria of the Via del Boccaccio where the cinema people go, Rossellini, Magnani. Afterwards we go every day . . . 19th August. Maria has gone on a jaunt to Naples with Rina's sister . . .

19th August. [Georges] Never met—never imagined even—a being of such exquisite elegance of feeling. Aldous's inexhaustible *gentillesse*, so natural so light, that it becomes almost invisible . . .

On the 22nd Maria writes to Matthew, "I cannot tell you how happy we have been here . . . the ease of the country . . .

There are many drawbacks. Such as the inefficiency and the dishonesty which in Naples reaches a point that is haunting—but one does not have to live in Naples . . .

Jeanne and Georges. The more we go on the more we are united in friendship, tastes, views on life etc. and also with our love for the child whom they bring up without an error.

24th August [George's journal] Aldous is not well, Maria had to go to a dinner at the Boccaccio . . and he dines all alone, on his vast terrace above the illuminated city of Rome, off a biscuit and an apple out of a paper bag.

He's delighted to have a visitor . . lively, gracious, mischievous. He reminds me of an old comedian playing tricks on an invisible schoolmaster. But his cheeks look hollow and he must have had a bad day.

On the 28th they left together by bus for Sanary, spending the night in Genoa.

At Sanary, Aldous and Maria found a house waiting for them. When Jeanne had sold the impracticable Villa Huley during the war, she had saved furniture and books and re-arranged them in La Rustique, the new house she had bought for them. The curtains were hung, the walls had been re-painted in the old colours; Rina was there, come to look after them:

Darling, now we are really at home. [Maria to Matthew] This house is so like the other without the disadvantages, that we forget it is new. All our things are there—cups, plates, books—it all seems very natural. Same old mosquito nets over the same old beds. Large rooms. Divine bathing—effortless swimming in a temperate sea which is just right. Sun air water wind combine to spoil us. Rina runs the house; she took time off from her own in-laws . . . The people in the village ask after you, and Renée is just as ever—I like her as much—and so would you . . .

Sophie came to join them. In the evenings they read aloud. The Letters of Mademoiselle de Lespinasse, Benjamin Constant, Diderot, Barbey d'Aurevilly, Novalis, Valéry, Baudelaire; Georges reading.

2nd September. [Georges] Aldous is installed on the terrace just outside his bedroom door. He is typing away at the end of his film.

4th September. Aldous has found a stack of canvases—his own paintings of fifteen years ago. Strange canvases . . . Evidence of his first effort towards the external world, towards contact . . . And now all day I hear the sound of hammering—Aldous and Maria hanging those paintings . . .

The one thing that really moved them was the discovery of their old walking sticks in the cellar which suddenly reminded them of all their walks in the past. And at once they set out on a long cross-country ramble.

Aldous and Noële adore each other. Yesterday Noële did her daily eye exercises under Jeanne's instruction. Aldous sat down beside her and, keeping time with her, went through exactly the same movements. A charming little scene . . .

10th September [Jeanne] Today in the lovely shady garden we fêted Coccola's 50 years.

Rina has made our stay a paradise of grace and comfort.

Walking sticks and canvasses—there was something else that Aldous re-discovered. The year before he had published an article, "If My Library Burned Tonight".[1] "Fortunately for me, it never has," he wrote; "But I have moved house sufficiently often and have had enough book-borrowing friends . . to form a pretty good idea of the nature of the catastrophe." Happily, books are replaceable—at any rate the kind of books that filled the shelves of *his* library. Aldous had never had any use for the collector's point of view, or the collector's items.

It is only about the contents of a book that I care, not its shape, its date or the number of its fly-leaves. Fire, friends and changes . . can never rob me of anything that cannot . . be restored in fullest measure.

Indeed; but what about such contents as one's annotations? What Aldous found again among his books in Sanary was the copy of Maine de Biran's *Journal Intime* extensively annotated by himself. Biran had always interested him; now the recovered journal became his spring-board for the long study of the philosopher that he presently began to ruminate.

By mid-September the film script was done and on the 19th Aldous and Maria left for Paris—a short fortnight at Mimi Gielgud's, interrupted by a couple of days in Brussels. Then England. On 2nd October they arrived in London (put up at Claridges by Rank Films). What Aldous thought and felt about this first return after eleven years, I have not the slightest idea. It is one of the things one encounters when trying to find a sequence in a life—three different views of some, possibly trivial, event on a given day, and so many many days unremembered, unrecorded. This, so far, seems to be the case about that return to England. I have come across no relevant letters. Julian, at Unesco, and Juliette were out of the country. Eddy Sackville-West, whom they saw, is dead. Georges and Jeanne had stayed on at Sanary. I was in Italy. The friends who did see Aldous then are no longer able to make a clear distinction between that

---

[1] *House & Garden*, 1947, republished in *The Weekend Book* of 1969.

visit and his many later ones. (There is a postcard from Maria to Betty Wendel from Rome, "We are leaving Italy too soon to suit us and are moving northwards . . . all rather sad.") They stayed in London for about three weeks, saw a good deal of Harold and Vera Raymond (and had looked forward to doing so), Aldous made a brief appearance on the B.B.C. on *In Town Tonight* and saw a performance of *The Gioconda Smile* which was still running. (The play in fact did very well, with an eventual full nine months in the West End.) We do not know what Aldous felt—nothing very much I would suspect; that return to England unlike some of his later ones was no sentimental journey—but we do know how he appeared to one of the most intuitively acute of his contemporaries: he was interviewed by Cyril Connolly.

> If one looks at his face one gets first an impression of immense intelligence, but this is not unusual among artists. What is much more remarkable and almost peculiar to him is the radiance of serenity and loving-kindness on his features; one no longer feels "what a clever man" but "what a good man", a man at peace with himself . . .[1]

They talked about their contemporary world—the bomb, radioactive contamination, famine, the possible technical and scientific solutions; but the real problem, Aldous said, would always be the soul of man and the ignorant cravings for pleasure and power which destroy it. They talked about baroque funeral sculpture; they talked about religion. And here Cyril seems to have managed to pin Aldous down to an unusual degree. He asked him how close his own brand of neo-Brahminism or Vedanta came to Christianity, Aldous answered:

> "I am not a Christian," he said, "but if I were, the sect which would appeal to me most would be the Quakers. They seem to me to be nearest the original truths of Christianity . . . As for my own religion—there have always been people who have tried to approach God without an intermediary; these mystics have been found in every church, but unfortunately it's very difficult to become one."

The interview took place in Aldous's sitting-room at Claridges. "He dressed," Cyril wrote,

> like an Argentine dandy who moves between Oxford and Rome, and he is adored by Chaplin and other Hollywood magnates, but

---

1 The interview appeared in the now defunct *Picture Post* with some very characteristic photographs of Aldous in the act of talking, by Elizabeth Chat.

often inaccessible to them. He eats fish, but not meat; will drink wine, but not spirits; goes to bed early, studies paintings corner by corner through a magnifying glass, enjoys seeing his old friends. Yet I know no-one more desperately concerned about the state of the world.

From Maria, there is one fragmentary line about London to Matthew, "But oh—le temps retrouvé."

In November they were back in New York. There they spent some weeks and intended to stay longer as Aldous had encountered an eye specialist, Dr Gustav Erlanger, who had done experimental physiology in Germany and London and developed a method of treating eyes by iontophoresis. Aldous began the treatment and thought that it resulted in a slight clearing of his old opacities; but he went down with severe bronchitis and had to desist. He returned to California and was ordered a three months' stay in Palm Spring Desert. There he and Maria settled down in a furnished bungalow at the Sun & Sage Apartments, Aldous trying his hand at an adaptation for the stage of *Ape and Essence*.

Chapter Four

Domestic Seesaw

ALDOUS'S bronchitis slowly wore off in the dry air and warmth of Palm Desert. Just as well to be there, as it turned out, for the rest of California that winter was having what Aldous called preposterous weather. The orange and the lemon groves were frozen; snow kept falling in the foot-hills, there was deep snow over the Mojave, five foot of snow at Wrightwood, with their house disappearing under a drift—"Well, we are lucky not to be inside it." Aldous is writing to Matthew. A long letter of paternal advice—should he change his job? There is the short-range prospect, says Aldous, of being condemned to a period of donkey work. Donkeyishness can be high even in "such apparently lively work as literary journalism. I remember the . . asininity of doing "shorter notices" of bad books on *The Athenaeum*.

> But the donkey work has got to be done and, in the nature of things . . it will be the new boy . . who has to do it . . I should, if I were you, certainly not be too much in a hurry to turn down the research job in the Conservation concern . . . it won't offer much scope for your gifts; but if there is a fair prospect of the job leading to something of greater interest and authority in the future, I am sure you would be well advised to accept it. [etc. etc.]

No more talk about Matthew's taking six months off to travel Europe with his parents, that great plan has slid into oblivion. He took the new job (with the Fairfield Osborn Conservation Foundation in New York) and stayed in it for the next three years. Aldous had finished the stage version of *Ape and Essence* (never performed) and some essays for his next book, one of them "Death and the Baroque" inspired by the Italian tombs he had visited that summer, to appear at once in Cyril Connolly's *Horizon*; and was turning now to the material for his study oı Maine de Biran. In February he writes to Julian,

> . . The prospects of reconciliation between East and West seem to be about on a par with the prospects of reconciliation between Christendom and Islam in the twelfth century. The best that can be hoped now is what happened then—a state of hostile symbiosis . . whereby the irreconcilable antagonists bound themselves, as a matter of practical utility, to respect one another's spheres of influence.

Man's life span being as long as it is, I suppose one cannot expect any major change in thought-patterns and behaviour patterns to take place in under one or two centuries.

Le Sourire de la Gioconde, in Georges Neveux's adaptation, opened in Paris in February (a moderate success).

Eventually the Huxleys went back to their apartment in Beverly Hills. Aldous hears of the death of his cousin by marriage, Ted (E.S.P.) Haynes. "The last time I saw him, in October, he remarked that he expected that he would die in the spring. He was a good prophet. Modern circumstances are such that we shall not look upon his like again; for he belonged to that curious and very delightful species of the English Eccentrics . . .

> Our world is too tidy to admit of marvellous disorder, the Dickensian leisureliness of an office such as Ted's. His death marks the passing not only of a friend, but also of an epoch of history and, one might almost say, a character in fiction.

On one of their evening walks, Aldous and Maria saw a house and garden in a quiet street. "Last night we were suddenly tempted", Maria wrote to Jeanne on 1st May.

> . . It is built in a way we like [all ground-floor in an inoffensive neo-Spanish style] it should be within our price . . there should be room for Noële. Would it look to you as if I were abandoning Europe? I think I could do as much for Noële here, perhaps more. Remember Sophie . . . If Noële could come . . . for her education, her health. She seems to be so near to us, so near to Aldous spiritually, intellectually . . .
> *Will* we buy a house in Los Angeles? I have an impression that we shall not settle again in France . . . I do not understand why I feel this—I have often had what I call a *"savoir"* an "I know it" . . . Aldous et moi, nous nous *voyons* ici dans nos vieux jours. Or ils sont bientôt là les vieux jours.

A week later they have plunged. "Coccola will have told you," Aldous writes to Matthew,

> The house—large, commodious—the garden—with big trees and plenty of space and privacy—and the location—in that curious country lane between Santa Monica and Melrose, full of huge estates and enormous trees—all seem ideal. And the price—ten thousand down with thirteen thousand to pay in ten years at $135 a month, is considered reasonable by all sensible people with whom we have talked. So there we are.
> I hope we shall be able to dispose of Wrightwood this summer. Nice as it is, it imposes too much of a strain . . .

Soon after they went up to Wrightwood for the summer. Krishnamurti will again be in the neighbourhood. "Aldous is in a happy mood, working hard and gaily. I . . well, rather moth-eaten; I have to admit it." Maria had a temperature which persisted through the summer and was dreading their next major house move, "the sheer muscular fatigue"; and there is more *va-et-vient* than ever; a few days in Los Angeles every other week or so. But they got a new car while they were about it, "I don't know why that means so much to me?" An Oldsmobile, 135 h.p. Rocket engine; no gear shift. By July they were able to spend the odd night in the new house.

Our house in town, 740 North Kings Road, L.A.46. WEbster 3 0455, has not yet had a defect [Maria to Matthew]. It is *large*; at last I feel at home again . . . The drains would not take a garbage disposal under 350 dollars so I do without . . It's still all up in the air. But we *love* it. We both purr in it. It is extremely cool and livable. Nothing too ugly. Nothing wildly pretty but all livable.

Edwin Hubble, the astronomer, received an honour from the Institut de France; Aldous composed his letter of acceptance in French. "We had a lot of fun over that because Aldous ended the letter à la façon de Gide.

So we knew there could be no error. When in doubt Aldous always goes back to that. The only letter I believe he ever had from Gide. [Who had ended it with "sincèrement votre" than which nothing could be more idiosyncratic.] But we composed the right thing, I believe, except for one sentence; but I did not insist . . And after all he is a foreigner, I mean Edwin. Their cat came and bit my legs. He is a strange cat.

This is perhaps the place to mention a comment Maria made, also to her son, on the company they kept. "Only the first-rate [intellectual] world is difficult . . That is why I learned to shut up so long ago—from the day I was sixteen it was first-rate most of the time. The second-rate bores *me*. And I shut up for another reason."

Aldous was asked to make some recordings,[1] and chose to read the story of the dwarfs from *Crome Yellow*, "Sermons in Cats" from *Music at Night* and the posthumous experience passage from *Time Must Have A Stop*. He wrote this comment on his own voice for the sleeve.

---

1 For a company called *Sound Portraits* formed then by two young Californian sound technicians, Mr and Mrs Barron.

For me, these records possess a certain historical . . interest. For, unless my ear and memory greatly deceive me, the way I speak is practically identical with the way my mother and her brothers and sisters spoke. Language is perpetually changing; the cultivated English I listened to as a child is not the same as the cultivated English spoken by young men and women to-day. But within the general flux there are islands of linguistic conservatism; and when I listen to myself objectively, from the outside, I perceive that I am one of these islands. In the Oxford of Jowett and Lewis Carroll, the Oxford in which my mother was brought up, how did people speak the Queen's English? I can answer with a considerable degree of confidence that they spoke almost exactly as I do. These recordings . . . are documents from the seventies and eighties of last century.

Wrightwood le 7 septembre

Darling . . we are breaking up here . . My desk has gone, so has my bed . . The books have yet to go and Aldous's desk . . Now there is no hope that we can sell the place so we shall shut it up; cut off water and gas and not come up at all during the cold weather. If we go to Europe as is decided next May, therefore to New York next April to have a month with Erlanger [the eye man] it will be shut a great deal . . you who like it so much may use it some day—or we may another summer—but that seems a long way ahead . . .

Aldous . . is of course less bouncingly well because of pushing to finish the work. No-one else would notice it but myself . . . We are all breaking up soon. Radha and Rajagopal go East on the 14th . . Rosalind and Krishnaji leave Wrightwood on the same day. So that will leave us free to leave as soon as it suits Aldous. Usually he has to leave about this time of year as the sage-brush is blooming, but so far the allergy is just in his nose and throat at the end of the day and does not keep him awake at night so we may stay until the M.S. is completed. I read most of this last Essay [Maine de Biran] which is one of his best ones.

Then we shall rush down, I with relief and delight. I really wonder what some of my friends mean when they say that Aldous does all I want . . When I think that I lived in this place for five years . . . I pray that the dampness of Kings Road will not be bad for Aldous. It is curiously damp . . . The large garden is watered a lot and the whole street has gardens . . also it is on the ground floor—how awful if we had to move another time . . .

Chapter Five

Themes and Variations

HAVING hung on at Wrightwood well into October, Aldous and Maria made the move for good into North Kings Road. Here, with the last book off his hands, he was able to turn to other matters, Orwell's *Nineteen Eighty-Four*, Julian's recent articles on Russian genetics in *Nature*. "Have you read them?" he asked Matthew. "If not, do so.

They are extremely interesting and contain a vast array of facts. The picture he draws is extremely depressing. One of the significant facts is that Russian geneticists no longer use the word "hypothesis", but always refer to "doctrines", exactly as the Schoolmen did in the thirteenth century. I suppose they will end up in the same sterility . . .

To Orwell, Aldous wrote this letter.

. . I had to wait a long time before being able to embark on *Nineteen Eighty-Four*. Agreeing with all that the critics have written of it, I need not tell you, yet once more, how fine and how profoundly important the book is.

May I speak instead of the thing with which the book deals—the ultimate revolution? The first hints of a philosophy of the ultimate revolution—the revolutions which lie beyond politics and economics, and which aim at the total subversion of the individual's psychology and physiology—are to be found in the Marquis de Sade, who regarded himself as the continuator, the consummator, of Robespierre and Babeuf. The philosophy of the ruling minority in *Nineteen Eighty-Four* is a sadism which has been carried to its logical conclusion by going beyond sex and denying it. Whether in actual fact the policy of the boot-on-the-face can go on indefinitely seems doubtful. My own belief is that ruling oligarchy will find less arduous and wasteful ways of governing . . and that these ways will resemble those which I described in *Brave New World*.

I have had occasion recently to look into the history of animal magnetism and hypnotism, and have been greatly struck by the way in which, for a hundred and fifty years, the world has refused to take serious cognizance of the discoveries of Mesmer, Braid, Esdaile and the rest. Partly because of the prevailing materialism and partly because of prevailing respectability, nineteenth-century philosophers and men of science were not willing to investigate the odder facts of

psychology. Consequently there was no pure science of psychology
for practical men, such as politicians, soldiers and policemen, to
apply in the field of government. Thanks to the voluntary ignorance
of our fathers, the advent of the ultimate revolution was delayed for
five or six generations. Another lucky accident was Freud's inability
to hypnotize successfully and his consequent disparagement of
hypnotism. This delayed the general application of hypnotism to
psychiatry for at least forty years. But now psycho-analysis is being
combined with hypnosis; and hypnosis has been made easy and
indefinitely extensible through the use of barbiturates . . Within the
next generation I believe that the world's rulers will discover that
infant conditioning and narco-hypnosis are more efficient, as instruments of government, than clubs and prisons . . . In other
words, I feel that the nightmare of *Nineteen Eighty-Four* is destined
to modulate into the nightmare of a world having more resemblance
to that which I imagined in *Brave New World*. The change will be
brought about as a result of a felt need for increased efficiency.
Meanwhile, of course, there may be a large-scale biological and
atomic war—in which case we shall have nightmares of other and
scarcely imaginable kinds.
    Thank you once again for the book.

For the present there were no very fixed work plans. Another
original script for the films, possibly, with Christopher Isherwood.
"If I don't succeed, I suppose I shall have to take a job in some
studio . . ." Aldous's post-war income from English book sales
was fairly high, if uneven. From £970 in 1936, up to over £3,300
in 1948 and to nearly £5,000 in 1949. But at this point the pound
had been devalued.
    The new book, *Themes and Variations*, contains perhaps some of
Aldous's finest work. The four variations on art and artists—on
El Greco, Goya, Death and the Baroque, Piranesi's Prisons
—have the elegance, the range and sparkle, the contagious
ardour, of the Aldous of the 1920s, with the confluence of ideas
enriched by experience and compassion, the intellectual play
sustained and clarified by unitive philosophy. The heart of the
collection is the study of Maine de Biran, "Variations on a
Philosopher". I often regretted that it was not given the impetus
of separate publication. Slightly longer than *Ape and Essence*, twice
as long as *Science, Liberty and Peace*, it could well have stood on
its own, a little book to be carried about, travelled with, annotated, as Aldous had annotated his copy of Biran's *Journal Intime*.
It is, I think, an extremely stimulating piece of work, leaping as
it does to every kind of question (without coming up too readily
with the literary or the preachy answer), lucid, yet aware of the
unfathomably queer and complex facts of human existence. The

life and works of Biran, a "spiritual positivist", were made to set off a man with Aldous's particular compass and talents: the man of letters who would keep breaking his own pattern, the man congenitally interested in science who was not a scientist, the man of thought who was not a professional philosopher; the man of religion who might not be pinned down to dogma or creed. "Variations on a Philosopher" is about man's nature and man's destiny.

> [Maine de Biran] is turning into a consideration of life in general [Aldous said to Hubble in mid-writing] as exemplified by what that particular man and thinker did, felt and thought, and also by what he didn't do or feel or think—for what is left undone is often as significant in a biography as what is done . . . I have become fascinated by the individual's relations with history and culture—the extent to which a man is in and out of history, like an iceberg in water . . .[1]

(Biran's own contention was that the individual's relation to history and society was normally that of victim to monster.) A major section of the biographical essay, Aldous's first, deals with Maine de Biran as "a Moralist, Metaphysician and Candidate for Salvation", a philosopher whose philosophy, spiritual positivism, was based upon carefully observed psychological facts:

> facts which, unlike almost all his immediate predecessors, unlike many of his contemporaries and successors, our philosopher takes as he finds them and refuses to explain away in terms of something else. For him, there is no hierarchy of facts. One datum of immediate experience is just as good as another. A fact belonging to the inner world is not less of a fact than one belonging to the outer world . . .

As a young man and during his early middle age, Biran—like Aldous—had been "never indeed a dogmatic atheist, but profoundly an agnostic. He wished and hoped that there might be a God and was only waiting to find some compelling reason to believe that there was. 'If', he wrote, 'If I ever find God and the true laws of the moral order, it will be by good fortune, and I shall be more credible than those who, setting out from a set of prejudices, tend merely to establish these prejudices by means of a theory.' A profoundly honest man, our philosopher knew that, if one is to explore the unknown, one must not start by pretending that it is already known . . ."

[1] This, and the next, quotation from "Variations on a Philosopher", *Themes and Variations*. Chatto & Windus, 1950.

Chapter Six

740 North Kings Road

MATTHEW HUXLEY was in his thirtieth year when he gave his father occasion to write him the following note.

9 December 1949

Dearest Matthew,

Your letter arrived this morning and gave us the greatest happiness, both on account of the news it brought and on account of the way you conveyed it. After thirty years of it, I can say I am definitely for matrimony, and I am sure that, if Ellen is all that Suzanne tells us she is, you too will be of the same opinion in 1980. Keep us posted on what's happening and on what you plan. Meanwhile this brings you the paternal blessing and every best wish for the happiest possible Christmas.

Your loving

Aldous

After a quiet first winter in their new house, Aldous alternately reading for the historical novel he never wrote and working with Christopher Isherwood on a script they did not sell, Aldous and Maria went to New York for Matthew's wedding. They had been delighted for their son; now they were enchanted by the girl. She was Ellen Hovde, daughter of Professor Bryn J. Hovde, president of the New School for Social Research. They found her charming, intelligent, life-enhancing, with great good looks thrown in. They also found a curious affinity, between Ellen and Maria, between Aldous and Ellen, it was hard to say who took most to whom; and meanwhile the two young people, as Aldous observed, were wildly in love with each other.

Matthew and Ellen went off to Europe and the Villa Rustique at Sanary (looked after by Rina) and a round of family visits in Belgium and France. Aldous and Maria spent a busy five weeks in New York, taking the new eye treatment with Dr Erlanger. *The Gioconda Smile* was to be put on in the autumn and Aldous was discussing and resisting changes proposed by the producer, Shepard Traube. On 9th May they sailed, again on the *Queen Mary*, and on the 14th stepped off the boat-train at the Gare St Lazare a few minutes before midnight. The three Neveux, with Sophie and Sylvia Nicolas, were there. "Tout le monde,"

Georges noted, "est ému." How true this must have been. No one had spoken of emotion on the first return two years before, the show of feeling became possible on the attenuated occasion. The weather was icy, taxis were found and the Huxleys conducted to their hotel, the Paris-Dinard in the rue Cassette, two steps from Jeanne's. Another stay in Paris: three weeks of museums, walks on the quais, theatres (Claudel's *L'Otage, Othello* in Georges's translation), a family celebration of young Sylvia's birthday. Then Italy: Siena, Rome. In early July Paris again and Aldous on his way to London, Maria on hers to central France where Georges and Jeanne have taken a house for the summer.

Julian and Juliette were in their Hampstead house and Aldous stayed with them. Maria sent minute details about tailor, shirt-maker, dry cleaners; Juliette was asked to keep him on a strictly vegetarian diet. ("I generally disregarded these instructions," Juliette writes, "and at the end we found that Aldous had put on a little weight.") What Aldous promised himself, besides English clothes, were new quacks. (He used the word without derogatory intention: "Don't wait," Aldous and Maria would say, "go and see a doctor or a quack at once.") He might go down to Brighton for a day or two to see Wilhelm Luftig who uses light therapy, plus homoeopathy . .

. . There is also another unorthodox eye man, called Brooks Simpkins, who has written a very good book on the mechanics of vision . . . He lives at Eastbourne. And perhaps I can look in on him too. And talking of unorthodoxies, I am asking a curious and interesting Danish acquaintance of mine, Dr Christian Volf, who is an expert on hearing, to send me, care of you [Julian], one of the special recordings he has made for relief of sinus trouble. One listens through ear-phones to a record of synthetic sounds in the lowest musical octave and the effect is to give an intense internal massage, vibrating the bones of the skull . . . I have heard of many people who keep sinusitis at bay simply by listening to the record every morning before breakfast. I am hoping that this thing may give you some relief from your miseries in this field. If, as I hope, Volf comes to London . . we will have a talk with him.

Aldous made some comment about that second return in two letters (one during, one after) to Christopher Isherwood.

. . England is much more cheerful than it was 2 years ago . . . Life is easier . . . Saw Stephen Spender several times—white-haired and wonderfully distinguished looking . . . expect to see Tom Eliot tonight and Cyril Connolly tomorrow. Poor Osbert has got Parkinson's disease . . . Edith a monument . . . Sybil Colefax, bent

double with her broken back, but indomitably receiving guests and
going out. The Jowitts—occupying an amazing Victorian-Gothic
apartment in the House of Lords, reserved for Lord Chancellors. All
very much *Le Temps Retrouvé*. "I show you sorrow and the ending of
sorrow"—with no ending in sight, of course, for any of us.

At a luncheon at Raymond Mortimer's Cyril made the follow-
ing remark (I am reporting this exchange exactly as he told it),
"Longevity is the revenge of talent upon genius."
Aldous "Who said that?"
Cyril "I"
Aldous "When?"
Cyril "Now."
Aldous "I think we must all applaud." And they clapped.
Julian and Juliette gave a family party—twenty-seven Huxleys
with their wives and husbands. ". . It was a pleasant and touching
experience," Aldous wrote to Peggy Kiskadden. "*Not* a bad lot,"
he kept saying to Juliette, "not a bad lot at all."
At the end of July Aldous went to join Maria at Sanary. They
remained there for the whole of August but without the sense of
rediscovery of the last time. There was a heat wave; material
existence had become completely normal ("How amazingly tough
the French way of life has proved itself!")—but somehow it did
not interest them very much. Julian and Juliette came; so did I.
On arrival I found Aldous doing a sister Anne—standing on the
lookout for a buyer who was to turn up that morning. They had
taken against the house and were determined to sell. (There was
indeed an odd sense of double *déjà-vu* about the place.) The buyer
did not come. In September they went to join the Neveuxs at
Juillac in the Limousin.
It was a cool old country house, if somewhat primitive, and
the five of them had an idyllic ten days in that prodigal region
of France—sitting under trees, picking mushrooms in the fields,
descending into grottoes, subterraneous rivers, magic caves at
Lascaux, Rocamadour, Padirac, Les Eyzies . . . In the evenings
Georges and Jeanne were introduced to the latest of the Huxley
interests, dianetic sessions. There was also their first meeting with
Dr Roger Godel, physician and philosopher, and his wife Alice,
who came all the way from Paris to meet Aldous.
The rehearsals of the *Gioconda* in New York were going badly
and Aldous decided on an early return. He and Maria left Juillac
on 10th September (it was probably then, on their way north,
that Aldous stopped and had his hard look at Loudun). In Paris
they put up at Mimi Gielgud's flat in Passy (a faithful friend
though long divorced from Lewis). "Dear ones," Maria scribbled
to Matthew and Ellen, "tomorrow at 8 a.m. we are off.

Everything has been quite an excitement as this day a woman appeared with money in her hand to buy Sanary—so we sold for 2 millions, 5,000 dollars. Not good but good riddance!!

So the looking-glass Villa Huley was sold, as Jeanne put it, for a mouthful of bread. The original house had cost them about 30,000 dollars. Thus Aldous and Maria achieved the near impossible—a loss in real estate in the South of France.

On 22nd September, Suzanne on board, they sailed back to America. They found the *Gioconda* "in the most frightful mess— the actors at daggers drawn with the director-producer, the rendering of the play unsatisfactory in the extreme . . ." (Aldous to Harold Raymond) Betty Wendel found him "enraged by changes that had been made without his consent. New York friends advised Aldous to demand that the opening be postponed, and that he should fight it out." Instead, the play duly opened on 3rd October (with Basil Rathbone as Hutton, Valerie Taylor as Janet Spence). Aldous did not go to the first night but, terribly nervous according to Suzanne, stayed at his hotel until he was telephoned that it was an apparent success. Next morning the notices in the *N.Y. Times* and *Herald Tribune* were bad. And a few days later Aldous and Maria drove off to California.

". . The *Gioconda* is dead," he wrote to Anita Loos from North Kings Road in November. "The move from the Lyceum to the Fulton [theatre] coinciding as it did with the universally bad businesses during election week, brought the receipts down to about seven thousand dollars . . So Traube decided to shut up shop . . . Now it is dead, it is dead, I suppose, for keeps.

. . It is a bore; for I would have enjoyed making some easy money. Now I must settle down to some honest work—and perhaps some dishonest work in the movies, if I can find it, which isn't so easy nowadays.

What was it like the play and what is it about?

. . the story has been developed in such a way [Aldous's own summary to Leon M. Lion in 1947] that the man who is falsely condemned for his wife's murder (. . the original short story . . was based on the Greenwood case of 1920) finds an internal solution by the acceptance of his fate, while the woman who actually did commit the murder and who seems to have successfully got away with it, refuses to accept the real state of things and thus breaks down into madness. By dividing the stage in the last act, I contrive to show, without interruption, alternating pictures of the one character on what, in spite of the circumstances, is the up grade, the other on a descending spiral . . .

So here we have a strong dramatic situation backed by the psychological spectacle of a conversion, a condemned man in his cell, seen modulating from stark fear of death to near serene acceptance. The play reads very well and its potentialities were, one is told, admirably brought out by the London production of 1948.

Since *Grey Eminence*, since *Maine de Biran*, Aldous was looking for some historical or biographical theme that would bring grist to his mill. Now he began to work on the material for that strange and revolting seventeenth-century episode, the diabolical possessions of Loudun. How did that come about? he was asked by John Chandos in 1961.

Years and years ago I read the account in Michelet's book *La Sorcière* of the Loudun case, and was interested—and incidentally found, when I came to look into the documents, that it was extraordinarily inaccurate, I mean [chuckle] this *great* historian was very slap-dash—and then I thought no more about it for many years, and then quite by chance I picked up in a second-hand bookshop the . . reprint . . of the autobiography of the prioress. And one of Surin's autobiographical things, and the late seventeenth-century book by [Pastor] Aubin which is an account of the whole episode. And reading those I was so fascinated—there was such extraordinary material there that I began collecting it, and found in fact that no historical episode yet has ever had so much documentation. There are autobiographical statements by the prioress, by Surin; a great many letters; all the exorcisms were taken down in shorthand, and a great many of them were printed. And a great many still remain unprinted. I have never read any of the unprinted material because I just can't manage those things. But I don't think it would have contributed anything. Most of the exorcisms were very like one another . . .

Then there were a great many accounts by outsiders who came to look at the possessions—I mean Loudun became one of the most popular tourist resorts of the seventeenth century. People went from all over the continent to see these nuns rolling about on the floor and screaming obscenities—it was the greatest fun.

. . So there was a great deal of material quite easy to get hold of.

It was also a great deal of material to get through (Maria still did much of the reading); days immersed in that labyrinth of witch-hunts, devils and hysteria were followed by other explorations in the evening, probings, by other means, into the workings of the sub-conscious and the super-conscious mind, the experimental sessions that became a standing feature of North Kings. Usually it was a Tuesday. First the participants would eat dinner at the counter of the World's Largest Drug Store, then assemble in the long main-room of the house, the music-room. Here—always game to try out anything that might come up, and what did not come up in Southern California—they would flash bright lights, make magnetic passes, turn on records of strange sounds, put the visiting hypnotist or medium through his paces. They would go into it with passionate interest but also critically, accepting that there might be fraud or multiple explanations. It was Aldous's open mind working both ways. That winter it was dianetics (which he thought might shed some useful light on the possessions of those nuns of Loudun). L. Ron Hubbard, the founder of the therapy, came to North Kings in person. The subconscious (if his theory may be roughly summarized) is presumed to function on several levels. There is a cellular level as well as a cerebral level. The cells are able to record words heard in sleep and even in pre-natal life. These recorded words, "engrams" in dianetic jargon, can act as obsessive commands—much like post-hypnotic suggestions—on an individual throughout his life.

. . The sub-conscious seems to take these verbal commands literally and unreasoningly, without regard to their context. [Aldous to Dr Roger Godel] The result can be disastrous, both mentally and physically. (If this is really the case, we may have here the rationale of magic spells, curses, anathemas and the like.)

Hubbard's therapy consisted of a procedure, called "auditing", which aimed at bringing those fatal recorded words and phrases into consciousness (and this without deep hypnosis or the standard psycho-analytical process). A patient who had brought his engrams to the surface was called "a clear". Aldous and Maria had three or four sessions with Hubbard. He and his wife came to dinner, "stiff and polite" the first time, bringing two pounds of chocolates which Maria described as *inutile*.

. . Up to the present I have proved to be completely resistant [Aldous wrote to Jeanne in an unpublished letter]—there is no way of getting me on to the time track or of making the subconscious produce engrams. Furthermore I find that there is a complete shutting off of certain areas of childhood memory, due, no doubt, to what the dianeticians call a "demon circuit" an engrammic command in the nature of "don't tell", "keep quiet", etc. Maria, meanwhile, has had some success in contacting and working off engrams and has been back repeatedly into what the subconscious says is the pre-natal state. Whether because of dianetics or for some other reason, she is well and very free from tension . . .

In any case, he concluded, the thing seems to be worth looking into and experimenting with.

They had settled into their pleasant, dignified, new house—respectable, Maria called it. It was certainly more conventional than either Llano or Wrightwood, where a tent pole had propped the ceiling of Aldous's room and the silvered caravan stood outside their door. It was comfortable, unpretentious, adapted to their needs—Aldous's study, the music-room, a breakfast-room, an arbour to sit out in. There were gadgets of all kinds, many contrived by Matthew; and Maria had at last succumbed to regular domestic help; indeed soon they were to have an excellent French cook. They still nipped out to their neighbourhood barbecue and there were the luncheons once or twice a week with the Stravinskys and a group of friends in the open air at Yolanda's in the Town and Country Market—booths and tables under pepper trees. The regulars were Robert Craft, the Reverend James McLane and his wife, an Episcopalian priest Aldous and Maria were fond of (great theological arguments went on) and a very young man, now Dr James Brainard Smith, who minded boutique (his words) for Mme Stravinsky and who recalls the arguments and the pleasantness of it all. These might be joined on any day by Peggy Kiskadden, by Gerald or by Betty Wendel or Christopher Isherwood. In the afternoons to book-shops and the L.A. Public Library, all blessedly within walking distance so that Aldous could go on his own, look into windows, browse among the shelves at his friend Jake Zeitlin's on Cienega Boulevard . . . To Mrs Corbett, for Aldous's eye training, they would go by car, and afterwards he and Maria would go for a stroll in "our cemetery", Rose Dale Memorial Park, a rural oasis a few miles south of mid-town Los Angeles, quiet graves below immense old palm trees . . . Then home. Friends for tea . . . Music . . .

PART TEN

"I Will Show You Sorrow . . .": 1951-1955

> . . There remained with him . . a
> haunting sense of the . . transcience,
> the hopeless precariousness of all merely
> human happiness.
>
> ALDOUS HUXLEY in *Grey Eminence*

> Each man's life is also the story of
> Everyman.
>
> IRIS ORIGO

Chapter One

Summer 1951—Winter 1952

Aldous has been on and off his book [*The Devils of Loudun*, Maria wrote to Matthew in March 1951], ever since he started it. He feels in an off mood and that he never has anything to say. It is a horrible shame that that play collapsed. He did deserve to earn some easy money.

MARIA assured him that if he never felt like writing a book again he still could earn his living with lectures and articles and so on; "not movies obviously as he has been trying in vain to get a job since we are back and *nothing* turns up. Anita tried . . Now they are dithering about some readings with Ethel Barrymore . . ."

A bad kind of flu was going round Los Angeles; Aldous and Maria caught it. The flu settled on Aldous's right eye, the bad eye, and for three days it was red and painful. Then the flu cleared up but the eye remained red, uncomfortable and vision deteriorated to nothing. This happened on 4th March. A month later "the eye was still no better," Maria wrote to Matthew in May,

. . though Aldous had gone to a very good specialist and been given drops of cortisone with the approval of Bill [Kiskadden] and [Dr] Hawkins and assent of Aldous. On April 24th this same excellent oculist put in some drops which were supposed to tear apart some old scars covering the pupil, this meaning that Aldous would see better. If it worked on the right eye it was to be tried on the left eye. The doctor had talked Aldous into trying this, without bullying him. The results were: for five days . . great redness, no vision and above all pains in the eye, the head and the neck. Psychologically it was the worst thing I have ever gone through. The pain would of course have been nothing had not Aldous been frightened and hating the doctor. The doctor telephoned from the hospital where he had fallen sick that it would be nothing, that obviously the medicine had been too strong, that the only thing to do was compresses. But of course and very naturally Aldous was frightened, very naturally I was equally frightened, and upset to see Aldous walking up and down, holding his head impatient, enraged, in fact so different from himself.

Bill came to see us on the Sunday and was definitely concerned; not because it was dangerous, but because one never knows. Once in a while things do turn out badly and Aldous is so evidently a *personage difficile* . . He was so rattled. It really was horrible.

Now [in mid-May] all is well. That is: the doctor will never try the rough medicine again . . . The eye is not *quite* recovered . . But in two weeks with Aldous's full wish, they are starting the gentle cortisone drops in the left, that is, the good eye.

Peggy is going east next week . . She will tell you about this; in fact I want you to ask her . . It is always interesting to hear two sides of a story . . Bill took it seriously enough to talk to Hawkins and tell him to look after Aldous properly; that is to come to see him here and take his time with him rather than slicing him between all the crowds in the office . . . For more than a week I thought I was very ill; then I discovered it was just the anxiety . . . Now we are well and happy and hopeful for the future. We plan nothing except a nice trip for the summer.

Aldous indeed was able to get on with his book, but had to say no to an invitation to go to India with his new friends the Roger Godels. Matthew and Ellen were expecting a baby in the autumn. Maria wrote "I have so much peace at heart since you are married. One does not know one's preoccupations till they are over; as with Aldous's illness . . .

But now all *is* normal. Vera Stravinsky rang up . . they could not bear going to another cinema, could they visit us? So I said yes the programme would be good but not the refreshments and they came at 9.

We are very fond of them, Stravinsky still looks like father and is very sweet really; always the same programme. Stravinsky, Bob Craft—almost an adopted son of theirs, 26 and very clever, knows everything, terribly nervous and not a pansy—and Aldous stays in the music room and Vera and I stay around somewhere else . . They play music and we chat . . Last night [12th May] Stravinsky arrived in an enchanting costume . . narrow effect in little blue jeans, and a blue jean zipper jacket open on a deep red wine jersey and silk scarf tied with pin. He looked enchanting and was really pleased with himself. I must not forget the always white socks and sandals. I do not know what he makes me think of, a voltigeur in the circus, a leprechaun with the little elegant legs or what? a cyclist? And Aldous *will* turn the heat off when I am gone and poor little Stravinsky shivers and dares not ask and Aldous notices nothing. So finally he came to sit on my bed, and Vera inside the open window in a decolleté dress under a lace shawl and velvet bows in her hair looked immense next to the little shivering elfish man. I am very fond of him and I like her and we are good friends. Bob too is very nice . . . They are all going to Venice where the world première of the opera on the *Rake's Progress* is taking place in September. [It was Aldous who had suggested that W. H. Auden should write the libretto.] I wish we could [be] there.

Gerald Heard had published an article on Flying Saucers, on which Aldous commented to Matthew: ". . in spite of Gerald's bad writing, there may be something there after all. I have no settled opinion so far, but keep my trap shut and wait." To Maria, the saucer business seemed "wildlier than we will ever grasp.

They may just be radar vortices, if you know what *that* is. I did not till two days ago when we walked with Gerald. These are just a vortex undetectable except by radar . . . then Aldous muddles it even more by telling me that we are only vortices but with a little more to it. And I give up.

Aldous had long been taking great interest in the Happy Valley School at Ojai, a small co-educational, non-sectarian and, of course, non-segregated, secondary school founded in 1946, of which he with Krishnamurti and Rosalind Rajagopal were the original trustees. The motto was *Aun Aprendo*, I Am Still Learning. Rose de Haulleville's girl Olivia was being brought up there; Maria hoped that Matthew would send his children, "Such a strong and happy atmosphere in the place . . . they have a Russian cook who is also a virtuoso on the piano; it sounds mad but it works." This June Aldous delivered the Commencement Address. *Aun Aprendo*—the process, he told them, goes on from cradle to grave and, doubtless, beyond. Or at least it ought to. Alas, in practice . . . "In all too many cases men and women do not wish to go on learning . . . They are like the young man of that ancient limerick . . who

> . . . . . said 'Damn,
> *It is borne in on me that I am*
> *A creature that moves*
> *In predestinate grooves;*
> *I'm not even a bus, I'm a tram!'*

And those people do not even say Damn."

Now they are all beginning to think about Christian names. This was Aldous's first contribution. "Dearest M, [to Matthew in an unpublished letter] Coccola tells me that you're floored for a name for the cub. Seeing that we embarked on the Evangelists with you, might not Mark be a possibility . . ? Or if it's a girl, there is Margaret—except that Miss Truman got there first. Or Frances,

> which was my mother's second name, as also the name of Matthew Arnold's youngest sister, who was alive when you were born and wrote me a letter to say how pleased she was that you had been called Matthew. My mother's first name, Julia, is also good. So is Elizabeth . . Or perhaps you had better do what was done in the case of the royal children of France—they were not named at all until a state baptism at five years old. Till then the Dauphin was called Monsieur, the elder daughter Madame, the second daughter Petite Madame . . . (We know all this as we are reading aloud a charming book, made up mainly . . from the day-to-day journal of Jean Héroard, the resident physician of Louis XIII. It gives a fascinating picture of nursery and adult life at the beginning of the seventeenth century . . .)
>
> When you are next at a news-stand, invest fifteen cents in a copy of the latest "See" magazine . . There is an article by Gerald embedded in the midst of twenty-six (I counted them) nearly naked women, whose photographs constitute the rest of the magazine. Gerald's bearded image sits there like St Anthony in the midst of his Temptations—or is it a prevision of the homosexual's purgatory, innumerable bosoms and not a boy in view.

This letter was dated 1st July. On the 27th, Maria had to write to Matthew and Ellen as follows:

> My darlings, I am sorry to have to give you less good news than usual but that right eye of Aldous's had an unaccountable flare up since ten days ago . . So we had a sad birthday and when your little gadget came this morning [a pocket telescope] it was wildly welcome but sadly so; as if you had guessed the need of it.
>
> . . . He was working well, very hard, I think too hard, and was very cheerful . . . Dow diagnosed iritis . . also telling Aldous he would not suggest removing this or that part of the eye. (I cannot quote in medical terms). This rather frightened me . . I wondered if Dow was preparing him for something very bad . . Hawkins . . suggested a consultation of other doctors to which we agreed. He however put Aldous on a general antibiotic drug, chloromycetin, in case there should be some smouldering infections of flu left. This was Wednesday. Last night about five there was enough improvement for us all

to hope that this general antibiotic was having good effects. So we were cheerful. Aldous slept very well until four; then woke up in great pain . . The trouble is that they cannot even give soothing treatments, no nursing or calming the eye seems possible.

I would not have written all this to you if your little parcel had not arrived this very minute and made us feel sad. Aldous is now sleeping with some aspirin.

The question is not . . whatever . . caused it—that would be a useless squabble . . Aldous is obviously one of those people on whom the usually successful treatments have unaccountable effects. Dr Volf, that charming man who has the deaf-curing, sinus-curing record is here for two days and according to his diagnosis Aldous is otherwise perfectly healthy, unusually so for a man of his age; so I hope that he will very soon now overcome this. I will let you know if it should not get better.

Three or four days later, Maria wrote again.

Aldous has had a terrible time. *Very much pain.* Now pain is over but congestion and inflammation still there—will last for weeks— Peggy and Bill a *great* stand-by. Do not worry about doctors—we have the best—all that is possible is being done . . . poor poor Aldous—it was terrible—now it is sad—we live in a dark house. We walk at night. He cannot work—I try hard and have much help. I *never* leave him. We read—he dictates—but of course it is not the same—poor poor Aldous, but he is patient . . sometimes very depressed—I am full of courage and not once was I [word illegible]— except on the night *before* it started—enormous fear—I knew something serious was coming . . . Iritis *and* glaucoma—if it recurs it means operation to relieve the tension . . . Aldous knows *Nothing of This*. Never mention anything specifically. It may be all right. Rose was here—she said "Ce n'est pas juste."

Unless you hear again it means progressing well . . .

Then to Jeanne on 2nd August:

After some frightful nights and days, I believe the menace is passing . . . if there hadn't been a slight improvement since 2 o'clock this morning, and if the improvement does not keep up, they will have to operate, an iridectomy . . . He has suffered terribly . . . for ten days, the last two days and nights were the worst—in spite of all the science . . . It is a consequence of the flu in March, iritis can also be a consequence of keratitis, which he did have forty years ago. Now no news will be good news. Otherwise Mère will write to you . . .

And on 18th August at last, to Matthew and Ellen:

> Well, my Dear Ones, I will write a real letter . . that of course means Aldous is better—poor Aldous, we shall never quite know what he went through. If he knew himself it might have helped—I mean I am *sure* that he was afraid of going blind, but he did not know he was afraid—I even suggested it. One time I suggested that *I* was afraid because in spite of what the doctors say one did not know what might happen—but it definitely brought no response. And I can *tell*. After 32 years I really can tell whether he is consciously worried-afraid. I think he feared for the good eye—and who would not? But oh! how he would not even tell myself that . . . The oculist agreed it was all right not to tell Aldous about the possibilities as long as he could tell me. I had warned him I was tough—but it is very extraordinary that a patient should not wish to know exactly the possibilities—the worse ones—of his case. I find it better to know because one is prepared for the lesser ordeals.
>
> But Aldous is much better today. Tomorrow he proposes to write a little in the morning . . .

From then, Aldous got well quite rapidly. (Though the affected eye, his bad eye, never properly recovered.) Maria says nothing of the hypnotic treatment which Aldous mentioned when all was safely over. (" . . I live in fear of a recurrence—tho' hope for the best," he wrote to Dr Roger Godel in December.) He had in fact two or three brief hypnotic sessions with the head of the Psychology Department of the University of Los Angeles which "undoubtedly helped me to sleep and to deal with the pain." He was not himself, he said, a particularly good hypnotic subject, but could get at least into a light trance.

> Moreover, [this is from a letter written the summer after in another context] by means of auto-hypnosis (which is an art not too hard to acquire if one has a good hypnotist for a teacher) and by treatments from Maria and our friend LeCron, the psycho-therapist, I was enabled to get over the very considerable apprehension which accompanied and followed the iritis—apprehension that the good eye might be involved and lose much of its vision . . .
>
> . . the benefits due to hypnosis are due fundamentally to the fact that it is accompanied by a high degree of relaxation, mental and physical. The ego is able to let go, to get out of the way, to stop interfering . . .

It was during the period of relaxation and relief after the iritis that Aldous and Maria were able to talk as follows. (In the remote past in Sanary, Maria once told me that there had been a third Huxley brother. "We don't speak about it.") Now, in the letter about Aldous's recovery, she said this to Matthew and Ellen:

[A few nights ago] I dreamed about Trev—at breakfast I asked more questions about him than I ever had—Aldous knows little enough about the causes of his death .. [Trev] was at a nursing home at the time while he and the family were on holiday in Scotland. There was some trouble with a woman . . . and also his graduation marks had been far below what he could have expected. He was very brilliant . . . Talking about [Aldous's] going blind, I asked who was there to comfort him, Aldous said, "People were very nice—and *there was Trev.*" So Peggy comes to tea and says you want to call the cub Trev. *DO.* We asked Aldous—it was so easy just after the morning's conversation—he would like it very much—and Matthew-kins, they say you are as [utterly illegible word] as he was—and Aldous says that Julian would like it too. I have wanted to suggest it long ago but feared you would think it too unusual. So write to Aldous what you decide. What about his "layette" have you bought it? May I pay for it? . . .

Three days later, Aldous took it up, beginning with a preamble, "I forgot . . to ask how you stood financially in regard to the blessed event. Please remember that, if you should need anything to cope with the emergency, I shall be only too proud and happy to advance it . ." He went on (in an unpublished letter),

I have been thinking more about names and asking myself why, in the event of the cub's masculinity, we shouldn't think of my brother Trev. Trevenen has the defect of being a bit out of the ordinary, but the merit of being euphonious and of commemorating a very rare being, whom we all loved . . .

A couple of days later Maria ran into "Lola the wonderful fortune teller who I thought was dead, but she is not practising anymore . . . But I did see an astrologer . . more educated and therefore less fun . .

but [he told me] there is more money in 1952 than there has been for some time and 1953 is really the money year. So we breathe a little more freely in anticipation . . yet how it goes—and now more doctors, more medicines, more treatments of all kinds. But so far we have at least got it. More than some people have . . .

On 21st October Mark Trevenen Huxley was born. Matthew telephoned the news to California early in the morning. His parents wrote:

Dearest M & E,
   I'm suddenly reminded of a letter I wrote to Arnold Bennett thirty-one years ago, in response to a note of his about Matthew's arrival—a letter in which I remarked that we literary gents might talk about our creative efforts, but that after all these creative efforts were pretty feeble in comparison with what our wives and le Bon Dieu contrived, between them, to achieve! Best love to all three of you.

And Maria,

God bless you Matthewkins—and Ellen and our little cub. It is already as if he had always been there and his name is so familiar in Aldous's voice—I hope that even if Trevenen is his second name you will use it—Aldous so definitely expects it—and it is a very pretty name. He was that before he was born—our cub . . .
   Aldous almost fell out of bed rushing to the phone—he guessed it was you—and he is so happy—he suddenly kissed me this afternoon and called me granny . . . How soon can we expect photos—I can "see" you three—and Ellen and Trev in her arms—as if I had been there. Ellen has a way of looking down which is so beautiful. In fact, this is as important to us as to you, Matthewkins, even though it is all your own and we are so far away . . . Are you Christening him? I mean—in some religion?
   I hope you can write soon—I have of course a most terrific headache—now realize how anxious I was—Goodnight My darling—

"Darlings—" in a large faint hand, the words painstakingly, legibly formed, "you are going to have a funny letter and I don't know how to begin because I feel shy and also want to be diplomatic—you see the limelights have been *on me* and you know I make faces . . ."
It was a letter from hospital, and the first Matthew and Ellen heard of it. The letter went on—five passages of re-assurance and admissions. There had been a cyst—Hawkins just kept at me—the usual paraphernalia of surgeons—it was done at a wonderful moment, Aldous being better than ever and taking his oxygen treatment from the maid who is a treasure, Bill Kiskadden keeping an eye on him. I shall recover 100%, there will be no recurrence. P.S. Will they telephone Constance Collier who will hear it anyhow and better from us direct—and just minimize it all you can.

PART TEN 1951-1955

On 26th January Aldous wrote to Jeanne (unpublished).

Maria is back at home and is getting on remarkably well, gaining
strength every day. The doctors are confident . . . No radiation will
be necessary.
. . Rose is now with us here, which is a great comfort, as she drives
the car . . & looks after things in a general way. In a few more weeks
I think that M will be back to normal, able to do everything . . .

But the cyst had been found to be malignant and the prognosis
was not good. The Kiskaddens knew this. So did Maria.
Aldous had finished *The Devils of Loudun* while Maria was in
hospital. The typescripts have gone off, she reported in her first
letter from home, now Aldous hopes to start soon on a film about
Gandhi with Gabriel Pascal, the producer of Shaw's plays, and
it might be necessary to go to India. By March, in fact, they
were able to go on a short trip to the Arizona desert, Maria
driving.

. . particularly wonderful at this time of year, with snow on the
higher mountains . . . and, in the warm plains, an immense profusion
of wild flowers, which come rushing out after the spring rains . . .
[Aldous in a long letter to a new correspondent, Mrs Elise Murrel,
whom Maria called "our un-met psychic friend in England"] And
here and there, in the most arid and naked plains, spring the desert
lilies . . with grey green leaves and a pyramid of perfumed blossoms,
snowy white with green veins on the outside of each petal. It is an
unforgettable spectacle—the good will of life, the tenacity of it in the
face of the most adverse circumstances, the patience of it (the lilies
will lie dormant for as much as ten or fifteen years, if there is a
drought). . the profusion, the beauty. And the yearly miracle takes
place in an enormous luminous silence. Huge spaces completely
empty of human activity, flooded with light and enclosed in an
immense crystal of silence, to which any sound—the song of a bird,
the noise of a passing car or plane—is completely irrelevant. It
remains unflawed . . .

Chapter Two

Watershed

WELL worth looking into and experimenting with—that, so far, had been Aldous's approach to dianetics and to how much else. One has to dream, as he said once or twice, in a pragmatic way. Now, there appears an escalation in his interest, one might almost say his need, for these pursuits, a precipitation set off perhaps by the events of the last months, a change from curiosity to conviction. Maria filled a supple role of leading and at the same time waiting. Since her return from hospital Aldous had been treating her with hypnosis, helping her greatly, he thought,

. . she has been in strikingly good psychological shape, with a serenity and a cheerfulness which have undoubtedly contributed to her excellent recovery.

Indeed, he had "become a rather good hypnotic operator . . ." (There is a corroboration by Stravinsky,[1] ". . Aldous's friendship was a great comfort to me, and more; Aldous is a healer, a skilful masseur who cured me of insomnia . . .") At present, however, it was the "E" Therapy that Aldous and Maria were absorbed in. This therapy ("E" for entelechy, or if you like, the informing spirit), though akin to dianetics, had been evolved from early Buddhist texts by an Oriental scholar[2] whom they knew, and was a therapy supposed to reach and affect the "deeper self". This self, Aldous expounded, "can generally be relied on to come up with something useful to the organism, if it is politely asked to do so—

e.g. some memory which requires to be talked out several times until there is no further emotional reaction to it, or else some symbolic image which may not seem significant at the moment, but will often turn out to make sense later on. This method of approach is, I believe, much better than any course of suggestions pushed in by the operator, or than a too busy probing of analysis. There is a part of the subconscious non-self which is much less stupid than the self and

[1] Igor Stravinsky and Robert Craft *Dialogues and a Diary*. Faber & Faber, 1968.
[2] A. L. Kitselman.

personal subconscious, and can be relied upon to provide help if asked . . .

. . . The procedure is actually a form of meditation, in which the meditator does not work alone, but is helped by the questions of an auditor. Why these questions should be helpful I do not exactly know. But the fact remains that they seem to assist the mind in its task of standing aside from the ego and its preoccupations, and laying itself open to the eternal consciousness. In a number of cases which I have seen the results have led to a remarkable increase in insight and improvement in behaviour.

There is a good deal more about this subject in Aldous's letters (from which I quoted fragments), to Julian urging him to have a go, to the Godels, later on to Dr Humphrey Osmond. Aldous's concern went beyond the immediate therapeutic results; the year before he had been working "with an interesting man, who was used, as a youth, as a hypnotic subject by a systematic investigator and goes down, under passes and suggestions, to a very great depth of trance—depths which are most uncommonly met with in ordinary hypnotic practice.*

The reports from these depths are most curious . . .

. . . Everything seems to point to the fact that, as one goes down through the subliminal, one passes through a layer (with which the psycho-analysts commonly deal) predominantly evil and making for evil—a layer of Original Sin, if one likes to call it so—into a deeper layer of "Original Virtue", which is one of peace, illumination and insight, which seems to be on the fringes of the Pure Ego or Atman . . .

Maria meanwhile was dealing with the thing in her own way. Aldous, she wrote to Jeanne, was quite evidently "blocked" and will take a long time to reach his "E" or deeper self. Whereas,

I, they say (and I know it's true) have a *rapport* with my "E" . . One feels oneself guided. I've always been profoundly convinced that we are guided; and had personal experience of it. During the first years of our marriage I used to say to Aldous (without knowing what I was saying) "God's hand will show the way"—it was about material matters then. When I knew him better—thought I knew him better—I didn't say it so clearly any more. Now, all this is so evident between us . . . I think with this therapy we may have got a simple and rapid way of getting to what the yogi recommend us, and the saints. E Therapy, like dianetics, is not an *end*, but at present it seems to be the best *means* . . .

And last Tuesday they had had another meeting of "interested and serious friends", LeCron, the psychotherapist and the Hixons,

* See note on p. 145

their dentist friend and his wife, "a very intelligent medium", with Aldous giving magnetic treatment to Mrs Hixon. And now, Maria went on "I must come to another aspect of all this. Aldous.

.. You do know for how many years we've loved Aldous and known his goodness and his sweetness and his honesty—but you also know how tiring, in spite of all this, he was to live with—sad to live with. Well now, he is transformed, transfigured. What I mean to say is that this change has been working in an intangible way and for a very very long time but that the result has suddenly exploded—and I say *exploded*. Aldous no longer looks the same, his attitude is not the same, his moral and intellectual attitude, his attitude to animals, people, the clouds, to the telephone ringing (and that's going very far)—no, let's go further and say that he even decides his own decisions— *qu'il répond du tac au tac à des articles insultants; qu'il se fait payer son dû et demande que l'on lui rende des services*—but he also *offers* his services, whereas up to now he has always been content to offer a little money rather than to pay with his person, or rather with his soul. At last he has reached the point of putting into constant daily practice everything he wants to practise, and this even without realizing it . . . He goes to doctor's meetings, he went to defend a friend of Matthew's in court; he telephones Mrs Corbett to ask how she is—he eats Marie's dinners with pleasure, even orders them . . .
.. His search for this road, we know, did not only come out of his philosophical interests; he helped himself by psychological experiments, by spiritual exercises . . . what we shall never know is where this virtuous circle begins and ends. My illness, which might have muddled and blackened and exhausted everything, has been both the starting point and the arrival of this development. Which once more goes to show that every experience has some positive value and that we must accept it constructively.
Aldous's illness, already, was a great step for us in the good direction—or let us say, an enlightenment . . And it encouraged me a good deal. We need not fear anything . . .
Next Tuesday we are going to make an experiment I suggested and Gerald will be here, but I don't know if this will be good or bad.

This letter to Jeanne was dated April, and in May Maria wrote that very curious one about her own visionary experiences to their "psychic friend", which Professor Grover Smith includes in Aldous's *Letters*. It begins:

.. Thank you for answering my question about prayer. I suppose I know all the answers in my head, but I only understand them when I know them in my heart; but that is all right too. Lately I am much more settled in my answers, and more believing in them. Just sometimes experiences are unbelievable because oneself is the experiencer when it seems that others would be more suitable—and deserving . . .

In the midst of all this Aldous went to see China Lake, the U.S. Naval Research station in the desert (he never missed the chance of any kind of sight, be it laboratory or sewage plant). "A thousand square miles of testing grounds. Sentries and F.B.I. men to check everybody going in or out . . ." Aldous was shown everything from million-volt X-ray cameras to refrigerated vacuum tanks and the insulated town

. . of twelve thousand inhabitants, mostly PH.D's, entirely air-conditioned, in the middle of the most howling of wildernesses. The whole directed exclusively to the production of bigger and better rockets. It was the most frightening exhibition of scientific and highly organized insanity I have ever seen.

One vaguely thought that the human race was determined to destroy itself. After visiting the China Lake Research station, one feels quite certain of it. And the whole world is fairly crawling with physicists in barbed wire compounds working three shifts a day *ad majorem Diaboli gloriam*. What a relief to turn to the book by [Konrad] Lorenz . .! Consider the wolves and the jackdaws . . .

Matthew was offered an interesting and well-paid job in an international organization, gave up his present one, found that the offer depended on further departmental decision and was left dangling. His father urged him to come out to California with Ellen and the baby on a long holiday. ". . Install yourself here, where I am sure you can make yourselves reasonably comfortable and have a reasonable degree of privacy [unpublished letter of 20th June]

Don't consider problems of expense. Your living won't cost much and money exists to be spent for productive purposes—and what purpose can be more productive than acquiring strength of body and peace of mind for a new beginning? . . . As for the job—it will come in due time. There are moments in life when it is imperative to behave like Mr Micawber and wait for Something to Turn Up, not try too hard to turn it up oneself, as though one were looking for a centipede under a stone.

Aldous, for his part, was in a similar position, the film on Gandhi for which he had been waiting these four months—"the

haggling has been going on since February"—having been called
off. Disappointment, vexation, but he tried to make the best of it.
"I .. shall have time and peace of mind . . ." He also was at last
getting the better of his chronic bronchitis by a pressure-breathing
treatment with a new device, an apparatus attached to a portable
oxygen tank, which he could take at home. Maria confirmed to
Jeanne that both she and Aldous are admirably well, that Aldous
is enlarging the range of his occupations, is speaking on the radio,
appearing on television and on platforms. He has agreed to give
a lecture on Art in Washington in 1954, "and even thinks that
he might be able to talk instead of read. Which is an enormous
step. In the past he simply would have ignored the possibility of
doing such a thing."

Maria's letters this summer always come back to the main
theme. To Jeanne she writes: "I am much comforted to know
that you are interested in spiritual things. Because for a long time
now it is only this which interests me and I feel entirely cut off
from those who do not share this in the ultimate sense.

Of course there are a thousand ways or rather as many ways as
there are human beings, of being spiritually concerned. But if it's
totally lacking I have no more contact. Rose is much nearer to it
than you would think—by way of the Catholic side. Suzanne, on
the contrary, is very far, I think; but the worst situation is Mère's.
If there is time I'll talk to you about Mère . . .

.. First of all I must tell you that pure "intellectuality" is as much
an obstacle as anything else .. it's a barrage . . .

.. *Savoir et pouvoir*—to know and to do—are two different things . . .
And we must look everywhere to find what we are looking for . . .
The Perennial Philosophy is the most helpful . . . And yet I've got
to tell you what Krishnaji indefatigably repeats—that it is in ourselves that we shall find the answer if we know how to listen. Where
Krishnaji doesn't give us any help is in learning to listen and how to
prepare the ground. Krishnaji has so well understood the error of
Theosophical directions by the .. Masters etc that he himself will
indicate no system. And yet we are all so buffeted by the speed of
living that it seems to me that a technique is necessary to eliminate
the *fragmentation, the unnecessary tensions,* caused by the details of daily
life .. You and I, and certainly women, have a more cluttered life
than the men of our class. When their work, which is essentially
concentrated while ours is dispersed, is over they are able to sit
back, they've earned their living. Whereas you have to be at the
disposal of your husband, your children, the housekeeping, have to
pay the bills, go to the hairdresser and the cleaners, sew a button ..
even to ask someone else to sew a button is a distraction and
interruption . . .

At this point there did come one indeed, and Maria had to resume her letter a few days later.

> I think that what I meant to tell you is that it was probably the search for their E—in that useful terminology of the E therapy—which made those so-called bigots always run to church. The silence of a church, and perhaps even the monotony of the litanies and the prayers prayed by the lips only, may calm the conscious, send it to sleep, so that we may arrive at the unconscious. So we should not criticise those pious old women too much, for as soon as one criticises one feels oneself superior and by this alone buckles oneself into an armour impenetrable even to our E.

Then, going back to the perennial philosophy, Maria speaks of Aldous's talent for choosing "important, comprehensible and practicable passages.

> .. [his extracts from] William Law, for example, have moved me so much, while read as a whole he is illegible, at least to me. The same goes for Benoit who is often arid, and also for Godel . . .
> .. I hope that if ever you feel a need for calm, for silence, such as I had in the desert, you will go and sit in a corner of St Sulpice and forget everything that may be troubling you. You will be surprised how much this will calm and "enlighten" you . . . I remember some of my most difficult moments, physically and emotionally—in New York with Sophie [in 1940] for her *bachot*.[1] The real war had started, but I'd promised to take her, I travelled under pressure, no news from Europe, worried about Aldous, with Sophie anxious about her exam, anxious about you, Mère and Rose, and you all God knew where. Well, it was in the cathedral, where I went to burn a candle for Sophie's success, that I found re-assurance—and I was far from realizing then how this could be possible . . . I think you understand what I am trying to tell you.

It was possible, even natural for Maria to write like this to Jeanne, herself open, alert to new theories and practices. How to approach a young man confident in the ways of the world? How to approach Matthew? Finally she wrote him a very long letter. It is the letter which began with, "Why, why in the world did Aldous choose me of the many prettier, wittier, richer etc girls? Why in the world did he come back to fetch me after two long years . . .? Knowing all the time . . that he could never teach me to write poetry or remember what I read in a book or spel . . ." It is the letter first mentioned, in the context of 1918, in the chapter

---

[1] Argot for *baccalaureat*.

called Strain. These questions were Maria's *entrée en matière*, the matière being the E therapy and all it stood for, and it now went on:

He told me yesterday [in 1952] that I *was* very pretty when I was young . . but I doubt it, I would have known it then, and the photographs would show it now. Anyway one does not choose and wait so long or stick so long to a woman who was pretty once.

And why did I who was horrified by those Garsington men (and women) I who was so squashed by the English and terrified of them, why did I let Aldous approach me . . ? Why, because, though I was not then in love with Aldous, even though he was in love with me, we could see all the underlying possibilities which are really facts. He could sense, shall we say, instead of see, that in spite of all he had been told, I was a steady one, and I could sense that I would be entirely devoted to his service for the rest of our lives. In fact we were fated to each other. And where psychology comes in is that we *acted* on it. And later on, in spite of life with a big L, we still stuck it out. Nothing is always perfect for anybody. So Aldous had to put up with me and I had to put up with him, or rather we had to put up with the difficulties life with a big L, as it does everyone else, got us into. Why we managed is because, underneath, our psychological sensitiveness knew better. Now, you are going to receive the same pamphlet[1] that Aldous sent Julian. Do read it; and do re-read it. Also re-read my letter after you have faithfully read the pamphlet; then you will say (because one needs some kind of speech) that our E's functioned. And that is what we think of yours and Ellen's.

Aldous's E functions chiefly in his work. But now, by developing it . . it works more and more in everyday life . . Aldous in fact, is being spontaneous . . . Aldous who could never *say* the right thing (I mean in the psychological sense and strains), now cannot say the wrong thing—and what is more, bubbles with the right things at the right moments and with the most difficult people and in the most difficult circumstances and in the most unaccountable positions. I will add to all this that his health has immensely improved with the treatments, but to that must be added that now he himself takes them, orders the new [oxygen] tanks, in fact he *runs himself*. In fact he lets his E or super-conscious run him. There is no more a blockage between him and his super-conscious.

In my case, all the attempts at the hand-writing, hand-reading, interest in fortune tellers, the fact that they read so well for me and *through* me; the fact that I do immensely know all the time what people feel, unfortunately too much sometimes . . (of course there is a reverse side to my medal as well) . . my spontaneity . . the fact

[1] A. L. Kitselman's on "E" therapy.

that in a whole life I cannot remember quarrelling with anyone (Ottoline when I was 17, because she said I flirted with Phillip who was . . not more interested in me than in every other young woman . . .). You probably never stopped to realize the terribly difficult position of an upstart little refugee getting away with the prize of the artistic English world—and keeping her prize—and at the age of twenty and without any schooling except failures. I did not ever come down to their levels of malice or sex, but that does not mean that I ever rose to their heights of intelligence and brilliance. Now, do you not realize that something helped us stronger and better than ourselves. Certainly not my *intelligence*; nor Aldous's. And from the E (to use the jargon, one must use some) everything is explained and explainable. And what an interesting novel; to write the life of people backwards, tracing their E. (It would have to be called something else, for public consumption—do not think we have become Faddists. Less than ever. We eat and drink and think and sleep and walk and work as everyone else does). In my case with more realization for the steps I take, and fall down upon too. But with no more despair and recrimination. I really have become patient. And those nerves were so very superficial. *I tremble to know* how you will both take it. Because we would lose nothing by your criticism as we know your affection is unlimited, but we would retard your realizing what we think is so important to realize. By putting you against it. And of course experience is the only thing . . I . . have always known it; Aldous knew it when he wrote the Perennial Philosophy, but at one remove so to speak; intellectualizing the whole thing. But it was in him; a few of us, Aunt Mary, and all his family, knew the treasure there was in Aldous, I sensed it, always as well as *knew* it, it was always ready for me, *under*, the superficial denseness, as superficial as my nerves and yours, but whereas one can get at nerves more easily by medications and by conscious will, one cannot get at that other thing so easily. Now the treasure is flowing in torrents of gaiety and openness, just sift it out while keeping in clear cool water. And as you can expect when the clearance hits Aldous it *is something*. Nothing ever was much buried in me, nor was there so much to reveal; but there is an easing for myself and all others which you would appreciate more than anyone else. And I *could* have been very ill and tiresome after the operation; some people remain rather stunted in their movements. Yesterday I actually managed to stand on my head again (it needs a terrific *stretch* in the arm). So you must *one day*, for we are as patient as we are trusting, come and see what you think of all this for yourselves and Trevenen.

Now, I hope this does explain a bit more. We are still using doctors, we are still using Bates, we still are imperfect, but we are at least working on improving ourselves, our output, and we do think there are many ways, and many of them unexplored, and their results are

widely and wildly fascinating and worthwhile . . I know, you are
afraid we go off the rails—don't. This has come to Aldous's help
because *his* danger was that the rails would stop in front of a cement
dam. You said as much when you were nervous in Wrightwood,
that he was just "sitting looking at his own navel" *that* was the
danger. Whether navel or otherwise, let us all look as far as we can
and that is unlimited.

As our loves,

Coccola.

Here one might come in with a fragment of corroboration by
Aldous. "There is a striking phrase by von Baader", he wrote to
Alan Watts, "the German philosopher of the Romantic Era, who
emended Descartes' Cogito ergo sum to cogito*r* ergo sum—we
think only in so far as we permit ourselves to be thought by the
immanent and transcendent X."

And this is how Rose—whose own marriage had gone to pieces
—saw her sister and brother-in-law at this very time (in a letter
to Jeanne).

. . . Maria et Aldous vont tous deux remarquablement bien. Très
calmes et très, très gentils et compréhensifs . . . Leurs études les
passionnent et semblent leur apporter beaucoup de paix. Ils sont si
gentils l'un pour l'autre que cela me réconcilie avec la vie: il y a
donc des couples heureux. Leur maison est un succès et enfin digne
d'eux.

A visit by Joep and Suzanne now, on their way back from a
journey in Mexico. They found Aldous in good form and Maria
more willing to let herself be waited on. Suzanne, too, approved
of the new house and the presence of a really first-rate French
cook—Marie Le Put, a Bretonne and a very kind and intelligent
woman. The Nicolas's joined the round of Stravinsky luncheons
("for Igor one had to have French wine, whereas ordinarily one
drank California wine"), gramophone music, walks. They did not
take part in the Tuesday evenings, in what Suzanne calls "les
séances de spiritisme et de chiromancie."

After they had left, Madame Nys sprained her arthritic shoulder
and a less harmonious family note is sounded by Aldous letting
off some steam to Matthew and Ellen (in September)

. . . she is making use of her trouble to get as much attention and
service out of both Rose and Coccola as she possibly can. Rose had
to rush in from the desert over the weekend . . and C is kept on the
hop all the time, fetching, carrying, shopping etc. This wouldn't be

so bad, if it weren't for the continual stream of emphatic and self-contradictory talk . . and for the elaborate and preposterous schemes and plots which BM [Bonne Maman] has only too much leisure to hatch. Coccola has never had a wide margin of reserve strength to draw upon, and since her operation this margin has shrunk to a point where her mother (who, for all her age and her rheumatism, has far more physical energy than her daughters) can easily push her over the edge . . .

The problem, Aldous goes on, is a difficult and many-sided one. There is first of all the psychological problem of an old woman who has consistently refused to be anything in life but a tourist.

BM resolutely declines to do anything useful, to co-operate in any way which would entail her making compromises and suiting her own convenience to that of others . . . Because she reads the *Figaro Littéraire*, she feels herself immeasurably superior to the general run of her neighbours . . She has quarrelled with the local Catholic church and so cut herself off from the social and benevolent organizations which it sponsors and in which she could certainly have found something interesting and useful to do. Age and disability make the full life of the tourist impossible for her; and she now spends her energies brooding and making life intolerable for Coccola and Rose. What can be done I don't know . . . In no circumstances would I think of installing her in this house. She would drive Coccola to death or madness in a few months, would make it impossible for me to do any work . . .

This last more than anything makes one realize what a penetrating personality Mme Nys has been. "Suzanne", Aldous concluded, "may consider herself extremely lucky to be three thousand miles away . . ."

Aldous's friend, Larry Powell, Librarian at the University of Los Angeles, asked him to give a talk on Bernard Shaw. Alas, Aldous replied, he felt wholly unqualified to talk about G. B. S., "whom I don't know at all well—perhaps because I have never found him very interesting. Did he, after all, ever know anything about human beings?"

In October, publication of *The Devils of Loudun*. The long, laborious job that promised, as Aldous said in mid-writing, to turn into something very substantial. It is a psychological study of "one of the most fantastically strange stories in all French history—the story [as he described it to Harold Raymond ten years before] of the demoniac possession of the nuns of Loudun,

which begins with fraud, hysteria, malicious plotting; goes on with the commission of a monstrous judicial crime, the burning of

Urbain Grandier, as the supposed author of the possession; continues posthumously with more diabolic manifestations and the
bringing on to the scene of Father Surin, one of the most saintly
ecclesiastics of his age, who tries to exorcise the Abbess of the
convent . . . [and] by a kind of psychological infection, himself
succumbs to possession and becomes half mad, but with perfectly
lucid intervals, in which he realizes the full extent of his misfortune.
Surin remains in this state for nearly twenty years, but finally
emerges into a serene old age of something like perfected sanctity,
during which he writes some of the most important spiritual works
of his period . . .

And nearly twenty years later, Aldous went on in the London
interview, "The strange thing is that the whole Loudun affair is
interesting only if you take the two sides together.

If you take the case of Grandier, and then the case of Surin. Between
them, the two episodes describe the religious life on every level—
from the most horrible to the most sublime. The whole gamut of
religious life is set forth in a kind of parabola in these two episodes.
Now the really extraordinary thing is that as far as I know I was the
first person to bring these two episodes together in a single volume.
Plenty of French people have written about Grandier, and in recent
times about Surin, but nobody has thought fit to put the two cases
together . . .
This is the whole message of this extraordinary episode—religion
is infinitely ambivalent. It has these wonderful sides to it, and these
appalling sides . . .
And here is a story which is strictly historical—and I really never
departed from the historical documents—which is at the same time
a parable. And *this* is what I'm looking for: an historical or biographical medium in terms of which I can think about all sorts of
general subjects.
I do strongly feel that philosophical and religious ideas are better
expressed not in abstract terms but in terms of concrete case histories
. . If you can find the right kind of case history . . And this . . is why
I am looking for another biographical historical personage or
episode on which to hang my ideas . . .

Before the turn of the year the long expected arrival of Matthew
with his family. Matthew was still between jobs, the delicate baby
in poor health, Aldous, though fighting bronchitis, at work again
—on the scenario of a popular film on the sun, a bread-and-
butter job. Once again, life with Aldous and Maria is seen through
a young woman in their household, Ellen, their daughter-in-law

(older than Suzanne at Paddington, younger than Jeanne or myself). ". . It's fascinating to see what can be recalled and what is gone.[1] I have strong visual pictures, almost like a camera— Aldous doing his Bates eye exercises in the patio outside his study door; Maria darting about, her feet scarcely touching the ground, as she sprayed Air-Wick throughout the house because someone had smoked a cigarette; Marie Le Put, smiling and smiling and making madeleines or a soufflé ('my God, the Huxleys ate well! . . the inside of their huge freezer, stuffed with breads and meats— they had given up being vegetarian on doctors' advice, and switched merrily over to the side of the carnivores; they even used to sneak hamburger to the Rajagopal's cat, because the poor thing was given only vegetables).

I suppose you have written about Maria and cars? I was astonished by her expertise with them . . . the incongruity of her small, feminine self being able to listen to her car engine critically, whip it into a garage, and give the mechanics a complete run-down on what was going on and how she wanted it adjusted.

They had a ring-toss game for Trev, a wooden rabbit with long ears and a set of rope rings you were supposed to toss on to the ears.

Aldous was deadly at this game—he was so used to concentrating what sight he had, when he wanted to use it, that he simply never missed. Though at other times of course he would run into things . . . Kings Road was a dark and gloomy house, with long corridors, not much sunlight . . .
We saw many people. They were tremendously hospitable, even to people they didn't know. Maria was major-domo and screened the visitors, but with so much tact and charm that everyone without exception felt better about themselves by the time they left . . .

Maria drove them out to Pasadena for tea with Edwin Hubble, "the astronomer of Palomar . . Fred Hoyle came too, being very intelligent and very bumptious,

the screaming was intense. Except for Hubble, that gentle, warm, touching man—in the middle of all the complex talk he wandered outside, came back to urge us all out ". . to see the evening star".

Edith Sitwell was in Hollywood that winter, and, as Ellen put it, "was around a lot. Maria would groan privately and say that

---

[1] The present Ellen Giffard writing to S. B.

Edith had always been in love with Aldous and wanted to marry him; Aldous said nothing, but was obviously enjoying himself.

He and Edith spent a happy day together touring Forest Lawn cemetery; they said they got treated with a lot of interest because they were both old enough to be serious candidates for a plot. *They* crowed when they found out that the bridal chapel was heated by heat generated by the crematorium.

And there were of course the North Kings Tuesdays. Aldous would take Matthew and Ellen to the pre-séance dinner at the mammoth drug store (mixed grill and phonograph records). Maria did not come: she never ate on Tuesdays.

. . She was in her element, very good at these things, completely in tune with her unconscious—Aldous went at it without preconception and with immense good will, but he was passive; his imagination didn't run naturally along those lines.

After these glimpses, Ellen sums up her main impression of that time. "Aldous and Maria dealing with being parents and parents-in-law and grand-parents, all three unfamiliar roles to them. They included us in their circle, were terrified Matthew wouldn't approve of the Tuesdays, doted on Trev, worried about Matthew's future, opened their hearts to me in the most generous way, suffered from their loss of privacy, couldn't believe how much we ate, thought us rather 'square', offered tremendous intimacy and openness. Maria never knew when to stop giving and start protecting herself, which would make her cross and exhausted at times—and she was full of forebodings about her health (typically, she discussed this with Marie the cook and not with the family; she had the deepest, strongest relationships with her servants [here I profoundly agree]. There is nothing she wouldn't have done for them, or they for her). So we got to know each other, and dealt with a lot of anxiety, and had great times together, and my remembrance is of untold tenderness and grace and love and good will . . ."

Matthew and Ellen left before the spring. On 25th February Lewis Gielgud died. His death came as a shock, Aldous wrote to Juliette, "we had been friends for half a century". And to Naomi Mitchison, that other companion of his young years, he wrote a month later,

His going seems curiously hard to take in . . He had been part of my Order of Things . . ever since we first met as new boys at our preparatory school in the autumn of 1903. He was a gentle man as well as a gentleman, with all the qualities of humaneness connoted by both expressions.

Lewis Gielgud—who at Eton had learnt Braille in order to be able to write to Aldous. Aldous too had been a faithful and affectionate friend. He was always that; in his great friendships and his lighter ones: inseparable by distance, time and the widening spaces of his own development. The thought that had flashed through Gervas's mind in 1914 as they said goodbye on the platform of King's Cross, cogitor, the thought which Gervas, as Aldous saw it now, had permitted himself to *be* thought—"If one survived one would never have to bother about communication with Aldous, there was something imperishable there," proved true. They all lasted as long as life, kept a freshness at the rare encounters: the friendship with Lewis, with Gervas (theirs was a double tie), with Eugene Saxton, with—to lesser degrees—Evan Morgan, Robert Nichols, Tommy Earp, the affective, companionable, exploratory friendships of his youth and the two great formative friendships of his maturer years, D. H. Lawrence and Gerald Heard. And now he was within weeks of one more of these precipitatory compatibilities, a relationship, this time, with a very much younger man whom he came to hold in affection and admire, Dr Humphrey Osmond. (One does realize that Aldous's most intimate friends, though men of high intelligence in their different ways and men of human quality (Lawrence of course stands entirely apart), were not the masters, the highbrows, the literary mandarins of his time, not, though he knew them all and was fond of many, Bloomsbury, not the Sitwells, not Morgan Forster or Tom Eliot.)

Dr Osmond, an English psychiatrist, was working at the time in a state mental hospital, Saskatchewan, on the Canadian Prairies. He, with Drs John Smythies and Abram Hoffer, were doing research in schizophrenia in the course of which they had been using mescalin. A paper setting out some of their findings had been published in medical and scientific journals. These Aldous read. He sent a friendly letter to the young doctors. Humphrey Osmond, who had kept a copy of *Texts and Pretexts* by him on Atlantic convoys and who had just read *The Devils of Loudun*, answered. Aldous wrote again. A month later, unexpectedly, Osmond had to attend a meeting of the American Psychiatric Association in Los Angeles. As unexpectedly, Aldous asked him to stay at North Kings. Later on he was told how it had come about, how at breakfast one morning Aldous had looked up and said, " 'Let's ask this fellow Osmond to stay'," and that Maria replied, " 'But he may have a beard and we may not like

him.' Aldous thought for a bit, and said, 'If we don't like him
we can always be out.' "[1]

On 3rd May the young man arrived. Feeling very shy. Maria,
of course, put him at his ease. She told him that he and Aldous,
being Englishmen, would get on. "To Maria, Englishmen were
largely incomprehensible except to each other."[1] (How true this
was.) Then, "Aldous glided towards me from the cool darkness
of the house into the sunshine of the front porch. He seemed to
be suspended a fraction of an inch above the ground like one of
Blake's allegorical figures . . ." They got on. Humphrey says that
what struck him from the beginning was the kindness and tolerance of this man, whose writings had led him to suppose that he
would be "disillusioned, cynical and even savage". Or solemn.
Humphrey took Aldous along to a session of his learned conference. They were standing in the foyer "when Aldous's voice
cut through the hubbub like a knife-blade, 'But Humphrey, how
incredible it is in a Marxist country like this . . .' It was 1953 at
the height of the McCarthy era . . ." Inside the hall, Aldous sat
"paying the keenest attention, crossing himself devoutly every
time Freud's name was mentioned . . Here was a congregation,
including many pious Freudians, so Aldous was kept busy. Luckily
my psychiatric colleagues were so absorbed by the incantations
that no one noticed him."

Mescalin, so far, had not been mentioned between host and
guest. (Mescalin, one might briefly recall, is a mind-altering substance, derived from the Mexican root peyote, that causes
hallucinations, visions and dreams. It was first classified in the
1880s by a German pharmacologist, Louis Lewin, who divided
all mind-altering agents into five groups: *euphorica, inebriantia,
hypnotica, excitantia* and *phantastica*. Mescalin and LSD belong to
the *phantastica*. Mescalin was synthesized about 1918. LSD—
lysergic acid diethylamide—a synthetic, was discovered only in
1943.[2] By the 1950s mescalin had been experimented with on
and off for the last seventy years, by Havelock Ellis, Jaensch,
Weir Mitchell among others. A number of psychologists and
alienists had taken it in the hope of coming to a firsthand understanding of their patients' mental processes, but these were a
small and limited category of guinea pigs, and the material
collected was still very inadequate. Aldous offered himself as a
possible new subject. He has given his reasons for doing so in a
letter to Dr Osmond (10th April 1953) which it is rather essential
to read if one wishes to understand what followed.

[1] Dr Humphrey Osmond, *Mem. Vol.*
[2] By the Swiss Scientist, Professor A. Hoffman, in the course of work on
ergot derivatives.

.. It looks as though the most satisfactory working hypothesis about the human mind must follow, to some extent, the Bergsonian model, in which the brain with its associated normal self, acts as a utilitarian device for limiting, and making selections from, the enormous possible world of consciousness, and for canalizing experience into biologically profitable channels.

Disease, mescalin, emotional shock, aesthetic experience and mystical enlightenment have the power, each in its different way and in varying degrees, to inhibit the functions of the normal self and its ordinary brain activity, thus permitting the "other world" to rise into consciousness . . .

Now Aldous comes to what for him was the basic problem of education—"How to make the best of both worlds—the world of biological utility and common sense, and the world of unlimited experience underlying it." He believed that a complete solution of this problem could only come to those who had learned about "the third and ultimate world of 'the spirit', the world which subtends and interpenetrates both of the outer worlds. But short of this ultimate solution, there may be partial solutions, by means of which the growing child may be taught to preserve his 'intimations of immortality' into adult life.

Under the current dispensation the vast majority of individuals lose, in the course of education, all the openness to inspiration, all the capacity to be aware of other things than those enumerated in the Sears-Roebuck catalogue which constitutes the conventionally "real" world. That this is not the necessary and inevitable price extorted for biological survival and civilized efficiency is demonstrated by the existence of the few men and women who retain their contact with the other world, even while going about their business in this. Is it too much to hope that a system of education may some day be devised, which shall give results, in terms of human development, commensurate with the time, money, energy and devotion expended?

In such a system of education it may be that mescalin or some other chemical substance may play a part by making it possible for young people to "taste and see" what they have learned about at second hand, or directly but at a lower level of intensity, in the writings of the religious, or the works of poets, painters and musicians . . .

Once under the same roof, however, the two Englishmen needed Maria to get it going. She told Humphrey Osmond that Aldous was waiting to take the mescalin, was looking forward to it and that his doctors had no objection. Aldous had already laid on a dictaphone for the occasion. Humphrey Osmond, who had

misgivings—What if it didn't work? What if it worked too well?
—could see no decent way of backing out. "Aldous seemed an
ideal subject . . . in spite of remarks that I sometimes heard about
'unfortunate mystical trends in his later years' I found him, both
then and subsequently, shrewd, matter-of-fact and to the point . . .
[and] Maria eminently sensible, and we had all taken to each
other, which was very important for a good experience . . ."[1]

Thus it came about [Aldous speaking[2]] that, one bright May
morning, I swallowed four-tenths of a gram of mescalin dissolved in
half a glass of water and sat down to wait for the results.

The session lasted for about eight hours. Dr Osmond and Maria
remained with him throughout. They, it goes without saying, had
not taken the drug. The experience was of profound significance
to Aldous. This he tried to put across in a small book, much
debated, *The Doors of Perception.*

[1] Dr Humphrey Osmond, *Mem. Vol.*
[2] *The Doors of Perception.* Chatto & Windus, 1954.

Note to p. 130

Aldous's interest in hypnosis began early. In 1937 he had published an
article on the subject in *Nash's Magazine.* "The very pleasant young man",
whom I called T., who was Aldous and Maria's neighbour at the Mount
Royal Hotel in London during that spring and who rescued Aldous from the
consequences of the botched operation on his jaw in Paris, did not entirely
agree with the article and said so to Aldous. Aldous told T., who is of course
Mr. Boris Trainin, the Harley Street dental consultant and analytical psychologist, that he very much wanted to be hypnotized but had never succeeded,
and he asked him to try. "It occurred to me [in B.T.'s own words] that the
previous failures might have been due to a wrong approach—i.e. asking him
to lie down . . . I got him to stand up and you might say I took him by surprise. He was an excellent hypnotic subject. This first experience may have
been the basis of his later development in this field."

Chapter Three

The Door in the Wall

HUMPHREY OSMOND left. Aldous and Maria went off on one of their car journeys—three weeks, five thousand miles, of nature and National parks in the vast American North-west. From Cœur d'Alene, Idaho, they sent a postcard to Anita Loos.

> There was a young lady of Bute
> Who was so indescribably cute
> That, each time she came out,
> All the boys gave a shout,
> With the Lesbians hot in pursuit.

Love Aldous

What more can one add!! M.

After their return Aldous was ready to get down to the small book. He finished it in a month. "So we are happy and working [I had a note from Maria] . . Last Sunday we had a fête, Aldous's 59th birthday." (The Hubbles, Stravinsky, Gerald, Eva Herrmann, Christopher Wood.) Work continued. Opportunely, *Life* magazine asked Aldous to do an article on parapsychology.[1] Matthew and Ellen were expecting a second child. What a good letter, Aldous said as he read the news.

What good children, I thought. [Maria to Ellen] What treasures . . .

With Matthew between jobs, the young Huxleys had been having the devil of a year but were getting the better of it now by making their own decisions. Matthew chose to specialize in a field that interested him and was given a scholarship at the Harvard School of Public Health. Once more, Maria was trying to impart to them something of what she had learned—about the give and take of marriage, about how to live—letters impelled, one feels, by a great urge and written in a tempo that is not that of the young and well. Perhaps that terrible year has brought them something, she wrote, "no experience, however painful, is not without its own reward: to Matthew it may have brought a patience towards grown-ups; and when he will realize that no one 'Knows better' but that we all 'Know differently', he will

---

[1] "A Case for Esp, Pk and Psi", *Life*, January 1954.

have reached what Aldous has reached now. And I believe that Matthew may reach it at a very much younger age than Aldous did."

Last winter already they had been "enchanted and surprised" by him and Ellen. "Never did you refuse to look at the things, however mad or new which came your way when you were staying with us." And once we realize, Maria went on, about this " 'knowing different', then we can apply to ourselves that which we can use, rather than waste our energies to teach others what we think we know better. Others can only use what we have to give if we let them use it in their own way. Of course one must also understand that some things might be left to the one who does them best ... in practical matters for instance. You cannot pack properly and leave it to Matthew." Yet even there they have a warning in her and Aldous's life.

Since I was exactly sixteen, I lived with those who could "think better" and also "speak better" .. but there was one field in which, when we were young, Aldous always turned to me—psychological matters. He used to say I was his personal relationship interpreter— and probably because he relied on me then, I took over too much; his efforts grew less and less until he gave it up almost completely and had to start the whole thing from scratch almost, about four years ago—I *could* have used my mind with more precision had I exercised it more—until that age my studies were very satisfactory ... Aldous is both being more and more practical and needs *no* interpreter ever now with human beings. It is a bit late for me to start training my mind in memorizing quotations which Aldous has at his fingertips, but I am sure that somewhere I am "still learning" ...

As ever the letter is packed with fifty other things: from Sophie being off to Ceylon on Unesco business, and the Kiskaddens well and cheerful, to Ellen's health—"Relax in a room as silent as can be, and pile cushions *under* as well as over the telephone ... but then we are so much older and of a different period that I do not realize what you need ... I wish I were the useful type of Grandmother ... My cooking is getting rarer and worse. [their French paragon did not come every day] Luckily Yolanda is reconstructed now and cool and open at night; the Stravinskys send their love." California has been hotter than anyone can remember but she stood it well, so now they *can* go to India any time Aldous wants to. He has finished his article on mescalin. Hutchins is reading it and was enormously interested and is going to try to get the psychology department to take an interest ... "Magic," the letter ends, "is advancing."

That was Robert M. Hutchins, then a director of the Ford

Foundation, now President of the Center for Democratic Studies at Santa Barbara, whom Aldous had been trying to persuade, now with Alan Watts, now with Dr von Bertalanffy, now with Julian, to carry out a variety of projects—research into the phenomena of the human organism as a whole, research into the role of language in international affairs, into non-verbal, non-conceptual education. The latest idea, suggested by Drs Osmond and Hoffer, was to record mescalin experiments with some fifty people of outstanding and diverse abilities. Hutchins himself was generally willing but unable to override objections from the heads of the concerned departments, the mesozoic reptiles, Aldous called them, who would not touch anything faintly controversial with a barge pole.

Hutchins's comments on how relentlessly Aldous pursued all technological change.

> He dragged me to Hollywood to meet a man who had a device that would slow down a phonograph to half speed and thus permit far longer and cheaper records . . .
> He dragged me to lunch with the founder of the Ampex Corporation to hear the tale of building an airplane untouched by human hands that could fly to any destination without a pilot . . .[1]

But he always raised the question of advantages or disadvantages to human life; once when someone held forth about the wonders of modern communications, Hutchins heard Aldous reply,

"When we didn't communicate with Japan, we didn't go to war with her, either."

During the summer the Huxleys got themselves involved in a farcical imbroglio. "Were you with us at Bandol when at the Casino there was a Fakir called Tahra Bey, sticking pins and needles and doing terrific other tricks?" Maria wrote to Matthew.

> Well, Tahra Bey has become a friend in distress. He is an M.D. of the faculty of Paris and Turkey (?). He is here and Aldous had a long talk with him . . . He is giving a show on Wednesday and we are all going . . .
> Maria has been very busy [this is Aldous, to Humphrey] trying to help a man we met twenty years ago . . a Lebanese doctor who learned all the tricks of the dervishes and has made a living all these years by giving demonstrations of being buried alive . . . A charming

[1] Robert M. Hutchins, *Mem. Vol.*

man—but unfortunately he contrived to spend more than two years in London without learning one word of English. This somewhat cramps his style when giving demonstrations here. He has been swindled right and left . . . he is finally in the hands of some Armenians . . . pork manufacturers, with a farm where five thousand sows work overtime eating the garbage of the city of Long Beach . . . our poor friend . . who was brought up in Armenia . . despises them as *marchands de cochons* and won't accept them as interpreters.

So his performance is a chaos of incomprehensibility . . .

And so it would appear, from accounts of persons on the scene, was the tale of Aldous and Maria's intervention: hilarious but too chaotic to relate here.

Now Julian appeared, on his way to Australia. "Julian came and went like a dream" Maria wrote to Matthew and Ellen. ". . Every minute of his stay was perfect and I believe he enjoyed it as much as we did. Poor Julian . . whenever he is not talking about his own affairs—and I must say very interesting—he has such a sad look in his face, perhaps that is why he must keep his mind crammed and crammed with outside business. But he looked well and was very calm and peaceful and *so like* little Trev —did you also notice that? . . Julian did not once *really look* at Aldous, ask how he was, what he was working at etc, really it is very extraordinary."

Their own great excitement was a new car. An Oldsmobile again, and "really almost everything that the advertisements say about power brakes and power steering is true. I was upset for 3 days at what it cost and could not sleep. Now it has all settled down—except for paying of course."

Edwin Hubble died on 28th September, very suddenly on his driveway in his car. Beside their own sadness Aldous and Maria were much concerned about his widow, their friend Grace.

Two years earlier, the Huxleys had decided to take out their first papers, to apply for American citizenship that is. They had been living in the United States for fourteen years. "We were *de facto* Californians, and it seemed the proper thing to become *de jure* Americans." According to Betty Wendel, their chief reason was that Matthew, himself a citizen since 1946 and raising an American family, would have liked his parents to do so. In the spring of 1953 Aldous and Maria had put in their final petition, and on 3rd November they came up for the routine examination on the American Constitution and other matters which immediately precedes the ceremony that would make them U.S. citizens. Betty Wendel and Rosalind Rajagopal were their character witnesses. It was a Tuesday and they set out before eight o'clock in the morning, taking Betty in the car.

Aldous looked *so* English [she writes], sitting by himself in the rear seat, those long legs folded, arms outstretched, head tilted back in the posture that signalled his willingness for small talk. And Maria looked so Maria at the driver's wheel, not completely disguised as an American businessman's wife by her dark blue suit and hat, white blouse, white gloves within reach for changing from chauffeur's pigskin. I presented each of them with a handkerchief with M.N.H. and A.L.H. embroidered in red, white and blue, immediately placed in pockets with monograms showing. To me the night before there had come a basket of champagne splits with the Maria-Aldous bookplate affixed. On the back of it Maria had written—legibly, ceremoniously: "Good health to you from two very old friends and very new CITIZENS."

Maria had been coached for the looming examination and it worried her that Aldous had not given her homework a glance. "Aldous, are you *sure* that you know American history?"

"Reasonably sure."

"Do you understand the principles and the form of government?" (In the rear-view mirror she saw him nod his prodigious head and smile.) "Of course they'll see how intelligent *you* are, and they won't question you the way they'll question *me*."

He teased her. "The examination can be as thorough or perfunctory as they choose to make it."

"They won't make it perfunctory with me," said Maria.

Aldous laughed. "They might ask you to swear that you speak English, but even if you fail to prove it, darling, *understanding* English is good enough. You can nod your head in English, can't you?"

"Now you're making me cross."

He leaned forward and patted her shoulder. "Your mother and Rose passed with flying colours. It's in the genes."

Presently they reached their destination, a court and offices on a floor of the Rowan Building in Downtown Los Angeles. (Rosalind Rajagopal was waiting.) "And there we were, Maria and Aldous standing in a line that led to an information desk with men and women of all ages and nationalities, flanked by their character witnesses to whom they spoke in foreign accents from slight to very thick." Betty and Rosalind were led off to separate cubicles where anonymous men asked them how long they had known Aldous Huxley? Was he, to their knowledge, a

man of good morals? regularly employed? on good terms with
his neighbours? Did they know whether he had any pressing
debts? Aldous and Maria meanwhile, having proved quite easily
that their knowledge of the Constitution was sufficient, were
required to fill in one more questionnaire. Among others, it contained these questions:

(a) Are you prepared to serve in the U.S. armed forces?
(b) Are you prepared to do non-combatant service in the U.S.
    armed forces?
(c) Are you prepared to do work of national importance under
    civilian control?

Aldous and Maria answered No to the first two questions and
Yes to the third. They were summoned to a court room. A judge
was on the platform, Aldous and Maria stood before him. (Betty
was seated directly behind them and later made a verbatim note.)

> The Judge: Mr Huxley, would you not bear arms in the United
>   States Army?
> Aldous: No.
> The Judge: Would you not drive an army truck transporting
>   armaments?
> Aldous: No.
> J: If the enemy were approaching your home, in defence of your
>   wife and in self defence, would you not pick up a gun and stand
>   by your front door, ready to fire?
> A: I would not have a gun in the house.
> J: Would you be willing to make bandages for the wounded.
> A: Yes.
> J: Would you serve in the Red Cross, as an ambulance driver?
> A: If the question applies to my willingness, yes.
> J: It does, Mr Huxley.

After the same questions had been put to and answered in the
same spirit by Maria, the judge asked them whether their objection to bearing arms was based on religious beliefs? On philosophical convictions, Aldous replied and Maria followed suit.
Religio-philosophical? said the judge. No, purely philosophical.

Now, in 1946 there had been a U.S. Supreme Court decision
to the effect that a person objecting to bearing arms might none
the less become a citizen. The judge explained, in what Betty
describes as regretful tones, that this decision had been superseded, or was held to have been superseded by most lawyers, by
the McCarran Immigration Act of 1952 which denied citizenship
to any person refusing to bear arms for any reason other than
religious beliefs. "The judge then gazed at Aldous with the deep
respect to which he was accustomed and asked if he was not a

religious man? Aldous said that he was indeed a religious man; his opposition to war, however, was an entirely philosophical one.

"The judge sighed. Maria whispered, 'Aldous, do say it's for religious reasons, let's get it over with.' Could he give his personal definition of conscientious objection? asked the judge. Aldous changed his stance from languid to making a stand, he looked directly at the judge, his face and hands became mobile (Maria perked up), his voice was at its most melodious . . . He smiled as he said that at the age of 59 it was unlikely that he would be drafted and have to claim exemption as a conscientious objector. Any trace of irony was gone as he went on to explain that his personal definition of pacifism was a deep conviction of the evil of war based on his philosophy, and not on the tenets of any religious belief, his own or that of any church or creed. Maria looked disturbed, but only for a moment. The judge sighed again and asked Aldous to consider the possibility that his philosophy was an extension of religion."

Aldous stuck to his guns. At the end the judge had no choice but to adjourn proceedings. "Aldous looked at his watch, not closely enough for him to see the time, but as his signal to Maria. 'I think we must be going,' he said to the judge, and then he reached across the table on the platform to shake hands. The judge gave Aldous printed sheets of paper, complete with addressed envelopes, and said 'I will send my report to Washington. At your convenience there will be a special hearing to determine what procedure will grant you naturalization. I am sorry that *postponement* is necessary.'

"Maria said, 'Thank you, your Honour.'

"When they left the building Aldous's face was white. He said with an entirely uncharacteristic show of feeling, 'They don't want us here!'

"On the way uptown there was little conversation. All three of us sat up in front of the car and I felt in the middle of more than the seat. Aldous loosened his necktie, ran his fingers through his hair, wiped his forehead with that foolish souvenir handkerchief from me. Worse, in the refrigerator at home lay three splits of champagne for a celebration luncheon. As we were nearing my house, Maria asked Aldous if he would rather go straight home, and he said, 'Yes, I would.' Stupidly I said, 'But we're having crab salad . . and brie cheese and melon.' 'Can't we have it tomorrow?' Maria asked. 'Not the same crab,' I said. Aldous said, 'I very much want to go home and go to bed.' Maria said, 'Betty, you understand, don't you?' I understood everything except the McCarran Act, and having seen leaving the building goodness knows how many brand new United States citizens happily chattering in the languages of their native lands now that they were Americans. None of them looked distinguished . . a few struck me as shady characters up to no good in our melting pot."

A few days after, Aldous wrote to Cass Canfield asking for his advice. "The current situation, so far as we are concerned, is as follows. We shall be called up for further examination, probably within three or four weeks.[1]

> If the examiner finds our position acceptable, we shall be allowed to proceed with our naturalization; if not the petition will be rejected.
> If it is rejected, we shall, I suppose, return to the status of resident alien. But in practice it will be difficult, perhaps impossible, to return to this country if we should ever leave it. Now I have various engagements in Europe next spring and do not wish to cancel them. Moreover the situation of not being wanted and not being able to come and go at will is one I would not be prepared to accept.
> So if the petition is rejected, I should feel bound, albeit with great reluctance, to wind up our affairs here and leave the country . . .
> . . The whole business has its absurd side, since it hardly seems probable that the armed forces would be very keen on having either Maria or myself in their midst. However, a law is a law.

They went off for a couple of weeks in Northern California. Here Aldous gave his first lecture on a subject that more and more engrossed him, Non-Verbal education, the training, that is, of the human entity by psycho-physical procedures. He spoke once at Palo Alto, once at a women's college (Mills), feeling, he said, like Daniel in a lionesses' den, a prey to innumerable questions about all that is knowable and a good deal that is not. For the rest they drove about enjoying that incredibly beautiful country-side. Aldous's work plans were quite unsettled. He might try to do some more short stories or novelettes, he wrote to Harold Raymond, or might try his hand on a book on human beings and what, if anything, can be done about them. "I have written one chapter of it and have others in my mind." (I think that the chapter may have been "Education of an Amphibian" which appeared later as the lead essay in *Adonis and the Alphabet*.) Alternately he might sit down to something he has had in his head for a long time, a novel extending from the mid-nineteenth century to the present.

It was only in December that Aldous mentions that Maria has had to have X-ray treatments and is going to have more. In two letters, to Humphrey Osmond and to Eileen Garrett, he speaks of

---

[1] Unpublished letter of 7th November.

how very badly the rays affect her, of the intolerable nervous strain, the physical exhaustion. There is not a word about it in Maria's letters to her family. (Only to the unmet psychic friend in England did she write already in October, "I am well too, but suddenly X-ray treatments come to shatter the wellness.")

Matthew had had a daughter, Tessa, in the autumn. First photographs arrived in the New Year, and Maria wrote

Matthew darling . . . Ellen my sweet—How beautiful those children are! Aldous's first remark was, "Aren't you proud of them?" And in the middle of dinner he suddenly interrupted the music to say, "I can't get over the beauty of those children.";. . It is more than beauty, it is peace and strength already that radiates from them—and *gay* happiness too. How we love you and what happiness your little family brings us. I can see what it means to Matthew to have you all. Did you see how little Trevenen crosses his legs just as Aldous does and already did in his 6 year old photo—and the repose in Trev's hands when he sits with you and Tessa . . . I am so grateful for everything . . . It is not good manners to say such things. I shall not say them again probably . . .

Aldous for his part had been moved to write:

Dearest M . . . I must say that between you, Ellen and you have done us proud. What really beautiful little human beings! "Heaven lies around us in our infancy"—and one can go a step further than Wordsworth and say that heaven sometimes seems to appear in us and through us. They really look like angels—though I suppose both have their share of original sin . . .

Presently Edith Sitwell, touring America, arrived again. Here is an original diary entry of Betty Wendel's.

Los Angeles, late afternoon of Thursday, Jan 14th.

With Maria and Aldous to visit Edith Sitwell . . . very high up in the Sunset Towers [then the tallest apartment building in Hollywood] Edith Sitwell in a garnet coloured robe . . centers a great divan, after indicating chairs that Maria and I should take, side by side, back of her, out of her sight. Without being told to do so, Aldous sits on the floor at her feet, suddenly becomes an English schoolboy, his sixty years gone except for twelve or thirteen, as he gazes adolescently up at his elder, enquiring about Osbert . . Sacheverell . . .

After being given glasses of sherry, Maria and I are ignored, while Aldous and Miss Sitwell chat and sip their sherry, poured from a bottle that stands on a table with another bottle of identical size, containing ink. Maria whispers to me, "He's always like that with the Sitwells." Out of sight, out of minds that are in England, there is no danger of our being overheard.

"Some more sherry, Aldous?"

"A little more thank you, Edith."

Maria suddenly rises and utters a sharp warning. "Edith! don't give Aldous *ink* to *drink*."

"Goodness!" says Miss Sitwell, "Let me get you another glass."

All at once reminded, Aldous looks from the face of Maria to that of his watch. "I'm afraid there isn't time, dear Edith—"

We thank Miss Sitwell for letting us come. After a private leave taking of Aldous, she asks him to come again.

"I'll bring him whenever he likes," Maria says, "and then fetch him."

For Aldous, quite an amount of external activities: on 31st January, with his new book about to come out and his article on ESP in *Life* Magazine to be reprinted in the *Readers Digest*, he answered questions on TV; the night before he had appeared on CBS with Dr Gustaf Stromberg of the Mount Wilson Observatory, "a nice old Swedish astrophysicist." (He was so good, Maria said, that Vera Stravinsky brought him a bunch of flowers.)

The new book was *The Doors of Perception*. The battle over the Bates Method is mild in comparison to the battle over Aldous's attitude to mescalin and later LSD. I certainly do not have the competence, nor the desire, to put forth an assessment or a personal opinion. My job at this stage—I shall have to come back to the subject—is to point again to the more ascertainable facts. (The *extent* to which his writings, and example, can be held to have been causative factors in today's drug scene is difficult, perhaps impossible to tell.) What did Aldous actually try to say, and why? What did he not say? *The Doors of Perception* is a short book, not hard to read (though hard to read perhaps with an open mind).

Aldous first took mescalin in 1953 when it was not exactly a household word. (Odd how often this reserved and quiet man would get himself into the thick of things ahead of his time.) He took the drug, under medical supervision, with a view to extending knowledge about the workings of the human mind. The book, essay rather, is an account of the experience itself with reflections on its philosophical, aesthetic and religious implications. It is a curious little book written, I would say, with utter sincerity and simplicity (though the simplicity of a very intelligent man), written, too, with evident passion—this whole thing was very

very important to Aldous and had moved him deeply—but the passion is balanced with detachment. It reflects a heart and mind open to meet the given, ready, even longing, to accept the wonderful. *The Doors* is a quiet book. It is also one that postulates good will—the choice once more of the nobler hypothesis. It turned out, for certain temperaments, a seductive book.

Now, what Aldous experienced under the drug was a change in *everyday* reality. Unlike other mescalin takers before him, he had no stupendous visions, saw no landscapes, geometrical structures or enormous spaces; *he* looked at familiar objects, his typing table, the books on the shelves, his flannelled legs, three flowers in a vase, and they were transfigured. The books glowed, the flowers shone:

> . . I was seeing what Adam had seen on the morning of his creation—the miracle, moment by moment, of naked existence . . . flowers shining with their own inner light and all but quivering under the pressure of the significance with which they were charged . . . Words like "grace" and "transfiguration" came to my mind . . .
>
> . . Being-Awareness-Bliss—for the first time I understood, not on the verbal level, not by inchoate hints . . but precisely and completely what those prodigious syllables referred to . . .[1]

He looked at a table, chair and desk, and the three pieces came together in a pattern that might have been by Braque or Juan Gris—but as he looked

> this purely aesthetic, Cubist's-eye-view gave place to what I can only describe as the sacramental vision of reality. I was back . . in a world where everything shone with the Inner Light, and was infinite in its significance. The legs, for example, of that chair—how miraculous their tubularity, how supernatural their polished smoothness! I spent several minutes—or was it several centuries?—not merely gazing at those bamboo legs, but actually *being* them—or rather being myself in them; or, to be still more accurate (for "I" was not involved in the case, nor in a certain sense were "they") being my Not-self in the Not-self which was the chair.

And again,

> . . Today the percept had swallowed up the concept. I was so completely absorbed in looking, so thunder-struck by what I actually saw, that I could not be aware of anything else. Garden furniture,

[1] All quotations in this chapter are from *The Doors of Perception*. Chatto & Windus, 1954.

laths, sunlight, shadow—these were no more than names and notions . . . The event was this succession of azure furnace doors separated by gulfs of unfathomable gentian. It was inexpressively wonderful, wonderful to the point, almost, of being terrifying. And suddenly I had an inkling of what it must feel like to be mad . . .

Confronted by a chair which looked like the Last Judgement . . . I felt myself all at once on the brink of panic. This, I suddenly felt, was going too far. Too far, even though the going was into intenser beauty, deeper significance. The fear, as I analyse it in retrospect, was of being overwhelmed, of disintegration under a pressure of reality greater than a mind, accustomed to living most of the time in a cosy world of symbols, could possibly bear. The literature of religious experience abounds in references to the pains and terrors overwhelming those who have come, too suddenly, face to face with some manifestation of the *Mysterium tremendum* . . .

Now in what way can a drug, a bio-chemical intervention, bring about this change in the quality of perception? Aldous inclined to a belief in the validity of a suggestion of Bergson's as expressed by the Cambridge philosopher, Professor C. D. Broad, a suggestion that the function of the brain and nervous system and sense organs is, "in the main *eliminative* and not productive. Each person is at each moment capable of remembering all that has ever happened to him and of perceiving everything that is happening everywhere in the universe. The function of the brain and nervous system is to protect us from being overwhelmed and confused by this mass of largely useless and irrelevant knowledge, by shutting out most of what we should otherwise perceive or remember . . and leaving only that very small and special selection which is likely to be practically useful." The assumption, in fact, that the brain transmits consciousness, rather than the assumption that the brain *produces* consciousness. From this it would follow, Aldous carried on, that each of us is potentially Mind at Large. "But in so far as we are animals, our business is at all costs to survive.

To make biological survival possible, *Mind at Large has to be funnelled through the reducing valve of the brain and nervous system.* [My italics] What comes out at the other end is a measly trickle of the kind of consciousness which will help us stay alive on the surface of this particular planet . . .

. . . Most people, most of the time, know only what comes through the reducing valve and is consecrated as genuinely real by the local language. Certain persons, however, seem to be born with a kind of by-pass that circumvents the reducing valve. In others temporary by-passes may be acquired either spontaneously, or as the result of deliberate "spiritual exercises", or through hypnosis, or by means of drugs. Through these . . by-passes there flows . . . something more than, and above all something different from, the carefully selected utilitarian material which our narrowed, individual minds regard as a complete, or at least sufficient, picture of reality.

Mescalin, for instance, reduces the supply of sugar to the brain. The brain is an organ that is in constant need of sugar. What happens when the normal ration is reduced? Aldous summarized what had happened to the majority of those (still few) who had taken mescalin under supervision,

(1) The ability to remember and to "think straight" is little if at all reduced . . .

(2) Visual impressions are greatly intensified and the eye recovers some of the perpetual innocence of childhood . . . Interest in space is diminished and interest in time falls almost to zero.

(3) Though the intellect remains unimpaired . . the will suffers a profound change for the worse. The mescalin taker sees no reason for doing anything in particular and finds most of the causes for which, at ordinary times, he was prepared to act and suffer, profoundly uninteresting. He can't be bothered with them, for the good reason that he has better things to think about.

(4) These better things may be experienced (as I experienced them) "out there," or "in here," or in both worlds, the inner and the outer . . . That they are better seems to be self-evident to all mescalin takers who come to the drug with a sound liver and an untroubled mind.

. . . When the brain runs out of sugar, the undernourished ego grows weak, can't be bothered to undertake the necessary chores, and loses all interest in those spatial and temporal relationships which mean so much to an organism set on getting on in the world. As Mind at Large seeps past the no longer watertight valve, all kinds of biologically useless things start to happen. In some cases there may be extrasensory perceptions. Other persons discover a world of visionary beauty. To others again is revealed the glory, the infinite value and meaningfulness of naked existence . . .

"This is how one ought to see," Aldous kept on saying during the experiment, "this is how things really are." And yet there were reservations. For if one always saw like this, one would never want to do anything else. Just go on looking at a flower, a chair, at flannel. But what about other people? they kept asking him. What about human relations? One ought, was the recorded answer, "to be able to see these trousers as infinitely important and human beings as still more infinitely important."

One ought—but in practice it seemed to be impossible . . . (how I longed to be left alone with Eternity in a flower . . and the Absolute in the folds of a pair of flannel trousers!) I realized that I was deliberately avoiding the eyes of those who were with me in the room, deliberately refraining from being too much aware of them. One was my wife, the other a man I respected and greatly liked; but both belonged to the world from which, for the moment, mescalin had delivered me—the world of selves, of time, of moral judgements and utilitarian considerations, the world (and it was this aspect of human life which I wished, above all else, to forget) of self-assertion, of cocksureness, of overvalued words and idolatrously worshipped notions.

Meanwhile Aldous's question remained unanswered.

How was this cleansed perception to be reconciled with a proper concern with human relations, with the necessary chores and duties, to say nothing of charity and practical compassion? The age-old debate between the actives and the contemplatives was being renewed . . . Mescalin opens the way of Mary, but shuts the door on that of Martha . . .

And now to the great drug issue itself. In the simplest terms, is it good, is it right, for people to have recourse to these Artificial Paradises (or Hells), or is it wicked, futile, destructive? Aldous's answer was that temporary escape from selfhood in one way or another *is* inevitable, and that therefore we had better see to it that the means of the escape shall be physically harmless, morally desirable and socially undisruptive.

. . Most men and women lead lives at the worst so painful, at the best so monotonous, poor and limited that the urge to escape, the longing to transcend themselves . . is and has always been one of the principal appetites of the soul. Art and religion, carnivals and saturnalia, dancing and listening to oratory—all these have served, in H. G. Wells's phrase, as Doors in the Wall. And for private, for everyday use there have always been chemical intoxicants. All the vegetable sedatives and narcotics, all the euphorics that grow on trees, the hallucinogens that ripen in berries . . all . . have been used by human beings from times immemorial. And to these natural modifiers of consciousness modern science has added its quota of synthetics—chloral, for example, and benzedrine, the bromides and the barbiturates.

Most of these . . cannot now be taken except under doctor's orders, or else illegally and at considerable risk. For unrestricted use the West has permitted only alcohol and tobacco. All the other chemical

Doors in the Wall are labelled Dope, and their unauthorized takers are Fiends.

We now spend a good deal more on drink and smoke than we spend on education . . .

Alcohol and tobacco—". . Lung cancer, traffic accidents . . millions of miserable and misery-creating alcoholics . . ." Yet the problem, "it goes without saying, cannot be solved by prohibition. The universal and ever-present urge to self-transcendence is not to be abolished by slamming the currently popular Doors in the Wall.

The only reasonable policy is to open other, better doors in the hope of inducing men and women to exchange their old bad habits for new and less harmful ones.

Some of these other, better doors, Aldous hoped, would be social and technological in nature, others religious, psychological or athletic.

But the need for frequent chemical vacations from intolerable selfhood and repulsive surroundings will undoubtedly remain. What is needed is a new drug which will relieve and console our species without doing more harm in the long run than good in the short.

A drug not only harmless and cheap to produce, but a drug with a constructive side, able to cause "changes in consciousness more interesting, more intrinsically valuable than mere sedation or dreaminess, delusions of omnipotence or release from inhibition." Did Aldous say that he considered mescalin to be such a drug?

Although obviously superior to cocaine, opium, alcohol and tobacco, mescalin is not yet the ideal drug. Along with the happily transfigured majority of mescalin takers there is a minority that finds the drug only hell and purgatory. Moreover, for a drug that is to be used, like alcohol, for general consumption, its effects last for an inconveniently long time.

But chemistry and physiology, he goes on, are capable nowadays of practically anything and can be relied upon to produce something at least more nearly ideal than what we had to make do with "in the wine-bibbing past, the whisky-drinking, marijuana-smoking and barbiturate-swallowing present."

Did Aldous say that mescalin was a completely harmless drug?

To most people, mescalin is almost completely innocuous. Unlike alcohol, it does not drive the taker into the kind of uninhibited action which results in brawls, crimes of violence and traffic accidents. A man under the influence of mescalin quietly minds his own business. Moreover, the business he minds is an experience of the most enlightening kind, which does not have to be paid for (and this is surely important) by a compensatory hangover.

Innocuous, then, to *most* people. Any warnings about others? Once or twice Aldous referred to the fact that the stuff must be taken in good health, under proper conditions and in the right spirit. He did mention the *sine qua non* of a sound liver.

. . The drug brings hell and purgatory only to those who have had a recent case of jaundice, or who suffer from periodical depressions or a chronic anxiety . . .

The warnings are there, though rather casually dispersed about the text; the proper conditions, the right spirit are only implicitly specified. Aldous used to say that he never thought of his potential readers as this would only interfere with his mental processes. If he addressed himself to anyone it must have been some shadowy beings very much like himself. He was also quite sceptical as to the influence, if any, of the (literate) printed word. Would it—and should it—have occurred to him that the contents of *The Doors* might trickle within the reaches of the half-baked, the under-educated, the unstable and indeed the pre-experienced, the young?
We do find this:

. . Of the long-range consequence of regular mescalin taking we know very little . . the available evidence is still scarce and sketchy.

Today we stand two decades later. In *The Doors of Perception* Aldous drew on what he had been told by workers in the field, on what he had read in the scientific literature to date, and on the one experiment upon himself. (It might be as well to anticipate and put on record here that later he took mescalin twice again and LSD and related substances at least seven, and possibly nine, times; which comes to nine to eleven times in all in ten years and a half.)
Lastly, did Aldous say that an experience under drugs could be a mystical experience? He did not.

I am not so foolish as to equate what happens under the influence of mescalin or of any other drug . . with the realization of the end and ultimate purpose of human life: Enlightenment, the Beatific Vision. All I am suggesting is that the mescalin experience is what Catholic theologians call "a gratuitous grace," not necessary to salvation but potentially helpful and to be accepted thankfully . . To be shaken out of the ruts of ordinary perception, to be shown for a few timeless hours the outer and the inner world, not as they appear to an animal obsessed with words and notions, but as they are apprehended, directly and unconditionally, by Mind at Large—this is an experience of inestimable value to everyone . . .

. . . the man who comes back through the Door in the Wall will never be quite the same as the man who went out. He will be wiser but less cocksure, happier but less self-satisfied, humbler in acknowledging his ignorance yet better equipped to understand the relationship of words to things, of systematic reasoning to the unfathomable Mystery which it tries, forever vainly to comprehend.

The response to the book when it came out was anything from excitement, discriminate and indiscriminate, moral and intellectual disapproval, shrugging-off, embarrassment. Drugs, dope, are emotionally charged concepts about which many of us have conditioned, and possibly quite sound, instincts. Yet it was not so much for advocating drugs that Aldous was decried in those early years. What people shied away from—or were attracted by —was the unfamiliarity, the way-outness of the whole thing. Really Aldous was proving himself too amphibious by half; from enfant terrible of *Antic Hay* to psychodelic acolyte he had been slipping through everybody's net. Self-respecting rationalists saw fresh evidence of quackery and intellectual abdication while the serious and religious were bothered by the offer of a shortcut; but I rather think that the people who were most angry were the aesthetes who were really outraged by Aldous's attempt to put art in its place. True enough he had paid the obvious tribute, "What the rest of us see only under the influence of mescalin, the artist is congenitally equipped to see all the time . . ." But look at *this*.

. . What sort of pictures did Eckhart look at? What sculptures and paintings played a part in the religious experience of St Joan of the Cross, of Hakuin, of Hui-neng, of William Law? . . I strongly suspect that most of the great knowers of Suchness paid very little attention to art . . . Art, I suppose, is only for beginners, or else for those resolute dead-enders, who have made up their minds to be content with the *ersatz* of Suchness . . .

The passages found most enraging were those where Aldous gazed with such rapture at the folds of his old grey flannel trousers. Those magic waves, those depths—

. . how rich, how deeply, mysteriously sumptuous!
. . . "The nearest approach to this," I said, "would be a Vermeer."

Grey flannel—how dared he? And thereby hangs a small tale.
After she had read the book, Betty Wendel asked him, "But
Aldous dear, you were wearing your blue jeans that morning. I
saw you." So he did, said Aldous. "Maria made me change it
in the M/S. She thought I ought to be better dressed for my
readers." Oh, what a disservice she did there to Aldous! Blue
cotton, blue linen, light-washed, sun-rinsed—who has not seen
those transfigured in impressionist and post-impressionist paintings; postmen's trousers, French railway porters' tunics, are
magical almost by definition. How much more tolerable, more
comprehensible, Aldous's raptures might have appeared had he
only been allowed to admit to his blue jeans.

Washington was taking its bureaucratic time and by the end
of January no news had come yet as to the next step in the
Huxleys' citizenship application. Since they were supposed to go
to Europe in April, it was "all very tiresome," as Aldous wrote
to Matthew, "all the more so as we have got into this imbroglio
quite gratuitously and of our own volition." This was certainly
true. There were no material reasons for them whatsoever to
change their status. The U.S. visa they had been granted in
London in 1937, an immigration visa, was still valid and would be
valid *in perpetuum*. A large number of persons have entered the
United States with such a visa and resided there ever after without
applying for naturalization. There are no strings attached. The
Huxleys were free to work, take paid employment, acquire
property, travel; only upon leaving for another continent they
required the formality of a re-entry permit. If they were guests,
they were fully paid up guests being subject to both Federal and
State income tax. The only things they could not do were to
vote, run for political office or enter the civil service. As for
non-material reasons ("We are *de facto* Californians . . ."), it does
seem gratuitous that a man of Aldous's a-nationalism and detachment should have chosen to make that kind of gesture of commit-
ment. Well it was not to be. In February there was still no news
from Washington. "If the papers come through," Aldous wrote
again to Matthew, "well and good; if they don't, well and good
also. Still I wish we hadn't let ourselves in for this bother and
confusion." A few days later he and Maria decided to drop the
whole thing. They renewed their British passports and, resuming
their *status quo ante* of resident aliens, applied for U.S. re-entry
permits. These they received at once. No problems ever arose

from their shelved application to become Americans. For the rest of his life, Aldous came and went at will. He remained what *naturaliter* he was, an evolved Victorian Englishman at home in the second part of the twentieth century, at home in Southern California, who walked alone.

Chapter Four

1954—1955

THAT whole business, on top of so much else, had been a strain for Maria. So were their travel plans—the Middle East: Egypt, Jerusalem, the Lebanon; Cyprus, Greece. "Je n'ose m'attendre à trop de bonheur", she wrote to Jeanne in early March, "*rien* ne marche facilement, ni agréablement en ce moment." Aldous has no book in sight, and is depressed . . Finances are low . . Fortunately Eileen Garrett's foundation is paying their passages . . . They may go to Switzerland as well, to see Jung who has asked them. "Perhaps in Switzerland—the country of good doctors—they may have different views on the subject of my health, which should be useful."

When it was brought home to Aldous that Maria might not be fit enough to undertake such a journey, he fell ill himself. He took to his bed for two weeks (Maria told Ellen). Indeed, we play strange tricks upon ourselves. Only a few friends knew that Maria was very ill. The Kiskaddens knew, Humphrey Osmond knew. Her family in New York and Europe feared but did not really know, as they had not been told. Aldous was given opportunities both for knowing or not knowing.

In the event, Maria's doctor told her that she and Aldous might as well go; so in March they went off to New York. There Aldous went down with a new attack of his bronchitis. He recovered enough not only to carry on but to start a new book, a short novel, a tale, which he managed to write—on ship-board, on hotel balconies, in gardens—at odd moments during the summer. On 7th April they sailed for Cherbourg on the *Queen Elizabeth*. Once more they arrived in Paris in the evening, once more there was the family reunion at the station, the taxi ride to the hotel. Maria looked radiant, very much *en beauté* (a press photograph taken as they stepped off the ship is there to prove it); Aldous looked ill. At the Hotel Pont Royal they all went into the bar downstairs and had a bottle of champagne. "Joie de les revoir," noted Georges Neveux. "Mais inquiétude." There was an undercurrent of anxiety—Aldous had to have an oxygen cylinder in his room for his pressure-breathing: had it arrived? Maria had an appointment with a specialist the following afternoon.

Next day they lunched together. "La joie de les revoir continue. [G. N.'s journal for 13th July] Aldous encore fatigué. Maria toujours pleine d'allant.

That afternoon Maria went to see (the late) Professor Mondor, the eminent French specialist who was still practising. Jeanne, with Noële aged thirteen, sat in the waiting-room. Nothing was said to, or before, the child but the experience haunted her for many years and may have played a part in the grave illness that followed some months later. Georges telephoned Professor Mondor in the evening. "He told us the truth," Jeanne noted simply. And Maria, too, had wanted to be told just that. (Mondor was a noted Mallarmé scholar, the two men knew of one another and he spoke openly to Georges.) "You must tell *me*" Maria had said to him. "You must *not* tell my husband. My husband has a book to finish and must have peace of mind." Rarely, Mondor said, had he met such fortitude.

That night Maria had dinner on her own at Georges and Jeanne's (Aldous was having a tray in bed at the hotel). She talked to them—her one and only time—of what was in their minds. She told them that she knew the seriousness of her case; she told them that she had become indifferent to the thought of dying. She expected death and was preparing herself. "But I can't give in, as I mustn't die before Aldous. How would he manage without me? It would be wrong of me to die before Aldous—I should have failed in my duty to him." And of course it must all be kept entirely from Aldous. And she talked to them, Georges says, in the calmest manner, in a peaceful, undramatic voice, sitting in their bedroom on the edge of a chair, interrupted now and then by Jeanne's having to answer the telephone. "So I must fight inch by inch, day after day, to keep alive so that Aldous will have me with him all his life, so that he shall never have to do without me . . ."

Elle parle de sa mort [Georges wrote in his journal] comme on discuterait de l'opportunité et de la date d'un voyage, calculant au mieux et avec réflexion. Quelle femme extraordinaire . . .

On 19th April Aldous and Maria flew south to attend Eileen Garrett's symposium on Philosophy and Parapsychology at St Paul de Vence. Professor H. H. Price of Great Britain read a paper on Philosophic Implications of Paranormal Cognition, Gabriel Marcel of France on Intersubjective Approach to Survival, Aldous on A Visionary Experience; there were papers and discussions by doctors and psychologists and philosophers from America and Switzerland and Germany . . .

. . no conclusions, of any kind, of course; [Aldous wrote from St Paul to Humphrey Osmond] but a lot of interesting things were said and there were occasions to greet very remarkable people. I liked

especially Price, [C. J.] Ducasse, Marcel and [C. W. K.] Mundle . .
Bender of Freiburg, Martiny and Assailly of Paris. Bender has a case
of demonic possession on his hands, which exceeds in horror and in
duration anything met with at Loudun—13 years of blasphemy,
split personality, stigmatization . . . and still no end in sight . . .

Both Aldous and Maria had a great affection for Eileen Garrett,
and she for them. She spoke to me of Maria's tiredness at that
time. "You should go home, my darling," Eileen told her. But
Aldous wanted to go on travelling (wanted everything to be
normal). She spoke of how much Maria did—"Always, always—
Aldous not realizing it." Of her hinting that he did not know
how to love, and Maria giving her one of those lightning straight
looks and saying with utter conviction, "Oh yes, he does!" She
spoke of her own answer to Maria's great anguish, What will
happen to Aldous? "It will turn out right."

On 3rd May the Huxleys flew to Egypt to keep the engagement
that meant most to Aldous, a stay with Dr Roger Godel at
Ismailia, where he was the Médecin en Chef of the Suez Canal
Company's Hospital. They had met in France in 1950 and
corresponded since. A very remarkable man, Aldous had out-
lined his expectations to Humphrey Osmond, "a heart specialist
who makes extensive use of psychological methods, a doctor who
is an eminent Hellenist, respected by other Greek scholars, and
finally a Western scientist who is interested in Enlightenment and
has written some interesting essays on 'L'Expérience Liberatrice.'"
He was not disappointed.

At last we have again found peace [Maria scribbled off to Matthew
and Ellen]—the first since before I started packing and passports in
L. A.
We arrived here last night after only 7 hours of excellent flight, in
the middle of a desert on the banks of the canal. Flowers, lawns,
silence and our dear friends the Godels. Now I know I am tired but
Aldous is well again.

And Aldous on 9th May.

We have been here nearly a week—a very extraordinary place in
company with a very extraordinary man. The house stands on the
edge of the canal (it was built originally for the Empress Eugénie at
the time of the canal's inauguration), and the ships pass practically
through one's bedroom—enormous tankers going to or coming from
the Persian Gulf, liners . . cargo boats of every shape and size . . .

Every day Aldous, disguised as a visiting doctor, went to the hospital with Godel.

. . It is a liberal education to accompany him through the wards with his interns and the young doctors who come from France or Lebanon or Greece to be his pupils. He succeeds in being . . . a physician who is also a philosopher and psychologist. Where patients are responsible for their own illness—and how many of them, here as elsewhere, are psychosomatics!—he treats them physically with all the resources of modern medicine, but tries at the same time to get them to recognize and, in so doing, to get rid of the underlying causes . . . He does it by Socratic questioning—often through an interpreter, for the poorer patients speak only Arabic—and it is wonderful to hear him patiently eliciting—exactly like the Socrates of the Platonic dialogues—fundamental answers about soul and body, about appearances and reality. And the thing works; for he gets amazing cures and enjoys a prodigious reputation. In himself he is a quiet gentle man . . .

And all this knowledge, Aldous added, "is applied in the most intelligent and humane way, for the service of his patients." One can imagine how captivated Aldous was, how satisfied by the nature of this work—at last something constructive, something worth doing, being actually done. "It would, I believe, be a wonderful thing if you [Matthew] cd come here for a few months and work with him."

Aldous and Maria, really longed to bring this about. There was so much to be learned . . . Godel occasionally did take laymen pupils—there would be room for Ellen and the babies—"the project is something you shd consider seriously . . . Even if you cd not get a scholarship it wd . . be worth thinking of coming here independently, as an educational investment . . . So ruminate and digest and make inquiries." And Maria in a (published) P.S. "This is a dream which I feel will materialize . . . I have not known a place and people so congenial at the same time. The beauty of the place passes belief, also the gentle climate . . . Perhaps we may even return for some weeks next year . . . I suggest that though it will not be necessary Ellen and I sell (not even pawn) our jewellery and Aldous his typewriter and the car and everything—because this seems the best idea for us all."

Maria had come to see Godel. They had some private talks— a part of her conscious preparation. Aldous later thought, and Jeanne, that this had been of great importance to her. To Matthew she wrote again after they had left Ismailia, "The greatness of Godel is not only to be a great doctor that people fly to consult but also a good man and a wise man."

On 11th May they went to Cairo. (Their first time.) "One can really form no idea of Egyptian art, wrote Aldous, until one sees it in the mass and at its best—the museum is fabulous, the pyramids . . beyond description . . ." Then Jerusalem, Beirut, Damascus . . . "Oh! everything has been such an education", Maria wrote,

> Such discoveries in all directions, as we knew nothing of the Middle East. Now we—not just jokingly—talk about retiring in the Lebanon which has a better climate than the South of France, is cheaper, and much more up to date than Egypt and is no volcano of politics . . .

Cyprus, Istanbul, Greece—also for the first time. From Athens Aldous wrote a very sombre letter to Eileen Garrett. ". . It has been a very wonderful journey through space and time—wonderful but very depressing; for I have never had such a sense of the tragic nature of the human situation, the horror of a history in which the great works of art, the philosophies and the religions, are no more than islands in an endless stream of war, poverty, frustration, squalor and disease.

> One sees the misery of the Egyptians huddled about the pyramids, the hopelessness of the inhabitants of Jerusalem for whom the holiest of cities is a prison of chronic despair, punctuated by occasional panic when the hand grenades start flying. And it must always have been like this—little islands of splendour in a sea of darkness,—and then, during the times of trouble, darkness unmitigated for a few centuries. The Near East is one huge illustration of the primal tenet of the Buddha: "I show you sorrow and the ending of sorrow" . . .

From Athens they flew to Rome. On the telephone (I was living there at the time) Maria said, "Oh, *I'm* very well indeed," quickly, emphatically, making quite sure that one would not ask again. "Aldous is superb." In the evening I walked up the Spanish Steps to the Hotel de la Ville where they had two rooms with a view. It was so—Maria had used the only word. I had not seen them since Sanary in August 1950: Aldous had changed. It was so evident, so disconcerting, that had it not been for his voice, Maria's presence and a kind of continuity in their atmosphere, one would have had the sensation of being, not with another man, but with another version of the man, a double, a brother. Now the point was that Aldous never *really* changed; he oscillated: no woman could have been more *journalière*—absurdly young, graceful, animated one day; sallow, tentative, withdrawn the next; his

pendulum might swing between the casual dandy and the old
man of Thermopylae. He did change, somewhat, in 1936 after
he had been taught by F. M. Alexander; he was changed a
good deal by the Bates treatment. *This* was a change in kind,
perceptible to begin with on the physical level. (I am putting
down what is only a personal impression, but it was a very
definite one.) Aldous looked robust; substantial; very much all
there; he had in fact filled out, though this was not in the least
like the thickening of middle-age (he was going to be sixty next
month) it was more like the filling out of a boy who is coming
into his own. If he looked young—he did—it was no longer
touching or unfledged young, but the youthfulness of full powers.
Never before had I seen Aldous look less vulnerable (nor since).
He was as gentle as he had been in all his phases, yet behind it
one felt authority. And there was a sleekness, a smoothed-outness;
he was glowing with it, as it were, and this had an extraordinary
peace-inducing effect as though one were sitting—if this is not
too fanciful—at the feet of a large and benign cat.

Yet he was not in the least remote. Pleased to be in Rome, he
talked about what they were going to see, he talked about their
journey. They had been overwhelmed by Egypt—the lighting up of
Aldous's face as he flung out his hands and said—s t a g g e r i n g;
disappointed by Greece. Several times he used the word squalor.
And I, while talking away myself, even then was trying to sort
out this new thing, trying—how stupidly—to find words, waiting
to put them before Maria. The summer before she had written
to me, "We are still exploring . . . also now exploring psychology
and para-psychology—*much further* than hands [those palm prints
they used to pore over in the Thirties with Charlotte Wolff]—
but they were the first steps." I had read the passage the way one
reads a letter . . . During that stay in Rome—two short weeks—
I understood a little what Maria meant. They *had been exploring*.
And whatever it was they had found, Aldous had tapped something, made a breakthrough. Into what? A potential Aldous? An
altered mode of being? How can one *say*. It was—obviously—on
a non-verbal level. There he *was*; and what he was, one felt,
was in some new way extraordinary. (Being with him had a
profound influence on me, of a kind that would be hard, and
that I don't really wish, to define. It lasted for some time, wore
off, at one point went into reverse, has not worn off entirely.)
Many of us in the course of our lives have found ourselves briefly
in the presence of a being of another order. The order might be
of various kinds but it is always *other* and always, unless we are
too besotted with cocksureness, recognizable. It is not usual to
make such a statement about a man who is the subject of a (I
hope detached) biography as well as an old friend, yet I think

that I should not leave unsaid that in Rome I had such a flash of recognition about Aldous. It is superfluous to add that it had nothing to do with the quality one commonly associated with Aldous, intellectuality. Sitting with him, the images that rose unwilled to my mind were sleek herds in serene countrysides. (This was not quite easy to understand or to convey, and when in due time I took it to Maria, I left-handedly said something about cows which took a moment to put right.) Maria, now, I did not find changed—she was herself to an nth degree. In appearance, she still looked as she had at Cherbourg, *en beauté*, animated, gay, with sudden sinkings into tiredness.

On their daily level, magic, to borrow Maria's saying, certainly was advancing. It had become as casual as taking aspirin. "You don't sleep well? Aldous, do give Sybille some of your Mesmeric passes." *Animal Magnetism*, I shied like a well-trained Pavlovian dog. Is *that* respectable? Aldous wrote down two books to read. ("You ought to be able to get them from the London Library.") And Esdaile; I should read Dr James Esdaile on anaesthesia by hypnosis. We didn't get down to magnetic passes in the first week, but what Aldous, rolling up his shirt-sleeves, gave me was a very competent spinal pummelling (against tension). He did this with his right hand only, while the fingers of his left rested lightly on the base of my neck like a violinist's hand on his keys. Aldous, what is that for? "Ah," he said, "I haven't the faintest idea, that's where the abracadabra comes in." At sunset we went up to the Roman roof above my flat where I had made a garden. On a slanting ledge I had built a stack of scrubbed empty flower pots resting on ochre tiles. "Now, this is *very* mescalin," said Aldous. At dusk we watched the opening of some large white moon-flowers on a trellis; I told him that what I loved to look at most though were their leaves. Aldous seemed pleased with this and quoted a *haiku*.

> *The flowers are easy to paint,*
> *The leaves difficult.*

Their days were long with sight-seeing. (It was hard to believe that Aldous should have required an oxygen cylinder six weeks ago, and yet he had. In fact, the new robust look notwithstanding, that swing between decent health and ill remained.) A friend drove them out to Frascati and Tivoli, Tarquinia and Etruscan tombs—"wandering through the ripening wheat," Aldous wrote to Matthew, "and popping down into the rock-hewn chambers with their still gay paintings of hunting, wrestling, dancing, even copulation and sodomy . . ."

Their niece Claire White was there, her husband having had

a prix de Rome. "They came for dinner," Claire wrote in a letter
to me fifteen years later,

> . . . Maria looked so frail . . I suddenly realized how terribly much I
> loved her and offered to walk Aldous about Rome to spare her
> fatigue, but she fought this off energetically. "It's much more tiring
> to be at home doing the housework," she said.

They went to see the international exhibition at the American
Academy.

> . . Aldous praised each young artist he liked with such kindness.
> Maria suddenly looked at me and said—"Tu es une femme forte,
> comme Ellen." But oh the exhaustion with which she walked home
> after that, barely able to lift her feet but still only concerned that
> Aldous should not stumble across a stone.

At the end of their first week Aldous and Maria went to
Florence for a couple of days; they went to say goodbye to
Costanza. Costanza Fasola, the first friend of their Italian youth,
was dying of cancer of the lung.

One evening as we were beating our way through the noise
up the Via Babuino, Maria spoke of a friend of theirs who
happened to be in Rome. (It was the young woman who had
taken them to Tarquinia.) Perhaps I'd like to meet her? This
she let fall so lightly that at once I was all ears. Maria never
forced, she suggested; one was left to choose. If there was no
response, she withdrew. (Where her sisters were concerned, this
was not always so.) In the sound-shelter of a café in Via Due
Macelli, she came back to it. Their friend was a rather remarkable
woman, interested in "our kind of things". An Italian, Aldous
took it up, a musician, concert violinist, who had become a
practising psycho-therapist—"She uses this rather curious method
. . and I must say it works . . I'm glad to say it doesn't take seven
years on the couch . . ." The one thing I became obscurely certain
of was that Maria wanted me to meet this friend.

The friend was Laura Archera. A couple of evenings later,
followed by Aldous and Maria, she came to my flat in Via della
Fontanella, not the forbidding esoteric therapist I had half
expected, but a young woman, feminine, high-spirited, full of life
and warmth. (She has herself described our meeting—with a
touch of extravaganza—in her book on Aldous.) The most in-
cisive memory of that first evening for me was what passed between
her and Maria. It was night, we were all up on that roof terrace,
my friend Evelyn Gendel put a kind of lucky-dip question to

Aldous: When does a grasshopper become a locust? Aldous took a deep breath. "Ah—" he said. "Well, now—" he said. "This is a very interesting question. My grandfather used to puzzle . . ." Aldous got under way. Maria and Laura disappeared. They had gone below to talk. They talked for a long time.

Up here the Roman night was what such nights can be. No traffic sounds could reach us. There was a scent of honeysuckle, jasmin, tobacco flower. There was darkness and patches of luminous leaves; to the north, almost on top of us, rose the cupola of one of the twin churches in Piazza del Popolo; to the east, across a gulf of night, one could see as far as the Pincian Hill; above us, garlands of vines and in their interstices the sky. There was Aldous's voice . . . Below in the quiet flat Maria was still talking to Laura. And I knew as surely as if I had been there that Maria was speaking at last about her illness.

Soon after I saw Laura Archera again—friendship came almost at once, Aldous and Maria having acted as the catalyst; Laura thought that they had wanted us to meet because she might be able to help me (I was struggling with a book and a multitude of anguishes); this indeed she did. Yet I am still convinced of what had been already present in my mind that night, that Maria was thinking a good deal further ahead.

Then, we finally did get down to the magnetic passes. Again no insistence, less than a hint by way of Maria; and I caught on that this was something Aldous would enjoy doing. I was very willing. (Before it, I'm ashamed to say, I dodged into the kitchen and quickly swallowed a glass of wine.) I lay down. Aldous stood over me making slow wave-like motions with his arms. Maria and Evelyn Gendel went on talking in another part of the room. I shut my eyes. Aldous in a slow seductive voice began the incantations.

> Presently you will be going out . . . You are going to spend a cheerful evening . . .
> And then tonight you are going to have a deep deep sleep, a restful sleep, a deep refreshing sleep . . .
> You are going to spend a cheerful evening . . .

I did not feel drowsy, I felt alert and peaceful. The sound of the words was soothing, full of promise, already I could feel the quality of that delicious sleep.

And presently we did go out, and it was a cheerful evening— dinner with Aldous and Maria in a tratoria, in a pool, as it were, of their own quietness, with the Italian waiters putting forth their *gentilezza* (but that was the *old* Huxley magic working as it had in all those years and times), a night stroll afterwards . . . How

one wished to remain in those hours! All the same I went home
as for a treat. The deep sleep did not come. I did not sleep at all.
Not a wink. An entire night of quite cheerful if rather astonished
wakefulness. I didn't sleep the second night, and very little in
the third. We were all more amused than distressed, though
Aldous was a bit puzzled and concerned; Maria advised against
our trying again. Later I learned that the same thing the other
way round had happened to Laura Archera some years before
in California; *she* remained in a somnabulistic state days after a
round of Aldous's Mesmeric passes. She has told the story charm-
ingly in her book,[1] and the gist of it was that Aldous had forgotten to wake her up.

At the time *Helen of Troy* was being filmed at Ciné Città, with
1,200 extras, Wooden Horse and all, and of course Aldous went
to have a look and as he did so he was recognized. (By Maurice
Zuberano, assistant director, who kindly wrote to me.) ". . The
writer of the screen play had laconically put down the words 'A
baccanale takes place.' I asked the director if he had ever been
to a baccanale and he said 'No,' he had been born and raised
in a small town in the Middle West. I had been born in New
York City but I did not know what they did at a baccanale either.

I was about to embark on a research trip when I looked up and saw
a tall man watching us shoot a battle scene on the back lot. I
recognized him as Mr Huxley . . . He was unattended so I offered
to show him the studio. We then took each other to lunch. He
showed great interest in my problem and went on for hours relating
what he knew about baccanales. As a result our baccanale was so
successful that the crowd people could not stop when the director
cried "cut" . . .

And then it was the last evening. 18th June. Sunset on the
roof, dinner near Piazza Colonna. Afterwards I went with them
as far as their hotel. At the door, Maria turned from me. "We
don't have to say goodbye," she said, "we've had our goodbye."
On the ship, on the *Normandie*. She did not have to say it. She
was gone. Aldous telephoned next morning. They were going to
Paris for a couple of weeks, then south to the Drôme to spend the
long holidays with Jeanne and Georges in a little country town
called Dieulefit. It would be a nice change, he said, to be sitting
still, he was looking forward to doing a piece of honest work.
Later perhaps they might pop down into Provence . . . Perhaps
we would meet later in the summer. He made some joke about

---

[1] *This Timeless Moment, A Personal View of Aldous Huxley.* Farrar, Strauss &
Giroux, 1968; Chatto & Windus, 1969.

the demons that interfere with sleep. And now they'd have to be off to the airport. Maria did not come to the telephone.

The house the Neveuxs had taken at Dieulefit was old and spacious, standing amid lawns and trees like an English country house. The Huxleys arrived on the 3rd of July. Aldous was enchanted; he installed himself in this garden, typewriter on knees, and got going again with his book. Through the Wrong End of the Opera Glasses was his working title; it became *The Genius and the Goddess*. But Maria had grown not only very tired but extremely nervous as if she had something on her mind. Georges and Jeanne's journals show that there was great tension in the house, an undercurrent of desperate unhappiness. Again and again Jeanne refers to it as the tragic summer. They did not speak of it at the time, Maria would not have it. And there was Aldous to consider, and the child Noële.

Aldous tape à la machine et adore le parc. [Jeanne's Diary] Maria n'est pas heureuse, c'est pénible. Elle est inquiète et d'un commun accord nous ne parlons pas de ce qui nous hante . . . et de notre impuissance. Je me sens coupable d'être bien portante. Mais nous faisons des promenades. Coccola cueille des fleurs et a toujours cette grâce qui est sienne.

. . . Pourtant Aldous semble ravi [Georges' Journal] il travaille dans le jardin et nous avons deux bons moments—la promenade sur la chemin de la crêe (ce pays est beau) et le soir la lecture à haute voix.

It was always Georges who read to them. This year, André Maurois's Life of Victor Hugo.

Il y a le thé de cinq heures [Jeanne] que Noële a tant aimé avec eux—mais maintenant Noële c'est la jeunesse et la vie . . .

Three weeks of this. On 23rd July they drove south to Vaisons-la-Romaine for the Festival. George's play *Zamore* was being given in the Roman Theatre next day. Sophie had come down from Paris, and Rina with her husband from Marseilles. They had taken lodgings in a vast renaissance mansion in the old town. After the play there was a dinner party. They returned to Dieulefit and celebrated Aldous's sixtieth birthday. Rina came back with them. There was no telephone in the house. On the 28th, Maria spoke not to Jeanne but to a friend of Jeanne's, Marcelle Rodenbach, telling her that she was concerned about

some symptoms; Mme Rodenbach arranged for her to telephone
in private from somewhere. Next day Maria was able to get on
to Professor Mondor in Paris, who told her to come to him at
once. The Huxleys decided to leave. Aldous was disappointed,
perhaps shocked. He had been so well there, he said over and
over again, but softly, so as not to upset Maria. Next morning,
30th July, they left in the Neveux's 2-Chevaux for Valence to
catch the Paris train. "Ce départ dans la panique." wrote Georges,
"a quelque chose de déchirant."

Professor Mondor advised Maria to return to America and her
own doctors as quickly as she could. That was 1st August. They
were not able to book any definite passage. Aldous left for London
and stayed with his brother and Juliette. Maria remained in
Paris on her own. ("I have no links with England," she had
written the year before to Elise Murrel, "nor in fact many links
at all.") So she stayed in Paris, the close-aired empty Paris of
the August holidays, wandering about the streets, eating in
students' restaurants. In the evenings there was Sophie.

One afternoon in the Hampstead garden Aldous told Juliette
about Maria's symptoms. Juliette, alarmed, asked him if he were
not worried. " 'Oh no,' he replied lightly, 'it is not at all serious.' "

Maria herself made light of her premature return to Matthew
and Ellen. ". . I really long to be home and the only doctors I
like are my L.A. doctors . . ." she wrote. She hopes that New York
will not be boiling, though at any rate the Warwick will be air-
conditioned. "We won't stay long but we must see *you* (Let us
swear to each other that if anyone has a cold we don't let Aldous
approach them, even you or Ellen or Trev or Tessa) . . . Paris is
expensive . . . Eileen is ill at St Paul . . . I want to see Jeanne
again, who has been wonderfully kind and patient . . ." An old
old friend, Luigino Franchetti, passed through Paris and they
had dinner together. "Luigino was touching in his affection . . ."
But it was Sophie who spent all her spare moments with Maria.
(She was tied in the day to her job at Unesco.)

> I think [Sophie wrote] that we were never more close to one another
> as during these days. I knew how ill she was. She did not know that I
> knew. Never once she complained or said a thing, but one evening I
> arrived at the hotel and found that she had ordered whisky and I
> was very surprised. Maria said very simply that she thought I
> would be hot and tired and might enjoy a drink (which I did).
> I took my glass and before I had had one sip, I saw that Maria had
> completely finished hers and that horrified me. I remarked upon it
> with amazement (she never drank) but she apologized and said that
> she must have been absent minded. I realized how distressed and
> "angoissée" she must have been.

Once they played tourists and took a *bateau-mouche* down the Seine and there, gliding on the river, Maria told Sophie how Aldous had proposed to her on the lawn at Garsington.

Finally they were able to get passages for 21st August on the *Mauritania*. On the 16th Jeanne travelled up to Paris to spend a few days with Maria. "We do not talk much. Maria does a lot of unnecessary errands. We spend hours at the hairdresser's. And I leave again. *Nous avons tenu bon toutes les deux . . .*"

Rina also came. Arriving at the Hotel Pont Royal after her night in the train, they told her at the desk, "Mme Huxley? Left by air." Rina experienced a moment of blank desolation. Shocked though she was, she had the wits to seek out Sophie at Unesco —Maria had merely flown to Nice for the day to see Eileen Garrett. So in the evening Rina took the bus out to Orly and waited, and saw Maria arrive, walk alone, unutterably tired, touched her arm at the exit and saw her face change. Rina stayed with her three days, sleeping in the same room in the hotel. Maria saw her off. After they had parted, Rina inside the station heard steps, saw her again—Maria had stopped her taxi and run back to embrace her once more.

(Later she found an envelope: reimbursing her fare and the words, "For Rina because she knows that friendship never can be paid.")

Maria had sent a little fur jacket of hers to a shop in the rue St Honoré. She was very attached to it as it was a present from Aldous.

When she went to retrieve it, [Sophie wrote] she found the shop closed for the rest of the month . . She was frantic. She made any amount of démarches to try to get the shop opened and regain the coat, all without result. I tried to calm her and I said I would send it on to her, but she was very upset at the thought of leaving it behind. Finally she had to, and I later on got the coat, and sent it . . and Maria had her little coat back. But the energy and will she put into moving heaven and earth to retrieve that coat . . . .

And on 21st August Sophie took Maria to the Gare du Nord and put her on the boat train. ". . As in a bad melodrama, we met friends on the platform and . . had to make polite stupid conversation with them. It was horrible. When the train pulled out, Maria was at the window crying. That was the only time she let herself go in all those days. I ran along the train as it pulled out and shouted to her, 'Ne pleures pas, voyons, tu sera avec Aldous dans quelques heures et c'est tout ce que tu désire.' She smiled then, 'Tu as raison, je suis une idiote,' and she waved . . . That was my 'vision' of Maria, wearing a silly little hat and leaning over the window of a departing train."

Aldous was on the ship at Southampton. Together they sent off a postcard.

Non posso dimenticare tua cara presenza a Orly e a Parigi.
A l'année prochaine,   M.

Aldous echoes,

A l'année prochaine, cara Rina,
Aldous H.

They landed on 27th August and remained in New York for fourteen days. Nobody had a cold and they were able to spend the time with the children and grandchildren. One night Matthew and Ellen took them down to the Battery; "New York est si belle!" Maria wrote. On 7th September they were back at North Kings Road and Maria began a series of X-ray treatments. On the 26th she and Aldous got away for a weekend with Rosalind at Ojai. "Krishnaji is here," Maria wrote to Jeanne. "I feel so much more calm . . . Aldous is admirably well, and stimulated and optimistic. On Thursday he is leaving for Washington and New York, by air, for 10-12 days, and alone! 1) Because it costs too much for two. 2) Because without me it's easier for him to stay with the professors. 3) Because I can't leave my treatments here."

So on 1st October Aldous gave a lecture in Washington at the Institute of Modern Art, went on to New York and on the 5th flew to Durham for the same lecture at Duke's University. Aldous and J. B. Rhine had met once before, on the Huxleys' very first trip across the continent in 1937.

The second visit [Professor Rhine wrote me] I had arranged . . . I found the English Department extremely eager to have Aldous . . and although he mentioned that he had not done much university lecturing, he consented to read a paper he had just written on visionary experiences. It was about the time he was especially interested in mescalin, but the paper was not directly concerned with that.

I recall that the anticipatory enthusiasm . . was great, and the largest hall on the Campus was completely packed.

Aldous had just come from the North . . at any rate he was dressed in woollen clothing, and the night was unusually warm . . I recall the doors were open, but it was still much too hot for his clothing. The chairman was dressed in summer clothes. I suggested to Aldous that he take off his coat, but he was reluctant. I took the chairman aside and . . asked him to lead the way by taking off his own coat. And there with that university audience (of pre-Hippy days at that) the two men marched onto the lecture platform with their jackets over their arms. It put everyone at ease immediately, and, anyhow, the audience was completely captivated. Aldous was a person, as you know, whom it was easy to like spontaneously. His gentle dignity and a suggestion of frailty, that perhaps came from his vision, made one lean a little his way in a helpful attitude.

During the reading some of his papers got out of hand and fell to the floor, . . and I know that everyone in the audience felt just as I did—they wanted to jump up there and help him. I myself was deeply impressed by the hold which he had upon that audience, by the remarks that followed in the days succeeding, coming even from persons I would not have expected would listen to such a topic. The next night he was scheduled to lecture at the University of North Carolina, and again the night was hot, and again he read his lecture in his shirt sleeves. In the hour that followed a discussion was held in the student lounge, Aldous sat in a big armchair, surrounded by piles of students on the floor, in every sort of posture, eagerly trying to catch every syllable. I remember that Aldous led a sort of parade back to my car when we had to leave.

. . . I like to think that these contacts with the students at Duke and U.N.C. must have impressed him with the warmth and appreciation American students so readily extended to him. To me it was a phenomenal experience indeed.

Aldous dovetails with (to Humphrey Osmond after his return) "Frightful heat in Washington and at Duke—97° with 96% humidity. But there were nice people in both places."

A few days later *The Genius and the Goddess* was done.

Aldous has just finished his best ever (I believe) long short story. [Maria to Matthew] 30,000 words and Oh Darling, there is Trev in it. I read it in M.S. . . it seems much "stronger" than anything else . . .

And a little later:

I can't help feeling that this love for Trev extends and makes the story so good—will make all of them so good . . . Because it *is* a great step ahead, or rather à-haut.

Aldous himself thought that the story had a good easy flow. ". . the easiness, I may say, [to Ian Parsons] was horribly difficult to get, and I have been writing and re-writing the thing for months, before, during and after our trip in the Near East."

Now Julian in transit blew in and delivered a lecture to the American Humanist Society. "He was sweet," Maria wrote to Matthew on 21st October, "though, poor man, how antagonizing he can be.

> And how ludicrous too when he talks as if only he were right—he shuts up even eminent people by contradicting something they know much better, and everybody knows too . . I was rather appalled, because even if he had been corrected on practical things such as time-tables . . he carried on repeating the correction as if he had always known. It must be a form of neurosis . . And he is *fundamentally so tired*. The actual delivery of the talk was excellent as well as natural (but rather too low-brow): dignified, clear, steady . . .

Humphrey Osmond was expected in November. "We plan more mescalin and a tour in the desert." Maria had decided to take the drug with Aldous. But when Humphrey came—it was their second meeting—Aldous had a mild bout of shingles, and Maria was under X-rays once more and suffering from a very painful lumbago (Aldous had lumbago too, "stealing my thunder," Maria said), so neither of them was fit enough to try mescalin. Humphrey experimented with Gerald Heard[1] and Hoynigen Huene, the photographer, instead. In Aldous's presence, ". . both of them very interesting [Aldous to Matthew and Ellen] albeit in rather different ways. Huene's reactions were wholly aesthetic, Gerald's mainly verbal and mediumistic—with other personalities talking through him from a variety of mental levels . . ."

(At this point, *The Doors of Perception* had been reviewed in *Pravda*. "It is like a parody of Dialectical-Materialist denunciation written, not by Orwell, but by someone a good deal less clever . . . [Aldous to Ian Parsons] Heavily funny—but how extremely depressing! For there is not the slightest evidence of any wish to discover what the other fellow is trying to say . . ."

Then much to their regret Humphrey went back to Canada. ". . he is a very remarkable young man, whom it is both a pleasure and a stimulus to have around . . . very able, imaginative and energetic, with a wide-angled intellectual lens . . ." What Maria said about him was, "Humphrey makes life more passionately interesting but busy. We both have a deep affection for him and miss him." And some weeks later, ". . We love him dearly—one does." While he was there she had spoken to him

---

[1] Gerald Heard, at least in his article in the *Kenyon Review* of 1965, puts the date as November 1953.

openly. About her concern for Aldous—"knowing that her time was short." She had said to him, "Aldous is a good man." (Humphrey later wrote to Aldous that he was so filled with grief that he wept for half an hour.) By this time Maria had begun to warn some of her friends. At the end of November Aldous had asked Betty Wendel to read the M.S. of *The Genius and the Goddess* and to meet them next day for luncheon at the Town & Country market to discuss the book. There Aldous asked her whether she would consider collaborating with him on a play dramatization. Betty burst into tears overcome by the compliment (this is her own account). Aldous asked her to work on her own for a few days, roughing out ideas for construction. It was very important to him, he said, to have her write the stage descriptions for the sets, as he did not visualize anything and wrote all his descriptions of places from those he had actually seen and re-membered. Betty did an outline of the play, and she and Aldous began working separately and together on the actual script. While this was under way, Maria asked Betty to lunch with her alone at the market, not letting Aldous know. "She told me that she was very ill and had been told in Paris that she was coming home to die. She had not told Aldous. She asked me to keep working with him, even when she became bedridden." (Some time before, Maria had written, "Betty Wendel is a wonderful friend and far from being a fool in spite of so much real *sweetness* and *kindness*.")

On 10th December Maria wrote to the children in New York. "Aldous is working passionately without taking a breath [extend-ing his paper on visionary experiences into what became *Heaven and Hell*]—making up for so many months of travelling." But, "It is sadder and sadder that we live so far apart, and nothing is going to budge Aldous from California; nor would any of us dare move until he wanted to—not only because we think he deserves having the few things he wants but also 'because it doesn't pay to have one's will'—I found that out so long ago . . ."

1st January 1955. Maria writes a long hand-written letter—they are all by hand now—to New York.

> My first love, my first thoughts to you as well as to Aldous, my 4 Darlings, and my very first letter . . .

But Christmas "was *not* very gay. I re-developed that lumbago . . . so things were a great chore. My maids are touching . . . Betty Wendel is our good angel . . ." She and Aldous had dinner alone on Christmas Eve then went over to take parcels to Mère and Rose and her children, and on Christmas Day they all came to a late lunch: "Marie is a genius because the skin of the turkey still

crackled; they all ate well and went off to the cinema while
Olivia walked with me. But I was getting older and miserabler
by the *minute, everything* ached . . . Then I was better until yesterday
when I was again 1955 years old, but Aldous repeated treatment
and gave me a lot of suggestions so I slept like a log and have
the courage to write . . ."

Also to write to Jeanne to rejoice with her over the recovery
of "our Noële" from a long and inexplicable illness.

A few days later "a remarkable personage, called Captain
Hubbard," turned up in North Kings Road—"the scientific
director of the Uranium Corporation, who took mescalin last
year, was completely bowled over by it and is now drumming
up support among his influential friends . . ." "He has everybody's
ear [Maria wrote] because instead of being a cranky literary man
he is a nuclear physicist, a businessman, a millionaire and an
ardent catholic. He gives the mescalin in small doses . . . Aldous
and Gerald and himself took it last night. I was too pained and
drugged to take it. And Aldous says it was totally different from
the first time and as immensely important . . .

This was the second (and apparently last) time Aldous took
mescalin. He had telephoned to Humphrey in Canada for his
approval. ". . since I was in a group [Aldous wrote to the Godels]
the experience had a human content, which the earlier, solitary
experience . . did not possess. For five hours I was given a series
of luminous illustrations of the Christian saying, 'Judge not that
ye not be judged,' and the Buddhist saying, 'To set up what you
like against what you dislike, this is the disease of the mind.' "

Now this letter to the Godels was dated 10th January and it
said first:

> . . . I think so often . . . of our stay in that magical house by the
> canal . . . and of our long talks, while the ships glided silently past
> the windows . . .
> Here [we] have been well—but not exuberantly so. Maria had to
> have a long series of X-ray treatments, which achieved the desired
> results . . . Recently she has been having recurrent and very painful
> lumbago—which now seems to be yielding to treatment . . . However,
> in spite of everything we are happy. I have done a great deal of
> work . . .

On the same day Maria wrote to Ellen:

> Aldous is still well and very cheerful. So is Gerald, and we walked
> with him yesterday, then he came home for tea and a "hypnotic
> instruction" by a record which sent him sound asleep, and he was
> refreshed for our dinner at the Stravinskys. We are such a happy

family with the S's. Vera and myself always the only women—red wine of good quality—only just enough of the main course but a large dessert . . . then music and books. They have wonderful art books. He works *very hard* and all those concerts are for the sake of money. They spend every penny and sometimes more but live easily. Vera has a one-man show in Rome and Aldous is to write the notice. We love what she does.

. . . Can you take a holiday, just all of you? We could meet you anywhere you choose—South of the Grand Canyon? Taos?

. . . We are rejuvenated by our new diet. I wish Matthew would try it for 3 days. [There follow two pages of charted meals which read like some resurrection of the Hay diet] Gerald won't; he's too much of a priest to give up his carbohydrates, and Mère is too much of a gourmet . . .

Two days later Aldous wrote to Humphrey, "Poor Maria has still got the lumbago. We have begun ultrasonic treatment . . . [by] one of the new German machines, and I hope very much that this may do the trick." And Maria to Jeanne on 13th January, ". . all our news is good at present: Suzanne and all her offspring, Mère, Matthew too . . ."

But on 16th January Aldous wrote to Humphrey:

Maria has just left for a couple of days at the hospital, where the doctors want to run a series of tests to see why, as well as this long drawn lumbago, she has been running temperatures every evening. I suppose it is some infection in the intestine or kidney, and hope they will be able to put their finger on it and get rid of it; for she has had much too long a siege of pain and below-parness.

While Maria was away Aldous worked on the play with Betty Wendel.

My Darlings . . . I have been stupidly careless with that lumbago [Maria reassured Matthew and Ellen on 18th January] so I am at the Good Samaritan again. It is hard on poor old Poppa—I wasn't much use with a back-ache, and now he must foot the bills . . .

There followed minute instructions for a present she wanted Matthew to get for a friend of his who was off on a long journey; and this is what Marie Le Put told me about her visiting Maria in hospital. It was a very cold day. "Elle m'a touchée—mon manteau—'Marie, est-ce que vous êtes assez couverte?' Toujours pour les autres, *toujours* . . ."

Maria returned on 22nd January. Some liver trouble was found, Aldous wrote Humphrey on the day, "but the doctor seems to think that much of this will disappear spontaneously as the result of helping the back. I think she is also embarking on a treatment of some kind. So I hope all will be well within a short time . . ."

Only a few days later Maria went back to hospital for more treatments. On 30th January Aldous still writes to Matthew and Ellen that he hopes "when they are over, next week, she will really start to get better." A day later he wrote to Eileen Garrett that the news hasn't been too good of late. "So please, dear Eileen, pray and think for the best outcome."

On 3rd February, he writes to Humphrey, ". . the news here is discouraging. Maria is not getting better . . ." Then two days later, poor Aldous at last is told, and Aldous sees. He wrote at once to Matthew, asking him to come. He wrote to Jeanne. That letter began:

> Je t'écris du fond d'une immense tristesse. Maria est très malade, s'il faut croire aux médicins, sans espoir. Elle rentrera à la maison après-demain car elle sera plus heureuse chez elle
> Pense à elle avec tout ton amour, et à moi aussi,[1]
>
> > Aldous.

Peggy Kiskadden (abroad these months) flew back from the Middle East when her husband cabled her and arrived in time to see Maria on her last day in hospital. Maria greeted her with an affectionate, mischievous smile, "I *knew* you would come," She said. "Aldous is letting me go home, isn't it kind of him?" and that afternoon Maria telephoned to Betty Wendel.

> She said to let me talk to her without interrupting because it was the last time she would ever talk to me. She asked me to keep Aldous working and gave me other instructions. The last thing she said to me was "Always, have a fresh ribbon on your typewriter so Aldous won't have trouble reading."

From hospital Maria wrote once more to Jeanne. The letter bears this postscript.

> Quant à toi Janin—nous savons ce que nous savons. Ne sois jamais triste *pour moi.*

[1] "I am writing to you from the bottom of an immense sadness. Maria is very ill and if we are to believe the doctors, there is no hope. She will be coming back to the house the day after tomorrow as she will be happier at home.

"Think of her with all your love, and of me too, Aldous".

Maria came home to North Kings Road on Monday 7th February. Rose was in the house, and Helen Halsberg, the nurse who had looked after her in 1952. Maria asked for the door of her room to be kept open so that she could hear the movements in the house. Aldous went over to an ironmongers and got rods and rings, and hung up a curtain in her doorway. In the afternoon their therapist friend, Leslie LeCron, came in for half an hour, put her into hypnosis and gave her some suggestions. Aldous repeated these suggestions later in the evening and from that time on she was free from any distressing symptoms.

It is Aldous who set everything down in an account he wrote afterwards for Jeanne and Julian and Juliette, for Gerald and Humphrey, of which copies were sent to a few other friends. (The account is published in full in Laura Archera's book as well as in a footnote in Aldous's collected Letters. I shall only quote essential passages.)

Matthew arrived on the Tuesday morning. Maria "was still able to find a great and fully conscious happiness in seeing her son . . .

> I [Aldous] spent a good many hours of each day sitting with her, sometimes saying nothing, sometimes speaking. When I spoke, it was always, first of all, to give suggestions about her physical well-being . . . I would suggest that she was feeling, and would continue to feel, comfortable, free from pain . . . These suggestions were, I think, effective; at any rate there was little pain . . .[1]

These suggestions for physical comfort were followed each time by much longer suggestions addressed to the deeper levels of the mind.

> Under hypnosis Maria had had, in the past, many remarkable visionary experiences of a kind which the theologians would call "pre-mystical". She had also had, especially while we were living in the Mojave Desert . . a number of genuinely mystical experiences, had lived with an abiding sense of divine immanence . . . This was the reason for her passionate love for the desert. For her, it was not merely a geographical region; it was also a state of mind, a meta-physical reality, an unequivocal manifestation of God.
>
> In the desert and, later under hypnosis, all Maria's visionary and mystical experiences had been associated with light . . . Light had been the element in which her spirit had lived, and it was therefore

---

[1] "It was only during the last thirty-six hours that sedation (with Demerol) became necessary."

to light that all my words referred. I would begin by reminding her
of the desert she had loved so much, of the vast crystalline silence . .
of the snow-covered mountains at whose feet we had lived . . . And
I would ask her to look at these lights of her beloved desert and to
realize that they were not merely symbols, but actual expression of
the divine nature; an expression of Pure Being, an expression of the
peace that passeth all understanding . . . an expression of the love
which is at the heart of things, at the core, along with peace and joy
and being, of every human mind. And having reminded her of those
truths—truths which we all know in the unconscious depth of our
being, which some know consciously but only theoretically and which
a few (Maria was one of them) have known directly, albeit briefly
and by snatches—I would urge her to advance into those lights . . .

So the days passed . . . her surface mind drifted further and further
. . so that she no longer recognized us or paid attention. And yet she
must have still heard and understood what was said; for she would
respond with appropriate action, when the nurse asked her to open
her mouth or swallow. Under anaesthesia, the sense of hearing
remains awake long after the other senses have been eliminated . .
Addressing the deep mind which never sleeps, I went on suggesting
that there should be relaxation on the physical level and an absence
of pain and nausea; and I continued to remind her of who she really
was—a manifestation in time of the eternal, a part forever un-
separated from the whole, of the divine reality; I went on urging her
to go forward into the light.

When Mère came, she found her peaceful, "Maria est très
calme, couchée dans son beau lit blanc . . . Je la suppose calme
sous la présence d'Aldous. Rose dit que s'il elle parle c'est en
français . . ."

Suzanne arrived on Thursday. Maria opened her eyes, "et
gentille comme toujours elle me dit, 'Tu as un joli chandail.' "
Then Maria said, "Vous êtes tous là. Comme à St Trond. C'est
comme la mort de Bon-Papa."

A little before three on Saturday morning the night nurse
called Aldous. "I went and sat by Maria's bed . . . I told her that
I was with her and would always be with her in that light which
was the central reality of our beings. I told her that she was
surrounded by human love and that this love was the manifestation of a greater love, by which she was enveloped and sustained.
I told her to let go . . . She knew what love was, had been capable
of love as few human beings are capable. Now she must go forward
into love . . . And she was to forget, not only her poor body, but
the time in which that body had lived. Let her forget the past,
leave her old memories behind. Regrets, nostalgias, remorses,
apprehensions—all these were barriers between her and the light.

Let her forget them . . . 'Peace now,' I kept repeating. 'Peace, love, joy *now* . . ."
Matthew was with them.

Those last three hours [he wrote to Ellen afterwards] were the most anguishing and moving hours of my life. It was just Aldous and Peggy and I. Peggy had put out the night nurse. And Aldous was whispering to her all during the time. Whispering the lesson of the *Bardo Thodol* . . . but framed in such a moving and personal way—illustrations from their lives together and incidences . . . and her own revelation of what the *Tibetan Book of the Dead* speaks about. "Let go, let go . . ."
. . . It was over so quietly and gently with Aldous with tears streaming down his face with his quiet voice not breaking . . .

Maria died at six o'clock in the morning on 12th February.

Maria was buried on 14th February in Rose Dale Memorial Park at Los Angeles. Aldous made the decision. Everyone thought, wrote Matthew, that Aldous would be the one who'd break down. "No, it was he, far more than any of us who held the family together . . It was his example that kept Bonne Maman going so wonderfully." Aldous decided that there should be some kind of service to satisfy Rose, Suzanne and Mère. Matthew believes that Aldous himself desired this. Matthew and Peggy saw to the arrangements. For some reason they stopped short of a Catholic ceremony. The service was conducted by their friend, Father McLane, a High Episcopalian, who was grief-stricken himself and who, in Matthew's words, "with almost unbelievable tact produced something so moving, so suitable to Coccola that even I who hated the whole idea was satisfied.

I now feel that the service had one profound and valuable effect—it acted as the great, the last catharsis, a kind of full stop, from which one *has* to look into the future; though the past is illuminated by the beauty and sweet remembrance of that being who for thirty years was the closest being in my life.

Throughout the ceremony, it was Aldous, frail as a ghost, who gave his arm to Mme Nys and who sustained her. The next day he and Matthew went away together.

Chapter Five

Telle Qu'en Elle-Même . . .

"WHAT is to become of Aldous? That is the greatest single question which is facing us." Matthew, point by blunt point, tried to work it out:

The immediate short-range problem [he wrote to Ellen on 17th February] from now until April when he intends coming to New York for the spring and summer with us in New England.

1) It looks as if I will not be able to persuade him to have anyone in the house with him. While the mechanics of running the house are working out very well—Marie [Le Put] will be there four times a week etc—he is not covered from 3.30 pm until the next morning. Quite apart from the gloominess of the empty house, there always exist . . problems and emergencies . . that Aldous will not be able to cope with. Possibilities: a full-time individual, or a part-time individual who comes in for the afternoon and evening, say, 2-9 pm. Or what he's presently thinking of, a pansy-boy—which he can't stand—but it doesn't have to be a pansy—to tootle him round in the car twice a week for a couple of hours . . .

The long-term problem. 1) This depends of course on where *we* are going after I leave H.I.P. at the end of the summer. Ideally, I think very definitely on Aldous's part, he wishes that we could come and live here in Los Angeles.

. . My thinking on the subject—I *must* have a job, but not just any job, but a job in terms of a career etc etc.

. . Would *he* be willing to move himself? I think he would: he gave me an indication when we were talking over what might happen to 740 [North Kings]—he thought he might move to a service type apartment or hotel, leaving us the house . . The house which in 4 years will be paid for . . .

Humphrey asked Aldous to come and stay with him and his wife in Canada; Frieda Lawrence asked him to the ranch. Anita Loos cabled offering financial help . . . Aldous resumed work with Betty Wendel on 23rd February.

Wednesday 23rd was the first day that we took up where we had left off. [Betty's diary] When I arrived Aldous said that he would like to have some music. Maria had always put on the record player for him. He had difficulties starting the machine—he fumbled with

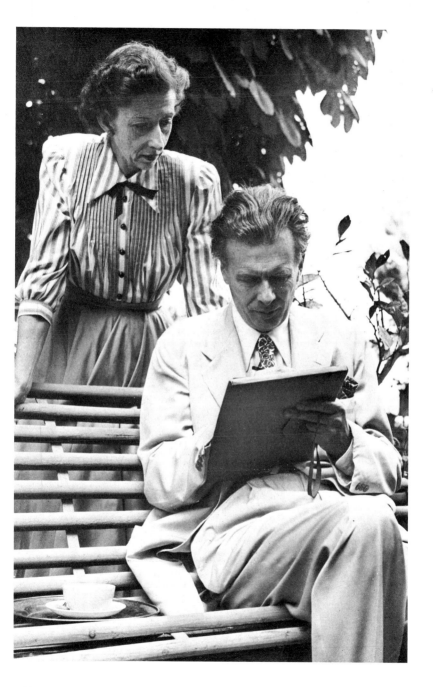

Aldous and Maria in Sienna, 1948

Left: Maria at Amalfi Drive *c.* 1942

Below: Aldous *c.* 1950

Opposite: Maria in April 1954 with a delegate at Eileen Garrett's Symposium of Philosophy and Parapsychology at St Paul de Vence

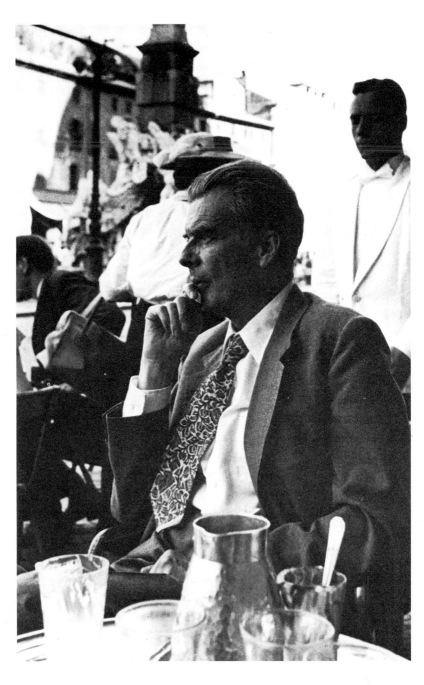

Aldous in the Piazza Navona, Rome, June 1954

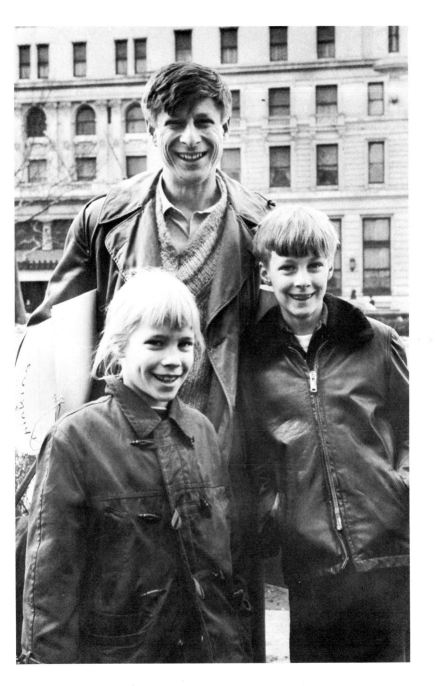

Matthew with his children, Teresa and Trevenen, New York, 1960

Inset: Aldous being interviewed by Cyril Connolly in 1948. *Above:* Aldous with Julian Huxley

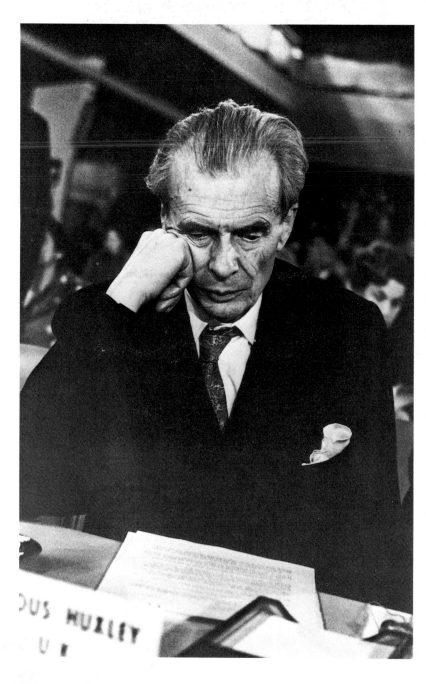

Aldous at an FAO meeting *c.* 1960

the arm—dropped it on the record—I felt I could not make a move
to help him; at last he got the music going.

Presently Matthew had to leave. Practical arrangements were
made more or less on his lines—Marie Le Put to cook and leave
food four times a week; Onnie Wesley, "a dear kind coloured
woman," to see to the house on one or two other days; a friend
of Gerald's to drive Aldous on three afternoons; and an old
Dartington school-fellow of Matthew's, Marianna Schauer to
come on alternate days for secretarial work and reading aloud.
As for the rest . . . The evenings, as Matthew put it, were un-
covered. He could do *nothing*, he wrote to his Aunt Jeanne, but
respect his father's wish for solitude. "I had to overcome my fears
and leave him alone in the house." Aldous had said to him, "For
the moment, I think, I will stay here with my work."

No book in hand. He persisted with the play, carried on with
some essays and the notes on the Utopian theme that had so
long pursued him; thought—the suggestion was Gerald's—of
writing something about death (anonymously), the whole problem
of death "and what can be done by those who survive to help
the dying, and incidentally themselves". One thinks back to the
boy of seventeen who struck by blindness retired into work.

He wrote to his friends, responded to their letters. Frieda he
told how often while he was sitting by Maria's bed he had thought
"of that spring night in Vence twenty-five years ago." (Frieda
wrote to her sister Else, ". . Maria Huxley is dead. A true true
friend . . .") He wrote to Maria's family, the family that had
become, that was, in the deepest sense, his own. To Claire, the
published letter in which he says, ". . in so far as I have learned
to be human—and I had a great capacity for not being human—
it is thanks to her." To Sophie, this unpublished one:

> I can't write a long letter—but am sending this little note to tell
> you that the thing which gave Coccola her greatest happiness during
> the last month of her life was the news that you were going to get
> married. She loved you and longed for you to be happy in growing
> to your full stature, in becoming your best, completest self.
>
> Telle qu'en elle-même l'éternité la change,[1] she hoped that you will
> become telle qu'en ell-même l'amour, la tendresse, la joie, la
> douleur, la change.
>
> Be as loving, sensitive, understanding and brave as she was—and
> be as happy, both of you, as we were.
>
> All my love

[1] This is of course a—slight—variant of Mallarmé's line; a line which had
long haunted Aldous.

To Yolanda, their friend of the market stall, he took a copy of his account of Maria's last days. This gave her the courage to come to him with something else. First she asked him not to be angry about what she had to tell. He promised. Whereupon she produced four hundred dollars in clean notes (Maria used to pick up dirty change with a tissue). This was her story. Last September Maria said to her, "Yolanda you are worried." Yolanda confessed to business trouble, money trouble. How much? Maria asked. Fifty dollars? Five hundred? "Oh," Yolanda said, "she had no money sense!" So there it was. Maria lent her the four hundred she needed, and now she was all right again, but Aldous must not mind that it was done behind his back. Aldous cried.

To Rina, he wrote first of all of the affection Maria had borne her; in Italian, he told her about the last days. And now "mi adatto ad una vita amputata. Non sa che cosa farò eventualmente. L'ultima malattia é stata, grazie a Dio, breve e poco dolorosa . . . *La fine é stata tranquillissima.*"

PART ELEVEN

Soles Occidere Et Redire Possunt: 1955-1960

"I don't think . . that we can be really happy until we have nothing to rejoice at—nothing, that is to say, specifically *Ours*."

ALDOUS HUXLEY

". . he always returned to the single theme that dominated his later years: the condition of men in the twentieth century."

SIR ISAIAH BERLIN

Chapter One

"Meanwhile Life Continues . . ."

ALDOUS stayed on alone at North Kings for over two months. On 19th April he and Betty Wendel finished their first draft of *The Genius and the Goddess* play; next day he left to spend the summer in the East. He travelled, the way he knew to travel, by car. Rose was going to drive. In Maria's car, the last new Oldsmobile. The afternoon before he went to tea with Mère. "J'ai constaté sa bonne mine," she wrote to Jeanne, "son calme, et certainement son soulagement de quitter la maison." He left her the itinerary of their route so that she could follow them on the map. It was the extreme Southern route, by the tip of Texas, the longest to New York and one that he had never taken, a point not lost on Mme Nys, who wrote how glad she was that Aldous would be spared "les souvenirs d'une route connue." Betty came to see them off. They were taking a picnic basket and a great many books.

> Rose was a little nervous. She told me. She hoped Aldous would like her driving. She wondered what it would be like sitting side by side with him all the way across the country. [It was not only, one must remember, that Rose was so much younger than all her sisters but that up to then anyone's contact with Aldous with a very few exceptions—Gerald, Humphrey, and even there, I would say, not a hundred per cent—had never been quite direct, with Maria always the conductor who got the circuit going.] Rose laughed when I presented them with a bottle of sherry each. When Aldous was out of earshot she said she would probably have her sherry alone and would need a drink at the end of the day. Plans had been carefully made; so many miles every day, reservations at motels . . .

Frieda, for once, was not at the ranch but in Texas, and so it was made natural for Aldous to avoid Taos and travel instead by way—a huge way—of Phoenix and El Paso down to Port Isabel on the Gulf to see her. From there they made their way up to Washington D.C., more or less following the coast, by Houston, Baton Rouge, New Orleans, Mobile and, after crossing Florida, Savannah, Charleston. Aldous turned out very sweet and companionable. They would start at about nine in the morning, stop for a picnic lunch, and they did drink their evening sherry together in one of their cabins at the motel. From New Orleans

Mère had word that Aldous was beginning to press on—"Il trouve le pays trop grand. [Mme Nys to Jeanne] Ce n'est pas le pays, mais l'absence de Maria et qui s'aggrandira d'heure en heure."

After twelve days and four thousand miles of it, they reached Washington. A couple of busy days—luncheon at the Indian Embassy, tea at Dumbarton Oaks, a visit to the National Institute of Mental Health, and on to New York. Aldous had been lent George Kaufman's[1] apartment on 1035 Park Avenue (Rose went on to Suzanne's) and there he settled down for the next eight weeks. "I live," he wrote to Betty, "in a style to which I am not accustomed—

> pent house with terraces overlooking the City, French butler and wife (admirable cook), Siamese cat and an enormous library of plays, mutely urging me to work—which I am doing now, like mad, for I cd do nothing en route. Have revised the first act and am now doing the second . . .
> . . Anita . . very sensible about producers, directors, actors etc . . .

He allowed himself one more interruption, a meeting of the "nut-doctors" at Atlantic City. From there—the American Psychiatrists' Association meeting—he wrote to Humphrey on 11th May. He was staying at an hotel called the Marlborough-Blenheim.

> Here I am in this Dome of Pleasure, floating midway on the waves, where is heard the mingled measure of the Electric Shock Boys, the Chlorpromaziners and the 57 Varieties of Psychotherapists. What a place—the luxury of early Edwardian days, massive, spacious, indescribably hideous and, under a livid sky, indescribably sinister!
> I am under the protective wing of a bright young researcher . . . They steer me through the tumult and introduce me to the Grand Panjandrums, who mainly speak with German accents and whose names and faces I can never remember for more than five minutes.
> . . Tomorrow we have an evening party with speeches about mescalin and LSD, at which I am supposed to hold forth for 10 minutes.

Humphrey came to New York later in the month for a few days and Aldous saw as much of him as he could. On the whole he kept himself busy in every available way. "I am leading a horribly social life," he wrote to Betty, "too many lunches and dinners, even when the people are pleasant and interesting there

---

[1] The American playwright.

is apt to be an expense of spirit." And of course there were negotiations about the play—these were to go on for a long time to come; now Aldous arranged for Helen Harvey of the William Morris agency to represent him and Betty and draw up a financial agreement. "We will split the hypothetical royalties," he wrote to her, "as you suggest—twenty-five and seventy-five. I hope they will be *very* large." This broke down as fifty per cent to Aldous as author of the novel on which the play was based, with the other fifty per cent divided half and half between Aldous and Betty as co-authors of the play. They agreed to share all expenses and they were to have equal rights and equal billing. On 2nd June he telegraphed for her. She arrived on the 6th. They sought every conceivable advice. "There were meetings, meetings, meetings," Betty said, "talk, talk, talk." At this point Alfred de Liagre, who had produced most of van Druten's plays, became interested. (He "is pleasant and a gentleman, and has a record of successes," Aldous wrote.) They conferred with him in Betty's room at the St Regis Hotel.

Delly [de Liagre] is handsome, stylish, rather formal [Betty's journal]. About four o'clock I asked if he would like some tea and he said he would love tea. He looked as if he was expecting me to phone for room service and appeared a little surprised when Aldous got up, opened my cupboard and produced an electric kettle, tea bags, cups and saucers, a grocery box of lump sugar, a package of cookies. Aldous told me to go on with play talk while he made tea. Delly quickly subdued his chic and urbane manner and matched Aldous's cosy simplicity. But at another meeting, which lasted until evening, as I was asking Delly if he would like a drink, he quickly got to his feet and insisted that we go downstairs to the King Cole Bar; I suppose he was beating Aldous to a trip after Scotch in my cupboard.

De Liagre suggested changes in the play which the authors half-heartedly agreed to work out, and Betty returned to California without anything being signed and sealed.

During this period Aldous wrote across the Atlantic to Elise Murrell (Maria's "psychic" correspondent)

Dear Friend,
    . . . Meanwhile life continues in its new, amputated context. Quite apart from everything else, there are certain mechanical difficulties; for, as you probably know, I am pretty blind and depended on Maria for many things requiring sharp eyes, such as driving a car, reading aloud, looking after the practical affairs of life. My old

friend Eileen Garrett—Irish like yourself, and a medium, and now the head of the Parapyschology Foundation, which finances research in ESP phenomena and organizes discussion of them by philosophers, psychologists and medical men—told me something very interesting about Maria the other day. M. has appeared to her several times since her death, and particularly vividly on two occasions, when she said two things which Eileen didn't understand, but which M. told her to pass on to me without fail. First "I didn't hear the whole of the Bardle" (this was how Eileen heard the message) "but the effect was to lull me and to carry me through, so that I was still with it on the other side." The other was, "I found the Eggart (again Eileen's version) very helpful."

Now, Aldous went on, he had *not* told Eileen about Maria's last days, had not explained that he had been repeating to her what resembled in a certain way the ritual for the dying described in the *Bardo Thodol* or *Tibetan Book of the Dead*, "and the word which Eileen interpreted as Bardle was obviously Bardo: for M. knew the book well and had a great feeling for it . . . As for Eggart —that was obviously Eckhart, whose tremendous phrase, 'The eye with which we see God is the same as the eye with which God sees us,' I had repeated.

Eileen also said that M. had always appeared in the midst of an intense ruby glow (the light of love, I suppose; for she was enormously capable of love); and that she seemed to be less attached to things here, less possessive about those she had loved, than anyone she had ever seen in this posthumous condition . . . Eileen's feeling was that she would not remain in this region for long, but would press onwards in the knowledge that she could do more good that way than by hanging about on the fringes of our poor old world . . .

Aldous mentioned Eileen Garrett's rapport with Maria to several people, Grace Hubble, Ellen, Jeanne (to whom he wrote, "Eileen . . se trouve assez souvent en contact, spontanément, avec Maria—la trouve heureuse, légère, gaie, jeune et extra-ordinairement *libre*"). And yet at about this time when Constance Collier's friend, Phyllis Wilburn (Constance had died in April while Aldous was en route) talked to him about survival and asked outright, "Do you believe in life after death?" Aldous answered "I do not know."

At the end of that long letter to Elise Murrell, though, we find a key passage:

I don't think . . that we can be really happy until we have nothing to rejoice at—nothing, that is to say, specifically *Ours*. Only then do we begin to have everything, impartially—the entire visible universe and the invisible too—being happy in all the countless reasons for happiness that exist in a world of infinite depth and beauty and significance, and not unhappy in the particular reasons for our own misery, however terrible they may be . . .

Of course, he ended, this is easy to say but "dreadfully hard to practise . . Illness (which is death in life) is much harder to cope with than death (which is life in death)."

At the end of June Aldous moved to New England with Matthew and his family. They had taken a house for the summer at Aldous's instigation, a beautiful eighteenth-century house called Newcomb, under great trees, on the banks of a tidal river, at Guilford, Connecticut. Aldous paid the rent (never mind if it's steep, "my *Esquire* articles will make it easy"). Matthew, working in Public Health at New Haven, commuted; Aldous was finishing off *Heaven and Hell* and spending his spare time with Ellen, their old affinity flowering in the daily companionship; the countryside was green, the township pleasantly rustic.

. . Aldous and I shopped together [Ellen wrote to me] and talked about food a lot, and discussed the children an incredible amount, and the weather almost constantly. It was atrociously hot and humid; the air simply sat there being re-breathed and getting damper . . . ["The hottest summer in the history of Connecticut," Aldous recorded] I made him a pair of pedal-pusher style shorts out of a pair of his old pants. He wore these a great deal, looking completely unselfconscious and at the same time like a stork wearing shorts. Edward Lear would have done a devastating drawing of him.
He worked, or foozled, in the mornings. Foozling, which was his term, was a way of avoiding work, and meant tickling the inside of his nose with opened paper clips—sometimes his desk was *covered* in opened paper clips—or recording bits of poetry, philosophy, literature that he liked, onto his dictaphone, and then playing them back again. But work he did, of course, and actually claimed that he became physically ill if he didn't work a good part of every day.

Little Trev and Tessa, though flourishing, were a handful. "How I admire people who can cope with children!" Aldous wrote to me." Ellen and Matthew do so remarkably well.

But, my goodness, how clearly (because they exhibit human nature with the lid off, or rather before the lid has been put on) children illustrate the four Noble Truths of Buddhism. Life is sorrow. The cause of sorrow is craving for individualized existence—and do they crave, poor little things! The extinction of craving puts an end to sorrow. And the means to that extinction are the prescriptions of the eightfold path. The path, of course, is out of the question for children, and all that can be done for them is to screw some reasonably acceptable persona over the seething mass of craving and aversion, which constitutes the human being in the raw . . .

"Lunch was always interesting," Ellen continues. "Aldous used it as a time to unwind, and would muse aloud about what he had been writing, or thinking about, or what was in the morning's mail, or what we would do in the afternoon." *How* like the summers at Forte, the summers at Sanary (*mutatis mutandis*) . . .

We both suffered from shyness, [Ellen] and our intimacy was often oblique. I remember particularly a lunch when he suddenly started to speak about visiting a medium in New York (I had picked him up at the station that morning). The medium had gone into trance and contacted Maria, and Maria had then poured out her feelings of love toward him, and told him that these feelings had widened into a completely accepting, non-clinging love . . . they would never lose each other, or what they had had together, and she now wanted to assure him that he had her permission and encouragement should he ever want to love someone else, and marry again. I realized that he was not only fascinated by the experience but also that he was, in his way, telling me that Maria would have wanted him to remarry, that he wanted to, and that he wanted my permission too. I was very moved, and told him that anyone who had participated in such a love would only be confirming that love by loving again. He agreed and seemed satisfied . . .

(Ellen had no idea that Aldous might be meaning something quite specific.)

We drove in the afternoons . . I was a horrible driver . . Aldous was my teacher . . he had a way of trusting me to do everything properly—when I slid, sweating with tension, into a tight parking space, he would pat me gently and say ". . . masterly, my dear, masterly!" I owed all my confidence to him. Anyway, we used to pack Trev and Tessa, and usually the cook's child too, into the back seat, and take off to the beach, to see Gillette's Castle, to visit neighbouring towns, to buy ice cream, to simply drive through the countryside . . he missed nothing and never seemed to tire of toodling around.

Once we rocketed up to Boston. I was delivering him to some conference or other, but we went a day early so we could see the

Fine Arts Museum and the Gardner and go to a play. He was fantastic with maps and deadly accurate about where we were at all times (I had never been to Boston, much less driven there), so he did all the navigating and enjoyed it enormously. I'm sure you have been through plenty of museums with him . . we simply galloped along, A. with his largest magnifying glass at the ready. I would read the labels, he would study the painting; he absorbed so much in such a short time that I felt I wasn't reading labels fast enough sometimes; later he would go on about the painting as though we had stood there for an hour. We went to an outdoor theatre in the evening. I don't remember the play, except that it was a Restoration comedy thing and it was very well done and some of my friends were in it—I mention it only because Aldous had such a good time, and I have one of those indelible mental-pictures of him standing backstage, hat pushed back onto the back of his head, a can of beer in his hand, laughing and talking with the actors . . . he was suddenly 25 years old.

Our other big activity in Guilford was walking. Matthew generally arrived back from New Haven in time for a glass of sherry and a talk with his father. I had a bath and changed—unbelievable luxury for me, I was used to cleaning up the children and feeding them and preparing dinner all at the same time. Now the cook did it, and the children ate in the kitchen, and we were served in the dining room, all elegant and civilized. After dinner we walked, as I said—my God he liked to walk. We knew every path and road intimately, and every silo, every cow, every bit of landscape. The air was so warm and damp that it was like walking through molasses, even late at night . . .

The *Esquire* articles, which helped to pay for cook and rent, require an explanation. Aldous had had a windfall. He had been approached at the beginning of the year with what he called a most surprising offer—"to send a monthly essay on anything I like to *Esquire*, that curious magazine which combines naked girls, men's fashions and a certain amount of literature. It is the only periodical, outside the most poverty stricken highbrow class, which will print an essay." (Two of his, "Sludge & Sanctity" and "The French of Paris", had already appeared in *Esquire* in 1953.) He accepted. "Thanks to the nude ladies, they can pay very well." In fact they paid him a thousand dollars an essay. Pretty high pay at the time, if not in the *Saturday Evening Post*, *Life* or *New Yorker* bracket; and extravagantly high, on the mass market, for that kind of writing—think-pieces they were called—published without interference. The money was very welcome, but, best of all, the arrangement gave Aldous a platform: the editors were as good as their word and he was able to write about anything he felt that needed saying—warnings about over-population, spoliation of our resources ("we are living like drunken sailors, like the irresponsible heirs of a millionaire uncle"), the misapplications of technology, about censorship by commercialism, warnings against the doctrine that in this universe of ours anybody can get anything for nothing. It was literary journalism at its most ungratuitous, for the last thing Aldous aimed at, the elegance and agreeable jugglery of these essays notwithstanding, was to adorn or to fill space. The first of the series appeared in July 1955 and continued with hardly a break until April 1957. The titles were part of the sugar-coating— "Usually Destroyed", "Doodles in the Dictionary", "Canned Fish", "Where Do You Live?", "Madness Badness Sadness", "Back Numbers" etc etc.

Aldous stayed in New England for two months, interrupted by some days and nights in New York, a trip to Boston and one to Maine to attend one of those parapsychological gatherings he was getting addicted to, Dr Henry Puharich's Round Table Foundation at Glen Cove.

> .. some days .. in the strange household assembled by Puharich ... [to Eileen Garrett] Elinor Bond doing telepathic guessing . . . Frances Farelly, with her diagnostic machine . . . Harry, the Dutch sculptor, who goes into trances in the Faraday cages and produces automatic scripts in Egyptian hieroglyphics; Narodny, the cockroach man, preparing experiments to test the effects of human telepathy on insects.

Aldous watched, open-minded certainly, not particularly credulous. "It was all very lively and amusing—

> and, I really think, promising; for whatever may be said against Puharich, he is certainly very intelligent, extremely well-read and highly enterprising. His aim is to reproduce by modern pharmacological, electronic and physical methods the conditions used by the shamans for getting into a state of travelling clairvoyance and then, if he succeeds, to send people to explore systematically "the Other World". This seems to be as good a new approach to the survival problem (along with a lot of other problems) as any of the rest, and may yield some interesting results.

And now we have only Aldous's own letters—often so resolutely on the surface, at times lightningly unreticent—to reflect his moods. In his birthday letter to Julian he was able to strike this positive note:

Dearest J,
    Many happy and happier returns! Yes, it is hard to feel old—to be

quite *sérieux*, as the ageing bourgeois ought to be! We both, I think, belong to that fortunate minority of human beings, who retain the mental openness and elasticity of youth, while being able to enjoy the fruits of an already long experience . . .

Yet the month after he wrote to Humphrey:

I too have had a birthday, this very day.

> How soon hath Time, the subtle thief of age,
> Stol'n on his wing my first and sixtieth year!

How little to show! One ought to have done much better. But perhaps it's never too late to mend. And what sad, sad, strange experiences since my last birthday, which was in France!

And to Ralph Rose (the author of a stage adaptation of *After Many A Summer*):

. . This has been a hard time for me too. There seems to be no remedy except to learn somehow not to identify oneself with the pains and losses one has to suffer, the bewilderments and darkness one has to go through—to accept them realistically as things that happen, but not permit oneself to be equated with them, not to forget that they do *not* constitute the entire universe and that we are capable, even in disaster, of being impartially aware of all the other non-disastrous aspects of the world.

To Eileen Garrett, very ill in France, some lines (in the course of a very long letter) showing his belief in the efficacy of benevolent thought, of prayer if you wish:

. . These last days I have been thinking of going with her [Maria] to your room at Le Piol and laying on hands. I hope the thought may have had at least some tiny influence for the good of your health.

To Noële Neveux, fourteen years old, he sends a warning against Proustian indulgence.

Hélas, le temps ne se retrouve pas . . . Rome, Dieulefit, tout le passé—il ne faut pas essayer de les revivre à la manière de Proust.

Instead, he tells the child, we must use the lost time in the present with the given facts of *now* and *here*, and in that way we might come nearer, perhaps very much nearer, to timeless eternity and to those whom we have loved and who have gone from us into death.

And embedded in a letter to one of his strangers, Mrs Barry Stevens, we find a confirmation of his long true ignorance (or his own conviction of it). Telling her that his wife died early this year, he speaks of her "four or five months of seemingly perfect health last summer, when we travelled in the Near East and in Europe."

At the end of August Aldous returned to California, making his own arrangements with some firmness. He was going by air (the car to be driven back eventually by some reliable person). Both his domestic helpers happened to be off on holiday; Aldous wrote to Marianna Schauer, Matthew's young friend who had been dealing with his post:

Dear Marianna,
    I am not supposed to know (since both Rose and her mother seem to think that I am too frail to take it!), but I actually do know that things are going very badly—Rose being ill etc. They both seem to be exceedingly disturbed about (a) the cleaning of the house, (b) the fact that neither Marie nor Onnie will be on hand when I arrive. Let us deal first with (a).

There follow commonsensical instructions about engaging house cleaners. ". . I do not want Rose, her mother and/or Peggy getting hot and bothered about something which can be handled so simply by a cleaning firm. If any of them start making a fuss, say that these are my instructions . . . I know you can handle this with tact and firmness—both of which seem to be needed at the moment!" And let nobody bother to meet him at the plane. As for Marie Le Put and Onnie's being away, he could easily manage breakfast and lunch for the time being and go out for dinner either to a restaurant or to friends. "So don't let anybody worry about that . . ."

On 1st September he was back at North Kings and to much the same life as he had led there in the spring. (The house, he wrote to Humphrey then, "is full of the presence of an absence.") His existence was compartmentalized, no one was allowed to see more than a part of it. Work solitary or with Betty in the morning. Marianna three afternoons a week. There wasn't much secretarial work, Aldous being very well organized with his letters.[1] They talked over tea. He asked questions about her life, her child . . . They went for drives, to tea at Mme Nys', to shop at Farmers' Market or browse in bookshops on La Cienega. Some evenings he remained alone in the house, others he spent with friends, at the Wendels, at Peggy and Bill Kiskadden's, the Stravinskys, with Eva Herrmann. "One never asked where he was going or where

[1] Marianna Schauer, the present Mrs Newton, talking to S. B.

he had been", Betty said. Friends drove him home at night but he would never allow himself to be seen into the house.

> There was a long dark drive with an irregular surface from street to home [Dr James Brainard Smith writing to S. B.] and yet he, without cane or whatever, was quite firm about sending me back to the car and *not* being led up it home. Not at all! And waited for the car to leave.

At the best of times Aldous had appealed to the maternal, the fraternal, the protective instincts, and now there were a good many people who could see themselves in the role of taking over. But Aldous was determined not to be looked after. As an adolescent he had shrunk from the help waiting for him in vulnerable positions. Later he became able to take help, physical help, daily and unremittent, from one woman (his brother Trev may have been, up to a point, another exception). Now he was quite deliberate in his intention to forego this help, not to allow that pattern to be repeated. He had received in the fullest measure what can be given by one human being to another, now he was going to learn to do without. He did not wish for anything like an attempt at emulation of Maria. And not for her sake, for his own. Here was something that went well beyond his need for privacy and the wish not to be fussed over; it was, I am convinced, part of a process towards renunciation. Quite rightly, from their points of view, Matthew, Julian, Juliette, his friends, were deeply and affectionately concerned. The Julians were in England, Matthew was tied to his job in the East, while Aldous by health, habit and inclination was tied to California; and it was in California that gently but unmistakably he drew a line, the invisible chalk circle: so far and no further.

Within a week of his arrival there occurred one of those frightful sudden California bush-fires that can ravage a whole countryside with such appalling swiftness. "Santa Barbara is surrounded by flames. Last night all roads going north were closed . . ."

Aldous's doctor, to whom he had gone for a check-up, declared him healthy; "I manage to do a good deal of work—mostly of a very exasperating kind." For they were by no means rid of the play yet, at the moment he and Betty were revising their revision, putting back some of the characters they had been persuaded to take out during the summer. *The Genius and the Goddess*, the novel, Aldous's first for seven years had come out (in June) and was doing very well. (A good start in America; twenty thousand copies sold in six weeks in England and a second printing ordered.) The novel, Aldous's shortest, is also his most un-Peacockian. The confluence of associations is there all right—that was as particular to him as breathing—but the dialogue and its apparent digressions are astringently subservient to the action. And he appears interested in telling a story, a story *sub specie aeternitatis* to be sure. The book is very far from what Cyril Connolly called the early brilliant, destructive period; the analysis of human motive remains ruthless, but the keynote is compassion, loving, not detached, compassion. (One interesting, technical, feature of the novel is that it has an all-American cast and setting, effortlessly as a matter of course, not Americans characterized as such but Americans as members of the human race.)

> I am glad you liked the little book, [Aldous wrote to me]. It was a favourite of Maria's, in its manuscript form. As you say, one could have gone on with it almost indefinitely; but on the whole I think it is better that the rest should be silence.

It was the last book of Aldous's Maria read. (". . . it seems so much stronger," as she had written to her son, ". . . a great step ahead, or rather à-haut.") Edwin Muir, too, thought it the best thing he ever did.

His original title had been *The Past is Prelude*, more expressive of mood and theme than *The Genius and the Goddess*; at one point it became *The Wrong End of the Opera Glass* (the main action being seen through receded time) which was discarded because of length. One may well ask why Aldous spent so much time on dramatic versions of his books. For one thing, he never let go of his *ignis fatuus* of the successful play ("which ought not be beyond one's competence", he declared when he was still an usher at Eton), the long stage run that would set one free, not now from actual financial worries because he had not had any to speak of since the end of the war, nor free from work as he would always work, but free to work at his own pace. According to Betty, he very much wanted to see a play of his produced and produced well. ("If one could see one's own dramatic ideas well realized . . the thrill would be enormous," as he had said twenty-five years ago when *Point Counter Point* was on the stage.)

> He talked to me about all this many times. [Betty] When crossing the ocean he had seen people reading his books, but they hadn't changed their expression turning pages, nor did they applaud at the end of a chapter, or walk away from their deck-chairs telling someone else about the book.

And yet he was so obviously bored by the mechanics of play writing—all this jigsaw work—unfortunately necessary. Never, for all his persistence, had there been less a man of the theatre.

About the sets [Aldous to Betty]. I confess stage sets have always left me profoundly indifferent. As long as they are not monstrously ugly or monstrously silly . . I don't care what they are like, provided they permit the story to be told . . .

All that is required is efficiency. ". . I had the hideous experience [in *The Gioconda Smile*] . . of what happens when you try to change a scene very rapidly by mechanical rather than optical methods.

Lights can go on and off in 1-100th of a second. Curtains take 5 seconds at least, and the setting up of realistic scenes may take long minutes. Hence I approve the idea of doing . . . with a minimum of machinery and a maximum of lighting effects. My own conviction is that no play (I am not speaking of a spectacle—ballet, musical comedy act) was ever made or marred by its setting . . .

Betty also remarks that Aldous, though perfectly aware of the power of dramatic critics, was no more concerned about them at the writing stage than he was about the book reviewers. Now, how did she and Aldous organize their collaboration? At their meetings—and in Aldous's long memoranda—they threshed out scenes; Betty, he insisted, was good at construction and at visualizing; she went off to write, then brought back her text to Aldous. "I loved his dialogue and he liked mine after he had inverted my sentences. After a while I started inverting my sentences myself and then Aldous inverted them back to where they had been at the beginning . . ." Most of their troubles with prospective directors arose from the fact that there was a play within a play. The outer play, they called it Conversations, consisted of Old John Rivers, the narrator, talking to a friend about the eminent physicist, the genius of the title, whose assistant he has been and in whose household he has lived as a very young man. The talk takes place the night of Christmas Eve in the present year of grace. Does his friend want to hear the official fiction, Rivers asks, the official biography, or the truth?

"The trouble with fiction is that it makes too much sense. Reality never makes sense."
"Never?"
"Maybe from God's point of view. Never from ours . . . In the raw, existence is always one damned thing after another . . simultaneously

Thurber and Michelangelo . . . The criterion of reality is intrinsic irrelevance."

. . "To what?"

"To the best that has been Thought and Said . . . Oddly enough, the closest to reality are always the fictions that are supposed to be the least true." He leaned over and touched the back of a battered copy of *The Brothers Karamazov.* "It makes so little sense that it's almost real. Which is more than can be said for any of the academic kinds of fiction . . . More than can be said even for Biography fiction . . ."[1]

The reality, the one damned thing after another, are acted out in the main, the inner play. De Liagre and other advisers felt that the Conversations should be shortened. "I seemed to be alone in clinging to the Conversations, [Betty] not only because they contained the most brilliant of Aldous's writing but also because they bridged the going from comedy to tragedy and back to comedy, and because they were in themselves dramatizations of the inner play. I suppose Henry James was right in defining the art of play-writing as a process of jettisoning the cargo so as to save the ship. But too much cargo was jettisoned. The version approved by Aldous and me has never been produced (or has not up to now). I am unconvinced, as Aldous was unconvinced, that the ship needed saving . . ."

By October they had done with the new revision; but a director, Joseph Anthony, whom Aldous had waxed enthusiastic about, had meanwhile taken on another engagement supposing—wrongly —that the authors would not mind delay.

Aldous at this time was busy with extensive reading for a talk —that grew into a long essay "Gesualdo: Variations on a Musical Theme"[2]—he had promised to give at one of Robert Craft's Monday evening concerts at the Southern California Chamber Music Society, a talk about the court of Ferrara and the "utterly amazing musical style" of the madrigals of Carlo Gesualdo, the psychotic prince of Venosa who had murdered his wife. Aldous delivered the lecture on 27th October.

. . When he spoke of Gesualdo's special brand of 16th century eroticism, [Betty's journal] the audience, mostly music lovers who sit with their eyes closed, or hands over face, or reading the score, tittered then laughed out loud. Aldous went on and on with story after story about the composer-flagellator . . increasing laughter sweeping through the auditorium . . . After the lecture when we were waiting to drive Aldous home and his admirers had dispersed, only

[1] From the opening of *The Genius and the Goddess,* the novel not the play.
[2] Published in *Adonis and the Alphabet.* Chatto & Windus, 1956.

one young man, very earnest and erudite, was lingering. He asked Aldous to tell him where he had found so much data on Gesualdo ... Aldous mumbled about journals and letters. The young man asked where they could be read. Aldous said to telephone him. Safely in my car, he said, "I have done the most dreadful thing—and I'll be caught ... I was carried away and invented all those stories except the first one. Never have I done anything so preposterous. Oh dear!"

Now another glimpse of Aldous, this time through Rose, On her birthday, he telephoned Mère asking himself to tea with Marianna, "sa gentille secretaire ...

Et voilà Aldous qui s'amène avec une énorme boîte sous les bras [Rose de Haulleville to Jeanne] ... un superbe manteau sport ... Il était allé avec Marianna dans un magasin choisi par lui, "Gifts for Men", c'est à dire pour tapettes mais où il y a des choses charmantes, et là lui-même a choisi ce manteau. J'étais émue aux larmes, surtout lorsqu'il m'a dit que c'était pour les jours froids et venteux du désert. Tu vois comme il est adorable, et tâche de nous remplacer Maria, mais avec tact et simplicité et sans sentimentalité. Il semble heureux; plein d'humour, et très décidé de ce qu'il veut et ce qu'il ne veut pas. J'ai admiré chez lui son nouvel aspirateur, dernier modèle et un nouveau deep-freeze ... Il est si beau à regarder, fort à l'aise se balançant un peu comme les éléphants et de temps en temps un geste de ses belles mains ... D'une certaine façon je le trouve "libéré." Comprends moi bien! Quant à moi je suis encore toute perdue ...

In November Aldous mentions that he is about to deliver a lecture "at the Swami's Tiny Taj Mahal" in Hollywood, this was the Vedanta Temple of Swami Prabhavananda, Christopher Isherwood's Swami, of whom Gerald Heard and Aldous saw a very great deal during their first years in California.[1] Shortly before Christmas Aldous, with Gerald and two others, took LSD for the first time. This he described at length to Humphrey Osmond (number 730 of the published Letters). Here I will refer only to his reactions to music.

[1] Swami Prabhavananda was good enough to receive me in 1969. He said, "Aldous was my disciple, he was initiated by me." I asked if I might have some particulars and the Swami told one of his monks, "May we have the file for Aldous Huxley's initiation." But there was no file. They kept no records at the Temple at that time. "A brilliant mind," the Swami said, "and a noble soul." He then expressed some discreet criticism of Aldous's experiments with LSD. This he mitigated with: "He had to follow many roads."

We played the Bach B-minor suite and the "Musical Offering," and the experience was overpowering. Other music (e.g. Palestrina and Byrd) seemed unsatisfactory by comparison. Bach was a revelation. The tempo of the pieces did not change; nevertheless they went on for centuries, and they were a manifestation, on the plane of art, of perpetual creation, a demonstration of the necessity of death and the self-evidence of immortality, an expression of the essential all-rightness of the universe—for the music was far beyond tragedy, but included death and suffering with everything else in the divine impartiality which is the One, which is Love, which is Being or Istigkeit. Who on earth was John Sebastian? Certainly not the old gent with sixteen children in a stuffy Protestant environment. Rather, an enormous manifestation of the Other—but the Other canalized, controlled, made available through the intervention of the intellect and the senses and the emotions. All of us, I think, experienced Bach in the same way . . .

The effect was quite different when they tried music of a lesser magnitude, a record of traditional Byzantine music, the Greek version of Gregorian:

To me at least, this seemed merely grotesque. The single voice bawling away its Alleluias and Kyries seemed like the voice of a gigantic flunkey kowtowing before a considerably magnified Louis XIV. Only polyphony, and only the highly organized polyphony (structurally organized and not merely texturally organized as with Palestrina) can convey the nature of reality, with its multiplicity in unity, the reconciliation of opposites, the non-twoness of diversity . . the Love which is the bridge between objective and subjective, good and evil, death and life.

. . . Meanwhile let me advise you, if ever you use mescalin or LSD in therapy, to try the effect of the B-minor suite. More than anything, I believe, it will serve to lead the patient's mind (wordlessly, without any suggestion or covert bullying by doctor or parson) to the central, primordial Fact, the understanding of which is perfect health during the time of the experience, and the memory . . of which may serve as an antidote to mental sickness in the future . . .

Aldous added that he felt it would be most unwise though to subject a patient to sentimental religious music "or even good religious music, if it were tragic (the Mozart or Verdi Requiems, or Beethoven's Missa Solemnis). John Sebastian is safer because, ultimately, truer to reality."

And in January 1956 Aldous once more took mescalin (it must have been his fourth time; there was a third in October 1955 to which I shall return). The present experiment was designed to test a possible short-circuiting of the mescalin effect by a new tranquillizer, frenquel; it was conducted by two M.D.'s, Dr Howard Fabing of Cincinnati and a young pharmacologist, Dr Barbara Brown, and is again described to Humphrey in the Letters.

By the end of the month Aldous had finished off his current volume of essays; Betty was in New York to see to their play business and new hope sprang in the shape of a young director, Arthur Penn, whom Betty was highly recommending and whose suggestions seemed constructive.

Chapter Two

Adonis and the Alphabet

THE sequel, to a certain extent, to *The Doors of Perception* was published in February 1956; it is well summed up in Aldous's own words, to S.B.

> I have a long essay coming out . . called *Heaven and Hell*, about visionary experience and its relation to art and the traditional conceptions of the Other World. It springs of course, from the mescalin experience, which has thrown, I find, a great deal of light on all kinds of things . . . I spent a good part of this summer writing a series of supplements or appendices—on painters such as Géricault and Georges de Latour [and how succinct and penetrating these are]; on popular visionary art (pageantry, theatrical spectacles, fireworks, the magic lantern, coloured movies in certain of their aspects) and the technology connected with it; on the bio-chemical conditions of visionary experience and the rationale, in terms of modern pharmacological and physiological knowledge, of traditional ascetic practices. It has been interesting to write . . .

And later in the same year *Adonis and the Alphabet*[1] appeared, a volume which contained, besides some of the *Esquire* contributions, two major essays, on the potentialities of education—what can we do about teaching man to fulfil his contradictory roles? *Man*, Aldous said over and over again, *is a multiple amphibian*. It was the development of what he had tried to grapple with already thirty years ago—*Oh, wearisome condition of humanity, Born under one law to another bound.*

> . . Simultaneously or alternately, we inhabit many different and even incommensurable universes . . man is an embodied spirit . . . [he] is also a highly self-conscious and self-centred member of a sociable species. We live in and for ourselves; but at the same time we live in and, somewhat reluctantly, for the social group surrounding us. Again, we are both the products of evolution and a race of self-made men. In other words, we are simultaneously the subjects of Nature and the citizens of a strictly human republic . . .
> Below the human level amphibiousness presents no difficulties. The

[1] The American title was *Tomorrow and Tomorrow and Tomorrow*.

tadpole knows precisely when to get rid of its tail and gills, and become a frog . . . With us, alas, the case is painfully different . . .[1]

We have to deal, to take but one of our problems, with "the troubles of an ape that has learned to talk—of an immortal spirit that has not yet learned to dispense with words." Yet words *are* necessary. Without words no scientific theories, no philosophy, no law, and without these we should be nothing but Yahoos. (Moreover, there is the basic twentieth-century fact that we live in a world where ignorance of science and its methods is the surest, shortest road to national disaster.) There is no substitute, Aldous goes on, for correct knowledge, and in the process of acquiring that knowledge there is no substitute for concentration and prolonged practice. Except for the unusually gifted, learning must ever be hard work. "Unfortunately there are many professional educationists who seem to think that children should never be required to work hard.

Whenever educational methods are based on this assumption, children will not in fact acquire much knowledge; and if the methods are followed for a generation or two, the society which tolerates them will find itself in full decline.

We are human because, at a very early stage in our history of the species, our ancestors discovered a way of preserving and disseminating the results of experience. Take classical education:

"The literatures of Greece and Rome provide the longest, the most complete and most nearly continuous record we have of what the strange creature *Homo Sapiens* has been busy about in virtually every department of spiritual, intellectual and social activity. Hence the mind that has canvassed this record is much more than a disciplined mind. It has come, as Emerson says, into a feeling of immense longevity, and it instinctively views contemporary man and his doings in the perspective set by this profound and weighty experience. Our studies were properly called formative . . . because their effect was powerfully maturing. Cicero told the unvarnished truth in saying that those who have no knowledge of what has gone before them must for ever remain children."[2]

So far so good. Yet if the letter is essential, the letter also killeth—"the paradox may be expressed in the statement that

[1] "The Education of an Amphibian", *Adonis and the Alphabet*. Chatto & Windus, 1956.
[2] Aldous is quoting from Albert Jay Nock's *Memoirs of a Superfluous Man* in "Knowledge and Understanding," cit.

the medium of education, which is language, is absolutely necessary, but also fatal, that [its] subject matter . . which is conceptualized accumulation of past experience, is indispensable, but also an obstacle to be circumvented.

> "Existence is prior to essence." Unlike most metaphysical propositions, this slogan of the existentialists can actually be verified. "Wolf children," adopted by animal mothers and brought up in animal surroundings, have the form of human beings, but are not human. The essence of humanity, it is evident, is not something we are born with; it is something we grow into. We learn to speak. We accumulate conceptualized knowledge and pseudo-knowledge, we imitate our elders, we build up fixed patterns of thought and feeling and behaviour, and in the process we become human, we turn into persons. But the things which make us human are precisely the things which interfere with self realization and prevent understanding. We are humanized by imitating others . . . by acquiring the accumulated knowledge which language makes available. But we understand only when, by liberating ourselves from the tyranny of words, conditioned reflexes and social conventions, we establish direct unmediated contact with experience. The greatest paradox of our existence consists in this—that in order to understand, we must first encumber ourselves with all the intellectual and emotional baggage, which is an impediment to understanding . . .[1]

What we must do—in Aldous's contention—is to balance that baggage with other, non-verbal, methods of education, by techniques for rediscovering "within ourselves . . a virgin not-mind capable of . . response to immediate experience." So far unfortunately organized education has done very little to help us in this task and we shall have to discover and re-discover the educators in psycho-physical health—F. M. Alexander, John Dewey, Yoga, Zen . . .

> . . The notion that one can educate young people without making any serious attempt to educate the psycho-physical instrument, by means of which they do all their learning and living, seems on the face of it radically absurd. Looking back over my own years of schooling, I can see the enormous deficiencies of a system which could do nothing better for my body than Swedish drill and compulsory football, nothing better for my character than prizes, punishments, sermons and pep talks, and nothing better for my soul than a hymn before bed-time, to the accompaniment of the harmonium. Like everyone else, I am functioning at only a fraction of my potential.

[1] "Knowledge and Understanding" cit.

Chapter Three

Here and Now

DURING the third week of March of 1956 Aldous wrote to his friends Humphrey and Eileen about this and that; nearer home he appeared to be taken up by new activity about the play: Arthur Penn, a prospective director, arrived from New York and Aldous dined with him at the Wendels on the 15th. On the 16th and 17th there were long meetings with Penn and Betty at North Kings (which went well, Aldous having taken a liking to the intelligent young man). In the afternoon Aldous went and bought himself a new shirt, a cowboy shirt with a gay pattern. On the 17th he dined at the Kiskaddens. On 18th March, a Sunday, Arthur Penn came again to the house and after he left Aldous sat down and wrote one of his detailed memoranda to Betty about changes in the play; over the telephone he told her that he was going away for a few days and would she please carry on the talks with Penn. Then he went out and had lunch with Gerald Heard and they, too, talked about this and that. When Marianna Schauer turned up for work the next day, 19th March, she found the house empty: she became at once intensely worried as she had known Aldous to be "the most considerate of men" (he had in fact written to her not to come, the letter through some muddle had been delayed); later that afternoon Betty, working on their notes, was rung up by someone asking whether she had heard the news? The radio had just been announcing that Aldous Huxley had got married to Laura Archera.

In the same way the news reached Matthew in New York. (And Mme Nys in Beverly Hills.) In Europe it was published next morning first in the *Continental New York Herald* and was soon conveyed to Julian and Juliette, to Jeanne, Suzanne . . . Meanwhile, within the hour, Betty's house became a storm centre of information seekers. United Press telephoned. Matthew telephoned. Anita Loos telephoned from New York, and Aldous's dramatic agent; Peggy Kiskadden telephoned and other local friends—not one of them would believe Betty that Aldous had never as much mentioned the name.

In due course Aldous's letters from Yuma, Arizona, dated 19th March, arrived.

Dearest Matthew and Ellen,

As you have probably read already in the papers—for the press was on hand within two minutes of our signing the licence—Laura Archera and I got married today ... You remember her, I am sure—a young woman who used to be a concert violinist, then turned movie cutter and worked for Pascal. I have come to be very much attached to her in recent months and since it seemed to be reciprocal, we decided to cross the Arizona border and call at the Drive-in Wedding Chapel (actual name). She is twenty years younger than I am, but doesn't seem to mind. Coccola was fond of her and we saw her a lot in Rome, that last summer abroad. I had a sense for a time that I was being unfaithful to that memory. But tenderness, I discover, is the best memorial to tenderness.

You will be seeing her in April, when we come East,

Ever your affectionate,

Aldous

On that same evening and in the same vein, he also wrote to Julian and Juliette, Mme Nys, Rose, Peggy, Betty, Jeanne: to her he started baldly,

Je me suis marié avec une jeune femme italienne, de 40 ans, Laura Archera ... Maria l'aimait et je sens qu'elle approuverait ce mariage qui n'est pas une infidélité à la mémoire de notre vie ensemble, mais la commémoration, la continuation de cette tendresse de tant d'années.

En attendant je suis toujours, chère Jeanne, ton très affectueux frère

Aldous

Amd a week later there was this word to Anita:

Thank you for your sweet message, which greeted us on our return from the local Gretna Green—to which I had resorted in the naive hope of conducting my private affairs in privacy ... We w'd have done better to have had a slap-up affair at St Patrick's with Cardinal Spellman officiating and Claire Luce as bridesmaid.

... But tho' I deplore the circumstances, I don't regret the event. Laura is very much all right.

They had met originally—Aldous, Maria, Laura—in 1948 when Laura, impatient of postal communication, had driven herself out to Wrightwood to get Aldous interested in making a film with her in Siena. She arrived in what her friends called *Laurissima*, a fast and temperamental old car, and there, greeted in Italian and following Maria down a corridor, "suddenly we were standing at the bathroom door.

> There, for the first time, I saw Aldous: unreasonably tall, washing his hands in a sink too little and too low, his strange light eyes looking at me, curious and amused, through a romantic lock of hair.[1]

Sporadic friendship followed mutual liking; the Huxleys became interested in Laura's techniques in psycho-therapy and had a go at it (Maria first, to try her out for Aldous, "My dear," she said "you do this very well"; Aldous in an attempt to regain access to some blanks in childhood memories—this did not work; it was he, instead, who sent Laura to sleep). They met again, though not often; all were busy, travelling. Six years later came the Roman encounter. They did not correspond. Laura returned to Los Angeles on 12th February 1955, a few hours as it happened before Maria died. Presently she wrote to Aldous; he replied, asking her for luncheon and a walk.

> I had many questions in my mind about Maria and he answered them without my asking . . .[1]

In the two months that followed Laura went to see Aldous quite often. "He was going through the most difficult period of his life," she wrote in her book.

> . . I saw then, for the first time, how Aldous applied his philosophy: Live here and now . . be aware of what is going on now. "Let go" . . . He succeeded much of the time. Once in a while he would lapse into a depressed silence. He did not speak much about his pain; he only said. "It is like an amputation."[2]

Nothing that had happened to him was allowed to be turned into self-pity. Aldous's own first, and only, mention of Laura before their actual wedding day occurs in a note to Marianna Schauer written from South Carolina in April 1955 on his drive East with Rose. He had forgotten his address book, would she please send him:

Kiskadden—phone and address.
Gerald Heard—phone and address.
Kent—phone.

---

[1] From Laura Archera Huxley's book on Aldous, *This Timeless Moment: A Personal View of Aldous Huxley*. (Chatto & Windus, 1969. USA Farrer, Straus & Giroux, 1968.)   [2] Laura Archera op. cit.

Archera—phone.
LeCron—phone.
Betty Wendel—phone and address.

During the summer Laura had been in New York; Aldous joined her, from New England, for some days or weekends. And in the autumn and winter after his return to Los Angeles:

> . . in the evenings he spent at home I was often there . . we would speak of everything under the sun. I was then very active in psychotherapy. We discussed that; we listened to music, experimented with cooking. Marie Le Put, the lovable and wise Bretonne who had helped Maria, came three times a week . . We always found delicious dinners ready in the refrigerator. ("Monsieur is eating so much," she said . . She did not know that often there were two eating her meals.)

In October Aldous had taken mescalin with Laura present.

> I decided it might be interesting [he wrote to Humphrey Osmond] to find out why so much of my childhood is hidden from me, so that I cannot remember large areas of early life. So I sat down to a session with a woman who has had a good deal of experience with eliciting recalls and working off abreactions by the methods of dianetics—which do in many cases produce beneficial results, in spite of all that can and must be said against the theorists of dianetics and many of its practitioners . . .

Laura, who had not taken, or seen anybody take, a psychedelic drug, asked him if there were anything she should know or do. Nothing, Aldous told her, "Just be as you are."

> I arrived at Aldous's home about nine o'clock. Aldous took the pills . . .
> . . . partly due to my experience in psychotherapy, I had expected—in spite, alas, of trying not to expect anything—that Aldous might speak of Maria. I had hoped he would . . .
> During that first [LSD] day the thought of Maria was often present. We were in her house, where nothing had been changed . . We had been silent for a long while listening to music. Now the record came to an end—I wanted to stop the machine to avoid the . . click of the automatic stop. To do this I had to walk a few steps . . . towards the record player. As I took the first step I felt suddenly that Maria was present. Present, but not outside of me—present in me. Amazed and fascinated, I knew that I was walking as Maria—that she, not I, was walking. It must have been at the third or fourth

step toward the record player . . that his voice reached and touched my shoulder. Extremely firm and gentle, the voice said, "Don't ever be anyone else but yourself."

Aldous did not have to remind me of that again.[1]

Again their attempts to recapture Aldous's childhood failed. ". . Very soon I gave up trying as I became aware that something awesome was taking place. I did not know what it was, but I felt that one had no right to disturb what was happening with the usual recall techniques of psychotherapy . . ."

. . . there was absolutely no recall [Aldous's own account to Humphrey]. Instead there was something of incomparably greater importance; for what came through the closed door was the realization . . . the direct, total awareness, from the inside, so to say, of Love as the primary and fundamental cosmic fact. The words, of course, have a kind of indecency and must necessarily ring false, seem like twaddle. But the fact remains . . . The result was that I did not, as in the first experience, feel cut off from the human world. I was intensely aware of it, but from the standpoint of the living primordial cosmic fact of Love. And things which had entirely occupied . . . my attention on that first occasion I now perceived to be temptations—temptations to escape from the central reality into false, or at least imperfect and partial Nirvanas of beauty and mere knowledge . . .

Another thing that I remember saying and feeling was that I didn't think I should mind dying . . .[2]

At one time in 1955 Aldous had asked Laura lightly, "Have you ever been tempted by marriage?"

I had never been asked that question in such a charming way . . .
. . . [It] launched me into an autobiographical narration of some aspects of my life. It ended with the mention of two men—but these are other stories.

What had chiefly kept her from marriage, she told Aldous, was a fear she had of losing her freedom. Brought up as a musical prodigy on the violin, giving concerts, studying "*avec rage*", her childhood and youth ruled by the disciplines of practice and performance, watched over by a loving and, one would guess,

1 From *This Timeless Moment* op. cit., as all following quotations unless otherwise stated.
2 The complete accounts of the experiences of that day can be found in Laura's book and in Aldous's letter to Humphrey Osmond.

possessive Italian family, Laura had been almost completely deprived of free activity of any kind (reading was regarded as a
sort of luxury, "like going to a masked ball"); and when at length
she did attain a degree of freedom, it was "not by the usual
rebellion . . . but by unflinching arduous work". Much later—
during the war in fact—she gave up the whole thing, her career
as a virtuoso, feeling that it was too life-devouring; and after
trying her hand at various things—breeding poodles, becoming
a professional film-cutter—found that she had got a second major
talent, psychology and its applications. She remained, she says,
attached to freedom in an almost compulsive way. Thus when
Aldous spoke of marriage, it was evident that for her this was not
an easy matter. As the months passed, though, the decision came
to look less formidable. One evening (according to Laura in
January 1956) they were having dinner at North Kings. Aldous
mentioned his lecturing engagements in the spring.

"It might be nice to be in Washington for the cherry blossoms,"
he had said nonchalantly earlier. And then, as if picking up an
interrupted conversation, he said briskly, "Well, now, what about
plans—shouldn't we decide the date we are going to marry?" The
tone was light and gentle . . .

By then they had been spending more and more time together,
had made a few short journeys; Laura had seen the way Aldous
ordered his days—marriage, at that point "would only have been
a confirmation". (To me, shortly after the event, Laura wrote,
". . it evolved as naturally as a Bach fugue.")

. . Aldous continued, "Don't you think we should get married?"
His tone was now more pressing, but not too pressing—he was not
going to force an answer if I were not ready for it. (. . I think he was
incapable of forcing.)

At length Laura answered. "I think it is very logical," she said.
So Aldous's choice was Laura, was not one of the candidates
resolved to enter upon a life of service—Laura Archera with her
misgivings and determination to cling to independence. What she
brought him was youth, drive, courage—her very particular blend
of inspiration and bravado in taking life head on; she brought
her Latinity; intuition, once more, rather than knowledge; discovery, challenge, *Le vierge et le vivace et le bel aujourd'hui*—renewal.
Off they went eventually to Arizona and the Drive-in Chapel.
In Laura's car, Aldous wearing perhaps the new sports shirt. The
forseeable slap-stick procedure, complete with random witness and
confusion over the ring, is described in Laura's book. At one point

she lost her nerve—might Aldous not expect from her "the same total dedication? I loved him and did not want to disappoint him." And now it was too late and public to go into this. She only managed a quick aside, " 'You know, darling, I love others too.' " Aldous with marvellous calm, shot back, " 'It would be awful if you didn't.' " After the ceremony they went to the nearest restaurant; they had hardly sat down when two local reporters swooped down on them. "Aldous was surprised and dismayed . . . [he] gave little satisfaction to the newsmen, but, we heard later, the news was on the radio within an hour.

> I was not worried about my family hearing the news. Aldous had written my father a month before and had received his answer. Ginny [Virginia Pfeiffer, Laura's greatest friend, in whose house she had been living for many years] knew that we were getting married . . I had taken it for granted that Aldous had made a similar arrangement. I did not quite realize that it was in Aldous's nature to act first and speak later . . .

Now she was a bit flabbergasted to hear that to Gerald yesterday Aldous had been talking about cockroaches and telepathy—"but not of our marriage!

> I thought Aldous seemed worried out of proportion by the sudden appearance of the journalists. As soon as they left, I understood why; he had not told his son yet and was deeply distressed . . .

They drove to the next resort and rented a bungalow. Did any thought of his own father come to Aldous's mind as he now addressed himself to the task of writing those letters? When Leonard Huxley had married again in 1912, his intentions, it has been said, were casually, or clumsily, revealed, and for his younger children at least there was an element of shock. (Aldous himself, though he insisted that there wasn't any one-to-one relation between Mr Beavis and his parent, worked off the theme of father breaking the news to son in *Eyeless in Gaza*.) The position of course was different. When Leonard married again, Aldous was an adolescent and his sister still a child; there could be no question now of Laura making another home for Matthew, a man in his mid-thirties and a father in his own right. The boot, here, was on the other leg: Matthew at his mother's death, if in psychological more than practical fact, must have felt that it was for him to continue her role as Aldous's shield. A natural role, on his side, given his affectionate nature and profound concern, and a role in which he had been trained implicitly since childhood by Maria. That this would never become quite feasible, second or no second marriage, because Aldous did not wish to accept protection—open and entire—for a second time, and because he too, like D. H. Lawrence, if in a different way, was a man who "needed to have a woman back of him", may already have been partly evident to Matthew. Only the situation would have been so very much more acceptable if the ground had been prepared; a post facto announcement by those we love is always hurtful. The actual mischief was caused by the media. Was Aldous to blame for not having thought of himself as newsworthy? (One remembers that when he met Stravinsky at the Town and Country Market, he introduced himself to the maestro as the uncle of Claire and Sylvia Nicolas.) Was he to blame for having misjudged the apparent obscurity of an improbable Western wedding-mill? However, the pouncing of the media would not have mattered if Aldous had exercised, not foresight about the workings of the press, but insight about human beings—Laura had told *her* best friend, had thought it proper for Aldous to bring in her father (by some elegant formula no doubt, and short of asking for her actual hand)—people like to be allowed to feel a part of things, and if Aldous's handling did turn out not to have been the most considerate to Matthew, it was also not the fairest one to Laura. Surely it might have been a good deal easier for all concerned, if his friends had already met Laura, seen them together, even if, or because, this would have led to talk? But then one of the few things Aldous was passionately attached to was his privacy (not withstanding the paradox of what he was capable of putting into a novel). In the event, the bad start was mitigated by the almost general good will. After an initial tremor, families and friends were glad to be able think of Aldous as no longer on his own. He and Laura returned to a North Kings filled with flowers and an accumulation of affectionate messages and good wishes.

Chapter Four

3276 Deronda Drive, L.A.

FIRST-RECORDED-INTRODUCTIONS were to Betty and
to Mme Nys.

> Monday, 26th March [Betty's journal]: Lunch with Aldous and
> Laura. I felt strange arriving at Kings Road. Passed the house and
> left the car on the street instead of parking in the driveway. When I
> rang the bell Aldous came to the door, as usual. We went no further
> than the living room instead of his workroom. In a moment or two
> Laura joined us. She came towards me with outstretched hand.
> She looked very serious. Aldous was completely at ease, I was not at
> the beginning. Laura said that Aldous had spoken of me often; I
> could *not* say he had spoken of her.

Laura told Betty that she had read the script of the play and
how much she liked it and hoped they would continue to work
on it together. A little girl of four ran into the room, she was one
of Virginia Pfeiffer's two adopted children whom Laura was
helping to bring up.

> They began to tell me all about Yuma and the Wedding Chapel.
> Laura stopped looking serious after a little while. We talked and
> laughed . . .

"Not as old friends of course . . It was much too soon for that,
but as new acquaintances who were getting on well together. And
it was the start of a new and lasting friendship." After lunch
Virginia Pfeiffer came to the house—" 'Ginny', Laura's great
friend—a pleasant looking, dark haired, dark eyed woman."
Mme Nys wrote to Jeanne that she found it "tout à fait normal
qu'il refasse sa vie." Laura telephoned her, thanking her "de mon
gentil message," demandant si je pourrais les recevoir l'après-midi.

> Aldous m'apportait des roses du jardin. J'ai embrassé Laura en lui
> souhaitant la bien venue . . . Aldous *si beau*, calme et communicatif.
> Assis à coté de moi, j'ai tout à coup dit à la jeune femme—Venez
> vous asseoir aussi à mes cotés et la main dans la main je les écoutais . . .

In the evening Mme Nys telephoned Matthew as he had asked
her to. "I said, it is hard for Laura to fill that place . . . It is up
to *us*, not to make the comparison."

In April Aldous with Laura went off to lecture, first at Lexington, Kentucky, then at Washington and Baltimore. They went on to New York to meet Matthew, Ellen and the children, and a number of Aldous's friends. (One of them told me how Aldous, helping Laura into her coat, said over her shoulder with great glee, "Laura does things in phases. She has had music. She has had dogs. Now she is—temporarily—having husbands.") After their return to Los Angeles Aldous, not yet settled in a book, was thinking of doing something practical about the population problem with Bill Kiskadden, who had been twice to India and Indonesia within the last three years and had "returned with a very urgent feeling that something more should be done about [it] . . than the writing of yet another report." What they thought of doing was to make a few pilot films for exhibition, by mobile projectors, in Indian villages. ". . . audio-visual propaganda . . to reduce the Indian birth-rate," Aldous wrote to Julian.

> . . Kiskadden has asked me to ask you if you would also give your name, so as to lend weight to the organization . . . Kiskadden is extremely *sérieux*, a great virtuoso surgeon, who has now, in his early sixties, turned to population control as the work of the rest of his life. He is a man of great determination . . .

Meanwhile Aldous had read the American Academy of Science's report on the genetic effects of radiation. How wonderfully close, he remarked, modern history is coming to the phantasies of the *Arabian Nights* and *Grimm's Fairy Tales*—

> the stories of the fishermen [to Matthew] who let the djinn out of the bottle and couldn't put it back . . . the more philosophical variant of the three wishes theme, W. W. Jacobs' "The Monkey's Paw", where the old people wish for a hundred pounds and get it, thanks to the magic paw, as compensation for the death of their son. Atoms will give us all the power we want, but at the price of multiplying the number of monsters and, perhaps, bitching up the whole human species.

Laura could not get herself accustomed to living in North Kings, so they found another house: high up in the Hollywood hills, in wild country. They would be within a few hundred yards of Virginia Pfeiffer's house, Aldous wrote to Matthew, ". . where there is a swimming pool, along with Virginia's adopted children, to whom Laura is much attached." On 16th July they moved.

Aldous, sending his new address to Humphrey, seemed delighted.
3276 Deronda Drive. Fire bricks to walk on,

> . . virtually no smog and an incredible view over the city to the
> south and over completely savage hills in every other direction, hills
> which remind me a little of Greece in their barrenness . . . Moving
> has been a job, and it will be a while before things are in order . . .

For Laura was completely redecorating the house, making of
it something light and bright. She was dreaming of "a marvellously
shining white surface.

> To throw out a new carpet [which had come with the house]
> would seem a needless extravagance to most husbands, but Aldous
> generously agreed . . .
> Aldous was fascinated by reflections of light, and that floor became
> an unending source of pleasure. Sometimes, coming home late at
> night, we would delight in finding the moonlight reflected on the
> living-room floor as on a pond.

They decided not to sell North Kings before the end of the
summer so that Ellen and the children could use it for a holiday.
("Matthew, poor wretch, has to remain in New Haven where
his boss's unexpected retirement leaves him in charge of the
office.") Aldous, too, was busy and beset with dead-lines: three
long articles for *Esquire* in one go, owing to the editorial timetable, and there was still much to be done to the play. No, he
wrote to Humphrey, he could not manage to take part in the
series of half-hour television shows on CBS; and even if he had
unbounded leisure he would decline on second thoughts—un-
welcome publicity, people stopping one in the street to say how
much they liked, or disliked, what you said. Particularly annoying
after a TV show on mescalin.

> Mescalin, it seems to me, and the odder aspects of mind are matters
> to be written about for a small public, not discussed on TV in the
> presence of a vast audience of baptists, methodist and nothing-but-
> men plus an immense lunatic fringe, eager to tell you about *my*
> revelation and to get hold of the dope on its own account. One gets
> plenty of lunatic fringe even after . . a two and a half dollar book . . .
> . . . I had a letter a few days ago from Mauritius, from a gentleman
> who went out there twenty years ago to achieve enlightenment and . .
> has now written the most extraordinary book on the world's history,
> and will I please write an introduction . . And I say nothing of the
> gentleman in Chicago who has discovered the Absolute Truth and
> sends letters and telegrams about it to President Eisenhower and
> Bertrand Russell . . . nor the young man from Yorkshire who ate a

peyote button . . . and for three days heard all music one tone higher
than it should have been . . .

  As you say . . we still know very little about the psychodelics, and,
until we know a good deal more, I think the matter should be
discussed . . in the relative privacy of learned journals, the decent
obscurity of moderately highbrow books and articles. Whatever
one says on the air is bound to be misunderstood . . .

  (*Psychodelics*. "About a name for these drugs—what a problem!"
Aldous had written to Humphrey a while ago. Could they call
them psychophans? or phaneropsychic drugs? "I have looked into
Liddell and Scott and find that there is a verb phaneroein, 'to
make visible or manifest,' and an adjective phaneros, meaning
'manifest, open to sight, evident' . . . or what about phanerothymes?
Thumos means soul . . . and is equivalent of Latin animus. The
word is euphonious and easy to pronounce; besides it has relatives
in the jargon of psychology—e.g. cyclothyme. On the whole I
think this is better than psychophan or phaneropsychic . .

> To make this trivial world sublime,
> Take half a gramme of phanerothyme."

However, Humphrey Osmond stuck to the name he had originally
come up with ("To fathom Hell or soar angelic, Just take a pinch
of psychedelic.") Psychedelic—to Aldous psychodelic—it became.)
  Busy; and at peace. "I, too am well," Aldous wrote to Victoria
Ocampo during the summer, telling her that he had married a
young Italian woman. ". . She gets on very well with my friends,
and they with her. I am very sure that you will like her. The
terrible sadness of Maria's last months . . [has] retreated, and my
memories of her are now happy, grateful, happy memories. And
that she survives and develops, I feel sure . . ."
  Aldous enjoyed Ellen's stay with Trev and Tessa, and the
ensuing family whirl—Rose and her children also camping in
North Kings, outings with Virginia Pfeiffer's little boy and girl,
hospitable gatherings round her swimming pool—and at the same
time (with workmen still in his own house) he was beginning to
come to grips at last with the long-hatched Good Utopia.

  I am now starting to work [to Humphrey] on the play revisions as
  well as on my phantasy, which begins, as I make notes, to take the
  rudiments of shape.

Even so he was still undecided whether to get on with it "full
blast," or to tackle a dramatic version of *Brave New World*—
B.N.W. "might be very profitable. Or it might not . . ."

  Frieda Lawrence died on 11th August. "How strange their

careers were!" Aldous was later moved to write to Victor F. White.[1]

The coalminer's son escaping, via Frieda, into the larger world, beyond his social conditioning. And the Richthofen, who had somehow blundered into marriage with possibly the dullest Professor in the Western hemisphere, escaping, via Lawrence into that same world and into an old age in that New Mexico desert which was, in some sort, a projection of her own deep nature. How improbable! But that is the charm and horror of human history: the impossible actually happens—all the time.

In September Julian and Juliette came for a fortnight's visit. The house was still unfinished.

. . We had the big bedroom downstairs [writes Juliette[2]]—no cupboards yet. Laura left after three days, taught me to drive that panther of a car, and went off with Ginny to the desert. Aldous took us to San Diego [to the incomparable zoo] to Disney Land, to see his friend Grace Hubble, the musician Porter . . I cooked for him and Julian, we fed in the little kitchen—very happy. Lots of talk between J. and A. . .

The brothers did the scientific sights, the new Salk Institute at La Jolla, John Lilly's experience with dolphins, which meant long expeditions by car "on the great speedways of California [Julian in his *Memories*[3]]. Juliette was often driving Aldous's leaping car with her heart in her mouth, amazed at Aldous's grasp of the map and his perfect direction: he had an unfailing memory of the landscape and of the maze of Los Angeles' motorways." They went to see the animal experiments at the University of California. These must certainly, wrote Julian, give the rats pleasure, and Aldous enlarged upon this to Humphrey:

. . rats and cats and monkeys with electrodes stuck into various areas of their brains. They press a little lever which gives them a short, mild electric shock—and the experiment . . is evidently so ecstatically wonderful, that they will go on at the rate of eight thousand self-stimuli per hour until they collapse from exhaustion, lack of food and sleep. We are obviously getting very close to reproducing the Moslem paradise where every orgasm lasts six hundred years.

[1] The late Dominican Philosopher and Psychologist, author of *God and the Unconscious* etc. etc.   [2] In a letter to S. B.
[3] Sir Julian Huxley, *Memories* Vol. II. Allen & Unwin, 1973.

"Though perched on the heights above Los Angeles, Aldous was far from leading a hermit's life.[1] While we were with him, there was a stream of visitors—Linus Pauling, Gerald Heard, Christopher Isherwood, Romain Gary . . Lesley Blanch . . Professor Harrison Brown, population expert . . Dr William Kiskadden . . Bertalanffy, Alistair Cooke . . . Aldous was the fulcrum of the conversation . . . He seemed to radiate what journalists now call *charisma*, which added quality to the moment, as we sat around on the terrace of his little house, watching the wide evening sky."

After the Julian Huxleys leave, Aldous is distractedly busy making up for time—he has got to write the outline for a TV film on over-population and a speech on the History of Tension for the N.Y. Academy of Sciences, and there is his usual article for *Esquire* as well as the first act of a musical comedy version of *Brave New World* to get on with. (Musical comedy, "for everybody tells me that [it] can never succeed as a straight play.") The Utopian phantasy has to be laid aside for the time being. In October he and Laura fly off to New York for his speech on the 18th.

> Our time in New York was a bit strenuous [to Humphrey]. The NY Academy . . have a publicity man so marvellously active that, on my arrival, I found no less than seven radio and TV appearances lined up for me, at hours ranging from six thirty in the morning to eleven fifteen at night. The conference on meprobamate [the tranquillizer] was quite interesting and I made some pleasant acquaintances—Dr [F. M.] Berger, the inventor of Miltown, and Dr James Miller, who heads a . . group at Ann Arbor, investigating human behaviour and trying to establish some kind of common language among psychologists, chemists, economists, sociologists and ministers. A commendable project . . .

(One eminent bio-chemist, according to Aldous, suggested—not entirely playfully—that the United States government should make a free gift to the Soviet people of fifty billion doses of the tranquillizer.)

Then within days of his return to Los Angeles Aldous left again for St Louis to attend a seminar on human potentialities, returning the same Saturday to do a TV show with Gerald the next day. He was obviously going through a streak of exceptionally good health (partly due perhaps to his desire to keep up with Laura; though he appears to have out-done her. "On these exhausting days [Laura wrote] when we returned to the hotel to take a breath and get ready for dinner, Aldous took me to my room, saying, 'You rest a little, darling. I am going to take a turn around the block and will be back in time to change my suit.' ")

[1] Julian Huxley, op. cit.

In December he did catch a bout of flu ("feeling low and mouldy"), but emerged before the year was out—the first act of the musical *Brave New World* was finished; Matthew had accepted an excellent new job; Mme Nys continued to report to Jeanne with unabated goodwill: "We must rejoice to see Aldous so calm and in such good form . . . I told him *combien Laura était bonne et gentille . . . Chaque fois que je la revoie je me réjouis qu'Aldous l'ait rencontrée.*" "May 1957," Aldous wrote to Humphrey on post-Suez Christmas Day "be as happy as the lunatics in the world's chanceries will permit . . ."

To Julian and Juliette he had this to say in January,

What we are paying for four hundred years of white imperialism—and how long, to all appearances, we shall go on paying! Asians and Africans do not forget and are so far from forgiving that, if they can thereby do some harm to the ex-imperialists, they will blithely damage themselves, even commit suicide. If I can spite your face I will cut off my nose. There is no appeal from these passions even to self-interest . . And the trouble is that these deep rooted passions can now be implemented in violent practice. The great truth enunciated by Hilaire Belloc:

> *Whatever happens, we have got*
> *The Maxim gun, and they have not—*

has unhappily ceased to be true. *They* now have the Maxim gun—and unless the West is prepared to out-trump the gun with atomic missiles, *they* will soon be in a position . . to win all the "little wars". If I remember rightly, Nostradamus prophesied that in the year two thousand or thereabouts, yellow men would be flying over Paris. It may easily turn out that he was right.

The Bates system once more has come under attack, this time in England by an article in the *People* by Philip Pollack, a Helmholtzian oculist (obviously, Aldous thought, of the old school "who regard the eye as an optical instrument and take no account of the mind-body with which it is associated"). Aldous writes to Ian Parsons that he thinks it best to do nothing about the whole business.

. . *The Art of Seeing* is about the mental side of seeing and the improvement of function—not by "exercises", as Pollack likes to call them, but by training in relaxed activity. *Even if there are no physical changes in the eye, seeing can be improved by proper function.* [My italics] This is something which someone who has never thought in terms of psychosomatic medicine cannot understand.

Aldous goes on to point out for the record that he has "never claimed to be able to read [without spectacles] except under very good [light] conditions." Incidentally he had just embarked on a new treatment aimed at getting rid of some of the scar tissue on his corneas—a combination of diet and the administration of a sulphur compound "(eyes with cataract and, in general, most sick and ageing eyes, have shown to be short of sulphur, which is normally in rather high concentration in the eye tissues) . . . The man who has developed this treatment is a very experienced old ophthalmologist, who has had many successes, both with cataracts and corneal opacities. It would be wonderful if the treatment had even a very small effect . ."

In February Aldous learned that his *Esquire* articles had to come to an end—the magazine was changing its format, more pictures, less reading matter.

> . . Evidently the majority of the public don't want to read, and now that so many cents in the advertising dollar go to TV, the magazine publishers (with the resounding crash of *Collier's* and *Woman's Home Companion* still ringing in their ears) must do everything in their power to increase circulation . . .
>
> . . So this convenient and well-paid pulpit has been pulled out from under me. I regret it very much . . .

Aldous agreed to work once more, briefly, at a Hollywood studio, UPA, doing an outline for an animated cartoon of Don Quixote; then involved himself—"goodness knows why"—in yet another dramatic project, an adaptation of *After Many a Summer*. One cannot say that he went into it with eyes shut. ". . This theatrical world is dreadfully exasperating [to Anita Loos]; and if I didn't have other things to do, I should find my present, small involvement in it very nerve-racking. To write a play is certainly to ask for trouble."

No clinching offer had been made yet for *The Genius and the Goddess* (Alfred de Liagre was still interested, and Arthur Penn; and Binkie Beaumont was thinking of doing the play in London). Now Courtney Burr, producer of *Seven Year Itch* and *Bad Seed*, came up with an advance of $3000 and a definite production date. Betty sped off to New York.

> Delly had been the one Aldous and I most wanted to produce that poor, poor play. And when Burr offered us that advance and promised us the world, we still wanted Delly to co-produce, and he was willing, but Burr wanted to go it alone . . .

By the end of March the agreement with him was signed.

Aldous, still in pursuit of staging *Brave New World*, wrote to

Robert Craft about the music. Whom would *he* advise? There was Leonard Bernstein of course, and someone had suggested sending the thing to Rodgers and Hammerstein.

> Needless to say, if the maestro felt inclined to take some time off to do something light—a little ballet music for the brave new worlders . . . I would be only too happy. But I hesitate to ask him—wouldn't want to do so before finding out what you think.

Stravinsky, apparently, did not take it up, for ten days later Aldous wrote to Leonard Bernstein. "As a very busy man with a large correspondence, I can well understand your annoyance at receiving yet another letter from a perfect stranger. But at the risk of being a bore . . ." (No composer for *Brave New World* has been found to this day.)

In April Aldous spent a week lecturing in San Francisco and at Stanford; in May, without Laura, he flew East, first for a weekend with Matthew and Ellen, then for lectures at Washington and the University of New Hampshire. In New York he talked to his new producer—"We have an excellent leading lady, Nancy Kelly, but not yet a leading man . . ." and saw people in various Foundations in the hope of getting someone to sponsor a TV documentary on over-population.

> . . (We have a little Foundation of our own, called Population Limited, rich in talent—my brother Julian, Harrison Brown, Kingsley Davies, the sociologist, Fred Zinnemann, the film director, Bill Kiskadden—but poor in money.) . . . I have written a synopsis of a film on Egypt—because it is better to attack the general through the particular, and because Egypt is a particularly painful case . . . Everyone agrees that the population problem is the most important problem of the present century; but nobody wants to get in trouble with the Papists . . .

On 15th July Aldous and Betty were summoned to New York to attend the first reading of the play.

Chapter Five

A Misadventure

AS matters turned out, Aldous was kept in New York through the worst of summer until late November. I shall not attempt to give more than an outline of the dismal tale. Things looked wrong from the beginning. Aldous and Betty found out that Courtney Burr, behind their backs, had engaged another collaborator (Alec Coppel) who was to be given programme credit and to whom they were to pay a quarter of their royalties. Betty wanted to go home then and there; Aldous persuaded her to stay. Now Burr, at first so enthusiastic about the play, changed his mind, insisting that it was unproducable in its present form. Aldous, on the assumption that he must know less than the professionals, reluctantly agreed to have the play re-shaped. Coppel dropped the play-within-the-play and turned out a weak domestic comedy with a single plot line and a happy ending; "a fairly slick piece of conventional craftsmanship," Aldous called it, but without depth and a weak and "somewhat phony" ending. He was assured by the experts that the new play was a better piece of dramatic writing and much more likely to be a commercial success. "Once again I made the enormous mistake of believing them."

Aldous and Betty, at the producer's request, were kept busy through the gruelling summer writing and re-writing and re-writing dialogue and scenes in an effort to infuse some quality and substance into the new version. "It was a pretty hopeless task," Aldous summed it up four months too late, "but I did my best. I listened to the suggestions of those whom I mistakenly believed to be more competent . . ."

He and Betty were at the Shoreham Hotel on West 55th Street, each in a bed-sitter with kitchenette. (By contract they were to receive $20 a day each for their living expenses. "Burr kept off paying us [Betty]; but at last began to do so when rehearsals started.") There was little time to see friends or do other things. In the evening they would often eat at one of the smaller French or Italian Westside restaurants; Aldous, in spite of heat and irritation, with a healthy appetite. When they got tired of each other's company, they would cook themselves a mess of vegetables on their hot-plates. (Aldous indeed had started eating meat again some years before, but as far as I know never tried to cook it.) On home nights he was apt to appear in Betty's door, steaming plate in hand—"If I give you half my mushrooms, will you let me have one of your artichokes?" and withdraw again to his own quarters with the loot. On the whole, he said, New York was not too bad; only four or five really equatorial days a month. He managed to go to the—"beautiful"—loan exhibition of French paintings at the Metropolitan, and look at the big Picasso show at the Museum of Modern Art "(what a lot of slapdash shoddy stuff surrounding the twenty or thirty masterpieces!)" Once or twice Laura came East to see him, and in September stopped on her way to Italy where she was going to remain with her father in Turin until the opening of the play.

One muggy day Betty, returning to the hotel, was met by the manageress, a kindly lady, in a state of agitation.

"I'm so glad you are back Mrs Wendel—have you seen Mr Huxley?"

"No."

"Well, he is up on the roof—and he ought to come down!"

Betty asked what was the matter.

"You'll *see* when you get up there."

From the tenth floor, where Aldous had his apartment, an iron stairway led to the roof—tarred and pebble flooring, a safety rail of sorts, clothes-lines, some tattered canvas chairs—there in the blazing sun was Aldous, barefoot, but otherwise completely dressed in a suit with the collar turned up, his long arms widespread and flapping as he was slowly revolving on his own axis, looking for all the world both like Don Quixote *and* the windmill.

"Aldous!" Betty at last managed to call out. She could tell that he had heard her by the changes in the tempo of his flapping, but he did not speak until his slow rotation let him face her again. Then he said, "This damned suit won't get dry."

"How did it get wet?" Betty asked; then, gathering her wits, "Why are you drying it *on* you?"

Still flapping and revolving, Aldous said, "I washed it on me under the shower and then trotted up here. The label says 'Wash & Let Drip Dry.' The only other suit I have for this damned heat is at the cleaners."

Eventually Burr's new director, Richard Whorf, arrived and the situation—"after weeks of irritation and ineptitude"—seemed to look a little brighter. But now new changes were suggested and "summarily made—mainly consisting of cuts, which reduced many scenes to a kind of digest of themselves." Rehearsals began in October, and on the 13th of November the play opened at New Haven, Connecticut with Nancy Kelly as Katy, the English actor Alan Webb as Maartens, and Michael Toland as young John Rivers. The week after it went on to Philadelphia. (After the first or second night there, Aldous sent a letter to his leading lady which is of interest because of what he so openly says about D. H. L. and Frieda. He was distressed, he wrote, to think that he had failed in the play to make his conception of Katy, the goddess, clear to her. It was very clear to him because he used to know very well a specimen of the breed.

This was Frieda Lawrence, the wife of D. H. Lawrence. I think I told you the other day about the miraculous way in which she raised Lawrence almost from death when he was ill with influenza (super-imposed upon . . TB) in my house. Katy's miracle with Henry is merely a transcription of what I myself saw, thirty years ago. (Incidently the miracle was chronic. Thanks to Frieda, Lawrence remained alive for at least five years after he ought, by all the rules of medicine, to have been in the grave.) Frieda (and Katy is a non-German and less Rabelaisian version of Frieda) was a woman of enormous strength and vitality, completely untouched by the neuroses of the Age of Anxiety. Everything that Katy-Frieda does, she does with her whole heart. With a whole heart she loves and admires her genius and with a whole heart she quarrels with him. (Frieda used to throw plates at Lawrence, and Lawrence threw them back at her. I have spared you this!) Again, it is with a whole heart that Katy-Frieda looks after her man when he is sick, and it is with a whole heart that she makes fun of him when he is being peevish or ridiculous. Frieda and Lawrence had, undoubtedly, a profound and passionate love-life. But this did not prevent Frieda from having, every now and then, affairs with Prussian cavalry officers and Italian peasants, whom she loved for a season without in any way detracting from her love for Lawrence or from her intense devotion to his genius. Lawrence, for his part, was aware of these erotic excursions, got angry about them sometimes, but never made the least effort to break away from her; as he realized his own organic dependence upon her . . .

Frieda . . was profoundly matter-of-fact, accepting events as they were given, in all their painful or delightful confusion. She had little patience with idealism or exalted ethical systems. Her essentially realistic view of life was expressed in Shakespeare's words in *King Lear*—"Ripeness is all." This ripeness of realism made some people feel, at a first meeting, that she was rather rough and even a little heartless. But her teasing . . was always profoundly good-natured. She would speak ironical words, but out of a depth of human kindness and sympathy. Another characteristic trait was her child-likeness . . product of her capacity . . for living fully in each successive moment, as a child does. And this gave her a certain superficial air of inconsistency . . . Finally, she had the most sovereign disregard for what people might think or say about her—a disregard based upon a certain native aristocracy, on the confidence of a very rich personality in its own essential rightness and excellence. This meant that she was never anxious, never apologetic, never tense or nervous. She did everything—baking bread, scrubbing floors, making her own clothes, tending the sick genius—with the unhurried, easy serenity of the heroines and goddesses of the Homeric myths. Her speech reflected the same spirit. She spoke slowly, deliberately, relishing the words she used (for she had a great command of language, even in a tongue which was not her own) . . .

At New Haven, the producer engaged yet another expert who wrote new lines and one entire scene; these were rehearsed—in secret—at Philadelphia. Aldous found out and "This final outrage was too much even for my long-suffering nature". He left for New York to consult his lawyer and his agent,[1] Betty remaining as his watch-dog. Meanwhile the unauthorized lines and scene were actually played on the last night in Philadelphia. On 23rd November Courtney Burr tried to keep Betty away from the performance on a pretext, but she went (upheld by Laura and her own husband, Sanford Wendel, who had arrived and rallied). On the 25th the play went on to Boston. Aldous, on professional advice, sent the following telegram to Burr on the same date.

You have flagrantly breached your minimum basic production contract with us by inserting material and making changes in the play without our consent . . . and have further and in various ways conducted yourself arbitrarily without regard to our rights as authors . . . we hereby demand that you correct the foregoing breaches within three days. If you fail to make such corrections within that period, all your rights in the play shall automatically terminate . . . Beth Wendel will remain in Boston during the three day period with authority of both of us to attend rehearsals and grant script approvals.

Aldous Huxley   Beth Wendel

On the same day Aldous exhorted Betty by letter to get hold of the script. "The only hope—and in view of what these people are it is rather a slim hope—lies in having a script, of which the more important parts can, if necessary, be photostated, so that we can produce them as evidence of what we have agreed to. They will of course want to discuss things; but my advice, and the advice of Helen [Harvey] and the lawyer, is, Don't. Just ask for the script."

Burr actually did remove the unauthorized material before the

---

[1] Mr Arnold Weissberger and Mrs Helen Harvey, who was then running the William Morris Agency.

end of the Boston run (4th December), but then inserted scenes
which had already been vetoed by the authors during rehearsal.
Aldous gave up and returned to California, having demanded
that their names be taken off the play. *The Genius and the Goddess*
opened on Broadway on 10th December, Aldous Huxley and
Beth Wendel appearing on the playbill. The play closed on 14th
December after a run of five nights.

Helen Harvey, fifteen years later, made this comment (the
actual business correspondence is already destroyed) ". . I do
recall that the production was horrendous. Many of the people
involved were as incompetent and inefficient as is usual around
the theatre, and Aldous Huxley simply could not believe that
these professionals really didn't know what they were doing! So
he went on re-writing, re-thinking and re-doing, until he himself
was just as confused as the rest of them."[1]

Aldous, then, peacefully ensconced once more in his Hollywood
hills, wrote an article, "Postscript to a Misadventure," then
thought better of it, decided to leave ill alone and put the M/S
into a drawer. A copy of it survived at Matthew's; there are one
or two nice bits which Aldous, I am sure, would not mind being
published now. "This story," he wrote, "a very commonplace
one, as I am assured by those who know their Broadway—has
several morals.

First, even during the frenzies of production, the writer should keep
his artistic head and retain what I may call (since "the courage of
his convictions" is not the right phrase) the obstinacy of his intuitions.
Second, he should be extremely sceptical of any claim to superior
wisdom on the part of those who call themselves experts . . . Third,
if he wants to go on writing plays, let him have them produced in
some place where the costs are less exorbitantly high than they are
on Broadway . . . exorbitantly high costs . . create, in the minds of all
concerned, the anxious sense of being embarked upon a very dangerous and deadly serious adventure, where humour and light-
heartedness are as much out of place as they would be on a burning
ship in the middle of the Pacific Ocean. A play should have something
playful about it. But how can anyone feel playful about a hundred-
thousand dollar investment? In the grimness of these desperate
theatrical gambles the amenities of life and even its common
decencies are apt to go by the board.

His private post-mortem Aldous wrote to Betty in a letter of
15th December. ". . all's well, or can at least be made fairly well,
that ends badly.

1 From a letter to S. B.

Weissberger has advised strongly against suing for damages, and I shall follow his advice. If the expense money can be extracted from these people, it will be a small triumph. If not, then it will be another loss that has to be written off. I have already had to write off four months of time . . . My motive for leaving the play at Philadelphia was disgust—the feeling that I didn't want to be associated any further with people who had broken their word and violated their written agreement. Writing articles and suing for damages, would be a kind of continuance of that association in negative terms, and I don't want to get involved in that.

Meanwhile what a comfort it is to be doing some kind of useful and interesting work once more!

There remains one question—what about the play? The final version of *The Genius and the Goddess* as written by Aldous and Betty? This version exists, but the question cannot be answered because (to date) it has never seen the foot-lights of an English-speaking stage.[1]

[1] It was televised in Australia, and in Germany and Switzerland in Herbert E. Herlitschka's translation.

Chapter Six

Towards a Topian Phantasy

FOR the next six months, the first half of 1958, Aldous stayed put, writing away quietly. He finished *Brave New World Revisited*, his short book—of some effect, he hoped—on the problem of freedom in an age of over-population, a series of articles—he called them that rather than essays—on governmental and economic power and all the means for reducing psychological resistance from brainwashing and advertising to (potentially) drugs and hyponoapaedia, and about what might be done to counteract these menaces by holding on to old fundamentals—"Every human being is biologically unique . . . The Sabbath is made for man"—and by new methods of education. He had also polished off a commissioned article for the *Saturday Evening Post* on the social and ethical implications of psycho-pharmacology.[1] It was work which Aldous could turn to at almost any time, material he had at his finger-tips, though it always remained hard labour to shape it into a lucid ("snappy" he hoped) and convincing form. And did it convince? *Was* it to some effect? Did his exhortations ever reach the right men in the right place? These were questions he was much aware of. "And, over and above the normal difficulties,

> I have to wrestle with the problem of not seeing properly [to Humphrey]—which makes all research and consulting of notes such an enormous burden. Which is all, no doubt, ultimately All Right—but proximately pretty fatiguing!

Julian touches on this in his *Memories*.[2] "How Aldous managed to absorb (and still more to digest) the colossal amount of facts and ideas which furnished his mind remains a mystery . . . Maria devotedly read to him for hours at a time; and with his one good eye, he managed to skim through learned journals, popular articles and books of every kind. He was apparently able to take them in at a glance, and what is more, to remember their essential content. His intellectual memory was phenomenal, doubtless trained by a tenacious will to surmount the original horror of threatened blindness . . ."

[1] "Drugs that Shape Men's Mind." October 1958.
[2] *Memories* Vol. II cit.

"But I am sick and tired of this kind of writing," Aldous said to Ellen when *Brave New World Revisited* was finished. Yet at least these months were even ones, a stretch of time without major anxieties or upheavals, no house move or hotel existence, and above all good health at home. Laura was doing her share for Virginia's children as well as being extremely busy with her patients. (Laura, Aldous said to Christopher Isherwood, "is becoming a walking Grotto of Lourdes.") It was in this New Year's Honours that Julian received his knighthood—"I'm delighted," Aldous wrote to him, ". . and hope that . . you will be able to feel as happy about it as I do." The one bad personal news was Bill Kiskadden's cardiac operation in February, a most frightful operation Aldous called it. "He has recovered—but is still in a sadly diminished state . . ."

Mme Nys, too, was coming out of a time of illness, "thanks to God, to Rose, to Laura and to Aldous."

"Laura telephoned . . ." "Quick dinner with Aldous and Laura before the theatre . . ." "Aldous et Laura dinent chez moi . ." ". . asked to lunch at Mrs Pfeiffer's . . ." "Laura has given [Maria's] Oldsmobile to Rose." "Dinner *en ville* with A & L, followed by a concert, Boulez, Stravinsky . . ." "Laura, without my having asked, took me to the cemetery on Maria's name-day." "Aldous came with books . . . brought flowers . . ." The letters to France are full of such amiable odds and ends, implicit reassurance to Jeanne.

Everybody seems to come out of this pretty well. What of Mme Nys? Was this Mère, the woman who had caused those agonizing conflicts in Maria (her favourite, her beloved daughter), and provoked so often even Aldous's strictures? The personality that arises from the correspondence appears a good deal more tolerant and sympathetic. Were they unjust to her, or had she mellowed? (Did not Maria write, only so lately, "Ma mère est devenue une femme bonne et douce"?) Matthew always loved her; she adored him (and had devoted herself to him when he was a little boy at St Trond). She was less pleasant to one or two of her grandchildren and she certainly made life exceedingly hard for Rose. Perhaps something of the truth can be got hold of in Jeanne's mature reflections: Mère was horribly difficult, horribly exigent and touchy in everyday life; she talked too much, she would not listen, she was always right—*Mère est odieuse!* the sisters used to cry. One could not live with her; they loved her from afar. (Mark that, unlike Maria or Rose, Jeanne and Suzanne were seldom under the same roof with her.) Yet she was also good and generous and resolute and capable, and these virtues she deployed particularly on what Jeanne calls the grand occasions: Mère was at her best in crisis, illness, war. Uncommonly self-centred, she could transcend self-interest—Elle avait des élans grandioses. She had profound affection and respect for Aldous; and after Maria's death recognized his choice and need, and accepted it with grace and fairness.

In the spring, with *Brave New World Revisited* off his hands, all was serene enough for Aldous to return to wider latitudes, yet he still found it hard to get the Utopian novel flowing. The present difficulty was not the subject matter, which was so very near his heart—and Laura's—a society in which serious efforts are made to realize human potentialities of sanity and happiness; nor the locale—a hypothetical island between Ceylon and Sumatra which due to a lack of harbour had had the historical luck of escaping colonialism; the difficulty was the working out of a story line to hold the thing together.

I don't know yet [to Humphrey in June] if I have a satisfactory fable, or how much of a fable will be necessary, or . . how reluctant people will be to read material which isn't straight story telling . . .

Meanwhile he went on feeling his way into the book— ". . the only thing is to go ahead, one step at a time . . ." He was also finding himself involved once more with the stage. The play was his, Laura was the producer, an undaunted one as it turned out. She put on *The Gioconda Smile* at Los Angeles through thick and thin, as Aldous said,

. . Like the generals of earlier days who used to have horses shot under them in their decisive battles, she has had about six complete casts shot under her in the course of her campaign—only to come up with better replacements, so that now we have a first-rate collection of English actors, highly competent and thoroughly trained . . .

Aldous attended rehearsals, listening with closed eyes (and congratulated his leading lady, Sylvia Marriot, on being word-perfect from day one). The play opened at the Beverly Hills Playhouse on the last Friday in June, (the Stravinskys in the audience) and ran for about six weeks, losing, as Laura put it, "a little bit of money".

The second half of 1958 was spent travelling. The Brazilian government invited Aldous to visit the country, he and Laura left for their first long journey together in July. They flew to Lima by way of Mexico City and spent some time in Peru. In

August they arrived in Rio de Janeiro where Aldous received a tremendous reception (one newspaper carried a daily column about him headed *O Sabio, The Sage*) and had to submit to interviews, official luncheons and a lecture at the Foreign Office. Then came the sights; they were taken to Brasilia, which expectedly he found inhuman, to Bahia, to São Paulo, and were flown up the Amazon in an army plane to the Matto Grosso to visit a tribe of stone-age Indians. They landed, unannounced, in the middle of the jungle and were swarmed upon by a horde of brown, stark-naked, friendly, shouting people, every which of them a good two feet shorter than Aldous, who moved about them fascinated, "all his antennae out." (It was he, before Laura did, who saw that they all had vaccination marks on their arms.)

. . a frail-looking white man . . came out of the jungle [an anthropologist officer of the Indian service]. He looked at Aldous as though he had seen an apparition . . . [He] stopped dead for a moment . . approached, "Uxley? Uxley . . . *Contrapunto* . . ." and burst into tears of joy. The two men embraced. Aldous, too, was moved . . .[1]

From Brazil to Lisbon. To Turin; to Sicily. To Turin again to celebrate the 80th birthday of Laura's father. In October, on his own at first, Aldous went to London. It was his fourth visit since the war; and for Julian it was "as always a time of intensified activity, social as well as intellectual.

. . Breakfast might go on to mid-morning before we tore ourselves away from these wonderful exchanges of ideas—how I wish I had had a tape recorder! . . .
From these encounters, I always returned to my work stimulated and refreshed, my mental and spiritual batteries recharged. I cannot remember a single subject, even in my own speciality, on which Aldous was not sufficiently informed to enable us to discuss it competently, enriching my own thinking in the process.[2]

Social and intellectual. Aldous saw old friends: Rose Macaulay (who died two days later); Bertie Russell; E. M. Forster; Tom Eliot ("who is now curiously dull—as a result, perhaps, of being, at last, happy in his second marriage"); Cyril Connolly (who interviewed Aldous for the *Sunday Times*[3]); Yvonne Hamilton,

---

[1] Laura Huxley op. cit.
[2] *Memories* Vol. II cit.
[3] Published on 19th October 1958

ex-Franchetti, ex-Palavicino of the young Florentine days; the Provost of Eton, Noële Neveux . . .

. . London looks curiously old fashioned after São Paulo and Rio— not a skyscraper to be seen and amazingly little re-building . . .

Noële, Jeanne's little girl whom he had not seen for these four years, was rising eighteen and at boarding school.

London yesterday to see Aldous. [Noële's journal] Zoo and National Gallery. A strange feeling—Aldous hasn't changed, he is only a little older. The English climate does not suit him. Rather shy at first with me, who, in a way is a witness of another part of his life. But I soon find again the essential Aldous . . . He is very elegant in a dove-grey suit, red tie, and a new wrist-watch he is unable to read.

Aldous appeared on a Brains Trust programme with Julian and Professor Ayer, and was interviewed by John Lehmann on TV.[1] On the Brains Trust, Aldous remained rather effaced, prodded now and then by Julian who kept trying to bring him in, only warming into animation by a question on metaphysics. On television he looked robust and sleek against a silvery, birdlike John Lehmann, and was very fluent. Writer to writer, they talked a good deal about the novel. He had always felt, John Lehmann said, "that it is really as a novelist you should be thought of first. Would you agree?"

Aldous: . . . I would certainly like to have written a very good novel; I don't think I ever have . . .

J. L.: . . . how delighted we all were with those early novels of yours in the twenties, you seemed to us the most sophisticated, witty entertainer, a debunker bringing things down to earth with a bump, particularly sex. But even then I felt . . . your desire . . to discuss strange ideas was very much in evidence. Did you have a feeling that you wanted to teach then, as well as to entertain?

Aldous: Well, I think I had a—always had a feeling that I *wanted* to learn, and maybe that this was the most effective way of learning— I mean, it is very often that the fact of getting things down is the best way of clarifying one's own mind. Maybe I am a little bit *pedantic*, but this has always been my desire, to learn, to explore.

J. L.: And when later on the—shall we say—the teaching side in your novels seemed to grow stronger . . . were you working out these new ideas of mysticism and the divine ground for yourself in these books?

---

[1] Broadcast on 12th October 1958.

Aldous: Yes, I—my problem has always been, of course, to find if possible some balance between the two sides. I don't think I've succeeded very well always, I think I have once or twice succeeded pretty well—not perhaps to my whole, entire satisfaction . . .

J. L.: You say in one of your essays that Balzac almost ruined himself as a novelist by trying to stuff everything into his novels . . . banking, science, politics, industry, mysticism. Were you conscious of—of this difficulty, this danger yourself?

Aldous: Well, it's certainly a temptation to which I've been very much subject . . .

John Lehmann asked him if he had lost faith in the novel?

Aldous: Not at all.

J. L.: And you don't think that the novel as an art form is on the way out?

Aldous: Well, a lot of people like to say so, but I cannot see any reason why this should be true; I think people will always go on using the narrative form, because it is the most extraordinary form . . . there are no rules, except to *do it well*. And I think people will continually adapt the narrative form to the problems which confront them at a given moment in history.

J. L.: Yes, but in a recent essay of yours you do say that serious novel writing was facing a very difficult future; and might have, in fact, to—to go onto gramophone records?

Aldous: I mean this is an economic problem . . . there is such a thing as may be called an economic censorship . . . and it's very grave . . . possibly, spoken literature may be a way out of this.

J. L.: It would be bound to change novels, wouldn't it, if they became spoken?

Aldous: I don't think you could have a very long novel. I think you could have shorter pieces which might go. I don't know. It is just a suggestion I made.

John Lehmann asked if it wasn't perhaps that other difficulties were more serious today for the novelist?

Aldous: . . There are—what may be called social difficulties. I was reading just the other day as I was travelling through Sicily, reading Trollope's *Framley Parsonage* and thinking how wonderful it was for novelists in those happy days to have a completely rigid framework. Everybody knew exactly where they stood, and it was possible to make your comments from an accepted ground—

J. L.: And that's quite gone today.

Aldous: It's quite gone today.

In due course they went on to lysergic acid, Wordsworth, heightened perceptions, tranquillizers—"You do of course anticipate this world . . of drugs in *Brave New World* to some extent," said J. L. Yes, said Aldous, but he projected these things five or six hundred years into the future—

> It is rather alarming to find that only twenty-seven years later quite a number of these forecasts had already come true, and come true with a vengeance.
>
> J. L.: Are you going to write a postcript to *Brave New World*?
>
> Aldous: Well, I've written a few chapters on the things which have already come true . . the menaces to individual liberty . . I think . . very grave threats, which although they may not be acute, particularly in the democratic countries, are potentially very grave indeed.
>
> J. L.: And unforeseen by you in *Brave New World*?
>
> Aldous: Some of them were foreseen and I think some of them I didn't have the imagination to foresee but I think there is a whole armoury at the disposal of potential dictators at the moment . . .
>
> J. L.: Do you think that can be mirrored in art? You say somewhere . . that art and the novel can't really cope with some of these problems that face the world today.
>
> Aldous: Well, I think there are very great difficulties in putting certain problems into the form of art . . . take the fact for example that poetry has very seldom had anything very significant to say about money.

And before the round-off, "Are you going to write some more novels?"

> Aldous: Well, I'm trying to write one, I've just begun one.
>
> J. L.: Can we ask what it's subject is?
>
> Aldous: . . . it's a kind of reverse *Brave New World* . . . an extremely difficult thing to write . . it's much easier to write about negative things—
>
> J. L.: It's an ideal?
>
> Aldous: It's an ideal. But I hope not a stratospheric ideal, what may be called a Topian rather than a Utopian phantasy, a phantasy dealing with a place, a *real* place and *time*, rather than a phantasy dealing with *no* place and time.

Now Aldous, after nearly two years of uninterrupted decent health, was again beginning to feel far from well; apparently it was not the English climate. Julian's doctor diagnosed a stone in the bile duct and prescribed drops and diet. Laura joined Aldous on 21st October and a week later they went to Paris.

Rue Bonaparte—Jeanne and Georges, not seen since 1954. Aldous goes alone at first, next day with Laura. Julian and Juliette are in Paris, too, and four of Aldous's five nieces, and Virginia Pfeiffer. There is a family luncheon in rue Bonaparte followed by a mass outing to the Impressionists at the Jeu de Paume, but Aldous feeling ill, looks ill; Georges finds him listless, Jeanne is upset and unhappy. Aldous refuses to talk on the radio, to appear on television; the one thing he was intent on was going to the Louvre lit up at night ("As soon as he puts foot in a museum, he comes to life" [Georges Neveux's journal] but the one evening he was free of the engagements heaped upon him was a Tuesday and on a Tuesday the Louvre, as they only realized in the taxi, is shut. Georges persuaded him to give at least one interview— "pour marquer son passage" (with A. Parinaud for *Art*). The three men met for luncheon at a bistro in the rue de Verneuil and here again Aldous came out of his shell. "Il est éblouissant —enfin il se reveille . . ."

But two days later he is down with mild flu or a bad cold and has to postpone his and Laura's departure for Italy. On their last night a small farewell dinner at the Neveux's with Sylvia and Sophie and her husband, Willem Welling. Georges described the end of it thus:

> Au moment de se séparer Aldous, qui est le dernier à partir, me regarde. On se regarde en silence. Il a comme des larmes aux yeux. On se donne l'accolade. Dans l'escalier il se retourne et me fait un grand geste vague . . .

In Venice Aldous went down with influenza and stayed in bed for a week. Later in the month he had to give four lectures (partly in Italian), the first in Turin, the second in Milan, the third in Rome. Here he had a relapse; bed again until he "had to creep down to Naples and there, hardly able to stand, deliver my final lecture." (One can see that Aldous would fulfil his engagements; why he let himself in for such increasing numbers of them is a more complex matter.) He and Laura flew straight back to Los Angeles, cancelling New York as Aldous feared the cold, it being now December. On arrival he felt so low and weak that he went into hospital for tests. It was found that the London diagnosis of a gall stone had been wrong.

> . . The main trouble [he wrote to Julian and Juliette on 14th December] seems to be the chronic emphysema in the right lung, aggravated by the flu. I'm taking the pressure breathing treatment that helped me so much in the past . . .

The weight loss is probably due to emphysema—tho' conceivably there might be TB [tests later showed that there was not] . . . No indication of cancer, I'm glad to say, and all well with heart, kidneys and pancreas.

And to Humphrey Aldous wrote a few days later that he was already emerging from his hideous state of tiredness and pleased to be back in the sun, able to do some honest work for a change —free at last from the swarm of interviewers who had plagued him both in South America and in Europe.

I was simultaneously touched and appalled to discover that I am now, as the result of having been around for so many years, a kind of historical monument, which sightseers will come quite a long way to inspect . . In Brazil it was as though the Leaning Tower of Pisa had just come to town . . and even in Italy I found myself talking to full houses in large theatres. It was really very odd and embarrassing.

Chapter Seven

Father to Son

ALDOUS recovered quickly. "Working hard and eating normally . . . regaining weight," he wrote to Julian in January 1959; his troubles must have been due to too much travelling and too much talking, on top of his old smouldering bronchitis. But now something else was happening that brought much sadness to them all: after nine years and many of them happy, Matthew and Ellen's marriage had gone wrong; they were about to part, at least for the time being. Their trouble does not concern us here except in so far as it affected Aldous. Enough to say that the fundamental cause was probably the kind of temperamental difference which two people do not mind when they are young and much in love, and are unable to put up with when they are older, yet not old enough to have come to tolerance and give and take. Aldous, who had come to that stage, was very much affected. "Your letter and Ellen's made me very sad," he wrote to Matthew the day after he received the news. He asked Eileen Garrett for advice about anything useful he could do.

. . Each of them has written; so I understand the story in its main outlines—the friction of dissimilar temperaments—Ellen spontaneous and adventurous, Matthew with his tendency to be rigid, rather censorious . . . But the details and the nature of the crisis which brought the trouble to a head are obscure to me . . . Ellen tells me that you discussed the whole thing with her and that you had been in touch with Maria in regard to what was happening. I should be grateful for any help you can give me, any advice you can offer as to the best way of helping them . . .

. . The news of the rupture has left me very sad; but sadness does no good and the problem now is to discover the best way of mending or ending, of changing circumstances within the marriage or outside it.

To Matthew he said more:

. . probably what you have decided is the best course in this unhappy situation. I know very well what you mean when you talk about dust and aridity and a hard shell that makes communication in or out extremely difficult. It was something that made the first part of our marriage difficult at times; but Coccola was very patient and in the long run I learned to get through the shell and let the dust be irrigated. Unfortunately, when you were a child, I was predominantly in the dust-crust stage, and so, I'm afraid, must have been—indeed, I know that I was—a pretty bad father.

And now what is to be done? . . .

Meanwhile would it be possible for you to get away from the office for a few days and fly out here? The tourist flights are relatively cheap and I will treat you to the ticket. So do come here if you can . . We would love to see you—and Ellen too, if she can come later on, when you or someone else can be with the children. It is quiet on the hill here and, in spite of smog, the sun still shines—a statement that carries more than a meteorological meaning.

I shall say nothing to Mère or Rose about all this, unless and until you want me to do so.

Laura sends her love, as do I.

A month later Matthew had not come; Aldous, who had accepted a visiting professorship at Santa Barbara for the spring semester, now spent two nights a week there. He urged Matthew to come out and meet him, but heard nothing for some time. Probably the best that can be done now, Aldous wrote to Eileen, "is to salvage a friendly relationship between E and M, and to see that the children get as good a psychological break as possible . . ." In April he had a letter from Matthew which made him feel that something better was beginning to emerge "from the sad confusion of the situation.

. . To become capable of love—[Aldous wrote in his answer] this is, of course, about two thirds of the battle; the other third is becoming capable of the intelligence that endows the love with effectiveness in an obscure and complicated and largely loveless world. It is not enough merely to know, and it is not enough merely to love; there must be knowledge-love and charity-understanding or prajna-karuna, in the language of Buddhism—wisdom-compassion. People have been saying this for the last several thousand years; but one has to make the discovery oneself, starting from scratch, and to find what old F M Alexander called "the means whereby," without which good intentions merely pave hell and the idealist remains . . ineffectual, self-destructive and other-destructive . . . It has taken me the greater part of a lifetime to begin to discover the immemorially obvious and to try, at least, to act upon the discovery. I hope it will take you only half a lifetime and that you will emerge from this excruciatingly educative ordeal with enough love and understanding to transfigure the second half.

To Humphrey Osmond, who had seen a good deal of both Matthew and Ellen, Aldous wrote that he, Humphrey, had

summed up their problem only too well. "Inhabitants of different
. . worlds *can* live happily together—but only on condition that
each recognizes the fact that the other's world is different and
has just as much right to exist . . . as his own . .

> . . there can be something very stimulating and liberating about
> the experience of being joined in a loving relationship with somebody
> whose universe is radically unlike one's own. . . I remember a very
> touching passage in one of my grandfather's letters about his own
> obtuseness—the obtuseness of an immensely intelligent man of the
> highest integrity—in relation to his wife's insights, immediate,
> non-rational and almost infallible, into human character . . .

In April Aldous went to New York now to receive a prize, the
1959 Award of Merit for the Novel by the American Academy
of Arts and Letters, then under the presidency of Mark Van
Doren. It is a reward that goes to a novelist once every five years;
Aldous's predecessors were Ernest Hemingway, Thomas Mann
and Theodore Dreiser. The prize, a gold medal and a thousand
dollars, was presented to him by Malcolm Cowley at a joint
ceremonial of the Academy and the National Institute on the
20th of May.

As his first semester at Santa Barbara was coming to an end,
Aldous was able to stay on in New York for ten days, Laura with
him. Both attempted what they could. Matthew's cousin, Claire,
much on the scene, thought that Aldous was very fair, very just
—equally concerned for both ("Laura was feeling sorry for Ellen
and I vehemently took Matthew's side"). "I wish our last evening
had been less sad;" Aldous wrote on his return to Deronda Drive;
"but sad it was. All that can be done is to try to make the best
of a bad job.

> I think the idea of calling in a lawyer to draw up some kind of a
> written agreement is good. Once it has been drawn up, you will
> both know where you stand. Ellen will know where she stands in
> relation to the future, to the overall situation. And you will have the
> knowledge that she knows, will have a framework within which you
> both can function, and . . play the day-to-day situation by ear, so to
> speak, without having to spend energy, and create friction, by having
> to insist on the overall situation and future contingencies. It will
> mean, I hope, that you will be able to meet with one another . . with
> the same preoccupation—the day-to-day well being of the children
> within a long-range scheme which has been worked out by a third
> party and which both of you accept.
> . . I hope, that both of you will be able to follow the gospel injunc-
> tion, "Judge not that ye be not judged"—one of the most important

and significant sayings in the whole corpus of Jesus's teaching. You will not have to judge Ellen for her reluctance to think of the future and the overall picture, and she will not have to judge you for what she regards as an undue preoccupation with things which, to a person of her temperament, seem merely mechanical, organizational, abstract . . . As in all human situations, there is a paradox here. "Judge not" . . . And yet, at the same time, choose what seems to be right, reasonable, decent. In other words, judge but don't judge— judge in the sense of discriminating, but don't judge in the sense of condemning. Even where there seems to be a moral evil, don't judge in a condemnatory way . . .

It is over half a century since Aldous's mother's last letter: "Do not be too critical of others, and love much." To his own son, he continued,

. . Huxleys especially have a tendency not to suffer fools gladly— and also to regard as fools people who are merely different from themselves in temperament and habits. It is difficult for Huxleys to remember that other people have as much right to their habits and temperaments as Huxleys have to theirs . . . So do remember this family vice of too much judging . . . Write to me from time to time to let me know how you are faring.

Aldous's own summer plans—after one more lecture on the 2nd of June, "my last, thank goodness"—were to get down "seriously and continuously" to the novel. As he was due for his second semester at Santa Barbara in September, he had three, not quite clear, months in hand. Georges Neveux was considering a French adaptation of *The Genius and the Goddess*. "Vous repensez à ma malheureuse pièce . . ." and here Aldous, too, was thinking again about that wretched play. He and Laura arranged a reading of it (in its original form) at the house. They had good actors; one of them Allan Napier who had played Everard Webley in the London production of *Point Counter Point* and taken part in Laura's Los Angeles *Gioconda Smile*. They read the play (he told me) to a private audience of about a dozen people, read it to a snore-snore obbligato by a fat woman who had gone to sleep and who was supposed to be a prospective backer. But the general effect was quite good, thought Aldous, who afterwards buckled down to make a number of new cuts, shortening the play by some fifteen pages. (Soon after he made what I think is a pertinent comment on an aspect of dramatic effectiveness. "Mindlessness and horror," he wrote about a film that had its quota of the latter,

. . Mindlessness and horror are all right provided that they be shown in relationship with the mind and the good that will keep the world from collapsing. Consistent mindlessness, such as one gets in Tennessee Williams' plays, becomes a great bore and is also completely untrue to life. (A Williams' play about mindlessness cd not be put on the stage except by a lot of highly intelligent people displaying all the qualities . . so totally absent in Williams's picture of the world.) Why intensely mindful people shd choose to portray only mindlessness is a psychological enigma . . . In doing so, they deny themselves, make the survival of humanity as a species completely incomprehensible . . and narrow the scope of art as a commentary on life.

One August night, on one of his solitary walks in the dark, Aldous stumbled over the kerb of the road and fell some eight feet on to a terrace below. It was a nasty fall in a steep and hazardous place, and it seemed a minor miracle to those who knew it that he got off with shock and a jolted back, trifling in comparison to what might have happened. Laura thought that he was mainly saved by his state of physical relaxation in falling. Aldous expressed himself profoundly grateful for a really providential escape. "If ever guardian angels were on hand, it was on that night," he wrote to Matthew.

A couple of weeks later, "as good as new," he was working away again on the Utopian novel.

. . wrestling with the problem of . . [not] becoming merely expository or didactic. [To Matthew] It may be that the job is one which cannot be accomplished with complete success. In point of fact, it hasn't been accomplished in the past. For most Utopian books have been exceedingly didactic and expository. I am trying to lighten up the exposition by putting it into dialogue form; which I make as lively as possible. But meanwhile I am always haunted by the feeling that, if only I had enough talent, I could somehow poetize and dramatize all the intellectual material and create a work which would be simultaneously funny, tragic, lyrical and profound. Alas, I don't possess the necessary talent . . .

Alas also, time was getting on. In a few days Aldous would have to turn his attention from the novel to the autumn's lectures at Santa Barbara.

Chapter Eight

Santa Barbara—Professor at Large

IN the past and particularly over the last years, Aldous had been lecturing with increasing response and ease in a good many American Universities; Santa Barbara now was his first experience of a visiting professorship. U.C.S.B.—University of California at Santa Barbara—had invited him to give a course for two semesters. From February to May, and again from September to December of 1959, Aldous delivered a lecture every Monday afternoon, followed the next day by a seminar. "My modest theme is 'The Human Situation.'" During the spring semester he attacked it on the large-scale level—planetary resources, population growth, advancing technicization, suicidal traditions of nationalism and so forth. He had put in a great amount of work collecting and organizing his material so that he was able, as he now preferred to do, to speak largely *extempore*. People gathered around him on these two weekly days and he had "to do a good deal of gibbering on the side—so much, indeed, that, last week, I almost lost my voice.

However, everybody seems to like it, and if I were to accept all the invitations that come pouring in, I should be talking non-stop for the next two years . . .

There were indeed full houses, great appreciation (I was told), but also opposition; some came from the English department, some from the metaphysicians . . . (One present faculty member, Donald Lent, who was a student at the time, wrote to me about the University, as he saw it, making a couple of mistakes: "They loaded the course on how good students' grades were, so you had a dull, efficient lot by and large—also amazingly brash; one pre-med student would preface his remarks with, 'well, you writers may think that, but *we* scientists think such and such'; another student . . suggested in a paper that went on for over an hour (Huxley-time burning up, I kept thinking) that the solution to the population problem was not birth control but the 'humane' killing off of the aged who filled our hospitals and rest homes . . . The second mistake was that they placed a professor in charge of the course. He saw that people did those awful papers and were graded etc . . .")

In the autumn semester, Aldous talked about The Human

Situation on the small-scale level—the make-up of the individual, his latent potentialities and what we might do about their realization, the relation between concept and datum, the nature of art . . . "It is an impossibly large project—but worth undertaking, even inadequately, as an antidote to academic specialization and fragmentation."

Worth undertaking . . . There is, on yet another level, something that remains of Aldous's passage in a few individual lives. Ten years after—if for once I may be allowed to intrude what was then the future, the better to conjure up the past—ten years after, Aldous and Maria's beloved friend Rosalind Rajagopal brought together some of the men and women connected with Aldous at Santa Barbara in 1959. The meeting took place in the house of Rosalind's daughter and son-in-law, Radha and James Sloss at Hope Valley on a night in January 1969. There were some twenty of us; we ate together and drank wine—the house, in that quiet countryside was spacious and attractive; our hosts' two adolescent children, so well known to Aldous, intelligent and graceful; animation, friendliness, generated. Later we settled in an informal circle. There were present, Dr Elmer Noble, University Chancellor in Aldous's first semester; faculty members, board members of the Ojai Happy Valley School, members of the Platonic Academy at Montecito[1], as well as two or three people who happened to be both Santa Barbarians and Aldous's friends. Dauwe Sturman, Professor of English and Philosophy, the man originally responsible for getting Aldous to U.C.S.B., took the chair (such as it was)—a youngish man, lean, very Nordic, being in fact of Friesian extraction, who gave the impression of combining a very acute mind with quiet, straightforward benevolence. Under a window halfway down the room, sat Jack Wilkinson, Professor also of English and Philosophy (at Montecito)—a little older apparently than Sturman, well-knit, of middle height, extremely intelligent, who spoke extremely well. Opposite him, Howard Warshaw, painter and Professor of Art, a big, dark man, brilliant, quick, coming in again and again with expressive brio. Everyone in that room had something to say; some spoke once, some often; there were no interruptions, a flow rather from solo voice to confluence, orchestral progression, initiated and sustained by these three men, Sturman, Warshaw, Wilkinson, who between them carried the evening.

There was no tape recorder (we decided against one). It was not essentially what was said—though some of it was fireworks—that was significant, but the kind of people who said it (Aldous

[1] "The Platonic Academy among the gardens of Montecito" was what Aldous liked to call Robert Hutchins's Center for Democratic Studies.

had had that knack of attracting quality, not only intellectual but human quality) and the way in which it was said: the under-current of emotion. How should we proceed, Sturman had asked me when we formed our circle? Did I want to ask questions, had I brought notes? No notes, no questions—let the thing develop. Warshaw began by telling an anecdote and it being taken up, a reminiscence here, fond recollection there—small things we know —Aldous's willing chauffeurs, his interest in cars, in gadgets, his knowledge of the map. It was usually Laura, they reminded one another, who drove him to Santa Barbara, the some eighty miles from his L.A. hilltop, on the Sunday night; or if she was too busy he might take the bus, or get a lift—"But, Aldous, how *did* you get here?" Oh, he said, pleased as punch "I just thumbed a ride." They talked about his voice, his courtesy; his utter professionalism . . . "but without assumptions—he always remained a private person." His patience and politeness with the students, his cease-less moral and intellectual energy; the ways, outlandish to Americans, in which he arranged his practical existence. He always put up at what they described, marvelling at such frugality, a fire-trap hotel, "the dear old Upham" (a wooden structure indeed, but really a charming, chintzy, old-fashioned residential hotel frequented by elderly gentlewomen). And those walks! how he *insisted* on walking. Well, at least this was in Santa Barbara, whereas in Los Angeles . . . And we recalled that several times Aldous had been arrested—let's say on the point of being arrested —by the police when out on his evening walks . . . Yes, and not only at night, once in mid-afternoon on Wiltshire Boulevard he had been stopped by the law: "Mister, where's your car?" and the silvery English voice, "I haven't got a car."

On Monday morning he would usually be fetched from the hotel by Eric Petrie, an English academic and husband of the sculptress, Marie Petrie, to whom Aldous sat for his portrait bust.[1] Mrs Petrie put him in a swivel-chair fixed to a revolving platform where she could look at him from all angles by giving the chair a push from time to time. Whoever had an hour to spare would come to the studio to listen to the captive Aldous who would talk about Vedanta, Brazilian architecture or the Pill— "Why don't they put in a few vitamins, that might be a way out for the Catholic Church?"—talk, as he was pushed from one profile to the other in his chair, about Pavlov, Schweitzer and Toulouse Lautrec, never stopping as he whirled. Luncheon after-wards at the Petries' under the figtree in their garden with some

[1] A very fine head, now in the possession of the late Marie Petrie's grandson, Mr Brian Petrie, in London. (A cast has been acquired by the Los Angeles County Museum.)

PART ELEVEN 1955-1960

eminent or amusing person to make a fourth. Later they would
drive him to the campus (Marie Petrie coming in the back of the
car, saying she needed the extra twenty minutes of looking at
Aldous's head and ears).

The lecture, Full houses—students, staff, the public (Santa
Barbara intelligentsia flocking in) . . . He used few notes—in very
big letters—spoke—dispassionately in manner—about ecology . .
dwindling planetary resources . . . Some said Aldous was crying
wolf . . . How *much* he anticipated, His *concern* about the human
condition—*that* came through. And yet, another day, privately,
he might retail, full of glee, some piece of hair-raising lore. Before
the bomb, before population catching up, he said returning from
some scientific conference, "there will be this virus conveyed by
air travel. Ah, the little microbes will get us first!" There had
been opposition to Aldous's appointment; not everyone at the
University was pleased; some of the metaphysicians looked down
their noses, calling his stuff old hat. Had anyone listened again
to the recorded lectures? Not yet. This was the first time, really,
that they were talking away like this; one could not have done
so before, not a few years ago, not so soon after his death . . . Now,
it was not too late—the memories were there, rediscovered, fresh.
The meeting[1]—or what should one call it? a party, group interview, memorial service or a séance, this fraternal and spontaneous
evocation of an extraordinary man? (thus had Gervas Huxley
evoked the Hillside schoolboy, the young man at Oxford) perhaps
symposium serves—well, the symposium then entered a discursive,
intellectual phase. Aldous's metaphysics. What exactly did he
believe? And how did he believe? The ends of man, Enlightenment, the Divine Ground—this Taoist agnostic whose element
was not rock but water, this inveterate empiricist, this modern
saint, who never ceased to ask "Where are we going?" who had
also said that one must dream in a pragmatic way—was he moved
by choice, by will, by faith? (Perhaps a part of an answer not
given that night can be found in *Island*: "Believing in eternal life
never helped anybody to live in eternity. Nor, of course, did
*dis*believing. So stop all your pro-ing and con-ing (that's the
Buddha's advice) and get on with the job.") Later still the talk
curved back into the personal, the reminiscent past. It was Santa
Barbara that had given Aldous his first honorary doctorate. He

[1] There were present at this meeting, besides our host and those already
mentioned, Professor Garret Hardin, biologist and author; Mrs Garret, Mrs
Noble, Mrs Warshaw, Mrs Wilkinson; Katherine Peak, Aldous's fellow board
member of the Happy Valley School; Frank Lacey, director of the school;
Harriette Van Breton; Aldous's old friend, Eva Herrmann; and of course
Rosalind Rajagopal and her sister, Mrs Louis Zalk and S. B. The date was
31st January 1969.

252

seemed *delighted* . . . He stood up in his new gown on the campus platform in the open air giving his acceptance address, his hair blown in the autumn wind . . . But later in the semester, he turned up for his lectures without the doctor's gown. "Oh!" Aldous said, "Well, Laura uses it for sun-bathing . ."

Chapter Nine

Menninger Foundation—Professor at Large

THE Julian Huxleys came for Christmas. Deronda Drive, which had still been in the making during their last visit in 1956, had reached its definitive stage; there was no spare room and they put up in a small hotel at the foot of the hill. Laura fetched them daily. "On approach, the house [through Juliette's eyes] looked like a squat grey toad, but inside it was charming. Laura had furnished it beautifully—white rugs, a large bed downstairs ensconced in a window, nylon curtains of many colours, a dining-table of shining black, white sofa and armchairs. Aldous had his room upstairs next to the second bathroom, and his study on the mezzanine floor—very *encombré*." (According to Mère, the number of Aldous's upstairs rooms was *three*; "small rooms, but not *mesquin*"; what she regretted was that he could not step from study into garden.) "The view incredibly lovely, over the whole plain, glittering at night with a million lights. Racoons came . . and were fed milk . . ." It was a Californian Christmas and they were able to swim in Virginia's pool. "Laura driving, though it was only 5 minutes walk. J. and I often walked back.

On Christmas Day lunch at the house with Mme Nys, Rose, the Capitano [Angelino Ravagli, Frieda Lawrence's second husband]. We exchanged presents; I can't remember *what* book A gave Julian . . . Mme Nys very lively. It was a happy day. We all sat outside in the sun.

Gerald Heard and Christopher came in one afternoon; there was at least one dinner-party with Romain Gary and Lesley Blanch, "Laura a good hostess, and the food nice"; all too soon their time was up. "It was wonderful having you here," Aldous wrote, "and I wish it could have been longer."

January 2nd, for Aldous, back to the Utopia—"the writing of which presents extraordinary difficulties". For Laura it was back to psychotherapy. Her work was most stimulating to Aldous, who transcribed some of her methods straight into the novel. She had, he said, "remarkable results in many cases: for she seems to have an intuitive knowledge of what to do at any given moment, what technique to use in each successive phase of the patient's mood and feeling." Among other things she had been using LSD "in a few cases where the method seemed to be justifiable."

Incidentally [to Humphrey], what frightful people there are in your profession! We met two Beverly Hills psychiatrists the other day, who specialize in LSD therapy at $100 a shot—and, really, I have seldom met people of lower sensitivity, more vulgar mind! To think of people made vulnerable by LSD being exposed to such people is profoundly disturbing. But what can one do about the problem? Psychiatry is an art based on a still imperfect science—and as in all the arts there are more bad and indifferent practitioners than good ones. How can one keep the bad artists out? Bad artists don't matter in painting or literature—but they matter enormously in therapy and education; for whole lives and destinies may be affected . . But one doesn't see any practical way in which the ungifted and the unpleasant can be filtered out . . .)

At this time Aldous asked Matthew's advice upon a point of business. The University of Texas had approached him—indirectly —about some of the manuscripts and literary correspondence in his possession. "This might be a good idea—sell some MSS now and put the money into the children's trust fund. What do you think?

I won't make any move until I hear what you feel about the matter. I've no idea what sort of price the U of T will pay: but if they offer a fair sum it might be a good idea to dispose of MSS rather than await my demise . . .

Matthew—as this would have benefited *his* children—did not respond, and, unfortunately, ironically, no action was taken in the matter.

Aldous's finances, incidentally, had been in a healthy state for quite some time. Between 1955 and 1958 his annual income from Chatto & Windus, U.K. and translation rights alone, averaged nearly £5,000. In 1959, he had just heard, the precise sum was £7,239—"a most surprisingly good showing". American royalties fluctuated, yet, again on the average, seldom fell below 75% of English ones. And on top of this, there were his not inconsiderable lecturing fees.

Present life was quiet. "Rose has retreated again to the desert —waiting for a very hypothetical job as a member of an archaeo-logical expedition to Yucatan with 2 gentlemen from Texas. Bonne Maman [an Aldous view of Mère] flourishes under the stimulation of successive disasters in France—the death of Camus, . . the Fréjus dam break, the news of which in the *Figaro Littéraire* . . excites her and keeps up her morale like a shot of adrenalin . .

What a strange creature! But what a blessing that it takes so little— the account in a newspaper of a French catastrophe (it has to be

French: nobody else's catastrophes cut much ice)—to keep her in good shape.

The Utopia was getting on—300 pages typed in February—though with no end in sight. "Heaven knows how much more there will be . . ." He had still not solved his main technical difficulty.

. . I became disturbed by the low ratio of story to exposition and am now, after discussing the problem with Christopher Isherwood, trying to remedy this defect by the introduction of a brand new personage . . .

(Could this character have been wicked, clever Mr Bahu, the envoy from the Bad Island?[1])

After more than a year of separation, Matthew and Ellen's dilemma had not been resolved. Aldous took a hand, writing to Ellen. ". . I had imagined that by this time you would have come to some definite decision—either to make a reconciliation or a definite break . .

. . This half way position with one foot in a marriage and one foot out strikes me as profoundly unsatisfactory—especially for Matthew who is essentially a family man with a deep wish for roots and stability and on whom the present arrangement imposes a rootlessness and a homelessness that for him are peculiarly distressing . . .

. . . Rose evidently feels very strongly that you should decide in favour of reconciliation. If you find it emotionally possible, I would also be for it—but I don't think it should be forced . . . The important thing, however, is to decide. If there is anything I can do to help you to come to a decision, let me know.

The decision was made, and it was to break. ". . there is no consolation," Aldous wrote to Matthew, "only the reflection that a mending . . on any basis short of a heartfelt 'marriage of true minds' might be an even sadder thing for all concerned.

The problem now is to make the best of the situation . . . [I] can only hope that you will soon be able to create for yourself a new home base, with its own internal relationships of love and affection, from which you can relate yourself to the children. *Their* well-being will be enhanced by *your* well-being: so it is as much for the children's sake as for yours that I wish and hope for your future happiness.

[1] C. I. does not remember.

And for the same reasons, I hope for Ellen's future happiness. Her letter to me was full of sadness . . .

> *Nel mezzo del cammin di nostra vita*
> *mi ritrovai per une selva oscura*
> *ché la diritta via era smarrita.*

Each of you must find a way out of the dark wood, for your own sakes and for the children's. And if I can help in any way, that is what I'm there for. Whatever may have happened on the level of the previous generation, the family still persists in Trev and Tessa . . .

There seemed to be almost nothing, wrote one of his medical friends, Max Cutler,[1] about which Aldous could not be curious. Yet on that vast circumference through which his mind swept, there were sectors of particular concern: health, for instance and the whole issue of medicine . . . "I had of course, before I went blind, intended to become a doctor" Aldous, for his part, said in the London interview of 1961. "I presume that if I *had* gone on with it, I would have gone into medical research. I don't think I would have been a very good *practising* doctor—Why? Well, I don't know that I would have been good enough in the personal relationships, which I think are tremendously important in a good doctor: I mean, I was diffident and shy and awkward then, I think I've slightly improved with age—but I think I would have been a fairly good medical researcher, I think I would always have been very interested in the research part of the thing . . ."

The following, for instance, had happened a few years ago. In Philadelphia in 1957—at the time of the unfortunate opening of the play—Aldous saw a young doctor he had known in California, Robert Lynch, who was experimenting with what at his hospital they called the French Cocktail, a mixture of Chlorpromazine, Phenacetin,[1] Aspirin and Demarol compounded by a French doctor and used for producing a form of hibernation. Administered in large doses, the Cocktail reduced temperature to ninety-two and lowered metabolism. A friend of Dr Lynch's, another young doctor, was afflicted with a horrible cancer of the lymphatic system, resistant to radiation, grown to the size of a football in his chest. Experts gave him a few months to live. Aldous and Laura urged trying the French Cocktail.

. . I argued [to Humphrey] that, since the cocktail greatly reduces the metabolic rate and since cancer cells require a great deal of

---

[1] *Or* Phenergen: the prescription differs in Aldous's relevant letters.

nourishment and probably don't like cold, there might be a chance of the malignant cells dying or being checked in their growth, while the healthy cells survived the hibernation process.

. . . We suggested combining semi-hibernation . . with intensive hypnosis, talking to the cells . . . wildly unorthodox . . . but conceivably it might work.

And it did. The summer after, Dr Lynch gave Laura the results. They were "extraordinary—complete disappearance of the tumour, acceptance of the young man as a full-time intern at the U of C hospital at Berkeley, complete recovery of weight, strength, vitality."

So when the Menninger Foundation, the main centre of psychiatric training in America, invited Aldous to spend two months with them in the spring—visiting Professor, no special duties "just hanging around and occasionally talking"—Aldous accepted with much pleasure. ("It will be interesting, I think, to penetrate the holy of holies of American psychiatry.") What he was actually being offered was the Sloan Professorship of the year, and he proposed to deliver a few lectures on subjects connected with psychology and discuss "the art of writing case histories" in a seminar. As to practical matters—

I shall be coming alone; but it is possible that my wife might come for a short time during my stay at Topeka—in which case she wd probably go to a hotel.

What I would like is a small apartment or motel room with a kitchenette. (One gets very tired of restaurant food, and I wd like to be able to make my own culinary mess when I feel like it. So a little kitchen wd be a *sine qua non.*)

Aldous arrived in Topeka, Kansas, in mid-March. The Middle West was under 18 inches of snow about to melt and "one waded about in rubber boots like a salmon fisher". He found "a vast psychotic population at large and in a dozen hospitals," an enormous hospital, a veterans' hospital, Dr Menninger's private hospital, schools for delinquent boys, for backward children, a large staff "—a lot of very able people . . (Gardner Murphy, Bertalanffy, for example) . . and some hundred and fifty young MD's and PH.D's taking a three years' course." Aldous was free to go anywhere, see anything he wanted.

. . much to admire [he wrote to Juliette] and also not a little to shake my head over in incomprehension. E.g. they treat hospital patients in a rational way, attacking their problems on all the fronts from the nutritional and gymnastic to the psychological: but their private patients they treat in the grand old Freudian way . . . by psychology alone, and psychology of only one, not too realistic brand. Very odd . . .

In what he regarded as the good hospitals, everything was done at once: psycho-therapy, work, play and music therapy, chemo-therapy, vitamins, diet . . "they really get to work on the person from every angle; and then you have a chance of getting the person out in quite a short time . . ." Aldous talked at some length about the subject a year later at the London interview. Strict Freudians can't really *do* very much with psychosis, he said. "There is no doubt that the whole organic approach is gaining ground—

I think it's pretty clear now that schizophrenia is an organic disease . . of chemical origin . . . and probably one could find chemical means of coping with it . . .

"The other day I was talking to Dr [William] Sargant who is the chief psychotherapist at St Thomas's, he uses entirely organic methods. And gets very good results. He wouldn't dream of using the sort of Freudian methods, because they just don't work . . But there is no *doubt* that we *are* on the threshold of some *very important changes* in treatment of mental disease . . .

"I was never as intoxicated by Freud as some people were, and I get less intoxicated as I go on. I think he omitted too much from his purview of human beings . . . We do know very well that there are many things on the neurological and bio-chemical level which *profoundly* affect our lives. But Freud—although he did himself say that finally all nervous disorders would turn out to be organic—he did say that in the meanwhile . . . we could treat them successfully by purely psychological means—I think this is absolutely *untrue*.

"His followers of course dogmatically insist upon this, in the most ridiculous way, the orthodox Freudians. Well, thank heaven, most psychotherapists are *not* orthodox Freudians now, they are eclectics and making use of organic and chemical methods, and psychological and sociological methods, which guarantee a cure which a pure Freudian just doesn't get with his eight years on the couch.

"As I said, I was never very intoxicated by it, and more and more as I learn what is happening now in the field of neurology and bio-chemistry, and in the general study of the human physique and the classification of human types, I feel more and more strongly that you have to have the total organic approach. We *have* to see the thing as *a totality*—we *have* to make the best not only of both worlds, *but of all the worlds*.

"*Man is a multiple amphibian who lives in about twenty different worlds at once.* [The italics are in Aldous's voice] If anything is to be done to improve his *enjoyment* of life, to improve the way he can realize his desirable potentialities, to improve his *health*, to improve the *quality* of his relations with other people, to improve his *morality*, we have to *attack on all fronts at once*.

"And the greatest, and what may be called the original sin of the human mind is *sloth*, it's over-simplification. We *want* to think that there is only *one* cause for every given phenomenon, therefore there is only one cure, *there is not!* This *is* the trouble: no phenomenon on the human level, which is a level of immense complexity, can ever have a single cause—we must always take at least half a dozen conspiring causal factors into consideration . . . The trouble with the Freudians is that they took only *one* set of factors into account, and of course their system doesn't work at all well.

". . . This is the sort of intellectual and scientific correlate to my feeling that the highest forms of art are those which impose harmony and order upon the greatest number of factors . . ."

Later again Aldous was to write on the subject in *Literature and Science*; here, and in the lectures he gave in the autumn following his stay at the Menninger Foundation, he developed his thought on these lines:

. . The interesting thing is that the ego remains very much what it was in Homer's day. It is this conscious, fairly rational creature which uses words, which is analytical, which pursues its own self-interest. It is the person, in the words of Robert Louis Stevenson, "The person with a conscience and a variable bank balance." But around this ego, around this person . . there are a whole lot of "not I's" . . .[1]

There are, for instance, Até and Menos.

Well, who and what is Até?[2] In the Greek tragedies the word stands for disaster, but in Homer the word stands for "the state of mind" which brings on disaster . . . the state of infatuation, the state of mind which leads to all kinds of absurd things against our own interests, things which make no sense to us whatever, and yet we still do them. And Homer personified this . . as an alien, super-natural force which came into man . . . Now, Homer . . makes it quite clear that there are also positive interventions from the

[1] "Modern Views of Human Nature" 2nd Lecture by A. H. at M.I.T. 13 Oct. 1960

[2] "Ancient Views of Human Nature" 1st Lecture by A. H. at M.I.T. 5 Oct. 1960.

supernatural world. In general these .. are made in the form called Menos, and Menos is that kind of accession of power and eagerness and strength and vitality which permits us to do the impossible. Even animals are capable of experiencing Menos. Horses every now and then .. do the most extraordinary things in the *Iliad*. Homer would have said that any particularly good idea .. any remarkable action of great insight, is given to us *from the outside* by a god who breathed his Menos into us . . .

. . . Today of course . . .[1] we speak about [Menos and Até] in terms of an active, dynamic unconscious. It's remarkable how recent this idea is. We now take it completely for granted, but actually it is an idea which William James dates exactly. [He] attributed the beginning of the new psychology, with its stress upon the dynamic unconscious, to the publication of a paper in 1886 by F. W. H. Myers [setting forth a theory of the sublimated self; later developed in Myers' posthumous *Human Personality*]. Myers was a profound student and describer of the unconscious mind, and I regard him as one of the best . . .

Nine years later, after experimenting with novel therapeutic techniques, Freud published his first book and formulated his famous theory of human behaviour in terms of libido, repression and a dynamic unconscious. Myers' fame became completely eclipsed. Yet Freud's hypothesis, Aldous thought, was less complete.

. . . for unlike his older English contemporary,[2] he paid very little attention to what may be called the positive side of the unconscious. Myers was more interested in Menos than in Até; Freud's primary concern was with the state of mind that leads to disaster . . . As a research physician, with a large clientèle of hysterical and neurotic patients, he had ample opportunities of observing the destructive activities of Até, very few for observing the influxes of Menos, the visitations of the Muses . . or the admonitions of the kind of daimon that spoke to Socrates.

. . . Freud,[3] so to speak, is talking all the time about the basement downstairs with the rats and black beetles, whereas Myers is largely concerned with the floors above the ground floor where the ego lives, and he would agree, I would think, with the mystical point of view that the topmost floor of these upper levels has no roof to it and is open to the sky.

[1] 2nd M.I.T. Lecture cit.
[2] *Literature and Science*. Chatto & Windus, 1963.
[3] 2nd M.I.T. Lecture cit.

Chapter Ten

Reprieve

AFTER the six weeks at Menninger's, more journeys, more lectures: Forest Hill, Berkeley, Idaho State College, the University of Arizona. It was well into May before they were settling down again, Aldous hoping to get on with his book, Laura to start one. For Laura had decided to write. One Sunday afternoon two young English scientists had come to tea to discuss ways of setting up some useful project. ". . It was a question of large sums of money, committees, laboratories and it seemed hopelessly long before any of this would have a practical application.[1]

> I . . could hardly imagine a million dollars, or a million people, but I was very clear-minded about the individuals in question—quietly self-liquidating in streets, hospitals and prisons, long before the project would even be out of the organizational stage.[1]

The scientists left. " 'Those are bright young men,' Aldous said. I was seething with impatience. 'Yes, they are bright—but it will be years . . .' And even before I had time to co-ordinate my thinking, I heard myself suddenly announce, at breathless speed, 'You know what I am going to do? I am going to write a book. I am going to make a book of my techniques—and everybody can use them right away, without a committee, and without a million dollars. And I am going to call these techniques, *Recipes for Living and Loving*.' " Aldous was delighted. A wonderful idea, he said, and a very good title. That was the beginning of *You Are Not the Target* by Laura Archera Huxley.

In a letter dated 18th of May, Aldous told Matthew that he hoped to finish *his* book before the next load of engagements in September; told him that Mme Nys was having dizzy spells and Matthew had better write to keep her cheerful; expressed pleasure about Matthew's plan to join an expedition to the Brazilian jungle, and enclosed a $20 bill for some vast and learned book he wanted sent. It was the usual even-toned and friendly letter, and no one could have told that Aldous was going through one of the most shattering experiences there is. He had just been in hospital for tests, and been given the diagnosis of a malignant tumour on the back of his tongue. Radical surgery, which might

[1] Laura Archera Huxley, *This Timeless Moment* cit.

have left him more or less speechless, had been recommended, or rather pressed on him as both urgent and inevitable. Aldous was against this, or at least against an immediate decision; so was Laura. And it was largely thanks to her quick good sense and resolution that he was spared this fate. She helped him to get dressed and actually whisked him out of hospital in the luncheon hour.[1] Then she telephoned Aldous's friend, Dr Max Cutler, for an appointment. They went on 19th May. Aldous asked, "Isn't there something else that can be done?" Cutler advised him to take a radium needle treatment.

Now, Dr Cutler is a very eminent cancerologist indeed. (Aldous had first met him in April 1954 when he was called in as consultant for Maria. He had seen her case as hopeless, and encouraged the last journey to Europe). Trained at John Hopkins and the Curie Institute in Paris, co-author with the late Sir Lenthal Cheatle of a medical classic, Dr Cutler had been for many years the head of the Chicago Tumour Institute before going into private practice in Los Angeles. Aldous wrote about him, "I find that both here and in Europe he is regarded among the greatest living surgeons and radiologists." Dr Cutler nevertheless insisted on a second opinion. Aldous with Laura flew to San Francisco the next morning; here he was examined by the Professors of Radiology and Surgery at the University of California Medical Center.[2] They advised him to take the radium treatment and to take it with Cutler.

Aldous's second decision was to keep the whole thing secret. He did not want to worry people necessarily or unnecessarily, and he wanted to protect himself from the inevitable atmosphere of apprehension and inquiry. *No* one was to know, neither his son, nor his brother, nor his friends, and above all not the press and the professional world. Laura entirely concurred (one should think of the burden this put on her). Thus Aldous's illness became known only to Virginia Pfeiffer and the Kiskaddens, Bill having long acted as Aldous's private medical adviser, and of course to the doctors concerned. On 31st May Aldous went into hospital for six days under the name of Mr Leonard, Matthew Leonard. The treatment was successful—the tumour was knocked out, and Aldous's speech remained perfect. The next ten weeks of convalescence at home were what he called unpleasant. Even so, he was able to take part in a symposium at Tecate, Mexico, as early as the 24th of June. In July he was at work again on his novel.

At this time Betty Wendel's daughter, Jeff Corner, a young and

---

[1] Laura's full account of these events and the nature of Aldous's illness can be found in *This Timeless Moment* op. cit.
[2] Drs Franz Buschke and Maurice Galante.

happily married woman, lost her husband in a sudden, meaningless accident. Aldous wrote:

> What can one say? There are no consolations; there is only the bearing of the unbearable for the sake of the life—your own and the children's—that has to go on and be made the best of.
>
> I never knew Doug well—but I always felt, whenever I met him, a renewal of the liking and respect that my first meeting had inspired. One had a sense when one was with him that there was an intrinsically good human being, decent, fair, kind . . with that blessed capacity for seeing himself with a humorous eye which is a true manifestation of the Christian virtue of humility. And now this dreadful, senseless thing has happened . . . As I said, there are no consolations; but out of my own experience I can tell you certain things which may be of some practical help. It is profoundly important to remember that, over and above the grief and the loneliness and the near-despair, there will be an organic reaction, closely resembling surgical shock. A bereavement such as yours . . . produces a state of psychic and physical shock—a state which may last for weeks or months. For so long as this state of shock persists, the mind-body requires appropriate supportive treatment in the form of adequate rest, a good diet etc. The bereaved person's tendency is to resent this—to feel that it is an ignoble kind of escape from the situation. But neglecting the amputated organism will do nothing to spiritualize the bereavement. On the contrary, it may physiologize it, transform it into a sickness that leaves the sufferer no power to think with love about the past or act constructively in the present . . . God bless you.

Before the end of the summer, the novel had to be laid aside for more pressing homework. In September Aldous left California to take part in a convention on medicine and ethics at Dartmouth College, then flew to Boston from where Matthew drove him in his microbus to Hanover, New Hampshire, to receive another honorary degree (Laura, busy with her own book, did not come East), thence he went on to New York, and to Pennsylvania to give a lecture at the University of Pittsburgh. And on the 23rd of September, Aldous alone—his equipment in two Revelation suitcases—boarded a train bound for the most glamorous of his academic appointments, Carnegie Visiting Professor at M.I.T., the Massachusetts Institute of Technology.

Chapter Eleven

Cambridge Massachusetts—Carnegie Professor in Humanities

"AN interesting job in an interesting place . . ." The Massachusetts Institute of Technology is known as one of the great purely scientific universities of America and the world. Less well known perhaps is the fact that it has also made a point of setting up an excellent department of the humanities, and that all students, whether they are going to be mathematicians, scientists or engineers, have to give twenty-five per cent of their time to literature, history and philosophy. This is how Aldous's appointment came about: Professor Patrick Wall, M.D. (now of the University of London), then a professor of biology at M.I.T., talking to Matthew, learned that Aldous would be interested in spending some time in a scientifically and technicologically oriented institution. Professor Wall approached John Ely Burchard, then Dean of the School of Humanities and Social Sciences, who took up the suggestion immediately. After a very brief correspondence Aldous agreed to come in the autumn semester of 1960, to give seven public lectures and take part in the Humanities Senior Seminar. He was to be designated Centennial Carnegie Visiting Professor in Humanities (M.I.T. was celebrating its 100th year), and to receive $9000 for a nine weeks' residence. (The funds came from a grant of the Carnegie Corporation.) Aldous accepted this large fee with pleasure, snapped it up it could be said. If there was one thing he was proud of it was to have been able to earn his living with his pen, and to this his growing lecturing successes now added another dimension as it were.

The major educational experiment under the Carnegie grant was the Humanities-and-Science, and Humanities-and-Engineering Curriculum, and the director of this was Professor Roy Lamson.[1]

> I was delighted to have Aldous at M.I.T., and our faculty, both humanists and scientists, were enthusiastic about the prospect. Dean Burchard asked me to take charge of the arrangements . . .[2]

---

[1] Roy Lamson, Professor of Literature, Director of Course XXI (Humanities and Science and Engineering) at M.I.T.

[2] Roy Lamson in conversation and a memoranda to S. B.

So Roy Lamson had flown to Topeka in the spring and spent four days at Menninger's with Aldous, whom he observed in action as the main discussant in a conference of the Constructive Uses of Anxiety. For the rest of the time the two men talked, about music, about art, about what Aldous wanted to do at M.I.T.; there was the beginning of a friendship. Aldous decided to make the subject of his lectures, "What a Piece of Work is Man".

It was Roy and his wife, Peggy, who found Aldous an apartment in Cambridge, three rooms and kitchen on the ground floor of a modern building, 100 Memorial Drive near the campus; and arranged for an office in the Hayden Library. ("Aldous took one look at the office and the Institute mail on his desk, and never returned to it.")

Aldous arrived. The Lamsons met his train at Back Bay Station in Boston. Roy stepped forward to seize the suitcases, dropped them and nearly dropped himself—the weight was staggering: not only were these expanding cases stuffed with books to breaking point, Aldous had packed his typewriter as well. He liked the apartment.

His first lecture was on 5th October, a Wednesday, at 8 pm (all of them, except one, were on Wednesday night). Beforehand the Lamsons took Aldous to dinner at the Faculty Club. Aldous ate and talked without the slightest sign of performer's nerves, "at precisely 7.40 pm finished a hefty meal" and went with Lamson to the auditorium a quarter of a mile away. They went in by the back door and up the stage lift.

When they came in, the auditorium was filled to the last seat, and so were the aisles. Under the fire regulations, anyone standing had to be asked to leave. Aldous said it would not disturb him to have students sit on the stage with him while he spoke, so two hundred students came up from the aisles. Dean Burchard introduced Aldous. Aldous introduced his lecture. What a piece of impertinence, he said, for "an encyclopaedically ignorant man to come to talk to extremely learned people." Yet really learned people are inhibited by their vast amount of knowledge from straying beyond the boundaries of their own particular province, and it is perhaps the function of the "widely interested literary man to go crawling about in the woodwork between the pigeon holes, and to look in here, and to look in there, and to try to make some kind of coherent picture of the whole elaborate system of compartments which has grown up in our academic worlds.

In this series, I propose to talk . . about our most profound, searching, and difficult problem, the problem of human nature . . .

"Aldous lectured from a small sheaf of notes[1]. Occasionally he would bring the notes very close to his face to read a quotation, but otherwise he seemed to be pouring out his well-planned essay. He was strict in his timing, keeping his lecture to three or four minutes under an hour. Following each lecture he met students, and faculty.

"The lectures were immensely popular. 'Kresge' Auditorium seats 1238; some 200 more sat on the stage. For the other lectures we put loud speakers in the corridor and also in the two rehearsal rooms under the auditorium, so that another 400 to 500 listened there. Attendance at these lectures is even today a record unsurpassed. . . The audience was mostly students—M.I.T., Harvard, Radcliffe, Boston University, Wellesley and the many schools and colleges in the Boston area."

Indeed the influx of these outside listeners was so heavy that they jammed traffic all across the Charles River into Boston, and extra police were called out to cope on Wednesday nights.

"A group of students complained that these outsiders were arriving an hour early and taking up seats. So Aldous offered to give an extra lecture just for the students.

"Once a week, on the Monday following last Wednesday's lecture, Aldous taught a seminar . . Thirty seniors, who had been studying for their degree of B.Sc. and had backgrounds in literature, history, philosophy and music, met Aldous and other members of the faculty for a two to three hours' session.

"At the opening meeting of the seminar on 10th October, in the Humanities lounge of the Hayden Library, the room was filled. Students enrolled in the seminar were given the front rows, and it was clear that we could not exclude the visitors, about fifty in all, faculty and students and some outsiders.

"Aldous often sat for a few minutes, head bowed, without a word. Then gave a short speech on a specific problem based on the general statements of the public lecture before. Then faculty and students pitched in with questions. At the end Aldous would often sum up the discussion or raise a new question and leave it to develop for the next session. The seminar was lively and often profound in that Aldous elicited comment from such people as Gyorgy Kepes,[2] Dr John Spiegel, psychologist from Brandeis, Huston Smith.[3]

"In addition Aldous offered to be at home every Tuesday from 2-5 pm to talk with students. His small apartment was always

[1] I am indebted for all quotations from these lectures to Roy Lamson's working copy, a transcription made from the tapes recorded at the lectures.
[2] Painter, Professor of Architecture, Director of the Center for Advanced Visual Studies of M.I.T.
[3] Professor of Philosophy of M.I.T.

jammed. Once I recall when students were in a cross-fire with each other, Aldous slipped out into the pantry-kitchen and made tea . . ."

Aldous's third lecture was introduced by Professor Georgio di Santillana, who said *inter alia*, ". . I happen to say at times to my students . . 'Gentlemen, you are the men from Mars, you are to get acquainted with this, our planet . . .' I should like, therefore, to pay my special respects to Mr Huxley, who was not only Master to my generation but . . the one who perhaps did most to introduce us to this planet. If I play a little with the time co-ordinate, one name comes to my mind . . it is the name of Plutarch with his moral essays . . Sometime, someone should draw that parallel . . He would find, for instance, that Mr Huxley has it harder as he's caught in the paws of progress while Plutarch is not . . . There is no . . end of the trail problem for Plutarch. All is quiet curiosity and serenity. On the other hand . . Plutarch . . lacks the definiteness that modern science has built into our thought and into our language . . . Of the great exponents of culture . . .

Mr Huxley is the one who has remained closest through the years to the scientific awareness. This is what gives point and relevance to his criticism, to his doubts, to his mystical conclusions . . .[1]

There was an immense excitement during Aldous's stay at M.I.T. ("It was an intellectual event and a 'worship' . . .")[2] A discovery for Aldous, too, who originally had been such a reluctant and not very effective public speaker, a reader rather of written speeches, when out of a sense of duty he had stood up for the Peace Pledge Union with Gerald Heard. Later he began to get some pleasure out of talking to learned institutions in America; the big change came in the 1950's when to Maria's astonishment he found that he would like to, and could, speak *extempore*. ". . he had made himself", Yehudi Menuhin wrote,[3]

into an instrument of music—concentrated as he was in the spoken word, his voice was the gentlest melody, ennobled beyond hate, violence and prejudice, yet not without passion, which sang of all that had ever touched his senses as of all the myriad impressions his mind had made its own.

. . . as pure in his maturity and ready to respond like a tuned violin

[1] I am indebted for this quotation from Professor Santillana's introduction to the M.I.T. transcript of the tape recording of the original lecture.
[2] Roy Lamson.
[3] *Mem. Vol.*

to a trained hand . . . this was a man in whom wisdom never destroyed innocence. He was scientist and artist in one—standing for all we most need in a fragmented world where each of us carries a distorting splinter out of some great shattered universal mirror. He made it his mission to restore these fragments and, at least in his presence, men were whole again. To know where each splinter might belong one must have some conception of the whole, and only a mind such as Aldous's, cleansed of personal vanity, noticing and recording everything, and exploiting nothing, could achieve so broad a purpose.

After nearly fifty years of solitary confinement at his desk, M.I.T.—like Santa Barbara and other Colleges before—must have been to a high degree rewarding and refreshing. (The fates, which so obstinately had refused him that successful play, at work in their mysterious way.) Even so, Aldous stuck to his sheet anchor, every or nearly every morning he stayed in and worked on the Utopia: *Island*; there was a title now . . On his free afternoons, he prowled about, often on his own. He walked across the long bridge into Boston, on the exiguous footway brushed by traffic; he prowled about the bargain-basement of Filene's department store, where you pay in scrip and the prices tumble week by week in some elaborate mathematical degression; he discovered a health-shop and carried home fruit, cereals and honey; he made his culinary messes of frozen fish and vegetables. Peggy Lamson did a certain amount of unobtrusive looking after him. Both Lamsons were a great asset to Aldous, and he was often in their house on Francis Avenue. The Wednesday night pre-lecture dinners at the Faculty Club became a ritual, Aldous eating through his three courses, finishing his stewed pears to the minute, Roy taking him across the campus, up the stage lift to the stand before the crowd of waiting men and women. Aldous stood as he lectured, "very erect, quietly commanding". The friendship with the Lamsons was also a private friendship, with them he could laugh as well as talk. In Peggy, herself a writer,[1] bright, gay, warm, he found the feminine company he always valued, they got on like a house on fire. They throve on nonsense, Aldous's riddle: The greatest invention of the twentieth century? The aeroplane? No, Scotch tape; an invented personage who was resident priest in a rosary factory; they thought of writing a sketch together (they did plunge later on into an actual dramatic project, the stage adaptation of a little known story of Aldous's called "Voices"; a good

[1] Author of *Few Are Chosen, American Women in Political Life Today*, and *The Glorious Failure, Black Congressman Robert Brown Elliott and the Reconstruction in South Carolina*, etc.

deal of work ensuing for both). When Peggy got a new Nash car and it wouldn't start, Aldous said, "try this", jiggled a button below the dashboard and it did. His own apartment was kept in order by a weekly cleaning woman. The cleaning woman demanded a vacuum cleaner; Aldous asked Peggy to lend hers. Every Tuesday morning, regardless of the needs of her own household, she drove into Cambridge, parked, and lugged the thing across the campus. Once, vacuum cleaner in arms, she ran across the wife of the President of M.I.T. "Why, Mrs Lamson?" "Taking my vacuum cleaner to Aldous Huxley."

As ever he wanted to see anything that was going and was driven about a good deal by the Lamsons (here again the same tale: when Roy lost his way, it was Aldous who gave directions). Wanting to do all he could, he took on supplementary activities, such as speaking to some of the organizations within the Institute.

> In all, he met with twenty groups—scientists, humanists . . . [Roy Lamson] He went to dinner with the chaplains but did not open his mouth except to the people on his right and left, and spent the rest of the—early—evening wrapt in one of his silences. One Monday he went reluctantly (because he had been in the Seminar from 2-5 pm) to talk to our commuters, a group not living in the campus. We promised one hour—no more, but Aldous found the group so responsive that he stayed until midnight, refreshed and vibrant.

Aldous also lectured at Boston University (arranged by Roy's son David Lamson), at Wellesley and at Harvard, and gave radio and TV interviews on WGBH, the educational station, and the most remarkable thing about this very heavy programme was Aldous's unhurried serenity.

The weeks moved on; Aldous was not going to stay the full semester but leave soon after his seventh and last lecture on 16th November, having to flee, because of that bronchial weakness, before the onset of the New England winter. Meanwhile he had visitors. Laura came; Matthew drove over in his microbus; Humphrey Osmond arrived for a three day visit on Election Day (Kennedy v Nixon). "I wish," Aldous had written to Matthew, "one cd feel much enthusiasm for Messrs Kennedy and Johnson.

> The thought of old Joe Kennedy, with $200 millions amassed . . . on the stockmarket, lurking in the background of the young crusader is very distasteful. But perhaps the man may turn out to be a winner and a good president—quien sabe? And do we need a good president!

To Humphrey, Aldous spoke of his illness. He said the doctor thought that he had a good chance; enjoined Humphrey not to tell any member of his family as they would worry and it would not help him. Then he dismissed the matter and read out a chapter from *Island*.

Aldous saw a good deal of Huston Smith, Professor of Asian Philosophy at M.I.T. Huston Smith had studied Zen in a monastery in Kyoto, looked after refugees on the border of Tibet; he had met Aldous once before, twenty years ago, when as a very young man he had sought him out in California. At the Los Angeles apartment there was only a Negro maid, who told him what wonderful people she was working for and directed him to Llano. There he found Aldous and Maria. Huston Smith talked to me about the quality of the days he spent with them in the desert. Of Maria . . . Of beginning it all by making up a bed with her . . . "It was so unexpected." Now at M.I.T. he accompanied Aldous on some of his out-of-town engagements, (with Aldous punctually appearing thirty to forty seconds before the arranged time and asking, "Anything unusually disastrous happened in the world today?") Four years after, Huston Smith wrote,[1]

More impressive than the range of the man's mind, however, was its sympathy and interest. Few major intelligences since William James have been as open. Huxley's regard for mysticism was well known by dint of being so nearly notorious. What some overlooked was equal interest in the workaday world . . . To those who, greedy for transcendence, deprecated the mundane, he counselled that "we must make the best of *both* worlds." To their opposites, the positivists, his word was "All Right, one world at a time; but not half a world!"

. . . If he lost his [literary] reputation, it was . . because he wasn't content simply to do what he could do well. His competence bored him. So the master of words moved on to what eludes them, remarking over his shoulder that "language is a device for taking the mystery out of reality." . . .

He could [relegate his writing, as it were] because he had so little egoism. A supreme unpretentiousness characterized him to the end. "It's a bit embarrassing," he said, "to have been concerned with the human problem all one's life and find at the end that one has no more to offer by way of advice than 'Try to be a little kinder.' " If, as he had earlier remarked, the central technique for man to learn is "the art of obtaining freedom from the fundamental human disability of egoism," Huxley achieved that freedom.

But this wasn't his supreme achievement, for his personal problem was . . pessimism—"tomorrow, and tomorrow, and tomorrow, creeps in this petty pace from day to day." His final victory, there-

[1] "A Tribute", *The Psychedelic Review*, Vol. I No 3, 1964.

fore, lay not in emerging selfless but in winning through to equanimity, to evenness of spirit and a generalized good cheer . . .

Aldous's M.I.T. lectures[1] are important. Much of their material was derived from previous sources, themes and expositions recurrent throughout his work[2]—the lectures are important because, in Roy Lamson's words, they *pull together* so much of Aldous's thought. And this is exactly what the lectures do. *Island*, contemporaneous to the lectures, also pulls together Aldous's thought, if perhaps in a more rigid mould. The great point about Aldous's spoken word—in which, I hope even on paper, one can hear his voice—is, I find, that it is looser, lighter, less didactic and a good deal more concise than some of the essays and expository passages in the novels; there is, as there was in his conversation, a kind of open-endedness about it: speaking as he was, assumedly, *inter pares*, he did not have to wrap it up; he was exploring, and so may we go on exploring after him . . .

Shortly before leaving, Aldous was dining in a small French restaurant in Boston with Patrick Wall and some other friends. "People at a nearby table got up.[3] Aldous was handed an anonymous note. (By the time he opened the note, the people had left.)

'Thank you so much for all the pleasure you have given us.'

"Aldous read it; showed it round; then put it in his pocket. His *look*."

This story brings to my mind the words of Aldous's niece, Claire.[4] How often had he not thought of himself as deficient in emotion; yet "When he died," she wrote, "he left such grief behind as only a man of great feeling could have evoked."

---

1 The Titles of the *What a Piece of Work is Man* lectures are: 1. Ancient Views of Human Nature. 2. The Contemporary Picture. 3. The Individual in Relation to History. 4. Symbols and Immediate Experience. 5. Why Art? 6. Visionary Experience. 7. Human Potentialities.

2 And indeed in some of his own previous lectures.

3 As told to S. B. by Professor Wall.

4 Claire Nicolas White, *Aldous Huxley, A Reminiscence*, in *Soundings*, N.Y. State University 1962.

PART TWELVE

Years of Grace: 1960-1963

He could hold his own in the world: even at his most aloof he has always been, as Degas said of the painter Moreau, "A hermit who knows the times of all the trains."

SIR JOHN COLLIER about
Aldous Huxley

Of all man's miseries the bitterest is this, to know so much and to have control over nothing.

(The words which Herodotus put into the mouth of the Persian who talked with Thersander at Thebes.)

Chapter One

"An Interesting Challenge"

AFTER Cambridge, Massachusetts, the Hollywood hills, another winter of sun, peace, hard work. "All goes well here . . . except that everybody is too busy, Laura with her disturbed and unhappy people (what a lot there are, my God . . .) I with my book and arrears of correspondence . . . I've been working like mad . . and hope and pray that I may get the damned thing finished by the spring." There was one more nudge about the literary papers that were stacked "somewhere or other" in the house, a note from Aldous's old friend, Jake Zeitlin, who had a customer for the MS of *St Mawr* which D. H. Lawrence had given to Maria. Again Aldous consulted his son. "Now what do you think? Wd you like me to hang on to it and bequeath it to you or the children in my will?

> Or shall I sell it and put the cash into the children's fund? I myself incline to the second alternative, as I have no collector's itch and don't feel sentimental about objects and mementos. But if you prefer, I will keep it.

The year ended well. Aldous had been seen by Dr Cutler and given a clean bill of health.

Of the book nearly all was done except the end and a going over some of the earlier chapters. "This matter of death—how badly we handle it! I have a whole chapter illustrating the art of dying, as practised by my hypothetical islanders—plus other passages concerning the fear of death and the training for its acceptance.

> My own experience with Maria convinced me [to Humphrey] that the living can do a great deal to make the passage easier for the dying, to raise the most purely physiological act of human existence to the level of consciousness and perhaps even of spirituality. The last rites of Catholicism are good, but too much preoccupied with morality and the past. The emphasis has to be on the present and the posthumous future, which one must assume—and I think with justification—to be a reality. Eileen told me that, in one of her contacts with what she was convinced was Maria, there was a message for me to the effect that what I had said had helped to float the soul across the chasm . . .

In January Aldous allowed himself a break, a week in Hawaii with Laura. ". . the motive a wish to look at the islands, the excuse . . some lectures" (at Honolulu). They liked the volcano and the forests but not the "frightful Hawaiian music" and the tourists. From this jaunt they went on first to a conference on Mind Control at San Francisco, then to Salem, Oregon because Aldous wanted to have a look at the mental State Hospital which was introducing the Open Ward system pioneered in England by Maxwell Jones. Then back, for another two months, to the grindstone: "All is pretty well here—tho' I am much too busy with this damned book as Laura is with her therapy."

An Aldous Huxley bibliography[1] had been compiled, and sent to him. "I stand appalled at the thought of all I have written over the years. 'What, Mr Gibbon! Nothing but scribble, scribble, scribble' . . .

"Even the bibliography will be thick, damned and square—and it is merely the logarithm of the millions of scribbled words to which it refers."

In the spring, Aldous went again to M.I.T. for a week of their Centennial celebrations. He stayed with the Lamsons, took part in a number of panels with distinguished artists, scientists, engineers, and gave an address on Education on the Non-Verbal Level. A day or two with Matthew in New York, and return to California to polish off the book before a long travelling summer —there were plans for London, France, a conference at Copenhagen, Italy with Laura; India in the autumn. By May, *Island* was nearly done, and Dr Cutler had just told Aldous that he was one of his most successful cases.

In the evening of Friday, 12th May, one of those murderous sage-brush fires sprang up in the Hollywood hills. Fanned by a gale the flames spread up the canyon and house after house was set a-blaze. By nine o'clock 3276 Deronda Drive was on fire, before midnight the house and everything in it was gone.

Aldous and Laura's movements on that night can be reconstructed about as follows. At 7.30 pm Aldous was at home and working; Laura went over to Virginia Pfeiffer's house (empty, as Virginia was away) to feed the cat. From there she first saw fire and realized that this house was menaced. She became strangely paralysed and for some valuable time did nothing, but eventually went to fetch Aldous. When Aldous came, he too stood speechless, though he rescued one box of Virginia's papers. Soon after the house began to burn. Television trucks and police cars began

[1] *Aldous Huxley A Bibliography 1916—1959* by Claire John Eschelbach and Joyce Lee Shober. Foreword by Aldous Huxley, University of California Press, 1961.

arriving though no fire engines. Aldous and Laura managed to get back to their own house—the road beyond already swept by flames—with the help of a stranger and his car. Here they found that the flames had reached the plants on the slope below their terrace; the house itself was still clear. Aldous went inside and upstairs and got out the manuscript of *Island*. When he came out he said to Laura, "Don't you think I should take some suits?" Laura said yes, but herself remained standing, looking. Aldous re-emerged with three suits on hangers, telling her that she too had better take some clothes. This she did, in slow motion, and also picked up her violin, a Guarnieri. An unknown young boy rescued their car. The fire took over. Still no engines. At midnight Aldous and Laura left the scene, drove down the hill and took refuge from sympathy and reporters in a modest hotel on Franklin Avenue.

Laura, in her book, tells of her own remarkable passivity: ". . something unexplainable happened to me. From that moment [of seeing the flames leaping up the canyon] until the end of the evening I behaved in a way totally contrary to my nature. In emergencies I have usually responded with immediate action. When faced with adverse circumstances, I have hardly ever accepted them; almost always I have tried . . applying whatever intuition, determination, logic I could muster. Here . . . what did I do? I stood immobile, fascinated by the wild grace of the flames . . .

Why did I not immediately take the hose and wet the roof and everything around the house?

At Virginia's house the swimming pool was full.

. . Why did I not call for help? Why did I not take clothes and valuables away? I could easily have packed dozens of suitcases with necessary and some irreplacable things. Instead, what did I do? First, I went into the kitchen, still propelled by my initial purpose of opening a can of cat food . . .

And in their own house, "I was looking—and only looking. How beautiful everything was! The flames from the outside were giving to the white walls a soft rosy glow . . .

'At last,' I thought, 'the perfect illumination.'

"I walked from one room to the other, touching the objects I loved . . . There were cases of letters and diaries and notes for future writings . . . It was usually Aldous and I who took the initiative. But in that moment we were stunned. If a friend had been there he could have awakened us to action. Cases and suitcases and drawers could have been put in the empty driveway, which remained untouched by the fire . . ."

Next morning Aldous and Laura went back up the hill and saw that indeed everything was gone. Poking in the ashes, Aldous found the one thing that remained, the marble bust of Maria, done when she was fourteen years old. He telephoned Mme Nys —the fire had been visible last night both in the sky and on the television screen—and reassured her, "d'une voix forte et calme". He spoke to Matthew in New York; Anita Loos, faithful friend in every crisis, rang up, to her he said, "It was quite an experience, but it does make one feel extraordinarily *clean*."

It was some days before they were able to take in their loss. Not only were Aldous and Laura homeless and, except for the MS, the three suits and the violin, without belongings, objects, household goods, but Aldous had lost his papers, notebooks, old letters, he had lost his books, some four thousand books with his own working references, annotations, markings, "I am now a man without possessions and without a past," he wrote to his son five days later.

> This last I regret as much for you as for myself; for what has gone is a piece of your life and heart as well as of mine. But there is nothing to do except try to start from scratch.

Not easy. "It is odd to be starting from scratch at my age—" he wrote to Robert Hutchins, "with literally nothing in the way of possessions, books, mementoes, letters, diaries. I am evidently intended to learn a little in advance of the final denudation, that you can't take it with you."

Talking to Humphrey later on, he put it even more starkly: "I took it as a sign that the grim reaper was having a good look at me."

Time magazine, too, had a word about Aldous's reaction to the disaster.

> Flames licked through dry grasses and gutted twenty-four luxury homes in Hollywood Hills. Destroyed were author Aldous Huxley's two-storey house, his manuscripts and mementoes of a lifetime. While firemen restrained the nearly blind British author from running into the blaze, Huxley wept like a child.[1]

[1] *Time* 26th May 1961.

This was one of the few occasions on which Aldous picked up the public cudgels.[1]

> Sir,
>
> As an old hand at fiction, may I congratulate the write-up artist who penned the account of my actions on the night my house was burned down (May 12).
>
> The facts are these. My wife and I started the evening at the house, a little way down the road, of an absent friend. Having rescued a box of her papers and tried in vain to locate the cat, we left this house in flames and were driven back to our own home by a friendly onlooker. Here we picked up a few clothes, my wife's Guarnieri violin, and the MS of the book on which I have been working for the past two years. By the time these had been taken to the car, the house was burning. There was nothing we could do, and all the local fire engines (though not the TV trucks) were somewhere else.
>
> So we got into the car and drove away—sadly enough, goodness knows, but (ignoring those conventions of the romantic novelette to which your write-up artist so faithfully adhered) not crying like babies, nor requiring to be restrained from running back into the flames.
>
> Aldous Huxley

Offers of hospitality poured in from the Kiskaddens, the Wendels, the Stravinskys; Aldous decided to hole himself up with Gerald Heard at Santa Monica and finish *Island* (". . 'tho at the moment writing seems difficult"). Laura with Virginia Pfeiffer, of course also homeless, moved into a rented house.

Besides Aldous's library and the fragments of two unfinished novels,[2] there had gone all those collector's items[3] he had failed to sell in time—a first edition of Voltaire's *Candide* which had belonged to Aldous's grandfather T. H. H. who had travelled with it across the world (as had Aldous), first editions of *Du Coté de chez Swan* and *Lady Chatterley's Lover*; signed volumes by T. S. Eliot, Pound, Wells and Gide; forty letters from D. H. Lawrence to Aldous and Maria, letters from Max Beerbohm, Virginia Woolf, Valéry, Elinor Wylie, H. L. Mencken, Wells and Bennett; a large number of MSS of Aldous's works, among them *Antic Hay* and *Point Counter Point*. The most valuable single item, always

---

[1] *Time* 16th June 1961.

[2] One of them most likely the historical one on Catherine of Siena.

[3] I am indebted for this listing to the kindness of Mr Jacob Zeitlin, who at the time made a valuation for Aldous. It is bound to be rather incomplete as it was based on Aldous's memory of his possessions.

from the bibliophile's point of view, was the MS of D. H. L's *St Mawr*. The irreparable loss for Aldous (and for Aldous's biographers) was Maria's pre-war journal and Maria's letters to her sister Suzanne; these were letters written during her last twelve years or so with the expressed purpose of leaving a record of Aldous's life (. . "pour raconter la vie d'Aldous . ."). How did these letters happen to be in the house? Because Aldous, beginning to think about writing his own memoirs had asked Suzanne for their return. They had arrived from Holland only a short time ago and were still in their original box or boxes.

Worse. "Yes," Aldous wrote to Eileen Garrett, "all the MSS were burned and all my letters from others and in the case of Maria, my letters to her." These were the letters Aldous had written to the girl he was in love with, from London, from Garsington, as a master at Eton, day after day during the years of separation in the First World War, after Maria had been whisked off to Italy by her mother; the letters Maria had re-read and tied up again and taken with her to America when they left the Sanary house in 1937. They are gone; as are the letters of that time to Aldous from Maria. "So there is no more tangible link with the past. It is an interesting challenge and I hope I shall be able to cope with it properly."

Chapter Two

London—Summer 1961

ON 15th June (*Island* finished) Aldous arrived in London.
Julian and Juliette met him at the airport. Having builders
in their house, they took him to a service flat in Kensington.[1] The
rooms gave on to a large garden full of trees, and he was delighted
by this and the country quiet. Aldous had not been in England
since the summer of 1958. It was a few weeks before his sixty-
seventh birthday: to his friends he looked thin, lath-thin, and he
had gone very grey; he still moved lightly, and he looked elegant,
dandified and at the same time of transcendant distinction. Here
is how he appeared to someone who had not seen him before,
Rosamund Lehmann:[2]

> . . . photographs had not prepared me for his extraordinary, his
> unique beauty. It was like being all at once in the presence of
> someone of another and higher planetary order. This may sound
> extravagant and trite as well; but there was really something angelic,
> in the strict sense, about his physical appearance: I mean he seemed
> at first sight a luminous intelligence incarnate.

It was the fifth return to England since they went away in
1937, his fifth return in twenty-four years. Maria once said that if
Aldous felt any nostalgia at all for Europe in their early American
days, it was not for Italy, not for France, but for English trees,
the English countryside. Then that too, she said, dried up. Aldous
passed through a period of indifference, the past became encum-
brance, indulgence; the first return in 1948—no eagerness about
it—was dealt to him by circumstances (involvement with a film;
almost identically the pattern that had originally brought him to
California). Now that, too, lay behind. He came and went at
ease; at home; detached; attached. This year he revisited scenes
of his childhood. The remarkable thing is that he was able to do
so—that corner of rural Surrey, the country west of Godalming
and Milford, where he had spent the fourteen steady years of his
happy, his very happy, late-Victorian and Edwardian childhood,
with its fields and woods and houses was still recognizable and
there: Laleham, the house in the parish of Compton, Aldous was

---

[1] At 4 Ennismore Gardens.
[2] In a B.B.C. broadcast, August 1964.

born in; Prior's Field, the school his mother had founded, its land intact and functioning as a school (the portrait of Julia Frances Huxley in the hall, WE LIVE BY ADMIRATION HOPE AND LOVE engraved upon the gate); Hillside, the Huxley boys' preparatory school.

On the Saturday after Aldous's arrival, Julian had to attend a meeting of the governors of Prior's Field and Aldous went with him. While they did their work, Aldous took himself for a long walk. When Julian joined him again, he found him full of joy—remembered haunts, the trees he had seen planted and which were now sixty feet high and looked as if they had been there for three hundred years. One of the oddest changes, he remarked, were the tangles of brambles and wild roses on what were once smooth grassy slopes; rabbits used to eat the young shoots as they came up, and now the rabbits were exterminated. Before going home Aldous asked to be taken to the cemetery, to Compton and the small hill-side graveyard where his and Julian's parents and Trevenen were buried in one grave.

We were both strangely moved [Julian in his *Memories*] to see that wild meadow saxifrage, one of Mother's favourite flowers, had sprung up on the grassy grave, and were in full bloom; they seemed a spontaneous tribute of the nature that both my parents had so much loved.

Here, Aldous was overcome with grief.

When presently he spent a long weekend with Gervas and his wife, Elspeth, in their house in Wiltshire, Gervas too drove him into Surrey to have a look at what had been their prep school. Hillside, at that point about to be converted, was a shell, yet Aldous was still able to place everything. Out here was the giant-stride . . Here was our cubicle . . Here was the stage (where the two boys and Lewis Gielgud did *The Merchant of Venice*) . . Here was the blackboard . . .

On his first Tuesday in London Aldous, on Dr Cutler's advice, had a consultation with a specialist, Sir Stanford Cade, the surgeon. "He confirmed Cutler's diagnosis, admired the excellent job Cutler did . . ." Aldous wrote to Laura. "So this is all very satisfactory." The same night Aldous went to the theatre to see *The Devils of Loudun* in John Whiting's adaptation which had been playing in the West End since February. (He thought production and performance excellent, and wrote to John Whiting to tell him so. On 27th June, he and Aldous had a talk about *The Devils* on the B.B.C.)

During the first minutes of our meeting, I, too, only saw the greyness and the frailty. When Aldous began to speak animation took over. The year before I had been reporting the *Lady Chatterley* trial and Aldous surprised me by treating the whole business much less solemnly than had our eminent literary and sociological experts in the witness box. He dismissed the four-letter words—"Poor Lawrence, well, I mean, this is simply one of the ways in which a novelist can *not* do it." He delighted me by his whole-hearted rejection of the new French novels of the Robbe-Grillet variety—"unutterably boring. Well, they just bore me stiff . . . I don't think they ever express *anything* . . ." The subject I could not help talking about was the fire, of which Aldous spoke with the detachment we find in the letters. How did he do it, I asked hoping to learn a way to stoicism, how did you begin again? "Well, I went out," he said, "and bought a toothbrush." Concern about Aldous's appearance waned because of the matter of fact energy he displayed. We had been dining at Rules off the Strand and afterwards walked towards St Paul's; from there we turned west again through Holborn and New Oxford Street (where Aldous commented on the fashion dummies in the windows looking like Jackie Kennedy this year); it was he who decided when to cross a road. At St Giles' Circus the traffic streams were particularly confusing; Aldous firmly stopped my dithering and steered me across. We wandered about Bloomsbury for a while, headed towards Regent's Park—the night was very warm; when we reached my door north of the Marylebone Road it must have been after the best part of a two hours' walk. Only then, with no sense of urgency, did Aldous decide that he might as well go back to Kensington in a cab.

Nor was it that his days were exactly inactive. He had to prepare his speech for the Congress on Applied Psychology in Copenhagen; he gave long interviews; he was not even altogether rid yet, as it turned out, of the book he had just finished. Ian Parsons and Cass Canfield had been corresponding about the length of some of the discursive passages in *Island*. They hesitated about approaching him. In their long publishing association with Aldous, neither had ever dreamt of asking him to change a comma. (As a point of fact, Aldous *had* once been given, and taken, Ian's advice, and cut some of the horror in the torture scenes of the English, though not the American, edition of *The Devils of Loudun*.) Ian decided to talk to Aldous and did so soon after his arrival. Aldous, to his relief, took it with calm professionalism, agreeing that some passages might well be too lengthy. He went through his text again and made some cuts, which must have caused some chopping and changing, as he appears to have had the book retyped. For the rest, he went about seeing people. He

looked up Dr Felix Mann, the young acupuncturist with whom he
had been in correspondence, "to talk acupuncture and, profes-
sionally, to be practised on." Previously he had written:

> I was glad to get your description of yourself. Long acquaintance
> with your namesake, Thomas, had led me to visualize you as an
> eccentric German of about 65. It is very gratifying to find that I was
> mistaken!

To Laura he reported that Dr Mann cures people "who can't be
cured by other doctors (mostly chronic cases). The state health
service pays him to spend a day each week acupuncturing difficult
patients in a public hospital—a good mark in favour of official
medicine in England. He felt my pulse, found general health
good, but detected a certain weakness in kidneys and liver, which
he tonified with needles in the foot and knee . . ."

Aldous had dinner with Dr William Sargant (having read his
Battle for the Mind) to talk psychotherapy; dinner with his friends
at Chatto's, Ian Parsons and Norah Smallwood, who gave a
party for him at which he met Iris Murdoch; went to see his old
friend Moura Budberg who was living round the corner, and his
old friends Harold and Vera Raymond in Kent; saw Huxley
grandchildren and cousins at Julian and Juliette's, went to tea
with Ethel Sands. And there was Enid Bagnold. They hadn't
seen each other for rather more than half a century.

> "I'm Enid Bagnold," I said.[1] "I was at Prior's Field. You were an
> odious little boy."
> Aldous (leaning about like a serpent) "I'm ODIOUS still!"
> But this time it was said with humour—like an indulgent bogey-
> man. I told him the little story. [About him, aged seven, snubbing
> her efforts of conversation at Mrs Huxley's table.]

He saw Rosamund Lehmann.

> . . He let me describe an overwhelming mystical experience. He
> told me I was very fortunate, said that he himself had never had one,
> adding with characteristic humility, "Perhaps I don't love enough."
> . . . I know that personally he radiated something that made it
> impossible to say one liked him—one had to think of him in terms of
> love.[2]

---

[1] Enid Bagnold in conversation with, and letter to, S. B.
[2] Rosamund Lehmann in B.B.C. broadcast cit.

People every day. Yet so many of Aldous's old friends were away or dead or ill, that he found London rather sad, he wrote to Laura. "Not all the time, however,

> for the colouring is so beautiful when the sun comes out, and the foliage and flowers are so rich that I find myself at moments almost in an LSD state. And I have met some very nice people; so don't let me complain.

It was Laura whom he missed very much—though here, too, he would not complain—and he wrote to her almost every day. (As well as being occupied with patients and her book, Laura was staying on in California to look after Virginia, who had broken her collar-bone.) He had been thinking of her all day, Aldous wrote in one of those letters,[1]

> with a strange kind of intensity—thinking how extraordinary you are in your power and your vulnerability, your capacity for loving and your "noli me tangere" passion for being left alone . . . I would like to feel that I could—would like to feel that I can love you with so much understanding tenderness that I shall always know what to do, or what to refrain from doing in order to help you in your strength and support you in your vulnerability . . .

This letter ends with,

> Be well, my sweetheart, and let us try to be happy and peaceful malgré tout—because of one another.

At Moura Budberg's, Aldous had met Professor Tolstoy (a distant relative of the great Tolstoy) come to London in charge of a Soviet scientific exhibition, who urged him to visit Russia. What about it? Aldous asked Laura. What about their both going for a week or two after Copenhagen?

> . . My own feeling is that we should go to Russia. I have never been anxious to go; but Tolstoy's extreme cordiality and obvious desire to be helpful have changed my feelings, and I think we ought to take the opportunity that is being presented to us. (Maybe this is one of the hints for which I have been waiting!) [Since the onset of his illness, since finishing Island, Aldous had been asking himself about the best use he ought to make of his life.]
> . . . Professor Tolstoy . . [would] arrange for us to see whatever we like. I told him that you and I were particularly interested in the

---

[1] Published, not in the collected edition, but in *This Timeless Moment*.

preventive medicine and mental health side of Russian life, and he would undoubtedly be able to get us into hospitals, rest homes, clinics etc. Let me know as soon as possible what you feel about this project . . .

. . . Goodbye, my darling. I don't imagine that either of us will ever be able to do what St Ignatius said he could do. [Father Ignatius's well-known reply when asked what he would do if the Pope dissolved the Society of Jesus and thus swept away his life work, "One quarter of an hour in orison and it would be all the same."] But even if the final All Rightness of the world may never be vouchsafed to us as a permanent experience (only perhaps in flashes), I believe we can do quite a lot—you complementing me, I complementing you—to achieve a relative all rightness for ourselves and a few other people in the midst of the awful all wrongness of what Keats called "the giant misery of the world." Ti voglio bene.

Laura was interested in the Russian visit, and Aldous went to the Soviet Consulate for his visa. "What a mess!

First of all half an hour's wait, because the consul hadn't turned up. When he did turn up, he was single-handed . . so everything took a very long time. Finally I asked for my visa: but it seems that unless one is travelling in one of the Intourist Groups, one has to have an official invitation to go. Of course I *could* get such an invitation from the Writers' Group there—but (a) there is not much time for this and (b) I don't want to go officially . . . meanwhile there is the problem of hotels, about which the consul was gloomy. So it really looks as though our Russian trip is off. Do you mind very much? Another year we will make the necessary arrangements 6 months in advance. Last minute plans are unworkable these days. Now I must go and see if we can get rooms at Gstaad.

For meanwhile Laura had given the date of her coming over and they planned to meet in Switzerland where Krishnamurti and the Yehudi Menuhins were going to be.

. . Krishnaji . . came yesterday to see me for a few minutes [Aldous to Laura]—looked well, but also curiously different from what he used to be; for he is now a small bright old man, with a bald head ringed by white hair. But I was very glad to see him . . .

The long recorded interview, often referred to in the course of this narrative, as the London interview, took place that summer—two long afternoons, punctuated by tea and sherry, in Aldous's sitting-room with the leafy view in Ennismore Gardens. The range of subjects was very wide; Aldous, as the case might be, responded to John Chandos, his interviewer, side-stepped or expanded. The point of the interview is that it has left us with such a characteristic record not only of Aldous's thought but of Aldous's way of expressing it; more informal still than his lectures, than his radio and television broadcasts—there was no time limit, no audience: he was talking to one man who himself talked a good deal—this record comes as near as anything to the way Aldous talked to his friends. *This was* his conversation. I shall come back to this record once again; here I would like to place a few of Aldous's comments and ideas on one thing and another. Some will sound familiar to all who knew him.

Writers. Writers of our time. Is there anyone, in your opinion, who will survive? who will be read?

Aldous: I don't know. A difficult question. [Pause] For some reason no *one* author has had a great influence over me. I get things out of all reasonably good authors and even out of some bad authors . . But as to naming any one of them who had a great influence on me—I've often been asked this question . . . I don't get as much out of James as some people say they get out of him. I never found him very interesting.

I used to get a lot out of Proust. I re-read some of it the other day and was rather disappointed—I don't know why. I read the last volume, *Le Temps Retrouvé*, it seemed to me curiously remote and—unbelievable and unreal.

And even the first volume . . which I thought was very beautiful in the early days—I didn't get very much out of it . . . It's very strange, because it moved me immensely when it first appeared. I must have another look at it.

Well, I think some of Hemingway's stories are *very* remarkable, his short stories. I haven't read any of the more recent books which I understand are not very good.

Nor have I read any recent Faulkners. I liked some of the early books very much. *Soldier's Pay* and *Light in August* and *Sanctuary*—but I confess I haven't read anything recently.

That subject soon ran dry. "Which do you find the most interesting art products in our time, music, literature, painting?"

I suppose there have been interesting ones in all, haven't there? I find myself out of sympathy with some . . . I personally get very bored with this endless repetition of non-representational expressionism, which goes on and on and on. But the trend towards abstraction was a very useful and valuable one in the earlier phases. I think it's *time we grew out of it*. But most painters don't. Music—

music is *very far* away . . . it seems to me that fully self-conscious and artistic music is far remoter from popular music than Tallis was remote from Greensleeves. It *was* remote from Greensleeves but not *nearly* as remote as Boulez, say, from *My Fair Lady*.

And this doesn't seem to me to be at all a healthy situation—when you have an immense gap between the ordinary taste and the taste of the highly refined and educated. It's a fact; but is it a *desirable* fact? There just is *no communication* . . . These are things which puzzle me extremely: I just have no idea what happens when you get this kind of *gap* between the masses of the people and the high priests of their culture? It's a most unfortunate phenomenon.

Literature?

Well, there is a slight tendency in the same direction. Extremely obscure poetry. But there, it seems to me, you get a number of good writers who *are* prepared to communicate to more people than the good composers as a rule are prepared to communicate.

The present trend of literary and historical criticism?

I do think it's inferior, quite definitely. After all, life *is* immensely complex, so why pretend that it isn't. Why not attempt . . . to make some kind of synthesis, some kind of meaningful pattern? . . . I find this new kind of criticism unspeakably *boring*. It seems to me so barren—and this hideous jargon they've invented—I don't know what it's all about—it *bores* me absolutely stiff, this whole thing. It seems so *trivial* . . .

Probably some of this work has to be done—this kind of very elaborate, meticulous linguistic work is probably useful, but regarded as the be all and end all of criticism it seems to be *absolutely absurd*.

Does anyone want to read him [the modern critic]? *I* don't want to read him . . . perhaps his fellow critics want to read him . . . Do people at large get much out of him? Perhaps they do. *I* don't happen to get much out of him.

. . Literary criticism is not the best way of criticizing life as it is today—there's a pharisaical element in it . . .

At one point they talk about the relation of content to style, the simple against the rich. Aldous says,

. . . I don't really like the bare bold classical style—because it is to my mind hopelessly over simplified and therefore not true. Life . . is incredibly complex and very very subtle—therefore I would say that any form of art which is as simplified as, say, the French tragedy of the seventeenth century is intrinsically an inferior art—it may be very elegant and beautiful—but if you can impose order on a much more complex mass of material as Shakespeare was able to do, this seems to me an intrinsically superior form of art . . . A great composition where enormous numbers of elements, both formal and literary in the widest sense, and emotional, are brought together and harmonized . . . is a higher form of art than the simple, elegant, so-called classical form.

A need for new forms?

Take composers of the grand period, like Mozart, or early John Sebastian Bach—they had this immense advantage that they had a tradition which they were quite prepared to exploit to the limit . . . and when you listen to both of them, you have this extraordinary sense of *good faith* in them, I mean they are never trying to produce effects for the sake of effects, they are never trying to produce originality for the sake of originality . . . They are content to work within a medium which they completely accepted and which they developed to the most extraordinary limits . . .

Now we have reached a point where we really don't accept any tradition without question and we run through an immense capital of artistic forms and are continually trying to amass new capital and exploit new forms, and so much of contemporary artistic effort is somehow *spent* in this *desperate* procedure of trying to find wholly novel methods of saying things . . . This is particularly true of music I would say, and also of painting, to some extent of literature—this kind of simple good faith in the expression of simple emotions in what appears to be a simple, but is in effect an extremely subtle mode: this is awfully difficult now. It is inconceivable now for us, you see, to write the kind of melodies, or the kind of contra-puntal arrangements, which Bach and Mozart did . . . It's really unfortunate—an enormous amount of artistic energy has to go into work which for the older composers had already been done for them . . the main structure had been laid down and they were ready to accept this, with minor modifications of course all the time . . In this sense we are curiously badly off in comparison with those people in the past . . .

What *is* the relation of the artist to his time?

The relation between life and art? *I don't know.* It's much less *clear* than some critics maintain that it is—there are other factors: this internal logic of art is of immense importance in the whole history of the development of the arts, and has very little to do with external events. Take Schuetz, for example, his life consisted of continually running away from the Thirty Years War, he lived in the middle of the most appalling circumstances—but you can see no trace of this in his music at all . . .

. . . I have this curious feeling that this extraordinary roulette wheel of heredity plays such a part in literature. Sometimes you get twenty-seven reds in a row at Monte Carlo, and this may happen in certain periods of history—with an extraordinary series of people turning up, who happen to have a fairly good environment and can do something with it. After all, the advances in literature *depend* on these purely fortuitous arrivals of extraordinary people. I mean, nobody could have conceivably foreseen Shakespeare . . Nothing in Russian literature could have told one that Tolstoy would come along . . .

Presently they discussed the Ideal Society:

Well, I don't know whether any age has done it completely. The Greeks did probably pretty well up to a point. But the Greeks had appalling limitations—their whole view of women was utterly unsatisfactory; they had no adequate kind of marriage, no view of permanent love relationships between the sexes. In that way they were frightfully limited. On the other hand they handled the problem of the irrational very well . . . I don't know enough about older civilizations . . Many of them obviously did it pretty well . . The Chinese did . . But I'm quite sure that we could improve upon it. I don't think that *we* do it very well.

The Church now, the Catholic Church—"How do you see its role in the history of Europe? As an instrument of repression? or of enlightenment?"

. . I'm not an historian, of course . . I should say it did both: it did *preserve* culture and learning, and it did *repress* learning . . . The whole thing is so ambivalent. In some ways it did good, in others it did an enormous amount of harm.

And if the Reformation could have been postponed?

. . . We would have had the rise of scepticism, of Voltaireanism—*les Libertins* rather than Protestantism and a second and even more violent and intense religion than the old Catholic one. The wars of religion might have been avoided. That would have been a good thing. Those wars were *unspeakably* horrible.

Is there a need of organized religion? Historically, it looks like that, said Aldous, then went off on his own:

I hope it's possible to have an a-septic mysticism. I think certain people can have it; but whether there can be a general atmosphere on the basis of a non-superstitious and non-dogmatic set of beliefs, I've no idea. I profoundly hope so. But at certain times I rather doubt it. I mean, the human mind *is a symbolific instrument*. It exists to manufacture symbols .. to turn immediate experience into symbols for the purpose of managing it in a fairly convenient way. The question is, can we get on with scientific symbols, realist symbols, and then concentrate on the immediate experience? I simply don't know whether this is a possible general attitude towards the world. It's certainly possible in isolated individuals . . . Whether it will ever turn out something that appeals to a great number of people, I have no idea.

. . . This whole problem of dealing with the irrational is surely to find out means by which these irrational drives can be given satisfaction without harming the person who has the drives and without harming his neighbours—it is not beyond the wit of man to devise these methods. This is something William James discussed years ago in his essay "The Moral Equivalent of War." This is an inadequate essay, but it touches on one aspect of an extraordinarily important way of dealing with human beings .. of dealing with the irrational side of man. Which requires satisfaction . . . The most difficult problem of reason is—how can we allow the irrational its proper scope within a general framework of rationality and benevolence?

Empirically all cultures have worked out various methods . . . The Greek method of Maenadism, Bacchic orgies and so on, were all methods of getting rid of these *intolerable tensions* in society in harmless and even beneficient ways . . . Carnivals, saturnalia . . . and I think that one of our troubles is that we haven't got enough of these devices. Christianity became so wildly respectable that it gave up *dancing*. Which was a *grave mistake*, it seems to me.

Muscular actions have great importance. It's very significant that the extremely, quotes, *spiritual* sect of the Quakers *quaked*. Here there was this voluntary quaking movement of the muscles which was an immense release . . . this was an empirical invention of great value . . . And any civilization that seriously takes account of man's nature tends to invent these kind of things; they've been invented again and again by primitive and even by quite advanced people, and we made the awful mistake of dropping the lot of them. The best we can do is Rock and Roll, which is something which the boys and girls had to invent for themselves—but there is no sort of social or religious sanction for this . . whereas in the past there was.

"To be satisfactory, haven't these activities got to be linked with some, let us say, religious authority?"

There is no particular reason why people shouldn't be realistic about them . . We didn't have to say that when the Quakers quaked or the Shakers shook this was necessarily the operation of the Holy Ghost . . They were getting rid of tensions . . . I think we can talk about this in realistic terms without invoking supernatural explanations. But at the same time, what we may call the sort of basic supernaturalism, what we may call the life force, are of value in so far as they permit basic sources of energy and enlightenment to flow freely through an organism which is constantly blocking itself up and obstructing itself by the operation of the conscious ego. There are *ways* of *getting rid* of the *conscious ego*, of *getting out of our own light.* Which is of course what everybody has been talking about since the beginning of time.

And I think we are now in a position to be able to talk about it in more or less naturalistic terms and not necessarily in these supernatural terms . . .

Every now and then the questions would take a personal turn. Literary plans?

I would very much like to find another good biographical or historical episode such as I dealt with in *Grey Eminence* . . and the essay on Maine de Biran . . . For the moment I haven't been able to find something which I could tackle well . . .

"Have you still any interest in writing for the theatre, Mr Huxley?"

Hm, yes, sometime I might write another play . . .

There were of course long passages dealing with immediate sociological problems. These, however, overlap, not textually but in substance, with another interview of that summer, a B.B.C. interview with John Morgan, telecast on 23rd July. Here one saw Aldous, looking fragile, gently attending to each question—the fraction of a pause, hear the flowing answer, the clear voice, often rising to a higher note . . . The programme was introduced by a few bars from the slow movement of Beethoven's A-minor quartet.

John Morgan: Mr Huxley, you've described that passage . . as the greatest music ever written—now why do you think that?
Aldous: Well, I would say that it's the greatest of its kind, though

unfortunately that was such a small snatch of it that we didn't get the full impression of this kind of sublime serenity in the music; and then of course it goes on into a very extraordinary passage where there's the counter-point of two melodies playing against one another, and doing this thing which only music can do, saying two things at the same time, something which, as a writer, I would long to be able to do, but the nature of language is such that one can't do it, one can't say two things at the same time.

J. M.: Would you like to have been a composer?

A.: Well, only if I'd been a prodigious genius—well, I would like to have been a prodigious genius in anything. But unfortunately, I love music but as for understanding what it must be like to be able to think in terms of musical sequences, I just don't know; I mean, I feel in relation to the great composers, as a dog must feel in relation to a human being. That those are creatures of another order altogether.

J. M.: . . . you've derived a very rich experience from a lifetime study of both art and society, would you say . . . more rich from art?

A.: Surely in a sense the two things are different. Art springs from . . . a very deep, what may be called an urge to order . . . an almost instinctive urge in human beings to impose order upon the profusion and chaos of existence . . . The whole problem of society is to find a way of imposing order, without imposing a too rigid order . . .

And from this, by way of *Brave New World*, they came to the menace of a technological take-over.

A.: . . I think when the . . scientific means are developed they just tend to be *used* . . . if you plant the seeds of applied science or technology it proceeds to grow. . . hence the sense which many people have . . . that man is now the victim of his own technology . . . instead of being in control of it.

J. M.: How could he be in control of it?

A.: . . . I think this is perhaps one of the major problems of our time. How do we make use of this thing? After all, this was stated in the gospel . . the Sabbath was made for Man and not Man for the Sabbath, and in the same way, technology was made for man, not man for technology, but unfortunately [we have] created a world in which man seems to be made for technology . . .

. . in the West we still remember John Stuart Mill, James Mill, Jefferson and so on, we still remember vaguely the precepts of Christianity, and we are a little reluctant . . to allow technology to take over. In the long run we generally succumb. I'm reminded of the line in Byron's "Don Juan" about this lady who vowing she would ne'er consent, consented . . . In the short run we sort of higgle-haggle about it and we are reluctant, but we tend to be pushed by the advancing technology in a certain direction . . . We do have to start thinking how we can get control again of our own inventions. This is a kind of Frankenstein monster problem.

J. M.: . . . You did say that over-population, over-organization were the great problems now?

A.: They're closely related. It's quite obvious that where you have a very rapidly rising population with its extreme pressures on food and production; upon problems of getting enough education, housing and so on, you necessarily must have a higher and higher degree of organization . . . you have to have organization comparable in complexity and tightness to the technology that has to be worked. I think the two things run hand in hand—technology, over-population, over-organization, are three factors which work together and which are all pushing us . . .

J. M.: . . . isn't it always possible, while human beings remain much as they are, that they will find means of over-throwing modern, scientific dictatorship?

A.: Well I would like to think so. But do reflect on this simple fact. For example in the revolution of 1848, when the crowds put up the barricades and resisted the soldiers, the arms on either side . . were about equal—they were just muskets. But now, on one side you may have muskets and on the other side you will have tanks and flame-throwers and, if the air force remains faithful to the regime, you will have aeroplanes dropping bombs and firing machine-guns from above. It is obviously much more difficult now to overthrow by force; the other thing is that the modern government has incomparably more efficient methods first of propaganda and then of information. I mean if you compare Napoleon's Chief of Police, Fouché, with any efficient police force today, it's childish what he could do . . .

Questions about *Island, Antic Hay*, D. H. Lawrence, Mrs Grundy, LSD, versus alcoholism, then back full circle to the "major problems of the rest of this century?"

A.: . . First of all there is this question are we going to blow ourselves up or not. I think and hope that we shall not. But if we don't then the most urgent problem of the next fifty and I would say a hundred years or more, is the problem of explosive population increase. In this country of course it's not a major problem, but when you go to countries in Central America or in South America, and find increases at the rate of three percent per annum, which doubles the population in twenty-four years, what on earth do you do if you're an under-developed country? Even if you can solve the food problem, which in many cases they probably can, what do you do about the housing problem, about the educational problem, how do you build enough schools, how do you find enough teachers—what do you do about the roads and sewage systems . . . ?

John Morgan asked if nevertheless it were not possible, given the will and abandoning preparation for war, to raise everyone's standard of living?

A.: I think it is. But the point is that it does look as if quantity were the enemy of quality on this matter. After all, it isn't simply a question of food, it's a question of is it pleasant to live in a town of ten million inhabitants such as Tokyo is? Is it pleasant to live in a place with fourteen hundred people to the square mile such as Barbados is? This seems to me the problem. Is life under such conditions as good as life where, as throughout nature, there is a balance between the birth-rate and the death-rate, where you have a kind of stable population, based on a low birth-rate and a low death-rate, where you can plan ahead . . and where it is possible to organize the good life much better.

J. M.: Are you hopeful or pessimistic about the rest of the century?

A.: I think I am both. We have it within our power, I think, *to do extraordinary things* if we want to. The question is do we want to enough? And also do we have enough—it's not merely a question of good will, it's a question of extreme intelligence . . .

Chapter Three

Travels—An *Amende Honorable*

ALDOUS left London on the 15th of July to go to Eileen
Garrett's for another of her parapsychological conferences at
Le Piol in the South of France. (A spacious house, terraces,
shade trees, flowering shrubs, a pool.) Eileen found him low in
spirit. When she suggested ways of replacing his burned books,
he discouraged her; he hadn't got enough time, he said. "You
have some time." "Not enough."

The conference started. Psychiatrists, neurologists, French,
Italian, Dutch, "Quite interesting group . . .

> a Swiss or two, the Englishman, Gray Walter [to Laura] . . very
> bright and well-informed. And of course Eileen in the midst of it—
> mostly silent, but sometimes describing her experiences very well,
> and making comments, generally very sensible . . .

On an off day, Eileen took Aldous for a long drive up into the
barren country in the mountains above Vence. There he talked
to her about D. H. Lawrence.

On the 21st, Jeanne Neveux with Noële came to pick him up.
They spent the night in Aix-en-Provence. "I had forgotten how
beautiful Aix is—a town with fountains and very sober, noble
17th-century houses. It was a pleasure to see [it] again." Next
day they drove up the valley of the Rhône to Vaison-la-Romaine
where once more a play of Georges Neveux's was being staged
for the Festival. "The countryside is very beautiful—vineyards,
orchards, wind-breaks of cypress trees.

> But the agriculture is becoming completely mechanized, indus-
> trialized, chemically controlled as in America. They have now
> reached a point at which they can make half a dozen different types
> of wine out of the same batch of grape juice . . .

At Vaison the lodgings were the same he and Maria had had in
1954. With the Neveuxs he went to Georges' *Voyage de Thésée* in
the Roman theatre, and the next night to *Triolus and Cressida*.
"Aldous very happy," noted Jeanne. ("If I dared to wish for
genius," he once wrote, "I would ask for the grace to write
Troilus and *The Canterbury Tales*.") In the mornings he waited

impatiently for the post. Rina came; proceeded to wash his shirts and generally look after him; he accepted it.

. . Rina, who came to us in 1924, when she was 13, turned up at Vaison to see me. Such a wonderful example of the most civilized and noble kind of peasant of the old school. She is now a woman of 50, married to a younger man (very happily) who has worked his way up to the head of a transport company . . Rina organizes the whole business and at the same time retains all her old qualities of simplicity, kindness, native common sense and goodness. One has a sad feeling that people of this kind are becoming rarer and rarer . . .

On their third day he had a long talk with Jeanne. He spoke about 1954; about the letters that were gone; about his feelings for Laura—the desire he now had to *give* . . . Jeanne offered to let him have her own letters from Maria. He said, We'll see . . . later perhaps . . .

On the 26th Jeanne took him to Orange to catch the early morning train to Geneva. Aldous was absent and remote and did not leave a forwarding address. He never returned to France.

Next day, in a hired car, he met Laura at the airport and they went on to Gstaad. The ten days in Switzerland were good ones. They had rooms in one of those large, old-fashioned hotels, the Palace; the weather was brilliant. "Laura has rejoined me [to Humphrey] and we breathe good air, eat large meals and listen to Krishnamurti . . ." The Menuhins were there.

Yehudi Menuhin and Aldous knew each other for a few years only. They met seldom but there was a kinship. When they were together, says Yehudi's wife, Diana, they were like brothers: "holding hands spiritually."

How sad those unforgettable reunions à quatre, so spread in space— from Gstaad through London to Los Angeles—should have been so confined in time . . .[1]

Krishnamurti was giving some talks at Gstaad; they were, Aldous wrote, "among the most impressive things I ever listened to.

It was like listening to a discourse of the Buddha—such power, such intrinsic authority, such an uncompromising refusal to allow the *homme moyen sensuel* any escapes or surrogates, any *gurus*, saviours, *führers*, churches. "I show you sorrow and the ending of sorrow"—

[1] Yehudi Menuhin *Mem. Vol.*

and if you don't choose to fulfil the conditions for ending sorrow, be prepared, whatever gurus, churches etc you may believe in, for the indefinite continuance of sorrow.

Aldous and Laura went to Turin on 7th August for a few days with her family, thence on to Copenhagen for the Congress of Applied Psychology. On their return they stopped at Basle and met Dr Albert Hoffmann who had first synthesized lysergic acid. Then back to Italy for some weeks with Laura's sister at Torre del Mare on the Ligurian coast. On 12th September Aldous went again to London, staying with Julian and Juliette; Laura flew back to California. He followed her at the beginning of October, by way of New York and a weekend shared between the Lamsons at Cambridge, Massachusetts and Colgate University at Syracuse, New York.

In Los Angeles, Virginia Pfeiffer had moved, with splendid courage, into a house quite near her old one. (The drought persisted and there was in fact that autumn another vast fire nearby.) Here, at 6233 Mulholland Highway, she offered hospitality to Aldous—"A simple, white-washed bedroom [Laura waiting] overlooking a large expanse of the still wild Hollywood hills."

However, Aldous's travels for that year were by no means over. On 7th November he and Laura flew off to Hong Kong on their way to what he called a headlong trip to India. They attended the Congress celebrating Tagore's centenary at New Delhi; spent a few days at Madras; stopped at Agra, Bombay, and Colombo; continued to Japan. "*India is almost infinitely depressing.*" (Aldous had used identically these words in 1926.) ". . there seems to be no solution to its problems in any way that any of us wd regard as acceptable . . .

. . And of course, so long as the more prosperous countries spend 40% of their revenues on armaments, nothing effective can be done about India and all the other places in the same fix. *Quos Deus vult perdere, prius dementat.*

"He was received, of course, with immense respect . . ." writes Isaiah Berlin,[1] who was a fellow delegate at the Congress. "We—Huxley, the American delegate Mr Louis Untermeyer and I—went to a reception at which six or seven hundred students came to do him homage and collect his autograph. There was dead silence as he stood, distinguished and embarrassed, looking beyond

---

[1] *Mem. Vol.*

their heads. An ironical young man broke the silence with some
such words as these:

'After the late Mr Gandhi the Taj Mahal is certainly the most
precious possession of the Indian people. Why then, did you, Mr
Huxley, in your book *Jesting Pilate*, speak in so disparaging a fashion
of it? May I inquire, Sir, if you continue to adhere to this unfavourable view?'

"Huxley was amused and faintly put out. He said that perhaps
he had spoken a little too harshly about the Taj Mahal, that he
had not intended to wound anyone's feelings, that aesthetics was
an uncertain field, that tastes were incommensurable, and then he
gradually slid from this perilous ground to his central Tolstoyan
belief—the unnatural lives that men lead today. But he wondered
afterwards whether perhaps he had been unjust, and so we
decided to re-visit Agra . . . We . . went together to Fatehpur
Sikri, Akbar's dead city. Huxley adored it. He moved with the
slow-footed, slightly gliding step of a somnambulist: his grave and
urbane charm was moving and very delightful.

". . he described his earlier visit to India in the 'twenties, when
he had stayed with one of his Oxford contemporaries, now a
member of the Upper House in India, a distinguished man who
had welcomed him on this occasion too. He described Jawaharlal
Nehru's father, Motilal, who, he said, was a man of exquisite
appearance and manners, and sent his shirts to be washed in
Paris; he had belonged to the rich and power-loving aristocracy
that had sought to use Gandhi for its purposes; but they found
that he had outwitted them . . . Huxley described the relations
of these distinguished and autocratic Brahmins to Gandhi with a
kind of benevolent irony, even-toned, slow, deliberate and
exceedingly entertaining . . . He was very simple, very serene,
very easy to talk with. The fact that . . his house and all his books
had been destroyed by fire seemed hardly to trouble him at all,
nor did he by the slightest allusion reveal the fact that he knew
that he was suffering from a mortal disease; he complained of his
eyesight—his old familiar infirmity . . .

"When he finally saw the Taj Mahal again, he relented; and
decided that it was not as unsightly as he had supposed, but on
the contrary, but for the minarets—'chimney pots' which he still
thought a mistake—it was a creditable building after all. We
spent the evening together; . . Monsieur Guéhenno, the French
writer, was also there . . Guéhenno, a melancholy, interesting and
idealistic man, was not likely—nor did he intend—to raise
anyone's spirits; the lights in the hotel were very low owing to
some permanent power failure. One might have thought that the

whole occasion would be one of extreme, if dignified, gloom and
depression. But it was not. Huxley was simple, natural and
unselfconscious, what he said was unusual and absolutely
authentic. Everything about him was so sincere and so interesting
that the occasion was wholly enjoyable, and inspired, at any rate
in me, a lasting affection and a degree of respect bordering on
veneration."

Chapter Four

Mulholland Highway & Professor at Large

ALDOUS and Laura now settled down at Virginia's. Laura's great friend proved a very good friend indeed to Aldous. She and her sister Pauline had belonged to that American *jeunesse dorée* of the Paris twenties, the world of the Gerald Murphys and the Scott Fitzgeralds and of *Tender is the Night*. The Pfeiffer girls met Ernest Hemingway; in due course Pauline became his second wife. Virginia travelled with them, shared boat and houses. More than mere sister-in-law, she was a fast friend of Ernest's. Their friendship outlasted the eventual divorce from Pauline, went on through the war and into the final bad years. "And now Hemingway's death," Aldous had written to Laura when the news had come last summer. "Where, you ask, is the All Rightness? Certainly not on the level where he lived and killed himself . . .

. . Would it be good for Ginny to remember all the good and the bad of the past times in the light of another LSD or psilocybin experience? It might be.

Ginny, Virginia: a quiet woman; observant, intelligent; of precarious health herself,[1] good with the ill, the depressed; helpful and self-forgetting in a crisis. Aldous liked her. "She has no Bovaristic angle," he would say. Laura thought that he felt more comfortable with her than with any other friend. (Once I was able to draw Virginia out about that pattern of her life, the link, the domestic proximity with those two literary men. Aldous was the best man, she said, she ever knew, getting better and better . . . Ernest: the opposite, he got steadily worse. "And they call him a hero.")

Virginia's house on Mulholland Highway was a light house with a large, light, high-ceilinged and high-windowed living-room downstairs. Deer came from the hills at night; if one kept still one saw the gleam of their eyes in the dark foliage of the bushes. Laura, running in and out, had her own studio on Graciosa Drive a couple of miles down the hill. Virginia's children, Pauline and Juan, were part of the household. Aldous took an interest in their development. Here an ambiguity persisted: he was at ease,

[1] She died in 1973.

300

often tender, with those (and most) children, we just heard how comfortable he was with Virginia, how easy to talk to he appeared to Isaiah Berlin; yet he could still create a field of silence, freeze. One of their local friends, Bernadine Fritz, introduced an admirer to Aldous who complained afterwards that he did not "get through".

I am distressed to hear that I can be so paralyzing to people—[in an unpublished letter to Mrs Fritz of 24th January 1962] a defect attributable to a certain shyness and difficulty in personal communication which it has taken me a lifetime to reduce to its present level and which, I suppose, I will never entirely get rid of.

Aldous slept and worked in his white-washed room with the view. There were two reproductions on the walls, one of Dégas's After the Bath and Rembrandt's Polish Rider. He was correcting the proofs of *Island*, preparing lectures and the nth revision of *The Genius and the Goddess* for an English production. Marie Le Put, the Bretonne of North Kings days, still cooked for them. Some days Aldous would ask her to eat with him; they would talk French; he liked the soups she made, knew every herb. Virginia read aloud to him. Laura tried once or twice. "It didn't work," she says. At times he read to *her*. He read to himself, that is he listened to recordings of poetry he had made himself. (This was an old habit.) From the house, he could take a walk he loved, the walk around the Hollywood reservoir. Often Gerald came. Topographically, it was possible to get about from Mulholland without a car—walking down the hill some twenty minutes to the nearest bus stop; a taxi home. Taking things as they came, was now a conscious principle with Aldous, Peggy Kiskadden affirms, and he lived up to it. He made no demands, ". . . ate the food set before him." Laura used the same words, "he ate everything he was given." Neither less nor more. This, too, was an old process. Peggy tells of an occasion in Maria's day when he had cleaned his plate of some revolting mess at someone's house. "Aldous, how *could* you?" Maria said as the door shut behind them. "Mortification."

Betty and Aldous had resumed their working luncheons. One day Betty, who has a lot of Boswell in her, asked him, "Aldous, do you pray?" "I always say my prayers—in the simplest possible words, I always begin 'Now I lay me down to sleep,' and my prayers are nearly always answered."

On 22nd January Aldous took psilocybin, monitored by Laura. Her tape recording of what was said during the session can be found in *This Timeless Moment*.

Many people had been offering help in remaking Aldous's

library. Cass Canfield asked him to accept a set of his own works and any book he chose from Harper's trade list. This he did.[1] He also responded to an offer from Mrs Lucille Kahn. Now, in 1947 Aldous had written a commissioned article for *House & Garden* on the subject "If my Library Burned Tonight." (This was republished after the fire.[2]) "If my library burned down . . ." Aldous wrote then, "fortunately for me, it never has.

> . . . To enter the shell of a well-loved room and to find it empty, except for a thick carpet of ashes—the very thought is depressing. But happily books are replaceable—at any rate the kind of books that fill the shelves of my library. For I . . have never been interested in first editions and rare antiquities. It is only about the contents of a book that I care, not its shape, its date or the number of its fly-leaves . . .
>
> In principle I would like to possess all the poetry worth reading in all the languages I have a nodding acquaintance with. But as an emergency measure, in the first few weeks after our hypothetical fire, I shall buy myself only the most indispensable . . .
>
> There will be Shakespeare—because, like the giraffe, there ain't no such animal . . . There will be Chaucer—because of all the great poets, I feel towards him the warmest personal affection . . . There will be Homer . . an absolutely truthful poet, who accepted life as it actually is . . . There will be Dante . . (though, as a human being, he seems to me second only to Milton himself in unpleasantness) . . . There will be Donne . . . There will be Marvell—because his small gift was perfect. There will be Wordsworth . . . There will be Baudelaire . . . Rimbaud . . . Mallarmé—because he was the most perfectly self-conscious of artists, and because his poetry has been, for me, a kind of obsession, ever since, as a boy of twenty, I tried my hand at translating his *Après-Midi d'un Faune*. There will be Yeats . . . There will be Eliot—because his is the most beautifully articulate voice of the generation to which I happen to belong . . .

As for the great novelists. There would have to be Tolstoy in Aldous's new library, and Dostoievsky, Dickens, Balzac, a set of Stendhal, Choderlos de Laclos, "the author of that extraordinary book, *Les Liaisons Dangereuses*, and that other romantic analyst, Benjamin Constant. Nor must we forget the eighteenth-century master of narrative—Henry Fielding, whom we must love for his truthfulness . . . akin to that of Chaucer and Homer;" and the Voltaire of *Candide*, and Swift. "As for Smollett—no; my sense

<hr>

[1] The list of the books chosen by Aldous can be found in a note by Professor Grover Smith to Letter 881 in the *Letters*.
[2] In *House & Garden Weekend Book*, 1969.

of humour is not robust enough to rejoice unreservedly in syphilis and broken legs. And as for Goethe's *Wilhelm Meister*—

the book, no doubt, is a work of genius, but full of so complacent an egotism that I never want to read it again. Returning again to the nineteenth century, I find myself very well able to support the loss of Scott and Thackeray . . . But I would re-possess myself of quite a lot of Trollope . . .

And what about Flaubert? What about Wells, Conrad, D. H. Lawrence? *Bouvard et Pécuchet*, certainly; but *L'Education Sentimentale*, one of his favourite books, sadly disappointed him on re-reading. Of Wells, only the scientific romances. A set of Conrad in spite of some reservations; D. H. Lawrence, unreservedly.

The essayists. Montaigne and Pascal inevitably. Thomas Traherne, John Dryden, Voltaire, David Hume, Samuel Johnson, Coleridge, Charles Lamb, De Quincey, "Macaulay who writes like a military band and is the best possible reading for a rainy afternoon. And Emerson who writes like an oracle and possesses authentic wisdom." Walter Bagehot, Sainte-Beuve, Matthew Arnold, Ruskin ("whom I must be allowed to read in selections, for he maddeningly mixes nonsense with the humanest social wisdom"). Schopenhauer, "one of the few great Germans who does not display the 'nimiety', or 'too-muchness' "; Heine; More and Babbit; E. M. Forster and Virginia Woolf.

Biographies, diaries, letters. "I can only name a few at random" —the letters of Keats, the letters of Byron; the note-books of Constant and Stendhal. The autobiographies of Alfieri, and of Lorenzo da Ponte. The Goncourt Journals . . The diaries of Scawen Blunt . . .

And now let us have a look at Aldous's actual requests when the hypothetical fire *had* occurred. He would like, he wrote to Mrs Kahn, "The poets first of all. A compendious Shakespeare and Chaucer. Then Wordsworth, Keats (and the letters as well as the poetry), Browning, Arnold, Hopkins, Yeats, Eliot—and Auden's anthology of English verse, plus the *Oxford Books* of 17th century verse, German verse, Latin and medieval Latin verse.

Then I'd like, if it isn't asking too much, some of the books on oriental philosophy and religion which I valued. Conze's *Buddhism* and his anthology of Buddhist texts. Suzuki's *Zen Essays* and *Zen Doctrine of No-Mind*, Evan Went's 3 books published by Oxford U. Press, *Tibetan Book of the Dead, Milarepa*, and *Great Wisdom* . . Also Zimmer's *Philosophy of India* and *Myths and Symbols of India*. Krishnamurti's *Commentaries on Living*. Benoit's *Supreme Doctrine*.

And from the West, Eckhart—the 1 vol selection by Blakney. William Law—selected by Hobhouse. Wm James, *Varieties of Religious Experience*. Russell's *History of Western Philosophy*.

And if anyone has a spare Dostoievsky or two, a spare *War and Peace* and *Karenina* and short stories of Tolstoy, a spare odd volume of Dickens, I shall be grateful to them.

Aldous had been nominated visiting Ford Research Professor at Berkeley. No functions were attached to the appointment and he hoped to use the salary to finance a reflective travel book about the West Coast, from Canada to Mexico, in the manner of *Beyond the Mexique Bay*. At the intervals of looking at scenery, sewage plants and lunatic asylums, he proposed to give a seminar. He went up to Berkeley for the spring semester of 1962 in early February. Laura drove him there and helped to find a pleasant apartment near the campus. Nothing turned out well. Aldous arrived with a cold in the chest and had to creep into bed, not much good for anything except listening to an educational programme on a portable radio found among the furnishings.

. . And in spite of this stupid little flu [he wrote to Laura], I love you—though it is difficult, when you were here, to manifest anything except a cough and a wheeze. That's one of the worst things about not being well: one's ailments eclipse one's feelings and shut out other people, even those one loves the most.

. . I have just been listening to a broadcast by an American historian on the life of the troops during the Civil War—a record of inconceivable incompetence and inefficiency, resulting in tens of thousands of unnecessary deaths and incalculable amounts of avoidable suffering. So this too is an old story!

Goodbye, my darling. Ti voglio bene.

The cold lingered on and on, then turned into pneumonitis and Aldous had to fly back to Los Angeles for a course of antibiotics. When he was on his feet again, he returned to Berkeley. Nothing much materialized, somehow things got mismanaged. For instance, the university was to have arranged for him to have the use of a car and student driver; neither appeared. Aldous let it go. Few people seemed to be aware of his presence. Julian turned up (from Reed College) and was shocked to see Aldous fending for himself. "Throwing all the food into a blender and messing it up—not nice. He was lonely, poor boy."[1] Betty Wendel went to Berkeley on 8th March with Frank Hauser of the Oxford Playhouse, the producer-director who was to put on *The*

---

[1] Sir Julian talking to S. B.

Genius and the Goddess at Oxford and with luck in London. They began their two-day conference by doing Aldous's washing up. Aldous, who described Hauser as an intelligent, sensitive and very professional man, promised to come to London for the West End opening if there were one. For the rest of the Berkeley semester, Aldous kept coming and going—breathers at Los Angeles, trips with Laura, endless journeyings to give lectures, attend conferences. Laura kept his engagement list.

March 14-16th	Santa Barbara	(Conference on Technology at Robert Hutchin's Center for Democratic Studies)
March 17-19th	Los Angeles	
March 19th-27th	Berkeley	
March 27th	Los Angeles	
March 29th	Alabama	(University lecture)
March 31st	Philadelphia	(Lecture)
April 1st	New York	(Luncheon and afternoon with Matthew; lecture at the Poetry Center)
April 2nd	Boston	
April 4-6th	Syracuse, N.Y.	(Conference on Hypnosis at Colgate University)
April 7th	New York	
April 8-14th	Berkeley	
April 14th	Los Angeles	
April 18-22nd	Portland, Oregon	(To meet Julian, who was lecturing there)

. . Julian seems well—though a bit tired [to Laura]. We drove out yesterday in beautiful weather to the Bonneville Dam. Magnificent country—and the fish making their way up the "fish ladders" at the side of the dam were fascinating.

. . talked with the professor of psychiatry at the Medical Center here—he is working on the problem of recognizing the children who will be specially vulnerable to schizophrenia and devising ways in which they . . may avoid the disease in spite of their inborn tendency. It was most heartening to find that anything so sensible is being thought of and worked at.

This morning we visited the zoo where a female elephant has just given birth to a 220 pound baby . . . The baby, I must say, is very touching—and it is fascinating to see the other female elephants as well as the mother, clustering round, like Aunts and Grannies, with an intense solicitude for the little creature (who anyhow weighs twice as much as you do!).

Tonight Julian speaks . . Now I must get ready for dinner. Goodbye, my darling.

And on a picture postcard a couple of days later:

> Here we are at the end of a most beautiful drive through pastures, wheat fields, rice paddies, olive and orange groves, forests and mountains . . Tomorrow we are to be taken round by a forester. Let's hope it won't be rainy.

The engagement list continued.

April 22nd-May 2nd	Berkeley	
May 2nd	Los Alamos	(Lecture to the scientists)
May 6th	Anaheim, Cal.	(Lecture)
May 7-17th	Berkeley	

And that was the end of what Aldous referred to as his Full Professorship of Nothing-in-Particular.

May 17th-21st	Los Angeles	
May 21-25th	New York	(Talk at the American Academy)

Here Aldous read the news of the death of Peggy Kiskadden's former husband, Curtis Bok[1], whom he had known long ago at Dartington. He wrote to her,

> . . These vital threads that link the present to the past—how many of them have already been broken, and how increasingly often, as one grows older, does one receive the news of yet another break! And the questions keep multiplying. How are we related to what we were? Who are we now and what were we then? And who were the others—in our minds, in their minds, in the mind of omniscience? There are no answers, of course—only the facts of living, changing, remembering and at last dying.

May 25th	Philadelphia	
May 27th	Los Angeles	
May 30th	San Francisco	(For the loan exhibition of Chinese Paintings from 900 A.D.)

Meanwhile *Island* had been published in March both in England and the U.S.A. Aldous had felt rather discouraged at the proof correcting stage. He found himself wondering, he had written to Humphrey, "if the book is any good, or at least more

[1] W. Curtis Bok, the American Jurist, author and philanthropist.

than spottily good. Heaven knows." Cyril Connolly opened his review in the *Sunday Times*, "This is Mr Huxley's most important novel since *Time Must Have a Stop*." On the whole, the reception was divided; the book was treated as a phantasy, a piece of fiction, science fiction at that. For once Aldous felt not indifferent.

Chapter Five

Summer and Autumn 1962

THERE had not been any recurrence of Aldous's original trouble of two years ago. Now, on his return from New York, he suspected that something was wrong with a small gland on the side of his neck. He saw Dr Cutler on the 31st of May who eventually decided to remove the gland, which proved malignant. Aldous took it calmly and wrote to Laura, who happened to be in Italy, in reassuring terms. Cutler had told him that, even at the worst, these kinds of metastases were not really serious. Yet he had a very unpleasant dream; a dream about some nameless, faceless person who was going to kill him and kept leading him from room to room. "So the unconscious evidently got a shock!

. . And meanwhile—perhaps just *because* death seems to have taken a step nearer—everything seems more and more beautiful, the leaves on the trees, the flowers, the sky . . . and my memories of you and all the people I have loved or felt concerned about.

The actual operation (in July) was quite minor; Aldous stayed in hospital for two days only. Again he went in as Mr Matthew Leonard. Afterwards he had a series of cobalt treatments as an out-patient.

Aldous had just been elected a Companion of Literature by The Royal Society of Literature, but was not able to come to London for the presentation as he had intended. (At the beginning of 1962 there were four living Companions of Literature: Winston Churchill, E. M. Forster, John Masefield and Somerset Maugham. The present Election added Edmund Blunden, Aldous Huxley and Robert Graves, who declined the honour.)

The Genius and the Goddess had opened at the Oxford Playhouse[1] on 23rd April, directed by Frank Hauser, starring Constance Cummings, Paul Massie and George Pravda. It went on to Manchester, Leeds, Streatham Hill and reached the Golder's Green Hippodrome on 28th May. No West End theatre being available at once, the opening at the Comedy Theatre was held over till 28th June. Again there had been cuts and changes, "detrimental and unauthorized", according to Betty Wendel,

---

[1] Produced by the Meadow Players Ltd, in association with the Arts Council of Great Britain.

who held the fort in England. Aldous's presence was urgently requested. But Aldous of course was ill and did not come. The notices were tepid and the play was taken off after twenty-one nights.

In August, well before the end of the cobalt treatment, Aldous was active—planning to go to the Argentine, to Brussels. With Christopher Isherwood he went to the aviation plant at Los Angeles to have a look at the Apollo moon-shot capsules and the latest missiles they were working on. "The plant executives were full of resounding phrases [Christopher Isherwood[1]] about Man's great mission and destiny in Outer Space. Aldous sat listening, his head slightly bowed, ghost-pale, aloof. He was like a ghost they had raised to speak to them of the future—but they hadn't bargained for what they heard . . ."

> All this concentrated knowledge [Aldous for his part to Humphrey], genius, hard work and devotion, not to mention all those incalculable billions of dollars, poured forth in the service of vast collective paranoias—and meanwhile our three billion mainly hungry people are to become six billions in less than forty years and, like parasites, are threatening to destroy their planetary host and, with their host, themselves.

At the end of August Aldous set out for Belgium on his own. (Laura was too busy trying to meet the deadline of her book; they arranged to meet in the Argentine in October.) The reason for the journey was the meeting of the new World Academy of Art and Sciences in Brussels, "started by a lot of Nobel Prizemen who would like to see that their science is used in a relatively sane manner." It seems worth trying at least, Aldous thought, "to do something to mitigate the current organized insanity . . ."

He looked up Maria's uncle Baltus; then went on to Holland, to Suzanne and Joep, and Sylvia. How well his other Nicolas niece, Claire, has described these autumnal wanderings[2] "from one member of his own and of Maria's family to the other . . New York, England, France, Belgium, Holland . . He sought them out, braving foul weather and bad trains, contracting bronchitis here, pneumonia there . . ." This was almost literally the course of the present journey—slow hours of cross-country trains to get to Tegelen in the Limbourg province. He looked too gaunt, too worn, for it to be taken as a casual visit. Nothing, of course, was said. Aldous was in an affectionate mood, took pleasure in Suzanne's garden, looked intently at an enormous black-faced

---

[1] *Mem. Vol.*
[2] Claire Nicolas White, "Aldous Huxley, A Reminescence", cit.

sunflower that had sprung up outside her kitchen door, went on long walks as they had done in their early days, walks at sunset along the wooden sandhills that form the natural border between Germany and Holland. They drove to Haarlem for a Franz Hals Exhibition. Here the September weather changed, an icy wind sweeping the town: Aldous began to cough in a terrifying manner. They took him to Amsterdam, put him to bed in a warm hotel, called in a doctor who prescribed penicillin. Suzanne and Sylvia kept him company. "Il semblait heureux d'être dorloté." He had started writing *Literature and Science*, and asked Sylvia to read the beginning out to him. These two had long talks, with Sylvia, a story-teller, able to make him laugh. From his bed he telephoned to Laura in California, asked Suzanne to say a word to her as they had never met. The chest cold cleared up after a few days, but he still felt weak and not only cancelled the Argentinian journey but gave up his plans for Paris—perhaps he could not face showing himself to Jeanne—and flew straight to London. There he stayed at Pond Street with his brother, under Juliette's admirable care. He gradually picked up. Nearly every day Juliette had friends to tea for him, never more than two at a time. His cousin Renée Tickell came, as on all his visits. And Jill Greenwood, the cousin who could have been his niece in age, whom he had not been able to take his eyes off when they first met at the Gargoyle night club and who had fallen in love with his portrait at the age of seventeen.

. . He asked me to bring my younger daughter Dinah, which I did . . .[1] He was lying in a chair looking just like an autumn leaf— you know, one of those skeleton leaves, very very gentle and quiet, and very sweet. He talked; and he talked to Dinah, which I thought was nice of him . . .

As ever, he went about his London business—publishers, haberdashers, quacks; saw about getting up a trust fund for Matthew's children; spent a weekend at Gervas's; wandered about with Humphrey Osmond. Humphrey, a Surrey man himself, was spending the summer in Godalming; with him Aldous again re-visited old haunts. Aldous was saddened, even angered, by the fact that there were no more birds in the hedges, "The insecticides have killed them all!" Once, when Julian was with them, Aldous described how as a boy he bicycled down the Devil's Punch Bowl towards Milford at forty miles an hour. Julian was sceptical. "I clocked it," Aldous said. And there used

[1] Gillian (Mrs Anthony) Greenwood, talking to S. B.

to be a sweetshop where they were able to get thirty caramels for a penny. "Very *small* caramels, Aldous," said Julian. "*Thirty* caramels, all the same," said Aldous.

One afternoon as Juliette was driving him, they passed Laleham. "He and I[1] got out of the car, A. leant on the gate silently. I saw a man in the garden, and said this was Aldous Huxley who was born there, and could he see the house, please. The owner said of course, and took us in and showed every room, including the old nursery upstairs, which A. thought very small and not at all as he remembered . . . The people in the house were very nice . . . So we drove back. I felt that Aldous was very happy."

The Huxley brothers met the Menuhins at Claridges. Julian was holding forth on the quality of genes—there was an aristocracy of genes . . . Aldous piped up, "You mean blue genes?" with a very long vowel in the blue.[2]

In late September Aldous was back in California, back in Virginia's house. It was now a year and a half since the fire. Did you not think of remaking a home? I once asked Laura. Yes, there had been plans to re-build—the site on Deronda Drive was still theirs—they had looked for something to rent . . . "He was docile, he would have done what I wanted . . . but the houses we saw—we looked at houses—were so unlike *my* dream . . . my design . . ." For some weeks Aldous worked away on his long essay on literature and science. All the essays on the subject, he wrote to Matthew, "from T. H. Huxley's and Matthew Arnold's in the 1880's (still the best in the field) to . . Trilling's and Oppenheimer's—are too abstract and generalized. I am trying to approach [it] in more concrete terms . . ."

Presently Aldous broke off for a month of lecturing in the Middle West and East. From New York he went to stay with Claire, as he so often did, at St James, the Stanford White estate on Long Island where she lived pastorally with her husband Bobby, the numerous members of the White family and her own four children (how Aldous had scolded her about their number! Yet he was fond of them, and had much affection for Claire's eldest son, Sebastian, a brilliantly intelligent boy). Matthew, too, since his divorce, had a home-base at St James. Aldous came equipped with rubber overshoes and an English umbrella which opened automatically when one pressed a button. He would join "our

---

[1] Juliette in a letter to S. B.
[2] In the words told by Yehudi Menuhin to S. B. I am afraid there is more than one story about blue jeans; Aldous was too fond of puns to let it go at that. I chose this version as the neatest.

tribal existence [Claire writing] with apparent enjoyment and great adaptability . . ." He shared in the children's games,

> tickled them with a long feather and then would sensuously stroke his own cheek with it. He sat on the sofa and read aloud . . from the *Doors of Perception* while the children listened spell-bound, and one of them drew his portrait.

And how lucky, he would say, to live in the country "to still be able to go for walks like these". Claire had been reading a life of Thomas More, and told Aldous that his visits reminded her of those of Erasmus, "that other avid traveller, keeping us in touch with the world . . . ." Later he wrote to her,

> It is always a great delight to see you and Bobby and the children . . . Alas for Erasmus! How I shd like to be like him! And how sadly I realize that his sweet reasonableness made him abhorrent to both parties, who went on with their wars and agreed only in denouncing the apostle of good will, intelligence and compromise.

In this same November, Aldous met Judy—Judith Wallet Bordage—Matthew's future wife. There had so far been no mention of a marriage, but Aldous was not born yesterday. Matthew asked him to have dinner with her at her apartment on 54th Street. It was a four floor walk-up and when the bell rang,

> I[1] thought it would surely be Matthew, a feeling that was confirmed by the tread on the stairs and the cough on the floor below. When Aldous rounded the corner I expected to be desperately nervous, but no.

There was a large and cherished tabby, who stole the cheese biscuits while they had their drinks. This helped.

> Matthew got there soon after and we had a splendid meal—you know I have an odd memory for inconsequential things—I remember making Julia Child's escalope de veau . . . and as Matthew told me after, Aldous adored eating well. Matthew was marvellous in helping the talk . . . he knew what to ask him, how to turn the conversation, how to keep the talk going. Finally Aldous left—Matthew put him in a taxi and came back up—it was after 11.30 and I asked whether M thought the evening had gone well . . . Matthew laughed and said that if it hadn't gone well, Aldous would have left at ten . . .

[1] Judy, the present Mrs Matthew Huxley, in a letter to S. B.

Next evening Aldous took them both to a Swiss restaurant, and they went on to see *Beyond the Fringe*. "This had opened about a week or two before, I think, and was a raving hit.

> . . we had house seats, something like seventh row centre. That was a heavenly evening—giggly and relaxed—the show, by American standards, erudite—a very Oxonian type show and Aldous rolled in the aisles along with the two of us. I remember suggesting afterwards to A. that he might go back to tell the young actors (Moore, Jonathan Miller . . .) that he had indeed enjoyed it—and A. answered that he didn't know them and it would be presumptuous (although that isn't the word he used) . . . After, we all walked up Sixth Avenue and then to the Plaza where he was staying—it was then the first time I was aware that he saw things very clearly—that he *looked*—seeing people, expressions, things that neither M. nor I saw because certainly we weren't looking—but that was when I realized that his sight was not impaired in the way I had always believed from what I had read.
>
> That evening we all walked arm in arm and—how do I say this?—nothing sexual, but very much the electricity of—maybe benign flirtatiousness is the right way to say it.

(Benign flirtatiousness is a very good way of describing Aldous's rapport with attractive women in his later years.) Next day, a Saturday, Aldous with Matthew, Trev and Tessa had a picnic lunch at Judy's apartment.

> . . . relaxed, lovely—we had a very good Italian delicatessen nearby . . and we had found all kinds of good things. When Matthew told the kids to sit up or not to talk with a full mouth, Aldous nodded approvingly and muttered, "Manners, manners . . ."

Then they went out to St James and spent the night at Claire's. Next morning Aldous had to catch a plane to Texas from La Guardia to give a lecture. Matthew cut it too fine:

> . . . a terrible drive [Judy's comment] . . . Aldous nervous and put out, obviously trying to control his irritation with Matthew. Aldous and I getting out at the proper airline, both of us rushing through the gate—on time. Great enormous hugs . . and off he went . . .

Chapter Six

1963—Winter, Spring, Summer

BACK to Los Angeles, back to work. Before Christmas Aldous had finished his short book, *Literature and Science*, Laura had finished her book, her first one, the Recipes for Living based on her psychotherapeutic methods. The title was to be *You Are Not The Target*. Aldous, who had taken a delighted interest, was doing the preface. Now, what next?

.. And tomorrow we start a new year [Aldous wrote to Maria Petrie]. Will the few scores of people who decide the world's immediate fate permit it to be a tolerably good year? And will the impersonal forces which determine our long-range destiny permit themselves to be controlled for man's benefit—and shall we even attempt to control them?

Meanwhile, wishes to his friends, wishes for good health, good work and *"malgré tout,* inner peace." And on 8th January Aldous writes to Matthew that he has a project for a "rather long and complicated novel." For the present: journalistic grind, proof-correcting, a working session at Santa Barbara.

It was Aldous's custom to request both his publishers, each January, to send a statement of his past year's earnings to his accountants so that they might work out his income tax. ("Faith, Hope, Charity—these three, and the greatest of all is Income Tax.") In 1962 Aldous's gross income from book royalties came to £6,496 and $26,646 respectively. *Island* had been doing well financially. But, in prosperous years or lean, he still did not really go into his royalty statements. He liked to hear that a particular book had been doing well, or being paid a nice round sum like $1,000 for an article; he enjoyed the size of his lecture fees; but he did not give much thought to his financial landscape as a whole. (He used to write his cheques without filling in the stubs. "My Bank will tell me when I'm overdrawn.") His rough view of the overall position was that he was fairly certain of a largish living as long as he was working, but that subsistence for himself or his dependents on earnings from past books was unpredictable at best. He never "accumulated a fortune" (he helped far too many people) and such savings as he had were accidental. He still had money panics ("We all get them," say his Huxley cousins), Laura would laugh him out of them. (Maria had skimped on

herself and worried, but could not learn to manage money;
Laura did not believe that there was any need to manage it.)

Matthew and Judy proposed to each other on St Valentine's
Day. Aldous was very happy about this indeed—"All seems for the
best." To Eileen Garrett he spoke of Judy as being just what
Matthew needed—"warm, intelligent and good."

On 9th March Aldous flew to Rome for the F.A.O. conference
on their campaign against hunger. In a letter to me, written on
the plane, he mentioned again that he was "feeling his way into a
kind of novel.

. . I don't yet know what it will really be like and proceed by a
process of trial and error, guided by whatever turns up, from
paragraph to paragraph.

He expected to be in England in the early summer.

In Rome Aldous had an audience with Pope John, who was
then already very ill. On his way home he stopped two days in
New York for Matthew's wedding on the 22nd. The day before
he spent talking to Humphrey Osmond; at night he dined at
Longchamps with the bride and groom. He was remote, and
Judy was disconcerted by their not being able to pick up from
where they had left off in November.

On the wedding day, Aldous was obviously not well. "He was
aged, we thought. Age being somehow acceptable." Matthew
had lunch with Aldous and Trev; Tessa helped Judy dress. They
met at an apartment on Park Avenue for the ceremony, performed
by a judge. Aldous was their witness. "Then crosstown to Central
Park West for the reception. A. tired. He sat in a small study off
the main room with Cass and Jane Canfield and Anita Loos,
apart from the sixty or so standing wedding guests, the cake and
the champagne . . ."

Los Angeles. Another of those brief talking trips: to Oregon,
Berkeley, Stanford. In April another tumour appeared on
Aldous's neck. Cutler told him; Aldous did not seem very alarmed.
He brought up a theory they had often discussed: the body's own
remarkable capacity to destroy cancer cells. "Cancer isn't always
the winner," Aldous said. Perhaps his body was building up its
own resistance. "If it isn't, there isn't much we can do about it,
is there?" But Dr Cutler was no longer hopeful; he told Laura.
Again he insisted on a second opinion. Aldous, Laura with him,
flew to New York on 23rd April for a consultation. Laura decided

that the time had come when she must tell Matthew. As it happened, a letter from him had arrived that very morning; they read it on the plane and it was such a happy letter that Laura lost heart. She could not bring herself, she wrote, to intrude. They had gone to New York unannounced and returned the same day, having made no attempt to reach Matthew. Perhaps it might have been better for him if she had; perhaps better for her not to have had to go on bearing that silence on her own, private silence, public silence, silence also now to Aldous.

On 1st May Aldous went into the Cedars of Lebanon hospital for a few days of observation. It should be said that medically everything possible was being done.[1] Throughout, Dr Cutler not only insisted on examinations by eminent colleagues in San Francisco, London, New York, he also corresponded about Aldous's case with such authorities as Dr F. Baclesse of the Institut de Radium, Dr Tailhefer of the Foundation Curie, Professor Guidetti of the University of Turin. Humanly, too, Dr Cutler was the right choice—gentle, kind and highly intelligent, he was very good at that personal doctor-patient relationship that Aldous had feared he would have failed in had *he* become a doctor. He was fond of Max Cutler, and the two men were able to talk to one another profitably.

You Are Not The Target was about to be published; Laura was faced with a painful dilemma.

. . I was scheduled to go to New York for a series of public appearances, synchronized with the publication of my book. Never was the duality of life more evident. On one side I was having every satisfaction that a new writer could wish for; on the other . . .
. . I did not want to go away even for a week. Yet my New York appearances had been carefully scheduled. They would acquaint a large audience with my book. If I cancelled my trip, I certainly would have to give a valid reason . . .

She asked Dr Cutler; he advised her to go. Aldous meanwhile carried on as usual, coming down to eight o'clock breakfast with Virginia's children, going back to his room to work, taking his afternoon walk; but Laura thought that he was being inaccessible and silent in a new way. Her book, which was a run-away success, was the one thing that distracted him.

L. is just back from New York [he wrote to Julian on 2nd June] . .

[1] Dr Cutler, with much care and kindness, not only talked to me at length but let me see the actual file on Aldous's case.

and making TV and radio appearances . . her book . . is turning
into a rampaging best seller. A second printing after a week—and
the computers predict a sale of 107,000 by August! . . The publisher
is out of his mind with joy and we are feeling elatedly flabbergasted.
   Otherwise there isn't much to report. I have just finished an essay
on the ambivalence of culture . . .

Aldous had never had a sale of such dimension and commented
on that fact with delight and glee.
   Presently it was decided to resort once more to radium therapy.
Between 13th June and 2nd July Aldous underwent twenty-five
exposures to radioactive cobalt, an extremely exhausting treatment which left him very low and weak. He had to cancel his
engagements. (He was to have lectured in Munich on behalf of
the British Council on 14th June and addressed the Royal Society
of Literature in London on the 22nd.) During July he regained
some little strength, and seemed preoccupied with his novel.
There was good news too: Matthew's marriage was turning out
extremely well. "He is happier now than he has ever been,"
Aldous wrote to Julian. And Ellen, also, was about to get married
again. So here all was for the best.

   . . and the children are thoroughly enjoying the experience of
having a father and a deputy father whom they like, and a mother
and a deputy mother with whom they get on extremely well.

And Matthew had a new job (on a planning committee at the
National Institute of Mental Health) and was moving to
Washington in September. "He is delighted at the prospect." Nor
had those computers been wrong, *Target* continued a best-seller—
"Laura is very busy signing books and giving interviews."

At the end of July Aldous was emerging from his low state just
enough to keep his engagement in Stockholm for a meeting of the
World Academy of Arts and Sciences. Laura came with him and
they flew by way of Greenland—twelve hours and eight time
changes—arriving on the 28th. Aldous had never been to Sweden
before and at once took strolls "about this pleasant town with its
mixture of rather solemn and respectably old-fashioned architecture and brand new . ." Humphrey Osmond arrived. Aldous
confessed to him that he had been unsure whether he could come
at all. "Yet he worked zealously to persuade members of the
Academy to study human potential." He succeeded, and was
asked to undertake, with Humphrey, the editing of a volume on

Human Resources for publication by the Academy. Aldous at once "set to and prepared an outline.

> I[1] sat with him while he was completing this in his hotel room. He was engrossed in his task. Watching him I felt that I might never see him again . . . I was uneasy when we parted, but tried to ignore my misgivings. He was to visit me in Princeton during October, which was only two months away . . .

After Stockholm Laura went to Italy, Aldous flew to London. ("It seems best for each of us," she wrote, "to visit our families.") Julian and Juliette met him at Heathrow; they saw at once that something was appallingly wrong. Aldous's colour was ashen and his voice down to half its volume. Yes, he said, he was very tired, having sat up all night drafting an outline for the Academy . . . He would soon recover, he assured them, by a quiet month in England.

> We brought him to Pond Street and settled him down [Julian's *Memories*], but soon saw that the promised improvement was failing to occur. In fact Juliette got so worried that she arranged a consultation with the best specialist at Bart's Hospital and took him there, rather against his will . . . he did not want us to know; indeed, we never had the slightest suspicion . . . He merely told us on returning from Bart's that the doctors had advised a quiet spell, and that his voice would soon be normal . . We were only too anxious to believe him.

"He was spectral, waxen, shockingly changed," Rosamund Lehmann said of him; "speaking only when he was addressed, and then replying with all his customary alertness . . . recovering his spirits once, for a brief time . . discussing the problem of world population . . ."
The Julians took him into Devonshire for a weekend at Dartington, that extraordinarily beautiful place, with its vast expanse of trees and lawns and gardens breathing peace. Leonard and Dorothy Elmhirst gave them a great welcome.

> . . Leonard Elmhirst has done wonderful things at Dartington [Aldous wrote—it was a very long time since he had whisked Matthew away from the school], which is one of the very few places in the world where one can feel an almost unqualified optimism.

They were taken out on Dartmoor, stopped by a small pond to watch a tame seal, "and the sun came out of clouds to sparkle on

---

[1] Humphrey Osmond in *Mem. Vol.*

the disturbed water [Juliette writing]. Aldous was silent as he walked away, then suddenly said: 'How could one describe that sun and water—the ripples catching the bright light . . .' A little further, on that wild moor, I saw high grass bowed by a sharp gust of wind just as a cloud passed over the sun, painting the grass with a shadow which looked as if it were bending the grass. Aldous stopped at once and looked intently until he had seen what I meant. He looked very tired when we returned to the car, but his face had a peaceful expression."

At night they listened to the Music Festival in the Great Hall. One evening it was early English music on the guitar, "the most tedious music possible. Aldous was boiling with rage—why didn't they play Purcell . . . The next evening Nell Gotkowsky, the young violinist, played Beethoven magnificently. After the concert the Elmhirsts took us to the artists' room . . . we made the usual remarks. Just as we were going away, Nell Gotkowsky rushed after us and flung herself on Aldous, saying that she had only just realized WHO he was, and breathlessly poured out her admiration for him . . . Aldous looked down on this brilliant young creature with a glow of pleasure, listened to her words with a sort of detached enchantment."

Later they went to stay at Lawford Hall in Essex, the home of their old family friends, the Nichols's. Robert, the poet, who had loved Aldous so well, was long dead; his brother, Sir Philip, who had been up at Balliol with Aldous, had died the year before. His widow, Phyllis Nichols[1] wrote:

. . When Aldous came here . . . his physical appearance was "transparent", and his mind detached from all worldly possessions and struggles. His face lit up with a radiance that was all the more striking because it shone out of a body that seemed like a half-discarded shell.

Lady Nichols's younger son had had a breakdown at Oxford and was suffering from insomnia and depression. When Aldous realized this he tried to help him. He talked to the young man and gave him some magnetic passes—a not unstrenuous procedure—to ease his state of anxiety.

. . I [Lady Nichols] asked Aldous what was his overwhelming feeling when in the visionary world of mescalin, and he replied, "Gratitude." This is the feeling I had after this visit in August 1963.

[1] Lady Nichols, who died herself in 1971, in a letter to Julian Huxley.

PART TWELVE 1960-1963

Again, almost daily, Aldous wrote to Laura.

I keep asking myself what I ought to do in the immediate future—
in the probably not very long future that is left me. How to be more
loving, more aware, more useful or (if that isn't possible) more
content and accepting. So far the answer hasn't come but perhaps
it will—especially if you help me to find it . . .

. . . I am feeling reasonably well—though not very energetic—well
enough to do what I have to do, but without the extra power to do
what one would like to do in the way of creating something or
initiating some new course of action. But one musn't complain. And
anyhow, unexpected things may happen—unforeseen changes
occur . . .

. . . you must forgive me, my sweetheart, for being so gloomy and
burdensome. I haven't yet learned to accept the fact of not feeling
very well, of being mentally and physically diminished—to accept
and to make the best of it. But I hope to learn. Meanwhile please be
patient with me and remember that underneath the gloom and the
sense of being lost, I love you very much . . .

. . . here it is unseasonably chilly and rainy—but the country is
beautiful and there are wonderful clouds when the sun comes out
between the showers—like Constables and Turners. And maybe I
have some good ideas for my hypothetical novel!

One day he went to Simpson's in Piccadilly and bought
himself a very smart new raincoat. The last country visit with
Julian and Juliette was to the Kenneth Clarks at Saltwood
Castle.

This mediaeval fortress had been made into a wondrous place . . .
from which narrow Gothic windows open on a wide courtyard
surrounded by a battlemented wall. At the further end of the
courtyard, K. had established his library in a large tower . . . The
library was a place of silence—striking in its harmony and beauty,
its scholarly atmosphere and the essence of so much that Aldous
loved. It made a deep impression on him—as did the house itself,
with all its modern and ancient treasures, and the feeling of continuity
with its historical past.[1]

Aldous wandered about the rooms and grounds, stooping to
smell the scented roses. He was gay at times, Sidney Nolan said
who was there, talked of Rimbaud . . . One evening it was
Nolan who went up to his room to call him, knocked at the door,
" 'Dinner is ready,' Aldous was reading in the twilight through

[1] Sir Julian Huxley, *Memories* Vol. II, cit.

his hand . . . looked up slowly with a remote smile . . . came back from very very far . . ."

Alas, Aldous did not see Gervas, who himself was ill.

I was so sorry to have missed you on this visit . . . I do hope you are making satisfactory progress towards complete health. "Growing old gracefully"—it isn't easy when the physiological machine starts to break down . . . One learns the Second Law of Thermodynamics by direct experience.

In the last week of August Aldous left England for Italy. "He never by any hint or murmur [Julian wrote] allowed us to guess his fate. He had made up his mind that it would be simpler just to ignore it . . . to let things come as they would. The last we saw of him was at the airport—he said goodbye, and opened his briefcase to take out some papers . . ."

Aldous joined Laura in Turin after [she wrote] "three long, and for me, anxious weeks." They took trips into the mountains, to Courtmayeur, a funicular ride half way up Mont Blanc, up the Val di Susa to Salice d'Oulx:

where an Alpine village is in process of being transformed into a town of 10 and 15-storey apartment houses . . We've come a long way from the Swiss chalet!

They were back in Los Angeles and Mulholland Highway on 24th August. Aldous counted on a full month of writing before starting for his next lectures in the East. On 4th September he sent his plan for the Human Resources volume to Humphrey, ". . I hope to come East early in October . . and hope to spend a day or two at Princeton discussing the book with you. After which we slip down to Philadelphia . . ."

Chapter Seven

Island and After . . .

"WE must dream in a pragmatic way." *Island* was not Aldous's testament; he expected to write more, to move on. Nevertheless it is the serious and deliberate expression of his thought on the for him over-riding theme of human happiness and the quality of life. Two-thirds of all sorrow is home-made and, so far as the universe is concerned, unnecessary. What can we do to avoid this sorrow? What can we do to make people more happy, more fulfilled, more loving? *Island* was intended as a not unworkable prescription of a good society in our age and on our planet. The locale is Pala, a hypothetical island between Ceylon and Sumatra which happens to have remained independent because of its rocky coast and lack of a natural harbour. In the 1840s Dr MacPhail, a Scottish surgeon of formidable intellect and character, saved the then Rajah's life by operating on him under hypnotic anaesthesia. The doctor remained, became the philosopher-king's friend, and the two men set out to change their society by adopting desirable features from different cultures of the East and West. This work was continued by the descendants of the Scotchman and the ruler for the next three generations. The book opens in the 1960s: we see and hear about the good society through the mediation of a ship-wrecked visitor from England. The island is beautiful and inhabited by a handsome race of human beings. "These things don't have to happen," our Gulliver is told (a highly civilized and very unhappy foreign correspondent). These things being hunger, war, urban squalor regimentation. "They happen only when people are stupid enough to allow them to happen . . . we're not overcrowded, we're not miserable, we're not under a dictatorship . . We chose to behave in a sensible and realistic way."

> "How on earth were you able to choose?" Farnaby asked.
> "The right people were intelligent at the right moment."[1]

Now, as Aldous used to say, it would be very nice if we were all good and happy and intelligent—but what on earth do you do to *implement* these intentions? How do you set about it? What sort of

[1] *Island*, Chatto & Windus, 1962. All quotations in this chapter, unless otherwise stated, are from *Island*.

322

upbringing? What sort of social, economic arrangements? What do you do about the problem of power? Of beliefs? And this is what he tried to work out in *Island*.

"And which are the best answers?"
"None of them is best without the others."
"So there's no panacea?"
"How could there be."

So Aldous has them try to make the best of all the worlds. There is enough to eat. "More than enough. We eat better than any other country in Asia, and there's a surplus for export." Why? "Lenin used to say that electricity plus socialism equals communism. Our equations are rather different. Electricity minus heavy industry plus birth control equals democracy and plenty. Electricity plus heavy industry minus birth control equals misery, totalitarianism and war." The population of Pala (about two million) has been stable for a century—due to a low death rate (advanced medicine and sanitation) *and* a low birth rate: two children per family the usual, three the limit. Agriculture is scientifically developed . . . "in the fifties we built the first super-phosphate factory east of Berlin . ."), the economy is neither capitalist nor socialist.

". . None of those blood-sucking usurers that you find all over the Indian countryside. And no commercial banks in your western style. Our borrowing and lending system was modelled on those credit unions that Wilhelm Raiffeisen set up more than a century ago in Germany. Dr Andrew persuaded the Raja to invite one of Raiffeisen's young men to come here and organize a co-operative banking system . . ."

In a word (Aldous does not go into it in detail) they have solved the economic problem. "It wasn't difficult.

. . Not being over-populated, we have plenty. But although we have plenty, we've managed to resist the temptation that the West has now succumbed to—the temptation to over-consume . . . And finally we don't spend a quarter of the gross national product preparing for World War III or even World War's baby brother, Local War MMMCCXXXIII . . . If war, waste and money-lenders were abolished, you'd collapse. And while you people are over-consuming, the rest of the world sinks more and more deeply into chronic disaster. Ignorance, militarism and breeding, these three—and the greatest of these is breeding. . . . Another ten or fifteen years of uninhibited breeding, and the whole world, from China to Peru via Africa and the Middle East will be fairly crawling with Great Leaders, all dedicated to the suppression of freedom, all armed to the teeth by Russia or America or, better still, by both at once . . .

Once or twice we get a glimpse of the other, the contemporary, the "real" world beyond Pala. Again through Farnaby Gulliver, the special correspondent, who remembers the cocktail party at the Foreign Office on Rendang, the neighbouring totalitarian island. "Everybody who was anybody was there.

All the local dignitaries and their wives—uniforms and medals. Dior and emeralds. All the important foreigners—diplomats galore, British and American oilmen, six members of the Japanese trade mission, a lady pharmacologist from Leningrad, two Polish engineers, a German tourist who happened to be a cousin of Krupp von Bohlen, an enigmatic Armenian representing a very important financial consortium in Tangiers, and . . the fourteen Czech technicians who had come with last month's shipment of tanks and cannons and machine guns from Skoda. And these are the people . . who rule the world . .Ye are the cyanide of the earth . . .

". . . Nice comfortable people just don't have any idea what the world is like. Not exceptionally, as it was during the War, but all the time. All the time." And as he spoke he was seeing . . . all the hateful scenes he had witnessed in the course of those well-paid pilgrimages to every hell-hole and abattoir revolting enough to qualify as News. Negroes in South Africa, the man in the San Quentin gas chamber, mangled bodies in an Algerian farm-house, and everywhere mobs, everywhere policemen . . paratroopers . . .

In Pala the political arrangements make it as good as impossible for anyone to dominate on a large scale, while the drive to power is already curbed on the individual level. "The power problem has its roots in anatomy and bio-chemistry and temperament." So has delinquency. Neither are hard to cope with if you start early enough.

Blood tests, psychological tests, somato-typing . . an EEG . . . And when they've been spotted, the potentially aggressive or retarded . . appropriate treatment is started immediately. Within a year practically all of them are perfectly normal . . . In your part of the world, delinquency is still left to clergymen, social workers and the police . . . With what results? . . A year in jail won't cure Peter Pan of his endocrine disbalance or help the ex-Peter Pan to get rid of its psychological consequences . . . what you need is early diagnosis and three pink capsules a day before meals . . .

Palanese medicine, likewise, is mainly preventive.

"Well, there was that group of American doctors [who] came last year [this is a young nurse speaking] .. They wanted to find out why we have such a low rate of neurosis and cardio-vascular trouble. Those doctors! .. they really made .. everybody's hair stand on end in the whole hospital."

"So you think our medicine's pretty primitive?" [asks Farnaby]

"That's the wrong word . . . It's fifty per cent terrific and fifty per cent non-existent. Marvellous antibiotics—but absolutely no methods for increasing resistance, so that antibiotics won't be necessary. Fantastic operations—but when it comes to teaching people the way of going through life without having to be chopped up, absolutely nothing . . . Alpha Plus for patching you up .. but Delta Minus for keeping you healthy . . ."

And what do you do to keep people well? "Chemical answers, psychological answers, answers in terms of what you eat, how you make love, what you see and hear . ." The Palanese, of course, are given early training in the perceptions (non-verbal education), training which allows them to realize the inter-connectedness of things; and their love making is encouraged to begin spontaneously, sensuously, free of guilt . . .

One must dream in a pragmatic way . . . An empirical way . . . A major point about *Island* is that Aldous was not indulging in pure phantasy. His epigraph on the title page is a dictum of Aristotle, "In framing an ideal we may assume what we wish, but should avoid impossibilities." Most of the Palanese social arrangements and techniques, from somato-typing to those Bismarckian co-operatives, had been, at the time of writing, thought of here, tried out there, experimented with at some university, laboratory, hospital or school. Take that operation on the Raja under hypnosis which started off the whole thing: this is an almost verbatim description of an operation performed by Dr James Esdaile[1] on 3rd June 1846 in Calcutta. Esdaile, who practised in India in the nineteenth century, was one of the pioneers of hypnotic or mesmeric anaesthesia. He performed some three hundred major operations without anaesthetics and without pain, and this with a staggeringly low mortality rate for the time. "Which shows", as Aldous once wrote to Humphrey, "what can be done by psychological means to minimize shock and increase resistance to infection.

---

[1] See Esdaile's *Mesmerism in India* (1846) and William Neilson's *Mesmerism in Relation to Medical Practice* (1855).

These facts have been known for more than a century. But nobody seems to have drawn the obvious conclusions or done anything about them [Esdaile and his fellow pioneers were attacked and, in some cases, hounded out of the medical profession] . . .

Or take the way the Palanese condition their infants in the novel (Pavlov for a *good* purpose). The mother strokes the baby while she is feeding it, and talks to him; then while it is sucking and being caressed she introduces it to the animal or person— dog, snake, father, stranger—she wants it to love, rubbing its body against theirs and murmuring the word, *good, good.* At first the child will only understand the tone of voice. "Later on, when he learns to speak, he'll get the full meaning. Food plus caress plus contact plus 'good' equals love. And love equals pleasure, love equals satisfaction." And so a conditioned reflex of a most valuable nature will have been built up.

We should certainly not be too proud to learn from people, however primitive they may seem. [Aldous remarked in one of his M.I.T. lectures] Their method seems to be an extraordinary brilliant invention, and heaven knows we have need enough of love in this extremely loveless world we live in.

Palanese schoolchildren start science education at the time of elementary arithmetic. Ecology—"Never give children a chance of imagining that anything exists in isolation.

Make it plain from the very first that all living is relationship. Show them relationships in the woods, in the fields, in the ponds and streams, in the villages, and the country around it. Rub it in.
And . . we always teach the science of relationship in conjunction with the ethics of relationship. Balance, give and take, no excesses— it's the rule in nature and, translated out of fact into morality, it *ought* to be the rule among people . . . children find it very easy to understand an idea when it's presented to them in a parable about animals . . .

And now for a condensation of some essentials Aldous tried to state.

"The point . . is to get people to understand that we're not *completely* at the mercy of our memory and our phantasies. If we're disturbed by what's going on inside our heads, we can do something about it. It's all a question of being shown what to do and then practising—

> the way you learn to write or play the flute . . . [to learn] a technique
> that [will] develop . . into a method of liberation. Not complete
> liberation, of course . . This technique won't lead you to the dis-
> covery of your Buddha Nature: but it may help you to prepare for
> that discovery—help you by liberating you from the hauntings of
> your own painful memories, your remorses, your ceaseless anxiety
> about the future . . ."

And here something which Aldous always emphasized in one
way and another:

> Public health and social reform are the indispensable preconditions
> of any kind of general enlightenment.

What chance is there of fulfilment of these pre-conditions?

> "One's justified [says the contemporary Dr MacPhail] in feeling
> extremely pessimistic about the current situation. But despair,
> radical despair—no, I can't see any justification for that."
> "Not even when you read history?"

No, says the doctor, not even when he reads history.

> "How do you manage to do that?"
> "By remembering what history is—the record of what human
> beings have been impelled to do by their ignorance and the *enormous
> bumptiousness that makes them canonize their ignorance as a political or
> religious dogma.* [My italics.]

And here a passage about our present historical situation. The
Palanese do not wish to produce or buy armaments, nor have
they the faintest desire to land on the moon. "Only the modest
ambition to live as full human beings on this island at this latitude
on this planet.

> . . If the politicians in the newly independent countries had any
> sense . . they'd do the same. But they want to throw their weight
> around; they want to have armies, they want to catch up with the
> motorized television addicts of America and Europe. You people
> have no choice—you're irretrievably committed to applied physics
> and chemistry, with all their dismal consequences, military, political
> and social. But the under-developed countries aren't committed.
> They don't *have* to follow your example. They're still free to take the
> road we've taken . . *the road that leads towards happiness from the inside*

out [my italics], *through health, through awareness, through a change in one's attitude towards the world; not towards the mirage of happiness from the outside in, through toys and pills and non-stop distractions. They could still choose our way; but they don't want to, they want to be exactly like you, God help them . . .*

From Mesmerism and bio-chemistry, from Taoism, Tantra, Zen, from the Bardo Thodol and Gestalt philosophy, from psychedelics, from the Greeks, the Chinese, the Quakers, from Victorian novelists and Christian saints, from Darwin, Mendel, Myers, William James, John Dewey, Sheldon, Alexander, Bates, from echoes of the E-therapy and Menninger and Laura's improvisations, from Aldous's own experiences, from all of these the Islanders derive their knowledge and their understanding and their practice, their techniques for living, for dealing with the young, the ageing, the well; their techniques for dealing with the pains of the heart, with loss, with *dying*, for coming to terms with the irreducible one third of sorrow. As in *Brave New World* there is no violence on Pala, no crime or cruelty or hunger, no material fears; unlike *Brave New World*, there is full consciousness of the basic *misère de l'homme*, the appalling possibilities, the certainties of unhappiness.

". . . Painless bereavement—no. And of course that's as it should be. It wouldn't be right if you could take away all pain of bereavement; you'd be less than human."

When Dr MacPhail's wife lies dying he, too, helps her through her last hours. Throughout *Island* there can be found traces of the private Aldous, as if he had wished to leave an auto-biographical squiggle here, a tribute there, a summing-up, a joke shared with himself . . . There is a glancing evocation of that very powerful memory of D. H. Lawrence's death at Vence. "Over there in the corner," says the dying woman, "I can see myself there. And she can see my body on the bed." There is a piece of defunct Aldous surfacing through Farnaby, the man from the West. Was he ever interested in power? they ask him. Never, he answers, "One can't have power without committing oneself."

"And for you the horror of being committed outweighs the pleasure of pushing other people round?"

"By a factor of several thousand times."

Defunct. Yet how much heart-searching it had caused the man who wrote *Point Counter Point*, who struggled over *Eyeless in Gaza*, that horror of his younger years of being committed, that desire to remain the spectator with the telescope, remain in the role he regarded as his guilty privilege and his prison. And here his

ISLAND AND AFTER... 1963

middle-aged view—how quiet, how detached—of having to live
in urban England.

> Well, you won't like the climate, you won't like the food, you
> won't like the noises or the smells or the architecture. But you'll
> almost certainly like the work and you'll probably find that you can
> like quite a lot of people.

And here Aldous's "favourite worst line of poetry", the oddly
unpronounceable,

> *Who props, thou ask'st, in these bad days my mind?*

which happens to be by his own Uncle Matthew.

There is Maria. "You used to say I was like a flea," the wife in
the book says to her husband before she dies. "Here one moment
and then, hop! somewhere else, miles away. No wonder you could
never educate me!"

"But *you* educated *me* all right," he tells her. "If it hadn't been
for you coming in and pulling my hair and making me look at the
world and helping me understand it, what would I be today? A
pedant in blinkers . . . But luckily I had the sense to ask you to
marry me, and luckily you had the folly to say yes and then the
wisdom and intelligence to make a good job of me. After thirty-
seven years of adult education I'm almost human."

"But I'm still a flea . . ." she says, "And yet I did try. I tried
very hard; I don't know if you ever realized it . . I was always on
tiptoes, always straining up towards the place where you were
doing your work and your thinking and your reading. On
tiptoes . . Goodness, how tiring it was! What an endless series of
efforts! And all of them quite useless. Because I was just a dumb
flea hopping about down here among the people and the flowers
and the cats and dogs. Your kind of highbrow world was a place
I could never climb up to . . . I never *knew* anything . . . I could
only *see*."

Why did Aldous choose—with indeed a good many misgivings
—to cast his prescription for the good society in the form of a
novel? (A philosophic novel, to be sure.) Because he believed, in
spite of contemporary cluckings, that the novel is the most
effective literary form. In *War and Peace* we learn more about war
and peace than we would from any documentary of comparable
talent. Aldous was only too aware that he would never write
War and Peace, but thought that even fiction on another level was
likely to be more persuasive, leave traces on a larger public, than
an essay. Up to a point his choice may also have been influenced

by the career of *Brave New World*. In fact *Island*, too, was to reach a large public; did it persuade? Aldous thought that it had not, that its propositions, on the whole, were not seriously discussed or looked at in the light of applicability. To a number of his readers Pala with its happiness and kindliness and good sense was immensely moving, made them long for a world in which such happiness was an aim within sight for themselves and their children. To a great many others, and this must be faced, the book was a boring tale of preaching goody-goodies. The attraction of Pala may well lie in the mind of the beholder.

Island, of course, is also a religious novel. The islanders are compassionate not by mere Pavlovian training. We cannot love our neighbour as we should, unless we love God as we should—the true end of their existence in this mortal world is the Perennial Philosophy, is contemplation, is religion, but religion held lightly, non-combatively, a religion without specific gravity, as it were: non-revealed, non-dogmatic, non-organized. "Mahayana Buddhism, with a bit of Shivaism on the side," as a Palanese remarks. When Gulliver presses him as to exact beliefs, he is told,

"That's one of the questions the Buddha always refused to answer. Believing in the eternal life never helped anyone to live in eternity. Nor, of course, did dis-believing . . ."

And there, I think, we come to another stumbling block. It is hard enough nowadays to write about religion, and here we have religion which is not only alien to both Christians and Agnostics (though goodness knows that Aldous's readers ought to be familiar with the terminology), uncomfortable to the unregenerate, to *l'homme moyen sensuel*, but at the same time so subtle and elusive that it seems nearly impossible to get it across to anyone who has not already "bought his ticket to Athens". It can and has been got across, of course, at times by music, a landscape, a flash of intuition in the night—Aldous had to do it in cold print. A great deal of cold print at that. This may well have been one of the causes for the resistance and impatience generated by the book.

There is one other thing. The inhabitants of Aldous's pragmatic dream use drugs. In *Brave New World*, it was *soma*, the forerunner of a tranquillizer cum euphoric, which the citizens were con-

ditioned into taking to stifle discontent with their own lot and
muffle cosmic questions; *soma*, in fact, was dope; Aldous deplored
it. On *Island* the substance is a perfected version of LSD used
sacramentally by men and women who desire to get out of their
own light and look over the wall. For Aldous—there is no getting
around this—the whole thing was tremendously serious and he
did believe in the possibility of a widely applicable mind-enlarging
drug. He derived this belief from the reports of researchers and
clinicians contemporarily using such drugs in cases of alcoholism
and neuroses, and primarily from his own experiences. This is
how he felt and thought about these in 1959, six years, that is,
after he had swallowed his first fraction of a gram of mescalin
and was waiting for the results with Humphrey Osmond and
Maria.

. . . I have taken mescalin twice and lysergic acid three or four
times [he wrote to Father Thomas Merton in January 1959]. My
first experience was mainly aesthetic. Later experiences were of
another nature and helped me to understand many of the obscure
utterances to be found in the writings of the mystics, Christian and
Oriental. An unspeakable sense of gratitude for the privilege of being
born into this universe. ("Gratitude is heaven itself," says Blake—
and I know now exactly what he is talking about.) A transcendence
of the ordinary subject-object relationship. A transcendence of the
fear of death. A sense of solidarity with the world and its spiritual
principle . . . Finally, an understanding, not intellectual, but in some
sort total, an understanding with the entire organism, of the affirma-
tion that God is Love. The experiences are transient, of course; but
the memory of them, and the inchoate revivals of them which tend
to recur spontaneously or during meditation, continue to exercise a
profound effect upon one's mind. There seems to be no evidence in the
published literature that the drug is habit-forming or that it creates
a craving for repetition. There is a feeling . . that the experience
is so transcendently important that it is in no circumstances a thing
to be entered upon light-heartedly or for enjoyment. (In some
respects, it is not enjoyable; for it entails a temporary death of the
ego, a going-beyond.) Those who desire to make use of this
"gratuitous grace," to co-operate with it, tend to do so, not by
repeating the experiment at frequent intervals, but by trying to
open themselves up, in a state of alert passivity, to the transcendent
"isness", to use Eckhart's phrase, which they have known and, in
some sort, *been* . . .

Aldous concluded this long letter, "There is, obviously, a field
here for serious and reverent experimentation." A year or so later

on, in his lecture on Visionary Experiences, he approached the subject in different terms.[1]

> . . . there are other directly chemical methods [for inducing visionary experiences]. There is an enormous history in this field . . . In the past the majority of these substances, these mind-changing, vision-inducing substances, have been dangerous. Opium, of course, is a dangerous substance; even dear old alcohol is a dangerous substance . . . the really startling fact about recent pharmacological developments is that a number of chemical substances had been discovered in recent years which permit . . enormous changes in consciousness . . without inflicting serious damage upon the body . . .
> . . Experiments, of course, have been made by eminent psychologists for a long time. William James, for example, made considerable experiments with nitrous oxide and incidentally was much blamed by some of his colleagues for such a frivolous undertaking and for taking it so seriously. James was defended by Bergson in his *The Two Sources of Morality and Religion*, where he said we must remember that the nitrous oxide was not the cause of Professor James's "remarkable experience," it was the occasion that removed certain obstacles which permitted this other material to come through. The obstacles could have been removed . . by other psycho-physical means, but this particular means did open the door, and the nature of the experience which came through is not affected by the nature of the key which is used to open the door. This is a very interesting passage in Bergson, and I think it is fundamentally true, although there seems to be something rather discreditable and unfair about the possibility of opening the door by a means so simple as psilocybin or LSD-25. There seems to be no reason to doubt that what comes through is of the same nature as what comes through via breathing exercises, or fasting, flagellation . . .

What *comes through*—after swallowing a powder or a pill—is it qualitatively, substantially the same as what comes through after weeks or years of asceticism and the more violent physical austerities? *Ought* it to be the same? As Aldous said, there seems to be something discreditable and unfair about it; indeed to many of us the whole thing is offensive or at least disquieting—it goes against the grain of what is left of our Christian or Puritan tradition. Professor Zaehner[2] stated this notion very simply after his own rather unrevealing experience (*trivial* was his word—"In Huxley's terminology, 'self-transcendence' of a sort did take

[1] This is a lecture Aldous delivered on several occasions. I am quoting from the text of Professor Lamson's working copy transcribed from the tapes at M.I.T. where Visionary Experiences was the 6th Huxley Lecture.

[2] R. C. Zaehner, *Mysticism Sacred and Profane*. Oxford, at the Clarendon Press, 1957.

place, but transcendence into a world of farcical meaninglessness. All things were one in the sense that they were all, at the height of my manic state, equally funny . . ."); the conclusion he then came to was,

> I would not wish to take the drug again, but purely on moral grounds . . . the more the experience fades into the past, the clearer does it seem to me that, in principle, artificial interference with consciousness is, except for valid medical reasons, wrong.

To which argument Aldous had already replied the year before, in *Heaven and Hell*,[1] "But in one way or another, *all* our experiences are chemically conditioned,

> and if we imagine that some of them are purely "spiritual", purely "intellectual", or purely "aesthetic", it is merely because we never troubled to investigate the internal chemical environment . . . Furthermore, it is a matter of historical record that most contemplatives worked systematically to modify their body chemistry, with a view to creating the internal conditions favourable to spiritual insight. When they were not starving themselves into low blood sugar and a vitamin deficiency, or beating themselves into intoxication by histamine, adrenalin and decomposed protein, they were cultivating insomnia and praying for long periods in uncomfortable conditions in order to create the psycho-physical symptoms of stress . . . or, if they were Orientals, they did breathing exercises to accomplish the same purpose. Today we know how to lower the efficiency of the cerebral reducing valve by direct chemical action, and without the risk of inflicting serious damage on the psycho-physical organism. For an aspiring mystic to revert, in the present state of knowledge, to prolonged fasting and violent self-flagellation would be as senseless as it would be for an aspiring cook to behave like Charles Lamb's Chinaman, who burned down the house in order to roast a pig . . .

In 1961, after eight years of psychedelic experiences, Aldous is once more on record. In the London interview he was questioned at some length by John Chandos, to whom the subject appears to have been novel—as indeed it then was to the public at large—and a trifle alien.

> "How often have you taken mescalin?"
> "I've taken mescalin twice, and LSD about five times, I suppose."[2]
> "Is the effect the same on everyone?"

---

[1] Chatto & Windus, 1956.
[2] After that point, Aldous appears to have taken a psychedelic drug twice, possibly three times, more. In the chapter on The Door in the Wall (Part X, 3), I put the total, including mescalin, LSD and psilocybin, as between nine and eleven times; Laura speaks of twelve times in all, and is very likely right.

"It varies. On the whole, no. Statistically about 70% get a good and positive and happy result from it, a certain percentage get no results, and a certain percentage get very unpleasant and hell-like results out of it. They get very frightened."

"And what were yours?"

"Mine were always positive . . ."

"How long does the effect last?"

"Eight hours."

"During this time, do you just sit, or do you move about?"

"You move about if you want to . . You spend a lot of time sitting quietly looking at things—getting some of these strange metaphysical insights into the world . . ."

"Is it a habit-forming drug?"

"No, no, absolutely not . . . Most people I know haven't any special desire to go on taking it. They would like to take it every six months or every year or something of this kind . . ."

"Is it not a condition one wants to be in, or continue to be in?"

"You couldn't be in it all the time . . . The world becomes so extraordinary and so absorbing that you can't cross the street without considerable risk of being run over . . ."

"But if this vision is so valuable, doesn't one want to go on . . .?"

"Well, I would like to take it about once a year. Most people . . who have taken it have no *desire* to sort of fool with it constantly . . . You *take it too seriously* to behave in this way towards it. You don't want to wallow in it."

"Would it be wallowing if it opened up a life . .?"

"Well, you need a good deal of time to digest this, I think . . ."

Much of this has a hollow ring today, twelve years after and more. Aldous, who foresaw so much, did not foresee much of the squalid, catastrophic sequel. *Anything* can be misused, he said, and stuck to his guns—self-improvement and insight are intrinsically valuable, to the individual, to the world as a whole, even if they are, like so much else, chemically induced. One way in which Aldous went wrong, I think, was in failing to take into account that there might be an extremely close relation between the quality of the man who takes the drug and the quality of the experience. Baudelaire, whose own excursions were more prolonged and terrifying, made this extremely important point.[1] (He is speaking of experience under hashish.)

. . . L'ivresse . . ne sera, il est vrai, qu'un immense rêve . . . mais elle gardera toujours la tonalité particulière de l'individu. L'homme a voulu rêver, le rêve gouvernera l'homme; mais ce rêve sera bien le fils de son père . . .

[1] Charles Baudelaire *Les Paradis Artificiels*, "Le Théatre de Séraphin."

[The intoxication, indeed, will simply be an immense dream . . . but it will always keep the pattern, the style, the quality of the individual dreamer. Man wants to dream . . . the dream will take charge; but the dream will be its father's son.]

Mine were always positive—the insights, the transcendence, the immense reality or dream that rose in Aldous's consciousness, were they not related, were they not conditional upon who or what *he* was?

To Aldous the dream was good; he wished, believed, that it could be shared. On the mundane level, to researchers, to friends, he counselled caution. ("Always Aldous emphasizes," Laura wrote, "how delicately and respectfully these chemicals should be used; and that they are only one of many means through which it is possible to increase good will among men.") One must not take them without doctor's consent, take them peacefully, deliberately, in the right health and frame of mind, at the right place and time, in friendly surroundings, wise company . . . Under no circumstances must one touch the dubious, adulterated substances peddled by crooks (which is, of course, precisely what the majority of drug-takers nowadays resort to). Aldous deplored the antics of young Timothy Leary, that enthusiast and high priest of the psychedelic cult. (He and Humphrey had first met Leary at Cambridge, Massachusetts, in November 1960, when he was conducting experiments with mind-expanding drugs at Harvard.) Aldous often tried to warn him; had urged him, for instance, without much success, to get his followers to desist from taking green LSD[1], a boot-legged liquid in plastic bottles which was circulating at the time.

. . Yes, what about Tim Leary? [Aldous wrote to Humphrey in December 1962] I spent an evening with him here a few weeks ago— and he talked such nonsense . . that I became quite concerned. Not about his sanity—because he is perfectly sane—but about his prospects in the world; for this nonsense-talking is just another device for annoying people in authority, flouting convention, cocking snooks at the academic world; it is the reaction of a mischievous Irish boy to the headmaster of his school. One of these days the headmaster will lose patience . . . I am very fond of Tim . . but why, oh why, does he *have* to be such an ass? . . .

I must now return to the question, to what extent Aldous can be regarded as a causative factor in the present drug scene? *Was* he a major link? Or an incidental, if much publicized, one? A seducer, a misleader? Or an alibi at second or third-hand? Was

---

[1] Dr Humphrey Osmond in letters to S. B.

he inadequately informed, should he and could he have known more about the potential dangers, physical, genetic, social, of these drugs? Evidence is elusive and the whole matter beclouded by emotion and by hearsay[1]—Aldous acclaimed as an apostle, Aldous deplored as wicked or gullible and woolly-minded; and of course Aldous no longer here to give his answer. I can only say, what I tried to say some two hundred pages earlier about *The Doors of Perception*, that I do not know. There *are* questions. Some, inevitably, quantitative. How many individual people, particularly among the serious, well-intentioned young, pinned their hopes on psychedelics, did actually take drugs in consequence of reading, or listening to Aldous? How many of them came to harm? How far did *their* example cause a further spread? Can one seriously assert that what is called the drug explosion would not be with us today had there been no Aldous Huxley? His public contribution consists of one distinctly highbrow book, *The Doors*,[2] passages of a lecture delivered in academic institutions and two scenes in a novel, *Island*, one of them a not entirely re-assuring description of a trip, the other a long, solemn account of a psychedelic rite. What weight is to be attached to these in the historical context—the waning of authoritative religion, the revulsion from consumers' existence, the perennial human longing to side-step the daily world, the aftermath of the Vietnam war? On the other hand, ought one to take into account the legend of Aldous's mescalin allegiance which may well have been more consequential than his actual words? And what of the future? Is the present messy, tragic footling with drugs a passing side-phenomenon, an *accident de parcours*, on the road to the beneficent pharmacological revolution Aldous liked to predict?

Leaving aside the accumulated mass of controversial material, I feel that I should mention the fragmentary comments by two people very close to Aldous. One is entire, almost casual, dismissal by Krishnamurti.[3]

Well, Aldous used to discuss it with me, but of course the whole thing is meaningless. Why go so far? We all know that human consciousness can be disturbed with stimulus. An alcoholic drink will do that much for you.

The other comes from Maria. Why are they making all this fuss, she is supposed to have said, in effect, to one or two friends when

[1] Such as people, whom he may not even have met, claiming to have been on trips with Aldous.

[2] *Heaven and Hell*, surely, is more of a cadenza on visual and visionary art.

[3] Talking to Chaman Nahal, from *Drugs and the Other Self* by Chaman Nahal. Harper & Row, 1970.

Aldous and Gerald Heard first described their transfigured world of mescalin. "I have known that it *is* like this all along." It has the ring of truth: Maria knew, did have the experience spontaneously (and one can hear her throw off that kind of remark). But I don't think it is the whole truth. I never had a chance to talk to her about it. In Rome, in 1954, *The Doors of Perception* came up for a few seconds (Aldous had dedicated it to her; of his whole *œuvre* only two books bear a dedication, *The Doors* to Maria, *Island* to Laura). Maria said little; what she implied, in her kind of shorthand, was approval, a feeling at peace with the book and all that it meant to Aldous.

Meant to Aldous . . . Let us give the last word here to him. Prefaced—irresistible temptation—by Baudelaire.

> . . . C'est une espèce de hantise, mais de hantise intermittente, dont nous devrions tirer, si nous étions sage, la certitude d'une existence meilleure et l'espérance d'y atteindre par l'exercice journalier de notre volonté . . .
> . . . C'est pourquoi je préfère considérer cette condition anormale de l'esprit comme une véritable grâce, comme un miroir magique où l'homme est invité à se voir en beau, c'est-à-dire tel qu'il devrait et pourrait être; une espèce d'excitation angélique, un rappel à l'ordre . . .[1]
> [. . . It is a kind of obsession, but intermittent . . from which we should extract, if we were wise, the certainty of a better life and the hope of finding it through the daily exercise of our will . . .
> [. . . This is why I prefer to regard this anomalous condition of the spirit as a true grace, a magic mirror where man is invited to see himself *en beau*, that is such as he ought to be and could be . . .]

Baudelaire wrote this more than a century ago, Baudelaire who came to the immense dream by a different road—poetic genius, private despair—but who, too, kept compass with the diamond clarity of his intelligence. Now to Aldous. In the course of the London interview, he had answered questions quietly, patiently; at one point he quickened—

> Different, yes . . . I mean the intensity of the experience is entirely unlike an ordinary experience . . . But on the other hand, it quite obviously resembles spontaneous experiences which certain artists and religious people have unquestionably had . . .
> . . It's an immense intensification, a transfiguration of the external world into incredible beauty and significance . . .

[1] *Les Paradis Artificiels*, "Le Goût de l'infini."

There is a quiet conviction in those words as they are spoken, something very simple, very moving; to get the feeling of this one ought to hear that happy, mellow voice.[1]

> . . . It's also beyond that kind of aesthetic experience—there may be . . a sense of solidarity with the universe, solidarity with other people . . . Understanding of such phrases as you get in the Book of Job, "Yea, though he slay me, yet I will trust in him"—this thing opens the door to these experiences . . Which can be of immense value to people. If they choose to make use of them. If they don't choose, well, this is what the Catholics call Gratuitous Grace: it doesn't guarantee salvation, it isn't sufficient and it isn't necessary for salvation; it can be collaborated with and it can be used in an intelligent way; it can be of immense help to people.
>
> And then there is the sense that *in spite of Everything*—I suppose this is the Ultimate Mystical conviction—in spite of Pain, in spite of Death, in spite of Horror, *the universe* is in some way A l l R i g h t, capital A, capital R . . .

Aldous wrote one more book, *Literature and Science*, begun in 1962, finished in the spring of 1963. It has perhaps been somewhat overlooked—another long essay, a slim volume—taken for the earlier, quite different, *Science, Liberty and Peace*; yet it is probably one of the most revealing of his later books, a re-casting and further distillation of the M.I.T. lectures, the most up-to-date as to his thought, and mood and stand. It is an unsolemn, ultimately optimistic book, good-tempered, easy to read, with a return to the wit and fun and playfulness of the early essays. The primary theme is stated in the three words of the opening sentence, "Snow or Leavis?" Aldous's answer can be inferred from his title, Literature *and* Science, not Literature *versus* Science.

> The world with which literature deals is the world into which human beings are born and live and finally die . . . the world of sufferings and enjoyments, of madness and common sense, of silliness, cunning and wisdom; the world of social pressures and individual impulses, of reason against passion, of instincts and conventions, of shared language and unshareable feeling and sensation; of innate differences and the rules . . the solemn or absurd rituals imposed by the prevailing culture . . .[2]

[1] I am delighted to be able to say that we *can* hear it. An admirable condensation of that interview on two gramophone records has been released by Denis Preston, the original instigator. "Personally Speaking."

[2] From *Literature and Science*. Chatto & Windus, 1963 (as all following quotations).

The scientist, as a professional,

> is the inhabitant of a radically different universe—not the world of given appearances but the world of inferred fine structures, not the experienced world of unique events and diverse qualities, but the world of quantified regularities.

The man of letters accepts the uniqueness of events, the diversity of the world, the radical incomprehensibility of existence,

> . . accepts the challenge which uniqueness, multifariousness and mystery fling in his face and . . addresses himself to the paradoxical task of rendering the randomness and shapelessness of individual experience in highly organized and meaningful works of art.

The medium of these works of art is language—*La poésie s'écrit avec des mots.* "There exists in every language a rough and ready vocabulary for the expression of the individual's more private experiences. Anyone capable of speech can say, 'I'm frightened', or 'How pretty!' . . . In good literature . . the blunt imprecisions of conventional language give place to subtler and more penetrating forms of expression. The ambition of the literary artist is to speak about the ineffable, to communicate in words what words were never intended to convey . . . [he] must therefore invent or borrow some kind of uncommon language . . ." And here Aldous, as he had so often done, invokes once more that potent line of Mallarmé's, "*Donner un sens plus pur aux mots de la tribu*—that is the task confronting every serious writer . . ." To purify, to enrich, the language of the tribe . . . For a few pages Aldous, recalling the serenities of *Texts and Pretexts*, returns to his old loves.

> . . There is the magic . . of unfamiliarly beautiful syntax and sentence construction; the magic of names and words that, for some obscure reason, seem intrinsically significant; the magic of well-ordered rhythms, of harmonious combinations of consonants and vowels. One thinks of such exquisite treasures of syntax as "Not to know me argues yourselves unknown," or *Tel qu'en Lui-même enfin l'éternité le change.* And at the other extreme of phrase-making one recalls the spell-like efficacy of such juxtaposed simplicities as "Cover her face: mine eyes dazzle: she died young"; as "I wak'd, she fled, and day brought back my night" . . .
>
> The supreme masters of syntactical magic are Milton and Mallarmé . . . *Paradise Lost* is Syntax Regained and completely remade . . . Elsewhere, and in lighter keys, we find such enchantments as "crossing the stripling Thames at Bablock Hithe", or "Amyntas now doth with Chloris sleep under a sycamore" . . . On a higher level of intrinsic

significance we find such Shakespearean marvels as "defunctive music", "sole Arabian tree", "multitudinous seas incarnadine." And what about Milton's "elephants endors'd with towers"? What about "sleek Panope" and "that two-handed engine at the door"! . . .

Some degree of verbal recklessness is characteristic of good poetry. There are slightly reckless good poets, and there are good poets who, at times, are extremely reckless . . . here is the final stanza of Yeats's *Byzantium*.

> *Astraddle on the dolphin's mire and blood,*
> *Spirit after spirit! The smithies break the flood,*
> *The golden smithies of the Emperor!*
> *Marbles of the dancing floor*
> *Break bitter furies of complexity*
> *Those images that yet*
> *Fresh images beget,*
> *That dolphin-torn, that gong-tormented sea.*

Now for the antithesis. "In the scientist, verbal caution ranks among the highest of virtues. His words must have a one-to-one relationship with some specified class of data or sequence of ideas.

By the rules of the scientific game he is forbidden to say more than one thing at a time, to attach more than one meaning to a given word, to stray outside the bounds of logical discourse . . . Poets and, in general, men of letters are permitted, indeed are commanded, by the rules of *their* game, to do all the things that scientists are not allowed to do . . .

The writer, then, must perform "the tasks for which his talents uniquely qualify him—namely, to render . . his own and other people's more private experiences . . [and] to relate these experiences in some humanly satisfying way to public experiences . . .

. . . Eliot is a great poet because he purified the words of the tribe in novel, beautiful and many-meaninged ways, not because he extended the field of subject-matter available to poetic treatment: he didn't. And this is true of most of his poetical successors. From their writings you would be hard put to it to infer the simple historical fact that they are contemporaries of Einstein and Heisenberg, of computers, electron microscopes and the discovery of the molecular basis of heredity, of Operationalism, Diamat and Emergent Evolution . . .

Whether we like it or not, Aldous postulates, ours is the Age of Science. And the question is, What can a writer do about it? And what, as a literary artist and a citizen, *ought* he to do about it?

. . For the non-specialist, a thorough and detailed knowledge of any branch of science is impossible. It is also unnecessary. All that is necessary . . is a general knowledge of science, a bird's-eye knowledge of what has been achieved in the various fields of scientific enquiry, together with an understanding of the philosophy of science and an appreciation of the ways in which scientific information and scientific modes of thought are relevant to individual experience and the problems of social relationships, to religion and politics, to ethics and a tenable philosophy of life . . .

The sciences of life have need of the artist's intuitions and, conversely, the artist has need of all that these sciences can offer him in the way of new materials on which to exercise his creative powers . . .

. . . Science, it seems hardly necessary to remark, provides no justification for slaughter and oppression. Hand in hand with progressive technology, it merely provides the means for implementing the old insanities in a novel and more effective way . . . To keep drawing attention to this grotesque and increasingly dangerous state of affairs is surely one of the functions, one of the prime duties, of the twentieth-century man of letters.

Aldous tried to convey something also of the tremendous implications of the new material available to the artist. " 'For the first time in history [he is quoting Werner Heisenberg, the physicist] man, on this planet, is discovering that he is alone with himself, without a partner and without an adversary.'

To put it more picturesquely, man is in the process of becoming his own Cataclysm, his own Saviour and own invading horde of Martians. And in the realm of pure science the same discovery— that he is alone with himself—awaits him as he progressively refines his analysis of matter. "Modern science," says Heisenberg, "shows us that we can no longer regard the building blocks of matter, which were considered originally to be the ultimate objective reality, as being 'things in themselves' . . . Knowledge of atoms and their movements 'in themselves', that is to say independent of our observation, is no longer the aim of research; rather we now find ourselves from the very start in the midst of a dialogue between nature and man, a dialogue of which science is only one part, so much so that the conventional division of the world into subject and object, is no longer applicable . . For the science of nature, the subject matter of research is no longer nature in itself, but nature subjected to human questioning, and to this extent man, once again, meets only with himself."

Presently Aldous comes to the point of how very little even the best informed philosophers and writers knew until very recently about man-the-species and man-the-product-of-culture. "The earth was largely unexplored, archaeology had not been invented . . .

Virtually everything we know about ourselves as the resultants of evolution, as the earth's dominant, wildly proliferating and most destructive species, as creators, beneficiaries and victims of culture, as the genius inventors and idiot-dupes of language, has come to us, during the last three or four generations, from paleontologists and ecologists, from systematic historians and . . the social scientists. And from geneticists, neurologists and bio-chemists has come, in great measure during the present century, most of what we now know about human beings as members of the animal kingdom, as living organisms with an inherited anatomy and an inherited chemical and temperamental individuality . . .

Then, "Who are We? What is our destiny? How can the often frightful ways of God be justified?

Before the rise of science, the only answers . . came from the philosopher-poets and poet-philosophers. Thus, in India the enigma of man's individual and collective destiny was unriddled in terms of a theory—implausibly simple and suspiciously moralistic—of reincarnation and *karma*. Present good luck was the reward for past virtue, and if you were suffering now, it was your fault . . .

In the Christian West the riddle was solved (or perhaps it would be truer to say that it was re-stated) in terms of some completely unobservable act of supernatural predestination . . . It was a matter simply of the arbitrariness of omnipotence, of God's good pleasure.

Men's destiny is a matter, among other things, of the observable differences between human individuals. Are these differences inherited or acquired, or inherited *and* acquired? For many centuries it seemed reasonable to debate the problem of Nature versus Nurture in terms of theology and metaphysics. Augustinians fought with Pelagians; Proto-Behaviourists, such as Helvétius, reacted against Jansenist Christianity by maintaining, in the teeth of all probability and on no evidence whatever, that any shepherd boy from the Cevennes could be transformed, by suitable tutoring, into another Isaac Newton or (if the tutor preferred) into a replica of St Francis of Assisi. "Everything," said Rousseau, "is good that comes from the Creator; everything is perverted by the hands of man." The Creator is now out of fashion; but environmental determinism remains the frame of reference within which many social scientists and many men of letters still do their feeling and their thinking. Theirs, surely, is an inexcusable one-sidedness; for the science of genetics has been with us for a long life-time and the unscientific study of innate human differences is as old as literature . . .

Manners maketh man, but on the other hand *you can't make a silk purse out of a sow's ear*. The old proverbs flatly contradict one another, but both are correct. Predestined by their heredity, human beings are post-destined by their environment . . .

From individual *karma* we now pass to the enigma of collective destiny. Kipling was probably wrong in asserting that there were lesser breeds without the law. But, along with other observers, he was probably right in thinking that the manifest differences in racial temperaments were more than merely cultural and must be due, at least in part, to hereditary factors.

The ways of God have never been justified, but they can be explained, at least partially, in non-theological terms. Why do these things happen to us? . . a number of fragmentary, but nonetheless useful and even enlightening answers to the riddle of human destiny are now forthcoming. And the same thing is true of the closely related riddle of human nature. Who and what are we? A complete scientific answer is still lacking. We know a great deal, but we do not yet know how to correlate what we know into an explanation . . .

To the twentieth-century man of letters science offers a treasure of newly discovered facts and tentative hypotheses. If he accepts this gift and if, above all, he is sufficiently talented and resourceful to be able to transform the new raw materials into works of literary art, the twentieth-century man of letters will be able to treat the age-old, and perennially relevant theme of human destiny with a depth of understanding, a width of reference, of which, before the rise of science, his predecessors (through no fault of their own, no defect of genius) were incapable.

Thought is crude, matter unimaginably subtle. [This is the final paragraph of Aldous's last book] Words are few and can only be arranged in certain conventionally fixed ways; the counterpoint of unique events is infinitely wide and their succession indefinitely long. That the purified language of science, or even the richer purified language of literature should ever be adequate to the givenness of the world and of our experience is, in the very nature of things, impossible. Cheerfully accepting the fact, let us advance together, men of letters and men of science, further and further into the ever expanding regions of the unknown.

Aldous's own philosophy was dynamic; he never said This is enough; he never stood still. He asked, Where are we Going? and Where Ought we to be Going? His beliefs were both immensely complex and quite simple, (. . *it's a bit embarrassing to find at the end that one has no more to offer by way of advice than "try to be a little kinder"*). He believed in knowledge, pursued it with the same ardour he had expressed when he went down from Oxford—I *should like to go on for ever learning*, straightforward knowledge (yes, yes, he did more or less read through the whole of the Britannica as anecdote will have it) *and* intuitive knowledge, intangible knowledge, the end of explorative experience.

. . . I do think that the whole idea of the cognitive value of music, and indeed of all art, is probably very important. [He said at M.I.T.[1]] In a certain sense, art is something which imposes forms upon the flux of reality . . but in another sense it is also discovering, not merely forms, but that which lies behind the forms . . this view, after all, is profoundly important in the ideas of Plato—that in beauty we discover something about the nature of the world; that in some way or another, an entirely ineffable and inexplicable way, beauty is built into the fundamental nature of things, and that art is a method of discovering this. Music above all, with its strange capacity for discovering a sort of pure incorporeal, dynamic essence of life, does perhaps provide the most powerful weapon for exploring this aspect of the ultimate nature of the world.

"What place has the supernatural in your own life?" (How convenient to be able to resort to John Chandos's questions.)

"Well, I don't know what people mean exactly by the *supernatural*. In practice, I would say that what people call the *natural* in our Western tradition *is in fact* our projection of concepts upon the world . . It is *our picture* of the world with its names and labels . . utilitarian and scientific . . the general day-to-day picture . . . The *supernatural* is the world as it comes to us in its mystery . . I mean, anyone who has ever had the experience of seeing the world without any labels and concepts, immediately has the impression of its being supernatural. In a curiously paradoxical way nature as it is in itself—and as much as we can ever know it—*is* supernatural . . . One is sometimes suddenly aware of *this bottomless mystery of existence*—sometimes *one is hit by this thing*. If you choose to call it the supernatural, I mean I don't know what other sense it has . . I mean, I don't believe in mysterious beings going around arranging things . . ."

"A mysterious Being going around arranging things?"

"Well, I do think [chuckling] there is a mysterious being . . but whether he arranges things is another question . . . *I just don't know* . . . I mean, one can be a complete agnostic and a complete mystic at the same time."

Chandos, still hoping to pin Aldous down, went on, "I want to

[1] In the 5th Lecture "Why Art?", on 2nd November 1960.

know whether you, yourself, felt you had any direct line . . to an individual upstairs . . ? As professing Catholics do?"

"No, no," Aldous said with utter detachment, faintly amused, "I certainly don't. I mean, what Blake calls 'Nobodaddy Aloft', I have no feelings about." And then again on the rising voice, the violin, "I am entirely on the side of the mystery. I mean, any attempts to explain away the mystery is ridiculous . . . I believe in the *profound and unfathomable mystery of life* . . which has a sort of divine quality about it . . ."

He was also on the side of happiness, as an absolute good, an intrinsic value. *The world is an illusion, but an illusion which we must take seriously*. He would say that people, adults and children could be made happier by decent living conditions, by love received and given . . . he thought that Bertrand Russell was right when he said[1] "Man is an animal and his happiness depends on his physiology more than he likes to think"; and at the same time Aldous's philosophy was governed by another equation—Man cannot be happy unless he is virtuous; man cannot be virtuous without God; God cannot be realized by man without virtue. "Virtue," he said, "is the essential preliminary to the mystical experience." And the mystical experience—enlightenment—is the supreme end of man.

The dialectic might be prolonged; one conclusion seems to impose itself, the conclusion that Aldous was a man who, for himself, had solved the question of how to live, for better and for worse, as a human being in this given world. To many of us he has left much to learn.

[1] In his essay "The Road to Happiness".

Chapter Eight

1963—September, October, November

ON the 6th of September Aldous was getting ready for his lecture tour in the East; on the 13th he cancelled it. There had been a relapse. He spoke of it as a secondary inflammation, an after-effect of radium. He was feeling pretty low again, he wrote to Humphrey, and would not be able to come and see him in October.

> Alas! But I think the sensible thing is to lie low and try to build up resistance and general health.

Whether he would be able to undertake the job of editing the Human Resource volume remained to be seen. "At present I have my doubts . . ." In a postscript he said, "I send you my news in confidence—so please don't mention it to Ellen or Matthew."

In fact Laura wrote to Matthew on the same day. "This is the letter I have been hoping I would not have to write . . ."[1] She told him what had now become evident, that Aldous was a very ill man indeed. ". . He may or may not write you and J. and J. I would prefer that he tell you in his own way and time. But now I feel you must know. *Nobody knows* . . ." What Aldous knew she could not tell. ("Never during the difficult days of his illness," Dr Cutler wrote,[2] "did he question me too closely concerning his own case.")

On 24th September Aldous did write to his son. (A three-page letter, unpublished, in his usual firm hand.) "The trouble began in 1960 . . ." As for the present, the secondary inflammation of a neck gland is "painful and debilitating . . . This state of affairs will doubtless wear off in time . . . so patience is the watch word. Meanwhile please keep this information as private as possible. It's appalling how quickly one's private affairs can get into the tabloids."

The stress of this privacy was mainly borne by Laura.

> . . To all appearances our life was the same . . . friends . . would call up, to make plans to meet. Invitations . . requests for interviews . .

---

[1] The whole of this long letter, and a very detailed account of these and the following ten weeks, can be found in Laura's *This Timeless Moment* cit.

[2] *Mem. Vol.*

continued as though Aldous were well. My own life had never been so involved with the public as at this time. My book was at its peak of popularity. I had been scheduled for lectures and appearances; I received calls and letters from people in urgent need, who hoped and believed that one or two meetings with the author of a book which had already helped them were essential . . Since spring I had put off seeing people who had been working with me previously. I could not bring myself to cancel their appointments unless I could give them a very solid reason.

But if she had, "Friends and admirers would have pressed around us with their love and encouragement—but also, unwittingly, with their grief . . I was afraid their feelings would affect me and rob me of that strength I was jealously keeping for Aldous . . . I did not want to be distracted by anyone's sadness, even if it were in sympathy with Aldous . . ."

On 29th September Aldous broke his silence to Julian and Juliette. He led on from remarks about the weather, "In my own case meteorology has been compounded by a spell of ill health." He gave a factual outline of the medical history. "Result: I have had to cancel my lecture tour . . ." He supposed it would not be manageable for Julian to take over some of his engagements? Another handicap is my persistent hoarseness, due to the nerve that supplies the right-hand vocal cord having been knocked out either by an infiltration of the malignancy, or by radiation. I hope this hoarseness may only be temporary, but rather fear that I may carry it to the grave.

What the future holds, one doesn't know. In general these malignancies in the neck and head don't do much metastasizing. Meanwhile I am trying to build up resistance with the combination of a treatment which has proved rather successful at the University of Montreal and the U of Manila—the only institutions where it has been tried out over a period of years . . . When this damned inflammation dies down, which it may be expected to do in a few weeks, I hope to get back to regular work. For the present I am functioning at only a fraction of normal capacity.

During those weeks and into October, Aldous though very weak, got up every morning, had his meals downstairs, went for walks, did a little work. He was beset by a number of varying discomforts, backache, shortness of breath, exhaustion, but no pain that aspirin could not disperse. Friends came to see him. Gerald of an afternoon.

.. We sat in the garden.[1] His thinness was extreme, his voice tended to tire, but the vivacity of interest .. and concern, the power to entertain showed no abatement. Agilely he had come down the flight of stairs from his bedroom study to sit with us in his garden. When we[2] left he came with us down the steep slope at the foot of which cars had to park . . .

There is a story going round that Aldous and Gerald in days of health had made a pact to discuss their impending death if either of them fell very ill, and that Gerald went to him then in dread of this discussion, and was relieved when Aldous talked to him of everything but death.

Jake Zeitlin came to lunch. "We talked of old friends—we ticked them off, this one and that one . . . We spoke of ourselves as survivors.[3]

We walked silently on Mulholland Highway for a while. He asked if I thought that men would learn to live in peace before it was too late? Before parting I told him a story of meeting his brother Julian in Texas in the 1920's and of our discussing Aldous's irreverent essay on Beethoven in *Vanity Fair*. Julian said, "But Aldous is very young, you know."

Literature and Science came out. Aldous had a copy sent to Mrs Hubble, the astronomer's widow—Edwin and Grace, two of Aldous and Maria's closest friends of the first Californian decade. Now he had not seen Grace for some time and her cat, whom Maria used to find uncanny, had died.

.. I think [he wrote to her on 2nd October] Edwin wd have approved of *Literature and Science*, and hope that you will like it.
.. I have been under the weather and have had .. to confine myself to the house and a regimen of not too *dolce far niente*. When things go better I hope we can make the Pasadena trip and drink a cup of tea with you. I shall miss Nicolas.

Aldous had been commissioned by *Show* Magazine to write an article on "Shakespeare and Religion" for the poet's quater-

---

[1] Again from his *Kenyon Review* article of 1965 cit. Gerald Heard was already a very ill man when I began my round of talking to Aldous's California friends in 1968, and I was not able to see him. So I never spoke to Gerald after 1941.
[2] I presume that the *we* refers to Gerald's friend, Michael Barry, who would have driven him to see Aldous.
[3] Jacob Zeitlin (to the best of my recollection) in an interview with George Wickes of Claremont University.

centenary in 1964, and this was what he was working at. On 3rd October Betty drove him to the L.A. public library. Aldous moved from shelf to shelf, knowing exactly what he wanted, where to find it, pulled out a book, got his reference, put it back, with swift efficiency. He insisted on going to the post office to mail a package, would not let Betty do it for him. It was a copy of the French edition of *Island* which Maria's cousin Marthe, married to Masurel the French tycoon, had asked him to inscribe for her husband's birthday. Aldous wrote his dedication in the post office, laughing when he read it to Betty who had met Masurel and knew his way of life.

For Ernest Masurel,
  A voyage to an island that cannot be arranged by Thomas Cook's.

On 9th October he wrote to Ellen, mainly about recorded literature; on the 10th he wrote to Jeanne. Lightly. She had thought of coming over but had given the idea up—"Je le regrette," he wrote, he would have loved to have seen her. He thanked her for a cheque she had sent to be put into an emergency fund for Mère—who, he was sure would preside over all their funerals, daughters', sons-in-law's, perhaps one or two grand-children's.[1] He hoped that *The Genius and the Goddess* would be at last produced in France, and had she noticed that those idiots of publishers at Plon's had given *Island* the title *L'Isle*, when it ought to have been *Isle*. "In Italy the book is called *Isola*, in Sweden *Ön* and in Denmark (miracle of brevity) *Ø*. Tendresses à Noële et à toi."

Of his own health not one word.

But by that time friends were beginning to know. On 11th October Laura went to Mme Nys to prepare her for the truth. That was also the day Aldous did not want to get up for the first time. In the evening Betty wrote to Jeanne.

. . Both your mother and Laura have asked me to write to you . . . your mother has written you her fears which have been mine too for many months—especially since he and Laura returned from Europe. I did not tell you, and until this moment have told no one, Jeanne dear, because I had no right to, and because I had the feeling that telling made *true* what I prayed some miracle might make untrue. About a week ago, however, Laura told me a long, heart-breaking story . . . and of Aldous's determination to get well, his faith that he would recover. He wanted no one to know because he was working, and still works for a while nearly every day.

---

[1] Mme Nys died in 1966.

He knows now that I know, from Laura, but we do not speak of it. I see him fairly often and *something* has made it possible for me to talk about all kinds of things—even gossip—and jokes.

It was then that Betty asked him. "Didn't you have a nick-name, Aldous, when you were small?" and that Aldous said, "They called me Ogie. Short for Ogre." He told her about life at Prior's Field, how at bed-time he used to run away and hide in his sister Margaret's room.

. . . At the post office a week ago . . . that was one of the moments I believed in a miracle, but I don't today . . . He looks dreadful, but has had no pain.

Jeanne was still debating whether to come or not—would her arrival be a shock to him? Betty was not sure. "My own answer to such questions—should I phone?—should I go there?—should I do this or that or nothing?—generally comes from wondering what Maria would have wanted me to do.

In the wish to help—with grapes or a book or a risqué story or an offer to go on errands—I haven't been wrong—so far. Maybe your answer will come from asking Maria. If you do come, please write Aldous a flock of lies . . .

On 15th October Aldous wrote to Humphrey at some length. ". . In our hypothetical volume on human resources there will obviously have to be a chapter—by you, no doubt—on the best emotional contexts in which the learning of new ways to use the mind should be placed.

The Indians tried to solve the problem by means of the guru system. But this lends itself to all kinds of psychological and social abuses (you should hear Krishnamurti on the subject of gurus!), and something less dangerous will have to be worked out.
. . I still don't know if I shall be able to undertake the work. At the moment I am so low . . . that I feel I shall never again be good for anything. But I hope and think this state of affairs will pass in due course. ("It will pass"—the only motto appropriate to every human situation, whether good or bad.)

The day before, a Monday, Matthew and Judy had arrived for the inside of a week, a visit disguised as a business trip. Aldous was propped up in bed in his white-washed room, his head in his hand, Matthew sat beside him, *his* head in his hand—the identical gesture (how many times we had seen it). Matthew talked to him about the book he was then writing about his experiences in Peru;[1] Aldous talked to him about his Shakespeare article—it was finished in his head but he didn't have the strength to tap it out on the machine. Matthew suggested that he dictate to him but Aldous, who had never dictated a line, who had always worked alone, thought he could not change his life-long method. There was time and vitality in those five days for Aldous and Matthew to have long talks by themselves. Once or twice Judy sat with him alone.

> . . Once he said something about would this end all right? [Judy in a letter to S. B.] And I said it would and we both knew I was lying and I felt terribly ashamed . . .

On their last afternoon Aldous was well enough to get up for tea.

> And there we were, he and Laura and Matthew and I sitting around the table in his room and Matthew getting him to talk about Forte and Sanary and people from the early days and Maria and the Fakir who got the lady's foot in his fly at the restaurant table—and when Aldous would tell one story, Matthew would say, but do you remember this—I think this is perhaps the first and only time I heard Matthew call Aldous Pa—and we all giggled. Aldous was the centre of the stage and Matthew the prompter—and I felt this was a father and his son—Laura and I were the spectators, but not shut out—we were able to share what those two men had known, and I thought this must have been what it was like that household when they lived in Europe . . . (When they lived in Sanary with Rina, Matthew said, they were settled and had things; from the time they came to America they were always gypsies . . .)

Next day, 19th October, Matthew and Judy left. Sandy Wendel took them to the airport. Betty went to look in on Aldous; they talked about his article. "He was full of enthusiasm, brilliant and funny . . ."

On 21st October Betty wrote to Jeanne again. "Poor sweet Aldous—and poor us—the doctor believes that he cannot live longer than a few months. He has promised Laura that Aldous will have no pain. She is distraught about his illness and in her cheerfulness with Aldous is being extraordinarily brave . . . He stays in bed and works for short periods nearly every day. To discourage him would be wrong. Telling him not to work would be telling him not to live."

On the afternoon of the 25th Betty found Aldous typing in the

---

[1] Matthew Huxley *Farewell to Eden*. Harper & Row, 1965.

garden in his pyjamas. She stayed and made some tea. On the 27th he was taken to the Cedars of Lebanon Hospital for observation. Betty visited him on the 1st and again on the 4th of November—Laura's birthday. She read to him and they discussed making a dramatic version of one of Aldous's early stories, "The Tilotson Banquet"[1] for TV. Christopher Isherwood came on the 5th.

Aldous looked like a withered old man, grey-faced, with dull blank eyes.[2] He spoke in a low, hoarse voice which was hard to understand; I had to sit directly facing him because it hurt him to turn his head. And yet—seeing what I saw and knowing what I knew—I could still almost forget about his condition while we talked, because his mind was functioning so well. I was nervous at first and talked at random. I mentioned Africa, and Aldous said that all the African nations would soon be governed by their armies. I mentioned V. V. Rozanov's Solitaria, which I had just been reading. Aldous promptly quoted a passage from it . . "the private life is above everything . . just sitting at home and picking your nose and looking at the sunset" . . .

Laura had told me that Aldous did not realize how sick he was. But now he began to speak about old age, and I couldn't help suspecting that this was a kind of metaphor, a way of referring to his own death. He spoke of it almost with petulance, as a wretched hindrance which prevented you from working. He told me that he did not think he would ever write another novel. "I feel more and more out of touch with people." And he added that when one is old one is absolutely cut off from the outside world. I told him, quite sincerely, that I have the impression that, as I grow older, my character gets worse and worse. This made him laugh a lot—not, I think, because he disbelieved me but because he found the statement somehow reassuring. We parted almost cheerfully . . .

On 6th or 7th November Aldous was taken home again to Virginia's house. Meanwhile, to his relief, Laura had telephoned New York and managed to extend the deadline for the Shakespeare article to 30th November. More than half of the first draft was down on paper, but now Aldous was no longer strong enough to type. He went on in longhand—large letters written with a marking pencil (he never went back to spectacles). There were a few things that still gave him pleasure. He could not listen to much music, but he enjoyed looking at objects if they were very near

---

[1] First published in the Cornhill Magazine January 1921; then in Mortal Coils. Chatto & Windus, 1922.
[2] Mem. Vol.

and in strong light. Once Laura took Rembrandt's Polish Rider off the wall and they looked at it together. ("The great confidence of the man," Aldous said, "is so wonderful, isn't it?") Every day Peggy Kiskadden came with roses from her garden and Laura would place one a few inches from his face.

Books remained. Virginia read to him by the hour, day after day. "It was his . . capacity to *listen*," Laura wrote, "that, more than anything else, made those last weeks bearable . . even in great discomfort, he was able to direct his attention to what was read to him . . ." Small doses of dilaudid[1] now supplemented the aspirin. There were two nurses; Cutler and two other doctors came daily. One can imagine the life of the house ("This illness, darling—" Aldous said to Laura, "this is the very last thing I wanted you to have to put up with"). Virginia took it on as a matter of course, coped with it admirably—with two children underfoot—coped with the nurses, the Spanish maid, the constant demands on every household resource, the coming and going of friends, the telephone, the deliveries. ("Virginia is my greatest help," Laura wrote to Matthew and the Julians, "particularly for the unobtrusive and nonchalant way in which she helps.")

Laura had by now alerted Rosalind Rajagopal, who came regularly from Ojai bringing the oranges grown on her ranch Aldous had asked for, sitting with him, giving him massage.

On the morning of 10th November, a Sunday, Aldous talked to Laura about his situation. He had not done so before. Laura was telling him that he should try to remember what was happening to him now so that he might use it for his writing. "Yes," he said, "it is important that I remember because this is such a different universe . . ."

. . then I said [Laura in a letter to the family of 17th November] "what do you make of this, what does it signify, your illness . . what sense does it have . . ?" And he said, "it doesn't seem to make any sense, it's just a sequence of events and it goes on and on . . ." But I kept insisting if he could not find more sense in this seemingly wasteful disintegration which he is going through, but he said "no, it's just impossible. I don't know what the answer is . . ." He was tired and I said, "before you go to sleep ask one question, maybe you get an answer." "Well," he said, "there are so many questions." So I said, find just one question . . . He said, "Well, the most natural question is that if I get out of this what am I to do with the few remaining years of my life? Because, as you know, I am living on borrowed time." "What do you mean by borrowed time?" "Well, a hundred years ago when this thing happened . . there would have

[1] A morphine derivative.

been no way to stop it and I would be dead by now. But now that we have been able to handle it, it means that I have more time to live, that I live on borrowed time, and the point is the best way for me to use this time that I still have." So that was the question with which I left him.

And later in the day I asked him if he had an answer, and he said, "obviously it is that—if I get out of this—those few years will be very important, because this experience that I am going through now will be of the greatest significance." And with that [the subject] was closed for the time being.

Over the next days it became physically impossible for him to write, and at times to speak. His mind was active, and Laura could see that "it was painful for him to keep this effervescence within and muted". Virginia had given them a tape-recorder and this was put by Aldous's bed with the idea that he might use it for making notes. (Laura also recorded what they were saying to one another, as well as some of Aldous's conversations with his doctors.) The unfinished article was weighing on his mind. On 15th November he began working with Laura. With the tape machine going she read to him the part already in typescript, he stopped her for corrections. A friend transcribed the tape. Laura read the transcript back to Aldous; Aldous made a new set of recorded corrections. And so it went on. It is only by listening to this tape that one can realize the painful laboriousness of the process. Aldous was almost completely deprived of physical strength and with hardly enough energy left to breathe; he was not used to dictating, nor was Laura used to being dictated to. His voice, interrupted by coughing, by fatigue, was often near inaudible; Laura appears bewildered by some of the Shakespearian words, misunderstanding, mispronouncing the unfamiliar. The whole thing was a nightmare. Laura carried on with great self-control. What made it harder for her was the actual text, of which she had known nothing—some of the most harrowing lines on death in English literature. Claudio's speech,

Ay, but to die, and go we know not where . . .

Next day they reached the hand-written part, one page and a half, and matters, if conceivable, became worse. Aldous realized that it was almost impossible for him to work; meanwhile Laura was having trouble with his script.

Laura: "Inter". It says here "inter". The first word—I already don't understand. [She is trying hard.]
Aldous: Interpretation?
L.: Is it "interpretation"? "Interpretation of . . ."
A.: What was all this about, darling?

L.: Well, this is the page you wrote . . .

A.: Oh, I see "Shakespeare divided . . .

L.: His . . his . . .

A.: Oh, wait. Wait a minute. "Interpreters of Shakespeare have divided his career. [He goes on quoting his paragraph from memory and comes to] . . history, biography and chronicle fiction." I think it is . . .

L.: "Chronic"?

A.: . . . I don't think it matters, but I can look it up in a place. "The time of the 'depth' " inverted commas "when . . ."

There were pauses between each word. At one point Aldous wanted to see for himself, and was trying to hold both the page and his magnifying glass; Laura was holding the microphone. Somehow they got through another paragraph. "It's the last period, the plays of the last period," he explained to her. Then in an almost inaudible voice, "I am exhausted."

On the morrow, 17th November and another Sunday, Aldous had a better day. He and Laura got to the end of the hand-written passage; after the words "In our religious context," Aldous began composing straight on to the tape.

He asked me to show him how to start and stop the recorder. He did not want me to hold the microphone for him, to have control over the machine gave him a greater feeling of comfort and independence. I stood silently by. He would think for a while, then press a button and speak a phrase, then stop the machine and think.

After two paragraphs he almost smiled. "I begin to see how one could develop a technique to write in this way . . . Yes, I can see how one could do this . . it is different . . quite different . . . One has to think the sentence through . . ."

Aldous used his new learned skill the same day, dictating a business letter about various dramatic rights[1] (he had written to no one since his letter to Humphrey on 15th October). In the afternoon, Gerald came once more. He brought an inscribed copy of his latest book; it was large and heavy, so he quoted George III's brother's remark to Gibbon, " 'What! Another big, fat book!' " Aldous pounced. " 'Another damned, thick *square* book!' "

The same evening he told Laura that something should be done to speed up his recovery. It was true, he said, that he was better, but it was depressing not to have the strength to do what one

---

[1] To Max Kester of Foster's Agency in London. This letter, according to Professor Grover Smith, remained on tape and was not posted.

wanted to. On Monday 18th he took some interest in his food, worked on the article and dictated a note to Victoria Ocampo.

> Thank you for your good wishes, which I certainly need at this time. I hope we may soon find an auspicious moment for our long delayed meeting and your first acquaintance with Laura.[1]

On the 19th, in the early morning, Aldous returned to the great longing he had always had for the unattainable in art, the bringing together of *all* the multiplicities. What he had stated in the hand theme in *Those Barren Leaves*, what he had tried to achieve with the concert at Tantamount House in *Point Counter Point*—the music and the fiddle *and* the fiddler; the sound, the ear, the mind, the given *and* the experience—"Almost the whole course of life" fused in one simultaneous whole. Now, he told Laura (in an unexpectedly strong, his own, his former, voice) that one could write the greatest book ever written, *if one knew how*, "By bringing it all in!" At the same time? Laura asked. "Somehow . . ." Aldous said, "around a central story with episodes."

> "You mean you want to do it like Bach . . .?"
> "Well, I mean Bach is music and this is something else."
> "Can you do your new novel like that?"
> "Well, it would be marvellous if I could."
> "Can you apply it to any little thing, even a little short story?"
> "No, I wouldn't want to."
> . . . .
> Laura: ". . . And yet it's different from a polyphonic thing, is it?"
> "Well, it has to be virtually analogous to polyphony."
> "But you cannot speak all at once."
> "Well, no, one can't, after all. It's not like Bach where you can have five parts going on. When you have words, you interrupt the thing . . each part blurs the other."
> "That's probably why people write opera . . ."
> ". . This is what Wagner hoped to do and didn't. Unfortunately, he was an unspeakably vulgar man . . ."

On that day Aldous finished the Shakespeare article except for the last paragraph. He dictated Prospero's speech.

> *Our revels are now ended* . . . .
> . . . .
> . . . . *We are such stuff*
> *As dreams are made on; and our little life*
> *Is rounded with a sleep.*

---

[1] This, again according to Professor Smith, was almost certainly Aldous's last letter.

Prospero is here enunciating the doctrine of Maya. The world is an illusion, but is an illusion which we must take seriously, because it is real as far as it goes, and in those aspects of the reality which we are capable of apprehending. Our business is to wake up. We have to find ways in which to detect the whole of the reality in the one illusory part which our self-centred consciousness permits us to see. We must not live thoughtlessly, taking our illusion for the complete reality, but at the same time we must not live too thoughtfully in the sense of trying to escape from the dream state. We must continually be on our watch for ways in which to enlarge our consciousness. We must not attempt to live outside the world, which is given us, but we must somehow learn how to transform it and transfigure it. Too much 'wisdom' is as bad as too little wisdom, and there must be no magic tricks. We must learn to come to reality without the enchanter's wand and his book of the words. One must find a way of being in this world while not being of it. One must find a way of living in time without being completely swallowed up in time.

> But thought's the slave of life, and life time's fool;
> And time, that takes survey of all the world,
> Must have a stop.[1]

The day after Aldous said, "I think we must finish on our subject matter, 'Shakespeare and Religion.'" He dictated the last paragraph to its ending—"How many kinds of Shakespeare."

Laura: You want an exclamation?
Aldous: Mark. Yes.
L.: But there are not many kinds of Shakespeare . .
A.: But darling, that's exactly what we've been talking about . . . and stop the damn thing now.

Next day, Thursday 21st, Aldous had the tape played back to him, "was slightly amused, added a comma." When Dr Cutler came he said again how different the universe of the sick was from that of the well, saying it, Cutler wrote, "in that wonderfully mellow voice . . there was no bitterness in his observations, only dispassionate objectivity . . We talked for a while of the nature of cancer . . a conversation between two scientists . . . Aldous had an incredible fund of medical knowledge . . . Although I was the doctor, it was he who kept up my morale and that of his wife . . ."
That evening Aldous told Laura that they could not go on

1 "Shakespeare and Religion" *Show* Magazine 1964 (Hardford Publications Inc., 1964). Republished in *Mem. Vol.*

imposing in this manner on Virginia; Laura tried to laugh him out of it, Aldous insisted: they must do something about it—take an apartment for the time being. He spoke with now unaccustomed energy; but only a few minutes later it became evident to Laura that he was losing ground.

Aldous slept through the night. When Laura saw him again at half past six in the morning of Friday, 22nd November, she felt that something was more wrong than usual, and telegraphed for Matthew. Towards 9 a.m. Aldous became very agitated; Cutler gave him something to ease respiration and he became more comfortable. Rosalind Rajagopal arrived and remained in the house. At 10 Aldous asked for a "big, big piece of paper." Laura brought him a writing tablet. "If I go . . ." he wrote. The pen did not work, Rosalind found a red one. Aldous wrote out instructions for an insurance policy to be transferred to Matthew. Laura promised to do what was necessary and Aldous appeared relieved not to have to take further action. A young man came into the room with a tank of oxygen. "These tanks are heavy," Aldous said; and when Laura looked about her, "there're some dollar bills in my trouser pocket in the cupboard." Peggy Kiskadden came in the course of the morning: Aldous took her hand and said, "Good bye, *dear* Peggy."

He grew weaker. At one point he murmured, "Who is eating out of my bowl?"

Around noon he asked again for the writing tablet.

LSD—Try it

intermuscular

100 mm[1]

Laura left the room to speak to Cutler. She found Virginia, doctors, nurses clustered round the television set in the hall, and was overcome by a sense of nightmarish irreality. She did not know that it was the hour of the Kennedy assassination.

After some hesitation Dr Cutler consented.[2] Aldous had not touched a psychedelic for the last two years; Laura was certain that he was deliberately choosing to do what he had written about in *Island*—taking a mind-enlarging drug *in extremis*, and she saw it as a sign of his awareness and acceptance. She gave the injection herself. (And a second one some two hours later.)

Aldous became very quiet. Laura felt that he was interested, relieved, at peace. She stayed by him, holding his hand, speaking to him, telling him to let go, to go with ease, helping him as he had Maria. The good black nurse was in the room, and Rosalind,

---

[1] See Appendix I.   [2] See Appendix II.

doctors were gently moving to and fro; all was peaceful. At twenty minutes past five, very quietly, Aldous died.

Matthew, delayed by the countrywide confusions of that frightful weekend, arrived late at night. Next day Aldous was cremated, without a service of any kind. No one was present. On Sunday afternoon, on Matthew's suggestion, they held a private ceremony; family and friends assembled at Mulholland Highway for tea and a commemorative walk. They were Laura and Virginia, Matthew and Judy, Mère, Rose with her son Siggy, Betty and Sanford Wendel, Peggy Kiskadden and Christopher Isherwood. They went for the walk Aldous had gone for every day as long as he was able to stand up, the track along the canyon with the view over the Hollywood hills and the tree-lined reservoir he had called the Lake.

In London, there was a Memorial Gathering at Friends' House on 17th December 1963. Yehudi Menuhin played the Chaconne by Bach; Julian Huxley, David Cecil, Stephen Spender and Kenneth Clark spoke.

Eight years after, in 1971, Aldous's ashes were removed from an anonymous depository and returned to England and to Surrey. Here, on 27th October, a warm and brilliant day, accompanied by Julian and Juliette, Jeanne, Sophie, Noële, his step-mother Rosalind and his half-brothers David and Andrew, Huxley nephews and cousins and a handful of his friends, Aldous's ashes were buried after a brief committal service in his parents' grave in the hillside cemetery at Compton. The year after, on 10th October 1972, the same service was held for Maria Huxley; her ashes returned to Europe and were put to rest by the side of Aldous.

CHRONOLOGY

1939

3rd September	England at war with Germany
September/December	Aldous and Maria live at 701 Amalfi Drive, Pacific Palisades, California, U.S.A.
	Aldous at work at Metro-Goldwyn-Mayer on an adaptation of *Pride and Prejudice*.
October	Publication *After Many a Summer Dies the Swan*
November	Sophie Moulaert, Aldous and Maria's niece, arrives from Europe. Lives with the Huxleys until 1944
December	Brief visit Gervas Huxley
	Christmas visit Julian Huxley

1940

January/December	At 701 Amalfi Drive, Pacific Palisades
January	Continues work on *Pride and Prejudice* for M.G.M.
February	On half-pay at M.G.M. Tinkering with a Utopian novel
April/June	Aldous in ill health. Unable to work
July	Decides to write a biographical study of Père Joseph, Richelieu's Grey Eminence
August/September	Research reading for *Grey Eminence*
October	Aldous starts writing *Grey Eminence*

1941

January/December	At 701 Amalfi Drive, Pacific Palisades
May	*Grey Eminence* finished. Aldous's Aunt Ethel Collier, the last of T. H. Huxley's daughters, dies
July	Film work at Twentieth Century Fox
October	Publication *Grey Eminence*
November	Aldous starts work on a new novel, *Time Must Have A Stop*

1942

January/February	At 701 Amalfi Drive, Pacific Palisades
February	Aldous and Maria move to Llano del Rio, a house in an oasis in the Mojave Desert
March	At work at Twentieth Century Fox on *Jane Eyre*
April	Novel laid aside. Starts writing *The Art of Seeing*

July	*The Art of Seeing* finished
October	Publication *The Art of Seeing*

1943
January/December	Main home base: Llano
March	Aldous resumes work on novel
	Matthew in U.S. Army Medical Corps
April	Matthew seriously ill in Army hospital
June	Matthew invalided out of U.S. Army
July	Aldous stays with Gerald Heard at Trabuco College
October	The Huxleys take a *pied-à-terre* in Beverly Hills, at 145 1/2 South Doheny Drive

1944
January/December	Llano and Beverly Hills flat
February	*Time Must Have A Stop* finished
April	Work with Christopher Isherwood on some film scripts
May	Starts *The Perennial Philosophy*. Writes Article on Dr William Sheldon's Human Typology
26th July	Aldous's Fiftieth Birthday
August	Publication *Time Must Have A Stop*
Autumn	Aldous learns to drive a car

1945
January/August	Llano and Beverly Hills
March	*The Perennial Philosophy* finished
June	Aldous and Maria buy a chalet in the mountains at Wrightwood, California.
	Matthew becomes a U.S. citizen
Spring/Summer	Writing *Science, Liberty and Peace*
July/August	At Wrightwood
September	Publication *The Perennial Philosophy*
October	Matthew at Berkeley University. (Takes degree in 1947)
November/December	Aldous works with Walt Disney on film of *Alice in Wonderland*

1946
Winter/Spring	At Llano
March	Publication *Science, Liberty and Peace*
Summer	At work on film version of *The Gioconda Smile*. At Wrightwood
September	Work on stage version of *The Gioconda Smile*

1947
February	Llano given up for good. Definite move to Wrightwood

361

January/March	Continues work of stage version of *Gioconda*
March	Work on a novel laid in 14th-century Italy (abandoned). First reference to a post-atomic novel
May	At work on and off at Rank on the *Gioconda* film
September	Aldous and Maria leave by car for New York. Their first absence from California since 1938
October/November	New York at 26 West 59th Street. Long weekends at the Joep Nicolas's house at Islip, Long Island
November/December	At Doheny Drive, Beverly Hills. Working on *Ape and Essence*
December	At Wrightwood

1948

January/December	At Wrightwood and Beverly Hills
February	Publication (U.S.) play *Mortal Coils* (Title later changed back to *The Gioconda Smile*)
	Release of Gioconda film under title *A Woman's Vengeance. Ape and Essence* finished
3rd June	*The Gioconda Smile* opens at the New Theatre in London (a 9 months run)
10th June	New York Hotel, St Regis
24th June	Aldous and Maria sail on S.S. *Queen Mary*. Their first post-war return to Europe
29th June	Arrival at Cherbourg and Paris
29th June/8th July	Paris at 82 rue Bonaparte VIme staying with Georges and Jeanne Neveux
9th July/2nd August	Siena at Palazzo Ravizza. Work on film of "The Rest Cure"
2nd August/28th August	Rome at Hotel de la Ville
30th August/18th September	Sanary at Villa La Rustique
20th September/2nd October	Paris at 67 Bld Lannes XVIme at Mimi Gielgud's flat
2nd October/Mid-October	London at Claridges. Interview with Cyril Connolly
October	Return by sea to U.S.A.
October/November	New York. Aldous has a new severe attack of bronchitis
November/December	At Palm Desert (Sage & Sun Apartments) on doctor's orders. Work on stage version of *Ape and Essence*

1949

| January/February | Palm Desert |
| February | *Le Sourire de la Gioconde* (in collaboration with Georges Neveux) opens in Paris |

February/May	At Beverly Hills. Collecting material for biographical study of Maine de Biran
May	Aldous and Maria buy a house in Los Angeles at 740 North Kings Road
May/September	At Wrightwood
October	*Themes and Variations* finished. Move to 740 North Kings Road
December	Matthew engaged to Ellen Hovde

1950
January/March	At North Kings Road
April	New York at Hotel Warwick. Matthew marries Ellen Hovde
	Publication *Themes and Variations*
9th May	Aldous and Maria sail for France on S.S. *Queen Mary*
May/Mid-June	Paris. Hotel Paris-Dinard
June	Rome, Hotel Flora, Siena, Palazzo Ravizza
July	Paris, Hotel Paris-Dinard
11th July	Aldous goes to London for two weeks. Stays with Julian and Juliette at 31 Pond Street, NW3
August	Aldous and Maria at Sanary. Villa Rustique
1st September/ 11th September	Juillac, Corrèze, Maison de Joyet with Georges, Jeanne, Noële Neveux
11th September/ 22nd September	Paris at Mimi Gielgud's
22nd September	Sail for New York
September/October	New York. Last weeks of rehearsal of *The Gioconda Smile*
3rd October	*Gioconda* opens on Broadway, Lyceum Theatre (5 weeks' run) Aldous and Maria return to Los Angeles by car. Visit Frieda Lawrence *en route*
November/December	North Kings. Aldous begins work on *The Devils of Loudun*

1951
January/December	At North Kings, Los Angeles. Work on *The Devils of Loudun*
March/April	Influenza effecting Aldous's eyes
July/August	Aldous has a severe attack of iritis
20th October	Birth of Matthew's son, Mark Trevenen

1952
January/December	North Kings, Los Angeles
January	Maria seriously ill
	The Devils of Loudun finished
October	Publication *The Devils of Loudun*

CHRONOLOGY

1953
January/December   North Kings, Los Angeles
                          Aldous at work on miscellaneous essays,
                            articles, film projects
February   Death of Lewis Gielgud
May   Aldous's first mescalin experiment with
                            Dr Humphrey Osmond
June   Car journey through the U.S. North
                            Western States and National Parks
June/July   Writing *The Doors of Perception*
28th September   Edwin Hubble died
October   Birth of Matthew's daughter, Tessa

1954
January/December   North Kings, Los Angeles
February   Publication *The Doors of Perception*
March   New York. Aldous starts *The Genius and
                            the Goddess*

7th April   Aldous and Maria sail for Cherbourg on
                            the S.S. *Queen Elizabeth*
12th-19th April   Paris, Hotel Pont-Royal
19th April/3rd May   St Paul-de-Vence for Eileen Garrett's
                            symposium on Philosophy and Para-
                            psychology
May   Ismailia; Cairo; Jerusalem; Beirut;
                            Cyprus
June   Athens; Rome
19th June/4th July   Paris
July   Dieulefit, Drôme and Vaison-la-Romaine
                            with the Neveux's
August   Aldous in London with the Julian
                            Huxleys. Maria in Paris
21st August   Aldous and Maria sail for New York on
                            the S.S. *Mauritania*
September   New York
7th September   Return to Los Angeles
October   Aldous lectures at Washington, D.C.,
                            Duke University and University of N.
                            Carolina. *The Genius and the Goddess*
                            finished. Visit from Julian
November   Visit from Humphrey Osmond. Aldous
                            starts play script of *The Genius and the
                            Goddess* and work on miscellaneous
                            essays

1955
January/April   At North Kings, Los Angeles
January/December   Work on dramatisation of the *G & G*,
                            miscellaneous essays and articles
12th February   Maria Huxley dies

364

April/May	Aldous drives to New York with Rose de Haulleville
May/June	New York at 1035 Park Avenue
June	Publication *The Genius and the Goddess* (the novel)
July/August	Aldous stays with Matthew and his family at Guilford, Connecticut. Finishes *Heaven and Hell*
September	Aldous returns to North Kings, Los Angeles
September/December	At North Kings

1956
January/July	At North Kings, Los Angeles
February	Publication *Heaven and Hell*
19th March	Aldous is married to Laura Archera at Yuma, Arizona
July	Aldous and Laura move to a house on 3276 Deronda Drive, Los Angeles
Summer	Aldous starts *Island*
September	A visit from Julian and Juliette
October	Publication *Adonis and the Alphabet* (U.S. title *Tomorrow and Tomorrow and Tomorrow*)

1957
January/July	At Deronda Drive, Los Angeles
July/November	New York, Hotel Shoreham working on the stage production of *The Genius and the Goddess*
November/December	Deronda Drive, L.A. Starts writing *Brave New World Revisited*
10th December	*The Genius and the Goddess* opens on Broadway. The play closes after five nights

1958
January/July	Deronda Drive, L.A.
Spring	*Brave New World Revisited* finished. Aldous returns to his Utopian novel *Island*
July/August	Aldous and Laura in Peru and Brazil
September	Aldous and Laura in Italy
October	Aldous in London, at the Julian's house in Hampstead. Publication *Brave New World Revisited*
October	Aldous and Laura in Paris. Later Venice
November	Aldous Lectures at Turin, Milan, Rome and Naples
December	Return to Deronda Drive, L.A.

1959

January/December	At Deronda Drive, L.A. Work on and off on *Island*
February/May	Aldous's first semester as Visiting Professor at the University of California at Santa Barbara. Delivers a course of lectures on "The Human Situation"
May	Award of Merit for the Novel by the American Academy of Arts and Letters New York
September/December	Second semester at Santa Barbara

1960

January/December	At Deronda Drive, L.A. Matthew and Ellen's marriage is dissolved
March/April	Aldous Visiting Professor at the Menninger Foundation, Topeka, Kansas
April/May	Aldous lectures at Forest Hill, Berkeley, Idaho State College, University of Arizona etc. etc.
May	Diagnosis of serious illness
June/July	Radium treatment and apparent good recovery
September	Takes part in a Conference on Medical Ethics at Dartmouth College; Boston. New York. Receives Honorary Degree at New Hampshire University. Lectures at University of Pittsburgh
23rd September	Aldous takes up Carnegie Visiting Professorship at the Massachusetts Institute of Technology
September/November	At M.I.T. Cambridge, Mass. Gives course of lectures and seminar on What a Piece of Work is Man
December	Deronda Drive, L.A.

1961

January/May	Deronda Drive, L.A.
January	Aldous and Laura in Hawaii
February	Aldous takes part in conference on Control of the Mind at San Francisco
April	Cambridge, Mass. Aldous speaks at M.I.T. centennial celebration
12th May	The house on Deronda Drive is destroyed by fire with its contents. Aldous loses his library and all his papers
June	Aldous finishes *Island*
June/July	Aldous in London at 4 Ennismore Gardens, Kensington. Gives important interviews

366

July	At St Paul-de-Vence. Takes part in Eileen Garrett's annual conference on Parapsychology
August	Laura joins Aldous in Europe. Stay at Gstaad in Switzerland seeing Krishnamurti and the Yehudi Menuhins. Copenhagen for conference on Applied Psychology
September	Return to Los Angeles. At Virginia Pfeiffer's house, 6233 Mulholland Highway
November	Aldous and Laura fly to India for the Tagore Centenary celebration at New Delhi. Aldous revisits the Taj Mahal. Brief stay in Japan
December	Return to Los Angeles

1962

January/December	At Virginia Pfeiffer's house on Mulholland Highway, L.A.
February/May	Aldous Visiting Professor at the University of California at Berkeley
March	Publication *Island*. Aldous takes part in conference on Technology in the Modern World at Santa Barbara
	Lectures: Alabama, Philadelphia
April	Conference on Hypnosis at Colgate University, Syracuse, N.Y.
	Stays at Boston and New York
	Aldous meets Julian at Portland, Oregon
May	Aldous lectures to the scientists at Alamos
	Lecture at Anaheim, California
	New York. Talk at the American Academy of Art and Letters
June	First recurrence of Aldous's illness
	Aldous elected Companion of Literature by the Royal Society of Literature. *The Genius and the Goddess* performed at Oxford, Manchester, Leeds and at the Comedy in London
July	Minor operation followed by cobalt treatment
	Aldous makes a slow recovery
August/September	Aldous flies to Brussels for the meeting of the World Academy of Arts and Science
	Stay with Joep and Suzanne Nicolos in Holland
September	London at Julian and Juliette's
October	Los Angeles. Working on *Literature and Science*

| November | A month of lecturing in the Middle West and East. Stay in New York |

1963

January/November	At Virginia Pfeiffer's, Mulholland Drive, L.A.
January	Aldous "ruminating a long and complicated novel"
March	Aldous flies to Rome for a conference of F.A.O. (United Nations Food and Agricultural Organisation.) Audience with Pope John XXIII
	New York for Matthew's marriage to Judith Wallet Bordage
March/April	Aldous lectures at Oregon, Berkeley, Stanford
April/May	Aldous has another relapse
May	Few days in hospital for observation
June/July	Radium treatments. Followed by very slow recovery of strength
August	Aldous and Laura fly to Stockholm for a meeting of the World Academy of Arts and Science
	Aldous accepts to edit a volume on Human Resources (with Dr Humphrey Osmond) for the Academy
	London. Aldous stays with Julian and Juliette.
	Visits to Dartington, to Lawford Hall (the home of his late friends, the Nichols's), to Kenneth Clark's Saltwood Castle
	Aldous joins Laura in Italy
24th August	Aldous returns to Los Angeles
September	Publication *Literature and Science*
October/November	Aldous writes "Shakespeare and Religion"
22nd November	Aldous dies (in the house on Mulholland Highway, Los Angeles). There is cremation by undertaker with no funeral service
17th December	A Memorial Service is held in London at Friends' House. Yehudi Menuhin plays Bach's Chaconne. Julian Huxley, David Cecil, Stephen Spender and Kenneth Clark speak

1971

| 27th October | Aldous Huxley's ashes returned to England and buried in his parents' grave at Compton, Surrey |

1972
10th October   Maria Huxley's ashes are returned to England and buried by the side of Aldous

CHRONOLOGICAL LIST OF WORKS
BY ALDOUS HUXLEY

The Burning Wheel	1916	*Eyeless in Gaza*	1936
Jonah	1917	*The Olive Tree*	1936
The Defeat of Youth	1918	*What are You going to Do*	
Leda	1920	*About It?*	1936
Limbo	1920	*Ends and Means*	1937
Crome Yellow	1921	*After Many a Summer Dies*	
Mortal Coils	1922	*the Swan*	1939
On the Margin	1923	*Grey Eminence*	1941
Antic Hay	1923	*The Art of Seeing*	1942*
Little Mexican	1924	*Time Must Have A Stop*	1944*
Those Barren Leaves	1925	*The Perennial Philosophy*	1945*
Along the Road	1925	*Science, Liberty and Peace*	1946*
Two or Three Graces	1926	*Ape and Essence*	1948
Jesting Pilate	1926	*The Gioconda Smile*	1948
Proper Studies	1927	*Themes and Variations*	1950
Point Counter Point	1928	*The Devils of Loudun*	1952
Do What You Will	1929	*The Doors of Perception*	1954
Brief Candles	1930	*The Genius and the Goddess*	1955
Vulgarity in Literature	1930	*Heaven and Hell*	1956
The World of Light	1931	*Adonis and The Alphabet*	
The Cicadas	1931	(U.S. title *Tommorrow and*	
Music at Night	1931	*Tommorrow and Tomorrow*)	1956
Brave New World	1932	*Brave New World Revisited*	1958
Texts and Pretexts	1932	*Island*	1962
Beyond the Mexique Bay	1934	*Literature and Science*	1963

All books were first published in England with the exception of the four titles marked thus* which were first published in the U.S.A.

SHORT LIST OF WORKS CONSULTED

BERTALANFFY, Ludwig von: *Problems of Life*. Watts, London, 1952

BRONOWSKI, J.: *Science and Human Values* (revised edition). Harper and Row, New York, 1965

CHEN-CHI CHANG, Garma: *The Practice of Zen*. Harper and Row, New York, 1970

FROST, Fr. Bede: *The Art of Mental Prayer*. Allenson, New York, 1940

GODEL, Dr Roger: *Essais sur l'Expérience Libératrice*. Paris, 1952

JAMES, William: *Varieties of Religious Experience*. London, 1902

LEARY, Timothy: *The Politics of Ecstasy*. Putnam, New York, 1968
High Priest. World Publishing Company, New York, 1968

MUMFORD, Lewis: *The Pentagon of Power*. Secker and Warburg, London, 1971

SHELDON, Dr William: *The Varieties of Human Physique*. Hafner, New York, 1940
The Varieties of Human Temperament. Hafner, New York, 1942
Varieties of Delinquent Youth. Hafner, New York, 1949

STRAVINSKY, Igor and CRAFT, Robert: *Conversations with Igor Stravinsky*. Doubleday, New York; Faber, London, 1959
Memories and Commentaries. Doubleday, New York; Faber, London, 1960
Expositions and Developments. Doubleday, New York; Faber, London, 1962
Dialogues and Diary. Doubleday, New York; Faber, London, 1963

VITTOZ, Dr Roger: *Traitement des Psychonévroses par la Rééducation du Controle Cérébral*. J. B. Baillière, Paris, 1907

WORTHINGTON, Marjorie: *The Strange World of Willie Seabrook*. Harcourt Brace & World, New York, 1966

ZAEHNER, Professor R. C.: *Mysticism, Sacred and Profane*. Clarendon Press, Oxford, 1957

ZAMYATIN: *We*. New York, 1924

APPENDICES to Part Twelve, Chapter Eight

Appendix I

See page 358; Aldous's written request for LSD is reproduced in *This Timeless Moment*. Some of the words appear very blurred; "LSD . . . Try it" and "100 mm" are entirely clear.

Appendix II

See page 358; Dr Cutler told me that he allowed Laura to give the LSD injection because at that stage it could have made no difference whatsoever. He could not say, when asked, whether it had had any effect. He confirmed that Aldous had died very peacefully. Yes, he said, after reflection, "*very* peacefully." This could be construed as meaning "exceptionally" peacefully.

When I reported this conversation to Laura (on the day it had taken place), she was surprised and taken aback that Dr Cutler had not told me that he had in fact observed a marked beneficial effect of the LSD. Her personal account of Aldous's last hours can of course be found in *This Timeless Moment*.

INDEX

INDEX

Literature in Paladin Books

Fear and Loathing in Las Vegas   £2.50 ☐
Hunter S Thompson
As knights of old sought the Holy Grail so Hunter Thompson entered
Las Vegas armed with a veritable magus's arsenal of 'heinous chemi-
cals' in his search for the American Dream. 'The whole book boils
down to a kind of mad, corrosive poetry that picks up where Norman
Mailer's *An American Dream* left off and explores what Tom Wolfe
left out.' *New York Times*.

Marx's Grundrisse   £1.95 ☐
David McLellan
A substantial set of extracts from the classic work in which Marx
develops an account of the process of alienation, analyses the nature
of work, and develops a vision of the fully automated society in
which social wealth could be devoted to the all-round development
of the faculties of each individual. Edited by one of Britain's leading
Marxist scholars.

The Stranger in Shakespeare   £2.50 ☐
Leslie A Fiedler
A complete radical analysis of Shakespeare's work which illuminates
the sub-surface psychological tensions.

Confessions of a Knife   £1.95 ☐
Richard Selzer
In this riveting book Richard Selzer seeks meaning in the ritual of
surgery, a ritual 'at once murderous, painful, healing, and full of
love'. In the careening, passionate language of a poet he speaks of
mortality and medicine, of flesh and fever, and reveals something of
the surgeon's thoughts and fears as he delves into the secret linings of
our bodies. 'I was awed and strangely exalted.' Bernard Crick, *The
Guardian*.

Notes from Overground   £2.50 ☐
'Tiresias'
Man is born free, and is everywhere in trains. More than a commu-
ter's lament, *Notes from Overground* is a witty, wide-ranging meditation on a horribly familiar form of travel.

To order direct from the publisher just tick the titles you want
and fill in the order form.   PAL8082

New Age in Paladin Books

Men and Beasts: An Animal Rights Handbook   £1.95 ☐
Maureen Duffy
A clear statement of the case for a more enlightened attitude towards
animals, based on equality and respect for their rights – a blueprint
for the way forward and a programme for action.

Entropy   £2.95 ☐
Jeremy Rifkin
Entropy is the supreme law of nature and governs everything we do.
In this powerfully argued book, Rifkin tells us why our existing world
view is crumbling and what will replace it.

Social History in Paladin Books

The Common Stream   £1.95   ☐
Rowland Parker
The history of a Cambridgeshire village from the first traces of human
settlement to the present day, and the common stream of ordinary
men and women who have lived and died there. 'Beautifully written,
imaginative and truthful.' *Ronald Blythe*

Men of Dunwich   £1.95   ☐
Rowland Parker
An imaginative reconstruction of the life of an ancient community
in East Anglia, which, over the centuries, took its living from the
sea, until finally the sea assailed, eroded and then engulfed the
community. Illustrated.

American Dreams: Lost and Found   £2.95   ☐
Studs Terkel
From Miss USA to an unknown New York cab driver – these frank
confessions, woven together by a master craftsman, represent the
authentic voice of America. A rum and original piece of social history
that will surprise, shock and move you.

To order direct from the publisher just tick the titles you want
and fill in the order form.   PAL7382

Politics in Paladin Books

Aneurin Bevan (Vols 1 & 2)   £2.95 ☐
Michael Foot   each
The classic political biography of post-war politics.

Karl Marx: His Life and Thought   £3.95 ☐
David McLellan
A major biography by Britain's leading Marxist historian. Marx is shown in his private and family life as well as in his political contexts.

The Strange Death of Liberal England   £2.95 ☐
George Dangerfield
This brilliant and persuasive book examines the forces responsible for the breakdown of Liberal Society in England. At once an exposition of the causes for the dissolution of a great period in English history and a reluctant threnody for the age of purpose and order. 'A brilliant analysis.' *The Times*.

War Plan UK   £2.95 ☐
Duncan Campbell
The secret truth about Britain's civil defence. The result of more than five years' research, the book reveals the incredible history of how one government after another has planned to protect itself and survive. 'An unprecedented break in the secrecy surrounding civil defence planning.' *The Observer*. Fully illustrated.

The Plutonium Business   £2.95 ☐
Walter C. Patterson
Concerned by the rarity of uranium at the dawn of the nuclear age, physicists came up with a compelling concept – the fast breeder reactor. But uranium is no longer scarce and a great vision has gone sour. In this searching analysis, Patterson argues that the plutonium people must be stopped – for the sake of all humanity.

To order direct from the publisher just tick the titles you want
and fill in the order form.   **PAL7482**

History in Paladin Books

Europe's Inner Demons   £1.75   ☐
Norman Cohn
The history of the vilification of minority groups as scapegoats, by the author of *The Pursuit of the Millennium*.

In Time of War   £4.95   ☐
Robert Fisk
In this exciting and brilliantly vivid narrative, Robert Fisk brings to life the little-known history of Ireland during the Second World War. Illustrated.

A History of the Great War 1914-1918   £3.95   ☐
C R M F Cruttwell
An intelligent and graphically readable account of the campaignings and battles of the 1914-18 War presented here for the general reader along with sympathetic portraits of the leaders and generals of all the countries involved. Scrupulously fair, praising and blaming friend and enemy as circumstances demand, it has become established as the classic acocunt of the first world-wide war. Illustrated.

Anatomy of the SS State   £2.50   ☐
Helmut Krausnick and Martin Broszat
The inside story of the concentration camps, 'probably the most impressive work on the Nazi period ever to appear'. *Times Educational Supplement*.

Blind Eye to Murder   £3.95   ☐
Tom Bower
A dispassionate but shocking indictment of Allied postwar policy. Bower dispels once and for all the myth that important Nazi criminals were removed from power. 'Devastating'. *Max Hastings*. Illustrated.

To order direct from the publisher just tick the titles you want and fill in the order form.   **PAL7182**

Folklore in Paladin Books

A Dictionary of British Folk Customs   £2.95   ☐
Christina Hole
Every folk custom, both past and present, is described with its
history, development and present-day usage. The book includes a
nationwide calendar showing what happens, where and when.

The Classic Fairy Tales   £3.95   ☐
Iona and Peter Opie
Twenty-four of the best known stories in the English language are
presented in the exact words of the earliest surviving text or English
translation. Lavishly illustrated.

The Lore and Language of Schoolchildren   £2.95   ☐
Iona and Peter Opie
The classic study of the mysterious world and underworld of
schoolchildren – the games, the chants, the rites and the rituals
performed generation after generation by children all over Britain.

The People of the Sea   £1.95   ☐
David Thomson
The haunting record of a journey in search of the man-seal legends of
the Celts. 'Enthralling, spine-tingling, cliff-hanging' *Financial Times*

Philosophy/Religion in Paladin Books

Mythologies   £2.50 ☐
Roland Barthes
An entertaining and elating introduction to the science of semiology
– the study of the signs and signals through which society expresses
itself – from the leading intellectual star.

Infinity and the Mind   £3.50 ☐
Rudy Rucker
In the wake of *Gödel, Escher, Bach* comes this exceptional book
which draws from a staggering variety of source material to explore
the concept of infinity and its effect on our understanding of the
universe.

Confucius and Confucianism   £2.95 ☐
D Howard Smith
A skillful and thoroughgoing study which illuminates the man and
his influence and the doctrines of Confucian thought.

Paladin Movements and Ideas Series
Series editor Justin Wintle
The series aims to provide clear and stimulating surveys of the ideas
and cultural movements that have dominated history. The first three
volumes are:

Rationalism   £2.50 ☐
John Cottingham

Darwinian Evolution   £2.50 ☐
Antony Flew

Expressionism   £2.50 ☐
Roger Cardinal

To order direct from the publisher just tick the titles you want
and fill in the order form.

Philosophy/Religion in Paladin Books

Mythologies   £2.50 ☐
Roland Barthes
An entertaining and elating introduction to the science of semiology
– the study of the signs and signals through which society expresses
itself – from the leading intellectual star.

Infinity and the Mind   £3.50 ☐
Rudy Rucker
In the wake of *Gödel, Escher, Bach* comes this exceptional book
which draws from a staggering variety of source material to explore
the concept of infinity and its effect on our understanding of the
universe.

Confucius and Confucianism   £2.95 ☐
D Howard Smith
A skillful and thoroughgoing study which illuminates the man and
his influence and the doctrines of Confucian thought.

Paladin Movements and Ideas Series
Series editor Justin Wintle
The series aims to provide clear and stimulating surveys of the ideas
and cultural movements that have dominated history. The first three
volumes are:

Rationalism   £2.50 ☐
John Cottingham

Darwinian Evolution   £2.50 ☐
Antony Flew

Expressionism   £2.50 ☐
Roger Cardinal

All these books are available at your local bookshop or newsagent, or can be ordered direct from the publisher.

To order direct from the publishers just tick the titles you want and fill in the form below.

Name _____

Address _____

_____

Send to:
Paladin Cash Sales
PO Box 11, Falmouth, Cornwall TR10 9EN.

Please enclose remittance to the value of the cover price plus:

UK 55p for the first book, 22p for the second book plus 14p per copy for each additional book ordered to a maximum charge of £1.75.

BFPO and Eire 55p for the first book, 22p for the second book plus 14p per copy for the next 7 books, thereafter 8p per book.

Overseas £1.25 for the first book and 31p for each additional book.

Paladin Books reserve the right to show new retail prices on covers, which may differ from those previously advertised in the text or elsewhere.